Korea

한국

Geoff Crowther
Choe Hyung Pun

Korea – a travel survival kit

2nd edition

Published by
Lonely Planet Publications
Head Office: PO Box 617, Hawthorn, Vic 3122, Australia
US Office: PO Box 2001A, Berkeley, CA 94702, USA

Printed by
Colorcraft Ltd, Hong Kong

Photographs by
Choe Hyung Pun (CHP)
Geoff Crowther (GC)
Deanna Swaney (DS)
H J M Goossens (HJMG)

Front cover: Old man in traditional dress, Seoul (Joseph Brignolo), The Image Bank
Back cover: View on Haein-sa, South Korea (HJMG)

First Published
1988

This Edition
April 1991

National Library of Australia Cataloguing in Publication Data

Crowther, Geoff
Korea – a travel survival kit.

2nd ed.
Includes index.
ISBN 0 86442 099 4.

1. Korea – Description and travel – 1953 – Guide-books.
I. Title.

915.190443

Geoff Crowther

Geoff was born in Yorkshire, England and started his travelling days as a teenage hitchhiker. Later, after many short trips around Europe, two years in Asia and Africa and short spells in the overgrown fishing village of Hull and on the bleak and beautiful Cumberland fells, Geoff got involved with the London underground information centre BIT. He helped put together their first tatty, duplicated overland guides and was with them from their late '60s heyday right through to the end. Since his first Lonely Planet guide (to Africa), Geoff has written or collaborated on guides to South America, Malaysia, East and North Africa, and India. Geoff lives with Hyung Pun, who he met in Korea, and their son Ashley, in the rainforests near the New South Wales/Queensland border. In between travel he spends his time pursuing noxious weeds, cultivating tropical fruit and brewing mango wine.

From the Author

The first edition of this book came together during 1982 and 1983 following two trips to Korea. Initially, the only grass-roots information I had to go on was what I could glean from the out-of-print Peace Corps guide to Korea kindly supplied to me by Patrick Linden of the USA and the many glossy, though very informative, leaflets and booklets put out by the Korean Tourist Office. These sources of help, however, quickly became of secondary importance after I met Choe Hyung Pun of Taejon. She travelled round Korea with me on both occasions, and without her enthusiastic support and suggestions and her ability to translate on numerous occasions, what followed might have been a hopeless muddle. I also must thank Mr Kwon Young Joung of Kyongju for his unmatched hospitality on both occasions that I visited and for his boundless energy in taking me to sites and places I would otherwise never have heard of.

The second edition was much more of a team effort by Choe Hyung Pun (who visited Korea once again for three months) and myself, together with much appreciated and valuable contributions by Hyung Pun's family members, Mr Kwon Young Joung and travellers out there on the road.

The third edition was another team effort by Choe Hyung Pun, her younger sister, Choe Hyung Soon, and their travelling companion, Helga Vogel, as well as myself and other travellers. It involved another sweep through Korea but with emphasis on the more out-of-the-way places.

This Edition

This fourth edition was compiled following two trips to Korea, one by Choe Hyung Pun and Debbie Wood just prior to the Seoul Olympics, and another in late 1989 by Choe Hyung Pun and myself along with our five-month-old baby, Ashley Chosun, who proved to be a very popular boy with everyone from hoteliers to restaurateurs to bus drivers!

For the technically/ecologically minded this book was written on a solar-powered, Kaypro 4 micro-computer using eight Solarex X100GT panels together with a bank of 12 BP PVSTOR 2 volt, 1000 amp-hour batteries and a Santech 2000-watt AC inverter. Lonely Planet continue to hassle me to upgrade my computer hardware yet these '50s state-of-the-art machines continue to soldier on regardless of heat, humidity, dust, cat hairs and mud-wasps and they need no line filter. I'd need an air-conditioned cell to operate anything else!

I would particularly like to thank Choe Hyung Pun's parents and her older sister, Choe Hee Ja, for their incredible hospitality and superb food on the several occasions when we stayed with them at their house outside of Taejon. No three people were ever looked after so well. And the same was true of yet another of her older sisters and her husband at their farmhouse outside of Puyo. Thank you Kim Young Dok and Choe Chun Young!

I'd also like to thank Mr & Mrs Lee, the owners of the Kwang Pyung Yogwan in Seoul, for their warm welcome and their tenaciousness in keeping open one of the best and most mellow travellers' hotels in Asia despite intense pressure from the high-rise developers. It will be a sad loss when they finally have to close. Lastly, I must thank Volker Brandt of Berlin with whom we became close friends on our several forays outside of Kyongju. He epitomised the essence of real travelling and his humour was an inspiration.

Travellers to whom I am indebted for their informative and, on occasion, abrasive comments include:

Tami Adam; Lars Albinsson (Sw); John Ander; William Balsamo; Claudio Berutti (I); Lee Geok Boi (S); Larry Borgerson; D F Bradford (NZ); Peter Byron (Aus); Paul Carpenter (USA); Peter Chalanish (USA); Pascal Decoussemaeker (B); Len Dobbs (Aus); Mike Duffy; Warwick Gibbs; Wolf Gotthilf (D); Paul Greening (UK); S E Hitchcock (UK); Susan Holtham (NZ); Damien P Horigan; Brigitte Jacobs; Lorraine Kapakjian (USA); Bill Kelly; Ruthli Kemmerer (USA); Cora Knutson (USA); David Kraiker (USA); Michelle Krause; Ann Kunderer; Mr Kwon (Kor); M Hickman (UK); Janet Martin (Aus); Rick Olderman; Robert Plautz; Julienne Richards (Aus); Steve Robinson (D); Daniela Schneider (CH); Sonja Thompson; Keith & Pauline Tobin; Henk Tukker (Nl); Robert Wilkinson (USA); Andrew Wilson (C).

Aus - Australia, B - Belgium, C - Canada, CH - Switzerland, D - Germany, It - Italy, Kor - Korea, Nl - Netherlands, NZ - New Zealand, S - Singapore, Sw - Sweden, UK - United Kingdom, USA - United States of America

From the Publisher

Back at Lonely Planet, Melbourne, this edition of Korea was edited by Katie Cody and Caroline Williamson, and proofread by Sue Mitra. Many thanks go to Sharon Wertheim for her help with the production and indexing of the book. Tamsin Wilson, working on her first desk-top book, designed and layed out the book, drew the computer maps and illustrations, and designed the cover. Thanks also go to Vicki Beale for her production assistance and patience.

Warning & Request

Things change - prices go up, schedules change, good places go bad and bad places go bankrupt - nothing stays the same. So if you find things better or worse, recently opened or long since closed, please write and tell us and help make the next edition better. All information is greatly appreciated and the best letters will receive a free copy of the next edition, or any other Lonely Planet book of your choice.

Contents

MAP LEGEND

BOUNDARIES

.—.—.—.— ....International Boundaries
—..—..—.. ....Internal Boundaries
.—..—..— ....National Parks, Reserves
– – – – – – – ....The Equator
....The Tropics

SYMBOLS

◉ NEW DELHI ....National Capital
● BOMBAY ....Provincial or State Capital
● Pune ....Major Town
● Borsi ....Minor Town
⌂ ....Post Office
✈ ....Airport
i ....Tourist Information
◖ ....Bus Station, Terminal
66 ....Highway Route Number
☪ ✝ ✝ ....Mosque, Church, Cathedral
∴ ....Temple, Ruin or Archaeological Site
⌂ ....Hostel
✚ ....Hospital
☼ ....Lookout
▲ ....Camping Areas
⊓ ....Picnic Areas
⌂ ....Hut or Chalet
▲ ....Mountain
+++ ....Railway Station
....Road Bridge
....Road Rail Bridge
....Road Tunnel
....Railway Tunnel
....Escarpment or Cliff
....Pass
.............................Ancient or Historic Wall

ROUTES

—————— ....Major Roads and Highways
– – – – – – – ....Unsealed Major Roads
—————— ....Sealed Roads
– – – – – – – ....Unsealed Roads, Tracks
—————— ....City Streets
+++++++++++++ ....Railways
●——— ....Subways
....Walking Tracks
– – – – – – – ....Ferry Routes
+ +++ +++ + ...Cable Car or Chair Lift

HYDROGRAPHIC FEATURES

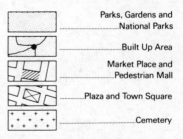

.................................Rivers, Creeks
– – – – ....Intermittent Streams
.....Lakes, Intermittent Lake
.................................Coast Line
....Spring
.....................................Waterfall
....Swamps
Salt Lakes, Reefs
....Glacier

OTHER FEATURES

Parks, Gardens and
National Parks
Built Up Area
Market Place and
Pedestrian Mall
Plaza and Town Square
Cemetery

Note: Not all the symbols displayed above will necessarily appear in this book

Introduction

Korea is still very much off the beaten track. Quite a few travellers get to the capital, Seoul, usually en route to somewhere else, and a few intrepid individuals make it to Cheju Island and Kyongju, but hardly anyone seems to take the time to explore the other attractions of the country. Undoubtedly the magnets of Japan and China serve to distract most people's attention, yet Korea is one of the most fascinating enigmas of the Far East. Its history is one of the world's most turbulent sagas of a small nation's struggle for survival against what would appear to be impossible odds. Sandwiched between vastly more powerful neighbours who, for at least two millennia, have frequently attempted to absorb it, it has nevertheless preserved its own unique character and cultural identity.

You might be forgiven for thinking that the most coveted gems of oriental culture are to be found either in Japan or China and that Korea merely offers a pale reflection of these. But you would be wrong. Korea has some of the world's most enchanting countryside - beautiful, forested mountains offering endless trekking possibilities which, while seen at their most colourful either in the spring or autumn, are misty and romantic even during the wet season. In the forests you will find sublimely crafted temple complexes whose origins stretch back 1500 years. A visit to any one of these hauntingly beautiful places will leave an indelible impression. Many of them are still functioning monasteries, and anyone expressing an interest in delving beneath the surface will find the monks not only very friendly but also hospitable. Then there are Korea's innumerable islands scattered like confetti off its southern and eastern shores, many of them with intriguing variations of the mainland culture. Very few of them have ever seen a visitor from abroad let alone had their paths tramped bare by tourist hordes.

And what of the people? Koreans are a proud, romantic, spontaneous and friendly people. You will not encounter that feeling of disinterest which Westerners often experience in China. Even in cosmopolitan Seoul you'll be regarded with curiosity. Wherever you go, but especially in the smaller places, you'll constantly be approached by people who want to strike up a conversation, whether they be soldiers, hotel proprietors, students, businesspeople or whatever. They will try their best, regardless of language or cultural differences, to establish some rapport with you, yet always with humour and never in an overbearing manner. If you respond with friendship and a little imagination you will often find yourself the recipient of the most unexpected and often disarming hospitality. It's not that Koreans don't have fairly rigidly defined rules of social conduct and public behaviour in common with other

9

Oriental people - they do, and you will often be aware of this - but for a foreigner they'll bend the rules double to spare you involvement and make you feel at home.

Not surprisingly, history lies heavily on these people. The cost of their survival as a nation has, at times, been devastating. The most recent example of this was, of course, the Korean War in the early '50s. Continually on the alert and prepared for invasion, the armed forces have always been an important element of Korean society. This is no less true today than it has ever been. It would be fatuous to ignore the ubiquitous presence of the army (and its American allies) in South Korea - conscription is a three year stint - but it would also be a grave mistake to allow these realities to prejudice your view of this country and its people. These people have felt the cold wind of superpower rivalry for centuries. Perhaps that's why they're so keen to establish friendships and exchange views with foreign visitors - but then again maybe it's just their natural disposition. Whatever the reasons, the line drawn between guest and lifelong friend is very much a question of your own attitude.

There's one last plus which ought to put Korea firmly on the traveller's route and that is its relative cheapness compared to such places as Japan and China. Even in central Seoul you can find places to stay for less than US$4 (sharing) or US$7 for a single and in the countryside it's often cheaper. Public transport is well organised and all but the most rural of roads are paved.

Korea is one of the unexplored gems of Asia. It once acquired the nickname of 'The Hermit Kingdom', after it closed its borders to all foreigners in the late 19th century as a result of what seemed like insuperable pressures from the outside. Once you have wandered round this country for a little while you'll realise what an inappropriate name that is for this exceptionally friendly and fascinating country.

Facts about the Country

Korean folk legends fix the date of the nation's birth from a semi-deity named Tangun at around 2333 BC, but according to the latest research its origins go back even further into the mists of time to 30,000 BC when migrating tribes from Central and Northern Asia first arrived in the peninsula. They brought with them their own folk myths and animistic religion as well as their own language, the latter a branch of the Ural-Altaic group which also includes Finnish, Hungarian and Turkish. This distinct language, though it borrowed Chinese script (until *hangul* was invented in the 15th century) and some of its vocabulary, has been of the utmost importance in maintaining Korean cultural identity down through the centuries.

The earliest influences assimilated by these nomadic tribes came from the Chinese, who had established an outpost near present-day Pyongyang during the Han Dynasty. Constant wars with the Chinese dictated the necessity for an early alliance between the tribes of the north which eventually led to the formation of the first Korean kingdom – Koguryo – around the 1st century AD, and the uniting of the northern half of the peninsula four centuries later following the demise of Han. Not being subject to the same immediate pressures, the related tribes of the south were slower to coalesce, but by the 3rd century AD two powerful kingdoms – Silla and Paekje – had emerged to dominate the southern half of the peninsula. Sandwiched between them for a while in the south was the loose confederacy of Kaya, but this had a relatively brief existence since the leaders of its constituent tribes were rarely able to present a common front when threatened with invasion.

Three Kingdoms Period

The next four centuries – known as the Three Kingdoms Period (Koguryo, Paekje and Silla) – witnessed a remarkable flowering of the arts, architecture, literature and statecraft as Chinese influences continued to be absorbed, reinterpreted and alloyed with traditional Korean ideas and practices. Probably the single most formative influence was Buddhism which, in time, became the state religion of all three kingdoms. Buddhism has immeasurably enriched Korean culture, and even though it was suppressed in favour of Confucianism when the Koryo Dynasty was overthrown at the end of the 14th century it remains an integral part of modern Korea. It has left an indelible mark on the language, manners, customs, art and folklore of the people.

The Three Kingdoms Period was also the time when the developments which were taking place in Korea began to be exported to Japan. Architects and builders from Paekje, for instance, were primarily responsible for the great burst of temple construction which occurred in Japan during the 6th century. This transmission of cultural developments naturally accelerated during periods of conflict and there were times in Japan's early history when there were more Koreans involved in influential secular and religious positions than Japanese.

There was, of course, much rivalry between the three kingdoms and wars were fought constantly in attempts to gain supremacy, but it was not until the 7th century that a major shift of power occurred.

Silla Dominance

The rise of the Tang Dynasty in China during the 7th century provided Silla with the opportunity to expand its dominion over the whole peninsula. An alliance of the two was formed, and the combined armies first attacked Paekje, which fell shortly afterwards, followed by Koguryo in 668 AD.

The alliance, however, was short-lived

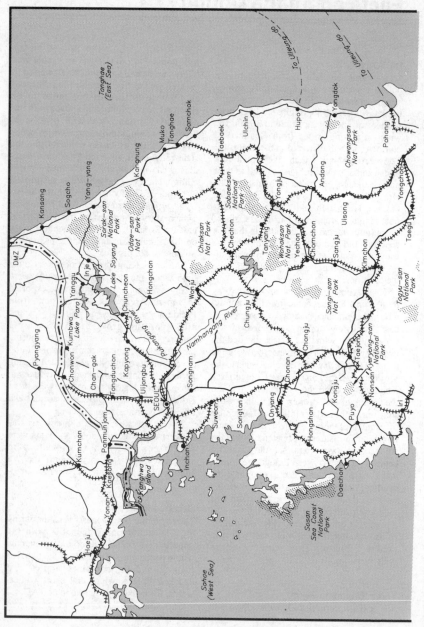

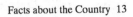

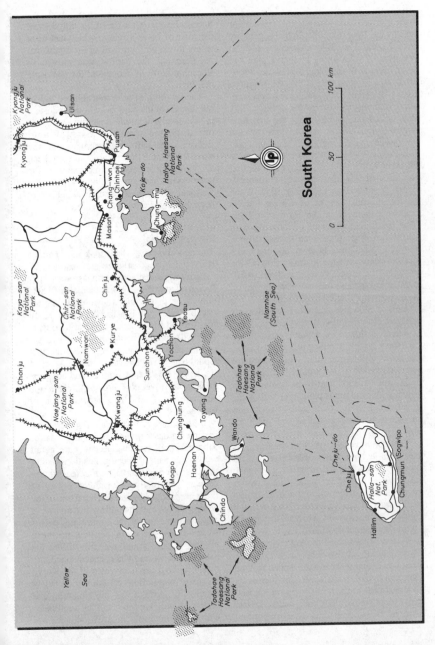

South Korea

since it turned out to have been a convenient ruse by the Tang ruler to establish hegemony over Korea. The Silla aristocracy had no intention of subscribing to such a plan and so, in order to thwart Tang designs, switched allegiance to what was left of the Koguryo forces. Together, the two Korean forces were able eventually to drive out the Chinese. Silla thus united the peninsula for the first time and this unification was to last through various changes of regime right up until partition after WW II. Yet Silla was to learn, as all other Korean dynasties have had to, that the price of this often precarious independence depended on the recognition of the vastly superior forces of China and its acknowledgement in the form of tribute. This traditional tributary relationship with China has more than once thrown Korea, through no action of its own, into the lion's den between contending armies from China at times of dynastic change, and left it vulnerable to Japanese military adventurism on its own territory and that of China's.

Unified Silla presided over one of Korea's greatest eras of cultural development, and nowhere is this more apparent than in the countless tombs, temples, pagodas, palaces, pleasure gardens and other relics which dot the countryside in and around Kyongju, the Silla capital. Buddhism in particular flourished, with state funds being lavished on the construction of temples and images, and monks dispatched to China and India for study.

The cohesiveness of Silla society was based on the twin pillars of *kolpum* – a rigid hierarchy of rank based on ancestry – and the *hwarang* – a kind of paramilitary youth organisation for the training and educating of the sons of the Silla elite. Yet it was the rigidity of this system which also brought about its eventual downfall.

By the beginning of the 9th century, discontent among those who were excluded from power had reached such a pitch that the kingdom began to fall apart. Threatened by rival warlords to the north and west, the end came surprisingly bloodlessly when the last king of Silla, unwilling to contemplate further destruction, offered his kingdom to the ruler of Later Koguryo which had been set up in the northern half of the peninsula. As a result, the capital was moved to Kaesong, north of Seoul, and the peninsula reunited.

The last king of Silla was allowed to live out the rest of his days as an honoured guest in his rival's capital. Kyongju sank into obscurity and remained that way until 'rediscovered' in the 20th century – in many ways a fortunate event since had there been a major conflict at the time many of the priceless archaeological finds now in the National Museum at Kyongju would have been destroyed, looted or lost forever.

Koryo Dynasty

The new dynasty, which took the name of Koryo, abolished *kolpum* and restructured the government, placing emphasis on a Confucian examination system for state officials similar to that which prevailed in China, except that eligibility for the examination was limited to the sons of the ruling oligarchy. With stability restored, the new dynasty prospered and it was during this time that Buddhism, through royal patronage, reached the height of its development and acquired considerable secular power through the acquisition of land and accumulation of wealth.

In time, however, the Koryo government became as despotic and arrogant as that of Silla, except that in this case it was the literati who monopolised the top positions rather than warrior-aristocrats. Disaffected military officers eventually reduced the power of these bureaucrats by assassinating one of the Koryo kings and installing his son as a puppet ruler. Yet, at the same time, events were taking place on Korea's northern borders which would radically affect the nation's survival as an independent kingdom.

Throughout the later years of the Koryo Dynasty, marauding Khitan tribes began making life difficult for the kingdom, and they were only kept in check by an alliance with the Mongols of China. The alliance was a reluctant one on the part of Koryo since it involved the payment of considerable annual tribute, and eventually it was broken off.

The reckoning didn't come until 1231 since the Mongols were preoccupied with their own internal problems, but when it did the decision to rescind the treaty proved to have been a disastrous one. The Mongols invaded with vastly superior forces, quickly took Kaesong and forced the king to take refuge on Kanghwa Island where he remained relatively safe but totally powerless while the Mongols laid waste to the peninsula for the next 25 years. A truce was finally arranged in 1259, despite opposition from a die-hard Koryo faction. The Koryo monarch was restored to his kingdom (minus Cheju Island which the Mongols used for rearing horses) on condition that Koryo crown princes would be held hostage at Beijing until the deaths of their fathers, that they would be forced to marry Mongol princesses and that the tribute would be restored.

The tribute demanded by the settlement was a heavy one for Korea to shoulder. It included gold, silver, horses, ginseng, hawks, artisans, women and eunuchs but that was not all that Koryo was compelled to provide. There were also demands to provide soldiers and ships for the ill-fated Mongol attempt to invade Japan between 1274 and 1281. These various exactions plus the powerful influence which the Mongol princesses wielded at the Koryo court led to intolerable strains being placed on the fabric of Korean society and were the root cause of the eventual downfall of Koryo.

Still, Koryo survived for a little while longer and reasserted its independence when rebellions in China led to the ousting of the Mongols and their replacement by the Ming Dynasty. There were reforms and wholesale purges of pro-Mongol aristocrats, but the rot had spread too far, and rebellions broke out which climaxed in the overthrow of the Koryo monarch and the foundation of a new dynasty by one of the king's former generals, Yi Song-Gye.

Yi (Chosun) Dynasty

The new regime staked its future on the ideals and practices of Neo-Confucianism which combined the sage's original ethical and political ideas with a quasi-religious practice of ancestor worship and the idea of the eldest male as spiritual head of the family. At the same time, Buddhism, regarded as an enemy and rival, was suppressed. The monasteries' estates were confiscated, their wealth sequestered and the building of monasteries limited to rural areas. Buddhism has never recovered its former dominance, as a result of these events, but it still wields considerable influence and its economic clout is definitely on the rise. Nevertheless, Neo-Confucianism remains the moral foundation of the nation though few Koreans would actually acknowledge it as their 'religion'.

The next 150 years were a time of relative peace and prosperity during which great strides were made under a succession of enlightened kings, the greatest of whom was probably Sejong (1418-50). It was he who presided over the invention of a phonetic script – hangul – for the Korean language. The new script was an outstanding achievement and, since it was infinitely simpler than Chinese, led to a vast increase in literacy. However, it was not introduced without considerable opposition among the intelligentsia, many of whom regarded it as subversive and worried about the reaction of the Ming court.

Japanese Invasion of 1592

The period of peace came to a dramatic end in 1592 when the country was invaded by a newly-united Japan under Toyotomi Hideyoshi, following Korea's refusal to join with them in an invasion of China. Exploiting to the full their superior weaponry – muskets supplied by the Portuguese – the Japanese overran the peninsula in just one month. At sea, however, they were soundly defeated by Korea's most famous admiral, Yi Sun-Sin, the inventor of the world's first ironclad ships (known as turtle ships or gobugson). In their naval encounters with

Admiral Yi Sun-Sin, the Japanese lost more than 500 ships in less than six months. Unfortunately the admiral fell foul of the Yi court and was dismissed, only to be recalled at a later date when his successor failed to match up.

The war dragged on for four years until Korean guerrilla resistance and Chinese intervention forced it to a conclusion. Nevertheless, the Japanese invaded again the following year, though this time the war was confined to the southern provinces, and came to a speedier end when Hideyoshi died and the invaders withdrew.

The Japanese invasion was an unprecedented disaster for Korea. Many craftspeople and intellectuals were taken prisoner and transported to Japan and almost all Korea's temples and palaces were burnt to the ground during this period. Yet there was to be no early respite.

Admiral Yi

The Manchu Invasion

The early 17th century was a time of conflict in China. The Manchus there were in the process of overthrowing the Ming court with whom the Koreans had treaty obligations. Though unsure which side to declare for, the Korean court decided to side with the Ming, thus incurring the wrath of the Manchus who, as soon as they had consolidated their hold over China, turned to invade Korea. The Korean forces were routed and severe restrictions placed on the country's sovereignty.

Korea – the Hermit Kingdom

Profoundly shocked and exhausted by this series of events, Korea folded its wings and withdrew into itself over the next century while the pace of change all around it continued to accelerate – largely due to the spread of Western ideas and contacts. Nowhere was this more apparent than in the number of converts to Catholicism and, later, to various sects of Protestantism. Frightened by the growing influence of these groups, the Yi court panicked and in the repression which followed hundreds of people were executed. But the major event which most shook their confidence was the occupation of Beijing by the French and British in 1860. In a vain attempt to shut off these dawning realities, the country was closed to all foreigners including the Japanese. It was as a result of this period that Korea acquired the name of the 'Hermit Kingdom'.

It was a policy doomed to failure. The late 19th century was no time to turn a blind eye to the increasing industrial and military might of the European maritime nations, the USA and Japan. Sooner or later, one or more of these nations would force the Koreans to open their doors. This happened some 25 years later as a result of independent occupations of Kanghwa Island by the French and Americans and a naval skirmish engineered by the Japanese which led to a so-called treaty of 'friendship'. The treaty was naturally biased in favour of the Japanese. Korean ports were opened to Japanese traders and the policy of excluding foreigners was abandoned. Suddenly, very ill prepared, Korea found herself blown like a leaf in the winds of imperial rivalry. Though she made a valiant effort to modernise and meet the challenge it was too late.

Japanese Control

The Tonghak uprising in 1894 – by followers of a new religious sect founded in 1860 by Choe Che-U which combined elements of Confucianism, Buddhism, Taoism and Shamanism – set off a chain of events which led to the Sino-Japanese War, the defeat of China and the installation of a Japanese-controlled government in Seoul. With China eliminated, Russia quickly jumped into the political arena and the Koreans became pawns in yet another struggle between giants. During this time pro-Japanese and pro-Russian governments followed each other in rapid succession in Seoul. Queen Min – the real power behind the Yi throne – was assassinated by Japanese agents, and for a year and a half King Kojong took refuge inside the Russian legation. In the end the struggle for supremacy was settled by the Russo-Japanese War of 1904 and Korea was occupied by the Japanese. Shortly after, in 1910, following public riots and serious guerrilla activity by elements of the disbanded Korean army, the Japanese annexed the country, abolished the monarchy and began to mould the country's economy along lines which would best exploit its resources and maximise returns for its colonial master.

With a long tradition of resistance to foreign domination, however, the Koreans did not simply lie down and accept annexation by Japan. After the failure of a Korean delegation to gain the right of self-determination at the Versailles Conference following WW I, an independence movement was formed by a group of patriots. They leafleted Seoul and provoked public demonstrations against the Japanese occupation. The unrest quickly spread to the rest of the country. The Japanese troops and police panicked, and in the brutal repression which followed over 7000 Koreans were shot and many thousands more seriously injured.

Cosmetic reforms were brought in to try and contain the uprising, but at the same time the ranks of the secret police were rapidly expanded and censorship tightened.

As WW II drew near, Japan's grip over Korea was tightened even further. The Japanese language was made mandatory as the medium of instruction in schools, all public signs had to be in Japanese, the teaching of Korean history was banned and hundreds of thousands of Korean labourers were conscripted to assist the Japanese army both in Korea and in China. It was a time which the Koreans quite rightly regard as one of attempted cultural genocide and the scars are a long way from being healed even today. Despite political shifts of power since WW II, Koreans still despise Japan for what it did to their country and rows between Seoul and Tokyo are not infrequent.

Post WW II

If Koreans had imagined that the defeat of Japan in WW II would usher in a new era of peace then their hopes were quickly dashed. A deal had been struck between the USSR, USA and Britain over the fate of postwar Korea in which the USSR was to occupy the peninsula north of the 38th parallel and the USA the country south of that. Though never intended as a permanent division, it soon turned out that way once the occupying troops were in position. Negotiations for a provisional government floundered when neither side was willing to make concessions which would result in the loss of its influence over the proposed new government. A UN commission was set up to try and resolve the problem and to oversee elections for a united government, but it was denied entry to the north and was forced to confine its activities to the south. The new government which was elected in the south declared its independence and provoked the Communists in the north to do likewise. The stage was set for the Korean War.

The Korean War

By 1948, Soviet and American troops had been withdrawn but while the Americans supplied only arms considered necessary for self-defence to the regime in the south, the USSR provided the north with a vast array of weaponry with which to create a powerful army. On 25 June 1950, the North Korean army invaded. The Americans responded by sending in troops who were soon joined by contingents from 16 other countries following a UN resolution supporting the American action. The USSR absented herself from the Security Council deliberations.

The war went badly for the UN at first and its troops were soon pushed into a small pocket around Pusan but, following a daring landing at Incheon under the command of General MacArthur, its fortunes changed and within a month the North Korean army had been thrown back to the borders of Manchuria. Such a development was anathema to the new Communist regime in China, still flushed from its recent victory over the Guomindang forces. In November of the same year Mao Zedong decided to intervene on behalf of North Korea. The Chinese poured troops into the war and the UN forces were pushed back below the 38th parallel. The conflict continued for the next six months with both sides alternately advancing and retreating until a stalemate was reached just north of the 38th parallel.

Negotiations for a truce were started but dragged on for two years, eventually leading to the creation of the De-Militarised Zone (DMZ) and the truce village of Panmunjom where both sides have met periodically ever since to exchange rhetoric and denounce provocations.

At the end of the war Korea lay in ruins. Seoul had changed hands no less than four times and was flattened. Millions of people were left homeless, industry destroyed and the countryside devastated. In the south, 47,000 Koreans had lost their lives and around 200,000 were wounded. Of the UN troops, 37,000 had been killed (most of them Americans) and 120,000 wounded. Combined military and civilian casualties in the north were estimated at 1½ to two million.

Post Korean War

North Korea North Korea went on to become one of the most closed countries in the world, ruled by the eccentric and uncompromising Kim Il-Sung whose position as head of state is maintained by a constant barrage of propaganda which gushes about his boundless wisdom, doctrinal purity and almost godlike qualities. If anyone deserves an accolade for having outdone Mao Zedong in the business of personality cults then it's Kim Il-Sung.

A similar barrage of self-congratulatory rhetoric is now being churned out for the benefit of his son who is being groomed for the succession. It is doubtful, however, that he will ever be able to match his father's grip on power. Plus, even North Korea cannot entirely ignore developments in the relationship between the superpowers.

South Korea In the South economic recovery was slow and the civilian government of President Rhee weak and corrupt. In 1961, following blatantly fraudulent elections, massive student demonstrations and the resignation of Rhee, a military dictatorship was established with General Park Chung-Hee emerging as its strongman. Pressures soon mounted for the return of a civilian government and so, in 1963, Park retired from the army and stood as a candidate for the Democratic Republican Party. The party won the elections and Park was named president. Park was re-elected as president in 1967 and again in 1971 though he only very narrowly missed defeat in 1971 at the hands of his rival, Kim Dae-Jung.

On the positive side, Park created an efficient administration and was the architect of South Korea's economic 'miracle'. But in October 1972, in an attempt to secure his position, he declared martial law, clamped down on political opponents and instituted an era of intensely personal rule. Like Kim Il-Sung, he created his own personality cult but his record on human rights grew progressively worse and, finally, in October 1979, he was assassinated by his own chief of secret police.

The 1980s

After Park's death, there was a brief period of political freedom in which popular expectations of reform were aroused. They were short-lived. In May 1980, a group of army officers headed by General Chun Doo-Hwan took control and arrested leading opposition politicians, including Kim Dae-Jung. Student riots erupted in Kim's home town of Kwangju and were brutally put down. Feelings were running high, however, and Chun's action merely inflamed passions further. This time the whole city rose against his government. A full-scale army assault was mounted and the insurrection savagely repressed. Realistic estimates of the dead put them at around 2000 though the government vigorously denied this and has maintained that stand ever since. Thousands more were arrested.

In the rigged elections which were held shortly after this, Chun secured his position as president but since more than 500 former politicians were banned from political activity during the campaign the result was a foregone conclusion. Kim Dae-Jung was tried for treason and sentenced to death, but so transparent were the charges against him that Chun was reluctantly forced to commute the sentence to life imprisonment following worldwide protests. Probably the single most important factor which saved Kim was Chun's need for a continued and substantial American military presence in South Korea (every main city has one or more American base). Though Reagan had just come to power and was intent on keeping American forces there, Chun's insistence on going through with Kim's execution was placing in jeopardy Congressional approval for Reagan's wishes. Kim Dae-Jung was released some time later in order to allow him to go to the USA for medical treatment. He stayed on there as a lecturer at Harvard University until his return to Korea in 1987.

Having consolidated his power base, Chun, on the other hand, lifted martial law, granted amnesty to quite a few detainees, and allowed the National Assembly to debate issues somewhat more freely than was ever possible during Park's presidency. Press censorship, nevertheless, remained tight under a 'voluntary restraint' system and the authorities steadfastly refused to allow any substantive discussion to emerge on the question of reunification. It was evident, too, that corruption and cronyism still existed within the government following the breaking of a scandal involving the embezzlement of millions of dollars of government funds by one of Chun's immediate family members.

While Chun survived the scandal, many high-ranking government ministers and army officers were forced to resign. He also miraculously escaped assassination in late 1983 whilst on an official visit to Burma. His fellow ministers were not so lucky. Almost all of them were killed in a bomb blast in Rangoon as they were arriving for a reception. Two North Korean army officers were later arrested and found guilty of the outrage.

The slayings returned relations between North and South Korea to subzero level despite an apparent slight thaw the previous year. Nevertheless, in late 1984, following devastating floods in the South, North Korea offered to help with substantial emergency aid such as food, tents and cement. The offer was viewed with prudent suspicion since it involved convoys of North Korean trucks crossing the border but it was eventually accepted and the aid delivered. There's little doubt that the motivation behind the offer was to score a diplomatic coup but it probably also had a lot to do with Chinese pressure.

The Chinese government exercises a major influence over North Korea and for a number of years it has been pressuring Kim Il-Sung to make genuine moves in the direction of an accommodation with the South in keeping with the continued Chinese expansion of ties with the West and especially with the USA. Just how far this will go remains to be seen. It's unlikely to go too far before Kim Il-Sung's death and a change of regime in Seoul, though the South did attempt to make substantial concessions to the North over a sharing of events for the 1988 Olympics in order to head off another boycott by Communist countries. In the event, however, North Korea refused the South's offers and became one of only two nations to boycott the Olympics.

While negotiations for the Olympics were going on, Chun announced his intention to step down from the presidency in February 1988. Shortly afterwards, Roh Tae-Woo, a classmate and confidant of Chun's, was nominated by the ruling party to succeed him. For a while it seemed that real democracy was still just a distant dream.

What happened next was largely unexpected but took the world by storm. Overnight, thousands of students in every city across the nation took to the streets to demonstrate. They were met by riot police, tear gas and mass arrests and within a matter of days the country was at flash point. The students were quickly joined by tens of thousands of both industrial and office workers and even Buddhist monks. The subways and streets of Seoul reeked of tear gas around the clock and gas masks became an essential item of equipment. Something had to give. Though threatening draconian measures to quell the disturbances, Chun largely took a back seat and left Roh to negotiate.

Under intense American pressure to compromise, and well aware of the obvious fact that the government wasn't just confronted with a bunch of radical students, Roh invited the leaders of the opposition Reunification Democratic Party to talks. The two figureheads of the opposition were Kim Young-Sam and Kim Dae-Jung.

Kim Dae-Jung had returned from exile in the USA the year before but had been kept under virtual house arrest ever since then. The two opposition leaders suddenly found themselves on centre stage but a deal with the government proved to be elusive. What was being demanded were free, direct, popular presidential elections, the release of political prisoners, freedom of the press and a number of other reforms. Roh felt he could not concede these demands and so negotiations were broken off. But not for long. While massive demonstrations continued on

the streets, the country was convulsed by a wave of strikes by industrial workers. Civil war and a military coup were getting dangerously close. Realising this, Chun gave Roh the go-ahead to concede all of the opposition's demands. The country reeled with a mixture of disbelief and ecstasy and the demonstrations stopped. Although strikes continued at various industrial plants over the next few weeks, they were mainly about wage increases and better conditions. At last it seemed that years of iron-fisted military rule, oppression, arrests, torture and censorship had come to an end.

The deal set in motion campaigns for the coming presidential elections by both the ruling Democratic Justice Party and the opposition Reunification Democratic Party. At first, it seemed that the two Kims of the opposition party would form an alliance and agree to one of them running for president in order not to split the opposition vote. A lot of pledges were made in this respect early on in the campaign but, in the end, they both announced their candidacy after touring the major cities and testing the depth of their respective support. In terms of gaining the presidency, this proved to be a fatal decision.

In the elections which followed (judged to have been the fairest ever held), neither of the Kims were able to match Roh's share of the vote (37%) though their combined total (55%) was considerably more than Roh's. Roh therefore became the next president and his party the government. There was a good deal of sabre-rattling during the election campaign with various army officers threatening a coup should Kim Dae-Jung win the election, but the one thing which probably restrained them most was the thought that the 1988 Olympics scheduled for Seoul might have to be cancelled if such an event occurred. As a matter of national pride, few people in South Korea wanted to see that happen.

Following the elections there were the inevitable accusations of vote-rigging and electoral fraud but much of this was simply sour grapes on behalf of the opposition. And there were the inevitable clashes between extremist student demonstrators and police. The failure of the opposition to win the presidency, however, was far more prosaic than sinister and was largely a question of egos getting in the way of practicalities. By failing to compromise and running against one another, the opposition was doomed from the start. Even Kim Young-Sam admitted as much when, after the result was announced, he publicly apologised to the country for having failed to reach an agreement with Kim Dae-Jung and field a single opposition candidate.

With Roh in power but restrained by two quite powerful opposition parties, some of the heat has gone out of South Korean politics – at least on the surface. Isolated student demonstrations still erupt here and there but it's perhaps true to say that they don't enjoy widespread support among the population at large. The one issue which has come to the fore and which refuses to bury its head is that of reunification.

With an intransigent military dictatorship out of the way, South Koreans are beginning to turn their thoughts to the reunification of the peninsula. Kim Dae-Jung has been in the forefront of moves in this direction but has been badly let down by members of his opposition party who have made clandestine trips to Pyongyang (they were afterwards forced to resign) without clearance from the party or the government-controlled National Security police. Even Kim has been hauled in for questioning, accused of prior knowledge of the trips, but released for lack of proof.

Throughout 1989, such trips to Pyongyang by various activists became almost daily news. Even Catholic priests having connections with farmers' and other labour organisations were discovered to have gone. In some cases it seems that Pyongyang was not only funding the trips but providing money to dissident organisations in the south. The whole sad affair – sad in the sense of a people's legitimate longing – came to a head with the well-publicised visit of Lim Soo-Kyong to the 1989 Pyongyang Youth Festival. Lim, a Seoul University student,

had gone there via Europe, made impassioned speeches in favour of reunification and then attempted, with the encouragement of the North Korean authorities, to return to South Korea via Panmunjom. No-one is allowed to do this without the approval of both the North Koreans and the UN and she was, at first, refused. Two weeks later, after a flurry of diplomatic activity, she was finally allowed through only to be promptly arrested and taken to Seoul. It was a measure of the degree of press and television freedom now allowed in South Korea that her trip was widely reported and included footage of her speeches in Pyongyang on the government-controlled KBS TV network.

While the government undoubtedly over-reacted – and in so doing made her a martyr to the cause – the issue won't lie down. Sooner or later it will have to be addressed seriously and major compromises made by both sides if reunification is ever to become a reality. It won't happen while Kim Il-Sung is still alive since his people have been fed an undiluted diet of vitriol designed to paint the leaders of the south as American puppets and capitalist roaders intent on keeping their people in poverty and chains. As such, they're ill-prepared to accept an about-face. But it's equally unlikely to happen while the South Korean military top brass continue to wield such an influence over the government of the south and while the police of the National Security organisation continue to conduct witch-hunts among opposition politicians in search of supposed North Korean 'agents'.

None of this will bring peace to the peninsula but it's probably true to say that it's the activists in the south, even if they're naive or just idealistic, who will be in a better position to deal with the issues of reunification when it finally gets a decent hearing than the dogmatic cadres of the north. Kim Il-Sung may think that the people of the south need 'liberating' and many people in the south may agree. But they have very little interest in exchanging one repressive regime for another and they're not impressed by Kim Il-Sung's political opportunism in exploiting idealistic young students from the south for his own purposes.

GEOGRAPHY

The Korean peninsula borders on Manchuria and the USSR in the north, faces China in the west across the Yellow Sea and Japan to the east and south across the East Sea (Sea of Japan). Its overall length from north to south is approximately 1000 km while at its narrowest point it is 216 km wide. In terms of land area it is about the same size as the UK. The peninsula is divided roughly in half just north of the 38th parallel between the two countries, North and South Korea. The great bulk of the country is mountainous, the highest peaks being Mt Halla on Cheju Island in South Korea at 2000 metres and Mt Paektu at 2800 metres in North Korea.

ECONOMY

In the south, agriculture is confined to the narrow, often terraced, valleys where the main crops are rice, barley, other cereal crops, ginseng and tobacco. Horticulture is a rapidly expanding primary industry. Cheju Island is the only part of the country where the climate is suitable for growing semitropical fruits – citrus, bananas and pineapples.

Most of the mountains are forested and South Korea is one of the world's leading nations in reafforestation. There's a lot this nation could teach the rest of the world about this even though some Korean companies do rape the forests of other nations.

The mainstay of South Korea's economy, on the other hand, is industry and this is dominated by the manufacturing industries concentrated around Seoul, Taejon, Taegu, Kwangju and Pusan. Despite the devastation of the Korean War these industries have made great strides as a result of which South Koreans now enjoy a standard of living rivalling that of the Taiwanese and Japanese. The main manufacturing products are iron and steel, chemicals, shipping, automobiles, textiles, and consumer products and they're rapidly moving into hi-tech. Many of these industries have become so successful over the last 10 years that they have forced plants in some of the older industrialised nations to close down.

Another major foreign exchange earner is the construction industry. South Korean firms can be found building highways, hotels, factories and residential complexes as far afield as Libya and Paraguay.

POPULATION

The population of South Korea stands at 42 million.

CULTURE
Courtesy, Names & Titles

Once you've tried to jostle your way through the rush-hour crowds of downtown Seoul and been buffeted from pillar to post by what seems like every third person without any murmur of apology, you might get the impression that Koreans are a rude bunch. The truth lies elsewhere and is to be found in the Confucian education system which lacks a code of behaviour for relating to outsiders. You simply don't fit into any traditional category so many Koreans have difficulty relating to you as they can't place you. It's not that any offence is intended – far from it – indeed it's probably true to say that embarrassment is the most common reaction to street collisions and that is to be avoided since it disturbs *kibun* (a feeling of wellbeing based on harmony in interpersonal relationships).

Even among Koreans, no-one merits special consideration in everyday activities unless they are members of the same family, the same club, the same company, the same school or whatever. Times are changing, of course, and you'll find that most Koreans will bend over backwards to be friendly, courteous and helpful to foreigners. Stand around looking perplexed in any bus station and there'll be someone beside you within seconds to ask if they can help.

Once you get to know people, however, as a family friend, business associate or colleague there's a dramatic change. When this happens you'll be treated in the manner appropriate to your position and you'll be expected to treat others likewise. Allowances, of course, are made for foreigners. You won't be expected to be an expert on social etiquette from the day you arrive. The secret to good relations is to keep everyone's *kibun* high.

Most Koreans will spare no effort to avoid impoliteness or rudeness even if they feel otherwise. Abrasive Western reactions to incompetence, delays, mistakes and dishonesty are totally unpalatable to Koreans. These people wear their self-esteem on their sleeves and are acutely aware of loss of face. Should this occur in front of others it can have a devastating effect. It's like letting a bull loose in a china shop. Bear this in mind whilst you are in Korea and if you have a sharp tongue, keep it in check.

Again, it comes down to Confucian strictures about the manner in which social relations ought to be conducted. Whether you think Confucianism is reactionary or not isn't going to make any difference. There is a fairly rigid social hierarchy and Koreans cannot even speak correctly without knowing who they are talking to. The form of the grammar used for addressing someone changes depending on whether you are talking to the president, your superior in the work place, an old person, a child, your mother or father, elder brother or sister, younger brother or sister or friend. In order to establish which form of address is correct, a Korean will want to know where you were born, how old you are, which school you went to, what position you hold in your job and several other things.

Titles and names are also important and should be treated with respect. Koreans always have three names. The family name (surname) is always placed first and, although there are some 200 family names in all, more than half the population is called Kim, Park or Lee. The latter may often be rendered as Yi, Rhee or Ee in English but they're all the same name. A person's second name is a generation name chosen by parents or grandparents sometimes with the help of an onomancer. It will have the meaning of good fortune in one form or another. Sometimes all the brothers and even

sisters of the same family will share the same second name though this isn't usual. The last name is a person's given name. Another thing to bear in mind is that Korean women do not change their family names when they marry but children born of a marriage always carry their father's family name.

Names are not used in the same way as they are in the West and Koreans regard their generational and given names as very personal possessions. Only very good friends of the same age would address each other using these names. Tradition and mutual respect demand that others address each other by their family names so you always call someone Mr Kim, Mrs Han, Miss Choe or whatever. And this isn't all. While a married couple will address each other as *yobo* (equivalent to 'darling') and be called Mr Choe and Mrs Han by people they don't know or don't know well, for instance, their neighbours will call them Hyung Pun's father or Hyung Pun's mother (if the name of the eldest child remaining in the family is Hyung Pun). When that child leaves the family, the father and mother will be called after the next eldest child. Most Korean children under high school age won't even know their father's or mothers' generational and given names because they will never have heard them. Even within a family, a younger sister or brother would not address an older brother or sister by name. Instead they call them simply 'brother' or 'sister'. On the other hand, older brothers and sisters address their younger brothers and sisters by name but they usually add the affix *see* to the end of the given name.

What happens if you don't know someone's name and you want to address them in a respectful manner? That's simple. Just use the most polite form of 'hello' (*anyong hasimnika* – very polite – or *anyong haseyo* – somewhat more informal) since the grammar itself indicates all nuances of social etiquette. With old people you can preface this with *harobo-ji* (grandfather) or *horomon-ee* (grandmother) before saying 'hello' if you want to draw their attention. With other adult men, the word is *ajosi* and for adult women it is *ajimah*. A young woman, on the other hand, is called *agasi*.

Lastly, when Koreans meet, they bow. The younger or less important person bows lower than the older or more important person. Hand shaking is a Western import but well-known and acceptable among city dwellers when meeting foreigners.

Entertaining

If you've ever been invited out for a meal or even just a drinking and dancing session at a club with Korean friends, you'll know how hard it is to pay for the bill yourself or even contribute to it. The same applies even if it's you that's doing the inviting. All manner of ruses will be used to beat you to the cashier even if it means that the person who pays is going to have to live on bread and water for the next week. It's a matter of honour and pride. The concept of a free lunch is alien. If you feel that it's your shout for the bill, you must *insist* on this but, at the same time, cater for the demands of honour by suggesting that, when you meet again, they can pay the bill. This can take a certain degree of determination. Even if your hosts are rich (in any relative sense) and you are poor and simply can't afford to pay the bill, you *must* offer. This gesture is most important but it won't be taken up unless you are adamant. The bill for a group is always paid by one person and one only.

Naturally, budget travellers simply won't have the funds to pick up the bill for a whole group. That's no problem so long as your Korean host is aware of your financial predicament. If you want to or feel that you ought to contribute then make these arrangements before you go out and square up after you leave. Never attempt to do it in front of the cashier. You will seriously embarrass your host. Indeed, by doing anything like this, you may embarrass them to such a degree that they'll never be able to return to that particular restaurant/club.

Don't take hospitality for granted. Koreans will not accept an invitation to a meal or night out unless they can at least pay a fair contribution towards the bill. I once made this mistake by inviting a student I'd met in a bar out to a meal with us. There would have been no problem if we had simply eaten *pekpan* (the basic Korean meal at a cheap restaurant) but we ate at a *pulgogi* restaurant. He was visibly embarrassed because there was no way his budget would have stretched to even paying his share of the bill despite the fact I had assured him it wasn't expected.

Having said that, what die-hards would describe as chivalry and radicals as male chauvinism still survives here. If you're a man taking a woman out for the night, you pay. She won't even offer. If you're a woman taking a man out, he pays. It's expected. Compromise arrangements are possible if both parties are poor and know each other fairly well.

RELIGION

Disregarding for the moment whether Confucianism is a religion or merely a code of morals and social conduct, Korea has four religions of major importance – Buddhism, Confucianism, Christianity and shamanism. There are also a few Muslims and even a mosque in Seoul.

Buddhism

Siddhartha Gautama, the historical Buddha, was born in northern India around 560 BC of a princely family at a time when Hinduism had lost its vitality and was weighed down by traditionalism, mystification and Brahmin privilege.

Having spent many years studying and rigorously testing various Hindu theories and practices, all of which were supposedly designed to result in enlightenment and release from the eternal wheel of reincarnation, he emerged with a sense of the futility of extremism. The exact nature of his enlightenment under the Bodhi tree at Sarnath is, of course, impossible to describe in words but he went on to found an order of monks and a religion of infinite compassion.

Amongst other things, he taught that there was no caste to whom all was revealed. Everyone was capable of knowing the truth.

He eschewed ritual and resisted the attempts of his disciples to institute them. Despite being a master of dialogue and dialectic, he refused to become involved in dualistic speculation on the nature of the universe knowing this was merely a diversion. His sermons addressed only the causes of suffering, their destruction and the path by which they could be destroyed. He rejected fatalism and defeatism and condemned all forms of divination and traditionalism. Enlightenment was a hard, practical path which avoided sentimentality, on the one hand, and indifference on the other.

The message was pure and simple, uncluttered by the usual trappings of religion. He also cautioned against any attempts to have him declared a god. He was simply one who had realised the ultimate truth and that possibility was open to everyone.

Gautama Buddha (or Sakyamuni Buddha as he is now known) said much about how enlightenment could be attained. Briefly this comes down to what is known as the Four Noble Truths and the Eightfold Path. The Four Noble Truths, though originally couched in precise Hindu terms, can be summarised as: suffering is a reality; it is caused by a drive for separate existence and fulfilment; it can be overcome; the means to overcome it are the steps contained in the Eightfold Path.

The Eightfold Path in turn can be summarised as: right knowledge, aspiration, speech, behaviour, livelihood, effort, mindfulness and absorption.

All these points can be interpreted in different ways – and they were. Moreover, Sakyamuni himself never wrote a thing and there was a gap of about 150 years before any of his teachings were written down following his death. Not only that, but some of his most important sermons were, to the lay person, totally esoteric. The most famous of these was the so-called Flower Sermon where Sakyamuni held up a lotus flower above his head but said nothing. Only Mahakasyapa among his disciples understood.

With no written records various sects of Buddhism flowered, based on different interpretations of his teachings and example. The most obvious of these are the Mahayana and Hinayana (Theravada) sects. *Yana* means raft or ferry but is sometimes translated as vehicle. *Maha* means great and *hina* small. Theravada translates as the Way of the Elders. The difference between the two comes down to whether salvation is an individual affair with wisdom being the key virtue or whether it is a social affair with compassion being the key virtue. Hinayana chose the first of these interpretations and Mahayana the second. The ideal, therefore, for the Mahayana is the *bodhisattva* – one who is on the brink of entering nirvana (the Buddhist 'heaven') but delays this in order to help others reach the same goal. There are many other differences and both claim to represent the true spirit of the Buddha's teachings. Mahayana spread across Tibet, Mongolia, China, Korea and Japan while Hinayana spread south to Sri Lanka, Burma, Thailand, Cambodia, Vietnam and Indonesia.

In contrast to Hinayana, Mahayana espoused a liberal interpretation of the Buddha's teachings and it was inevitable, given this attitude, that it would itself divide into subsidiary sects in its spread across Central and North-East Asia. There are five main schools of Mahayana Buddhism, all of them placing different emphasis on some aspect whether it be faith, study, politics or the intuitive. All, save the intuitive, share one thing in common: despite Sakyamuni's entreaties, it was not long after his death that all the trappings of traditional religion came pouring back with a vengeance. The only school which resisted these tendencies and kept the message relatively pure is that of Zen – known as *Son* in Korea.

Though Sakyamuni Buddha died around 480 BC, it took over 850 years for the religion to reach Korea and a further 200 years before it reached Japan. By that time the different sects of Mahayana were clearly defined. The peninsula was also divided into the three separate kingdoms of Koguryo, Paekje and Silla. Koguryo was the first to adopt Buddhism as the state religion but this quickly spread to the remaining two kingdoms and was to become the central guiding force for the first major flowering of the arts in Korea.

Little remains from these early days in terms of surviving structures but the temple of Hwangyong-sa became the centre of Buddhism for the whole of Silla and was the largest temple in the nation. Many famous monks studied there including Wongwang (531 to 630), Wonhyo (617 to 686) and Uisang (620 to 660). Like the ruling families who promoted Buddhism and funded the building of many magnificent temples, these monks were not content to wait passively for the arrival of transcripts of the Buddhist scriptures and of masters from China. Instead, they took off in search of the originals – in search of the essence of the teachings before they had been processed through Confucian China – and returned many years later, often to become extremely influential at court.

The early forms of Buddhism which had been transmitted to Korea via China had naturally acquired a great deal of baggage on their journey across northern Asia and it was the realisation of this which motivated Korean monks to go in search of a purer form of doctrine. Luckily, it was still to be found in the form of *Son*. *Son* traces its origins back to the Flower Sermon and to Mahakasyapa. His insight was transmitted through 28 masters in India and carried to China in 520 AD by another monk, Bodhidarma.

Son arrived in Korea towards the end of the united Silla period and was instrumental in revolutionising Buddhism in the country.

Son emphasises that words are never adequate, however benign their intention, to describe immediate and direct experience. While they can make a positive contribution to understanding, they ultimately obscure the intensity of the experience. They tend to stereotype and camouflage actual feelings in honorific titles. Rationality is regarded as merely a comfortable verbal closet. *Son*, in common with all major religions, insists that suprarational experience remains a paradox

and beyond the call of language but it remains the lifeblood of enlightenment and salvation. Though *Son* has its scriptures, the essential message is one which is transmitted *outside* of the scriptures and not *through* them. This is one reason why *Son* is very difficult for people who rely greatly on rationality to accept.

Such unadulterated insights into the Buddha's message didn't, however, prevent elements of Korean shamanism from being incorporated into Buddhism during the Koryo Dynasty which succeeded Silla. Nevertheless, it contributed to a further flowering of Buddhist culture and its influence can still be seen today as can some of the Taoist baggage which was picked up from China and even India during Buddhism's spread across the continent to Korea. Though most Korean temples give pride of place to gold images of Sakyamuni (*Sakyamuni-bul*), Amitabha (*Amita-bul*, the primordial Buddha), *Miruk-bul*, the Buddha of the future, and Avalokitesvara (*Kwanseum-posal*, the Bodhisattva of mercy), you will discover many themes derived from shamanism in the wall paintings and door decorations of the same temples.

With the downfall of the Koryo Dynasty in 1392, Buddhism slowly declined as the new rulers of the Yi Dynasty fell under the sway of Confucian bureaucratic philosophy. Many restrictions were placed on the religion and temples were forced to relocate in remote mountain regions. At times, monks were not even permitted to enter the capital city.

The situation changed slightly for the better following the Japanese invasion of 1592 when many Buddhist monks fought bravely against the invaders throughout the peninsula. This was, however, a very sad time for Korea since most of its temples were burned to the ground and many religious and secular art treasures carted off as loot to Japan.

Buddhism again enjoyed a renaissance period during the Japanese annexation of Korea from 1910 until 1945 but, though the religion was encouraged and supported financially by the Japanese, many treasures were carted off to that country's museums where they remain to this day. It's a bone of contention which flares into the open from time to time with Korea insisting that the treasures be returned.

Since liberation in 1945, various South Korean governments have recognised the cultural importance of the many Buddhist temples, shrines, pagodas, figures and rock carvings and many of them have been classified as national treasures. Millions of dollars have been spent renovating and rebuilding temples and the religion seems to be undergoing a renaissance. The largest of the 18 sects of Mahayana Buddhism represented in South Korea is the Chogye Order – a *Son* sect – which has some 14 million adherents and almost 12,000 monks and nuns. In recent years it has been sending missionaries abroad and there are now Chogye temples in the USA, Japan, Hong Kong and many European countries. The total number of Buddhist adherents and monks in South Korea is 20 million and 25,000 respectively. This represents a good half of the total population.

South Korean monks are not permitted to eat any meat or fish and must remain vegetarians throughout their life. They are also not permitted to smoke or consume liquor of any kind. Monks of the Chogye Order must also remain celibate though those of the T'aego Order are allowed to marry. A monk begins his apprenticeship by studying the *sutras* – the Buddhist scriptures – and follows this up by travelling to many different temples to further his education in meditation.

There are daily services at all temples every morning and evening. The former is usually well before dawn – sometimes as early as 3 am – and the latter is usually around 6 pm. Services are also held to mark births, deaths, marriages and to celebrate certain events during the lunar year. One of the most important, and certainly the most colourful, festivals of the year is that of Buddha's Birthday. On this day, thousands of people flock to the temples to buy a candle

which they light and place inside a paper lantern which is then hung up inside the temple courtyard. By dusk, the temples are a riot of colour and light. It's a sight not to be missed if you are there at that time.

Since Mahayana Buddhism is a syncretised religion – unlike Hinayana which worships only the statue of Sakyamuni Buddha – many Buddhas, Bodhisattvas and other images are to be found in their temples.

If you'd like more detail on Buddhism in South Korea then hunt around for the book, *Korea Buddhism* (Chogye Order, Seoul, 1986). This is a beautifully illustrated book in full colour which covers most of the major temples of South Korea. If you can't find it then get in touch with the Korea Buddhism Chogye Order, Kyongji-dong 45, Jong-ro, Seoul. Their headquarters is a large building and you can't miss it.

Paper lantern hung to commemorate Buddha's Birthday

Confucianism

Confucius (Kongja to the Koreans and Kong Fu-zi to the Chinese) was born in 551 BC in the Shandong Province of China and died in 479 BC at the age of 73. In his early years he held a series of unimportant government posts and later struck out, tramping from state to state, offering advice to various rulers on how to improve their administrations and better the lot of the common people. He wasn't very successful but he did acquire many disciples who valued his insights highly. No doubt he could have become rich, powerful and influential had he been willing to compromise his integrity but he was cast in the Socratic mould and steadfastly refused to do this.

Just how this man whose famous, though didactic and pedantically unexciting, series of anecdotes came to personify something as vast and important as the Chinese civilisation remains an enigma. There was nothing otherworldly about him and he did not address the transcendental so, in a sense, he was not the founder of a religion, though Confucianism does display many attributes of a religion. Certainly a form of deification set in after his death, but the reasons why his philosophy became the central pivot of Chinese civilisation is perhaps to be found in the conditions which prevailed in China when he was alive.

At this time, the Zhou Dynasty had collapsed and China was ruled by a series of warlords who fought amongst each other for a greater share of the cake. Social anarchy was the order of the day and brutality common. A unifying philosophy simply had to be found in order to induce social harmony and make the country governable. The constraints of tradition had failed to deliver this and all manner of contending remedies were being bandied around.

Confucius was drawn to tradition and even occasionally idealised it but he was no antiquarian. Tradition to him was not the passive, unconscious variety handed down from generation to generation but a dynamic force which, while it might take pains to preserve continuity with the past, had to take into account new factors which could well make customary responses inappropriate. Every possible means was to be used to get people to internalise the new traditions, ranging from proverbs, stories, music, schools, theatres and temples. Leaders and rulers were required to be the standard-bearers of this new morality so that the common people might imitate them.

Confucius' philosophy was based on five factors.

The first of these was *Ren* which translates roughly as 'goodness'. It defined the ideal relationship between people and its most important virtue was humanity towards others and respect for oneself. Such an attitude, he said, would lead to magnanimity, charity, good faith, courteousness and diligence.

The second was *Chunzi* which is the idea of the 'superior man'. Such a person should be fully adequate to the task in hand, relaxed, poised and schooled to meet all contingencies with fear or favour and be able to accept success or failure with equanimity. It was the converse of the petty, the mean, the vulgar and the violent.

The third principle was *Li* – a condition of propriety, grace and urbanity regardless of circumstances. It defined the nature and roles of social intercourse. Compromise was an important part of this principle and it eschewed excesses of temperament, pleasure and indulgence. Respect for age was its cornerstone, and Confucius went to great lengths to define the relationship which ought to exist between father and son, elder brother and younger brother, husband and wife, elder friend and junior friend and subject and ruler. It's obvious that the sage regarded the family as being of prime importance.

The fourth principle was *De* which defined the power by which people are ruled. Confucius considered this to be grounded in justice – economic sufficiency, military sufficiency and an administration which would have the confidence of the people. Rulers were required not only to be honest but to be seen to be honest and thus engender respect among their subjects.

The last pillar of his philosophy was *Wen* which is generally translated as the 'arts of peace'. Confucius had much respect for the arts and he considered them to be an instrument for furthering moral education.

While none of the principles can be considered to address direct spiritual aspirations they do so in a reflective way and this is one reason why you will find shrines dedicated to Confucius in China, Taiwan and Korea. There are no images in these shrines and they're quite plain.

Confucius died relatively unknown, yet some 250 years later Confucianism became the state religion of the Han Dynasty and, in 130 BC, the exclusive means of training officials for service in the government. It remained as such until 1912 when the Republic was declared and it can safely be said that, Mao Zedong and the Red Guards notwithstanding, it still exerts a powerful influence on the everyday lives of the Chinese people.

Confucianism came to the fore in Korea with the overthrow of the Koryo Dynasty in 1392. The new Yi rulers staked their future on an updated version of Confucianism and went to great lengths to suppress Buddhism which had become corrupt and politically divisive and was regarded as a threat and a rival for the allegiance of the people. Examinations for the state bureaucracy were set up which, in theory, any male could sit for and which might lead to the highest offices of state. Not only that, but a great deal of effort was made to eliminate favouritism. In practice, however, the highest ranks of the bureaucracy were dominated by those from aristocratic backgrounds.

Nevertheless, the system was initially successful and Korea entered into a new era of progress, although not all the Yi rulers embraced Confucianism to the same extent. Some even converted to Buddhism but it has remained the dominant force in education to this day. Like all systems, however, it gradually lost its dynamism and became a dogma of suffocating conformity which intruded into every aspect of daily life. The same sort of thing happened to Confucianism in China

but, because that country was so large, regional variations prevented the same inflexible interpretation and application of the sage's philosophy. This was not the case in Korea since it was far easier to police and root out dissidence.

All the same, South Korea is probably the most Confucian nation on earth even today and it may well be that this was the key factor which induced Chun Doo-Hwan to concede opposition demands for genuine democratic elections in 1988 rather than face wholesale violence and social anarchy.

Shamanism

Many Koreans, especially those in the cities, will deny that shamanism still exists and, as a visitor, you are unlikely to come across it unless you stay with a family in the countryside for a period of time. If it's a thing of the past, however, then it's been a long time dying. The fact is that it still flourishes throughout the peninsula in many different guises ranging from 'spirit posts' (similar to totem poles) at the entrance to villages; to packets of pine needles under the main beam of the house; to scarecrows in the rice paddies; and strings of chillies, charcoal and pine needles over the entrance gates of houses where a son has recently been born.

Nature spirits exist everywhere and they must be cajoled and placated if a family is to enjoy good health and good luck. Even a family's stash of *kimchi* jars in a corner of the courtyard comes in for ritual attention. A bowl of uncooked rice is placed before them and a lit candle inserted. If the candle burns evenly, all is well. If it burns unevenly then watch out! The spirits are not content.

Much of the minutiae of South Korean shamanism are similar to the vestiges of pre-Christian paganism in the West – 'superstitions' like not walking under ladders, horseshoes above doors and flicking spilt salt over one's shoulder. Where it differs radically is that Korea never experienced the witch-hunts and burnings at the stake that eclipsed folk religion and medicine in medieval Europe and, at the same time, secured for men a position of ultimate authority over women. In South Korea, witches – known as *mudang* – are alive and well and treated with great respect. While it's true that shamans fell into disfavour when the Yi Dynasty brought in Confucianism, there were no wholesale purges and they continued to command the respect of the women at the royal court.

Though nature spirits affect both men and women alike, when the intercession of a *mudang* is required it is basically a women's affair. A *mudang* is frequently consulted about relatively mundane things like a son's educational and employment prospects or a daughter's suitor in much the same way as we might consult a fortune teller. But when something major strikes a family which cannot be cured by more profane methods then a full-scale *kut* – a sort of exorcism – is called for. These can be elaborate affairs and go on for two days or more without a break. They involve dancing and music, special garments, sacrifices to the spirits and wailing exhortations. Some shamans work themselves into a trance and roll around with their eyes bulging, announcing the presence of the spirits and making disconnected comments on everything real, apparent or imagined. It's certainly a compelling performance and can be quite frightening. One thing they all have in common, however, is the noise. You can't mistake the sound of a *kut* in progress with the clashing of cymbals and the banging of drums.

There are even festivals of *mudang* in certain parts of South Korea, the most famous being that in Kangnung which goes on for a whole week and resembles a medieval festival. Don't fail to get there if you are in South Korea at that time. The festival is held on the fifth day of the fifth lunar month (early June on the solar calendar). There's also a smaller version of this in Seoul at the same time on the banks of the Han River.

While shamanism retains a distinct life of its own in South Korea, many elements of it have also found their way into Buddhism and Christianity, in the same way that all the major religions of the world have been mod-ified by local traditions when they have been exported far from their point of origin.

Christianity

You might wonder what a section on Christianity is doing in, of all places, a book on Korea. The fact is that over 16% of South Koreans are firm Christians of various sects and the numbers are increasing yearly. You can't fail to notice the pairs of earnest young men in smart white shirts and zippy slacks with a bible tucked under their arm in any city street. These proselytising Mormons on their door-knocking rounds are just part of the wave of Christian missionaries flocking to South Korea in search of converts. The born-again Christian sects are probably the keenest in this respect but they still have a long way to go before their followers will match those of the Catholics and the various Protestant sects in number. Seven million might not seem a lot in terms of the total population but Christianity has a high profile in South Korea as the number of churches – even in rural areas – bears witness.

So why are there so many Christians in a country which otherwise you would regard as being Buddhist or Confucian?

Korea's first contact with Christianity came with the Japanese invasion of 1592. It's not a well-known fact that one of Hideyoshi's generals was a Christian in command of Japanese troops of the same persuasion and travelling with them were two Jesuit priests, one Japanese and the other a Spaniard. Not surprisingly, they didn't make many converts and most of those who did convert followed the Japanese army back to Japan at the end of the war.

Korea's next brush with Christianity came in 1777 when a young scholar called Yi Tuk-So converted to Catholicism after studying a book on the subject – probably obtained from Beijing where there were Western diplomats and Christian missionaries. After he persuaded an influential family to adopt the religion it began to spread but attracted the attention of the Confucian rulers who were far from pleased by the development. The court reacted by periodically rounding up Korean converts, torturing them and, in many cases, executing them. Likewise, foreign missionaries were frequently deported although there was no actual ban on their entry into the country.

The crunch came in 1866, by which time there were around 15,000 converts. It was a time of considerable rivalry between Catholic France and Orthodox Russia in this part of the world. The Korean court decided to play one off against the other and arrested eight French priests, including the bishop of Seoul. These eight were publicly beheaded followed by a further 8000 converts over the next three years. The executions precipitated the brief French occupation of Kanghwa Island though this action brought no restitution for the deaths of their fellow countrymen.

The Protestants, for their part, made a brief but inconsequential visit in 1832. Only in 1884 did they start to make headway as a result of the arrival of the Protestant US ambassador to Korea, Horrace Allen. Much of their success was a direct result of their dedication in establishing schools, particularly at a time when Korea was beginning to realise the importance of Western technology. Allen was followed by a veritable onslaught of Protestant missionaries of all persuasions but especially Methodists and Presbyterians.

It may be hard these days to understand quite what was the attraction to Koreans of these various Christian sects whose differences to most contemporary Westerners are hardly worth a second thought. It should be remembered, however, that the late 19th century was a time of Bible-bashing fervour. It probably also has a lot to do with the spiritual vacuum which late Neo-Confucianism had bestowed on Korea and the fact that Buddhism was not readily accessible, since the temples had been banished to remote rural areas at a time when communications were primitive and when most Koreans neither had the time nor the money to make regular visits to a temple. Though Christianity is certainly not losing ground in modern South Korea, it is obvious that with increasing affluence and excellent communications, Buddhism is also making a tremendous comeback.

FESTIVALS & HOLIDAYS
Solar Calendar Holidays
January
> *New Year's Day* (1st) is a public holiday though most Koreans celebrate the new year according to the lunar calendar.

March
> *Independence Day (Samiljol)* (1st) commemorates the day in 1919 when the Korean Proclamation of Independence against Japanese rule was first read.

April
> *Arbor Day* (5th) South Koreans are urged to go out and plant trees to assist in the country's reafforestation programme.

May
> *Children's Day* (5th) is a public holiday in honour of the youth of South Korea. On this day children are dressed up in traditional costume and taken on excursions to national parks and the like.

June
> *Memorial Day* (6th) commemorates South Korea's war dead. Services are held throughout the nation, the largest one being at the huge National Cemetery in Seoul.
> *Farmers' Day* (15th) honours agricultural workers and is celebrated by feasting and drinking along with traditional folk music and dance appropriate to the occasion.

July
> *Constitution Day* (17th) commemorates the proclamation of the Constitution of the Republic of Korea in 1948. It's an opportunity for South Koreans to demonstrate their patriotism by joining gatherings in town squares and other public places.

August
> *Liberation Day* (15th) commemorates the day in 1945 that Japan surrendered to the Allies thus bringing to an end 36 years of colonial domination by that country of the Korean peninsula. It's a day of speeches and parades and another opportunity for South Koreans to demonstrate their patriotism.

October
> *Armed Forces Day* (1st) honours South Korea's defence forces. The day is taken up with colourful military parades and low-level fly-pasts by the air force.
> *National Foundation Day (Tangun)* (3rd) is the celebration of the birthday of Tangun, the mythical first king of Korea. Legend says he ruled from 2333 to 1122 BC.
> *Hangul Day* (9th) honours the commissioning by

King Sejong of the country's indigenous alphabet in the mid-15th century.

December

Christmas Day (25th) is a national holiday because although South Korea is a predominantly Buddhist and Confucian nation, there are a large number of Christians.

Lunar Calendar Holidays

April

Han Sik-il falls in the middle of the month on the 105th day of the lunar calendar. It's a day when Koreans visit the graves of their ancestors with offerings of rice cakes, fruit, wine and other dishes.

May

Buddha's Birthday falls in the middle of the month on the 8th day of the 4th lunar month and is celebrated with colourful parades and temple rituals. One of the main rituals is the 'feast of the lanterns'. Towards the end of the day, Buddhists (and even many non-Buddhists) go to a temple and buy a paper lantern and candle. By the time it is dark, temple courtyards become festooned with row after row of flickering lanterns. In certain places this may be followed by a long lantern parade which winds its way through the streets of the town. It's a fairly recent festival which only became a public holiday in 1975 though the Buddha's birthday itself has been celebrated for centuries.

June

Tano falls at the beginning of the month on the 5th day of the 5th lunar month. On this day Koreans visit their family's ancestral shrines with offerings of summer food specialities. It's one of the most important celebrations of the year.

September

Chusok is celebrated around mid-September on the 15th day of the 8th lunar month. This holiday is the equivalent of Thanksgiving in the USA. It's a day for putting on traditional costume and for visiting ancestral shrines with offerings of food.

LANGUAGE

The Korean language is a member of the Ural-Altaic group which includes Mongolian, Turkish and Finnish. Some researchers also claim that it has similarities with a number of North American Indian languages. The spoken language has been around for over 5000 years but it was only in the 15th century that the alphabet, known as *hangul*, was invented. This took place in 1446 during the reign of King Sejong, a scholar of the Chinese classics and probably the greatest of all Korean kings. *Hangul* is one of the most phonetic alphabets in the world and can be learned virtually overnight. Once you've learnt it you'll be able to read any sign or menu though, of course, you won't necessarily know what the meaning is in your own language. The invention of *hangul* led to a dramatic increase in literacy among the population at large. Before the invention of *hangul* Koreans used Chinese characters and, even today, they borrow liberally from that language, as do the Japanese, but these characters are only used for expressing concepts. These borrowed characters, known as *han-ja*, can be found in newspapers and books and they are what makes reading publications difficult for foreigners.

There is a basic list of *han-ja* numbering 1800 which the government has approved and they have to be studied by all school children. That doesn't mean that they remember them all and you'll often see Koreans referring to a specialised dictionary of *han-ja* particularly when reading good literature or books demanding a high level of education. Maps, other than those produced in foreign languages for the tourist trade, are also frequently entirely in Chinese. Naturally, there are far fewer *han-ja* in newspapers since these have to be understood by a much wider section of the population.

The continued use of Chinese characters in both Korean and Japanese has led to a widespread misconception that the three languages are closely related. This is not the case and the similarity ends with the borrowing of characters, which itself dates back to the times when no indigenous writing systems existed. There have, of course, been close cultural connections between the three countries but Korean grammar and inflection are totally different from Chinese, though similar to Japanese. Linguists are at odds as to how similar Korean is to Japanese. Certainly the grammar is similar but the pronunciation of indigenous words in each country is completely different. The most likely explanation is that while Korean and

Japanese had separate origins, they were both subjected to the same cultural forces which led to a restructuring of their grammars along similar lines.

Korean Alphabet

Hangul originally consisted of 28 characters but that was later reduced to 24. There are 10 vowels:

a	아	ya	야
ŏ	어	yŏ	여
o	오	yo	요
u	우	yu	유
ŭ	으	I	이

and 14 consonants:

k	ㄱ	n	ㄴ
t	ㄷ	r, l	ㄹ
m	ㅁ	p	ㅂ
s	ㅅ	-, ng	ㅇ
ch	ㅈ	ch'	ㅊ
k'	ㅋ	t'	ㅌ
p'	ㅍ	h	ㅎ

Pronunciation

The basic consonants **k**, **t**, **p**, and **ch** are pronounced as g, d, b, and j, respectively, when occurring in the middle of a syllable. The letter ㄹ is sounded like **r** when it comes at the beginning of a syllable and like **l** at the end.

When the letter ㅇ precedes a vowel at the beginning of a syllable it is not sounded but when it is added at the end of a syllable it is similar to the **ng** sound.

You will occasionally come across a number of doubled-up consonants like ㄲ, ㄸ, ㅃ and ㅆ, but only rarely. You'd need an extensive knowledge of Korean to be able to use or speak them so beginners can ignore them.

Transliteration

In some ways, Korean is an easier language to learn than any of the European languages because there are fewer tenses, not as many particles and there is no such thing as subject-verb agreement. The grammar is, however, very difficult and you have to listen to the whole of a sentence before you can understand the full meaning. This is because the verb comes at the end of a sentence and the verb ending which is attached to the stem is of crucial importance. It determines, for example, whether you know a person is doing, will do, plans to do, won't do, did not do, wants to do, does not want to do, etc.

One source of confusion you'll have to come to terms with in Korea is the way the language is romanised. There are two accepted systems of doing this. The more usual one is the internationally recognised McCune-Reischauer system. The other is that used by the Ministry of Education. To illustrate the differences between these two systems a few examples are necessary:

Pusan	=	Busan
Chong-no	=	Jong-ro
Halla	=	Hanra
Poshingak	=	Bosingag
Cheju-do	=	Jeju-do
Kyongju	=	Gyeongju
Kangnung	=	Gangneung
Sorak-san	=	Seolag-san

This should give you the basics of which letters are interchangeable. It should also explain the use of the diphthongs **eo** and **eu** (Yeosu = Yosu and Cheonan = Chonan, for example). This comes about because Korean has 10 vowels whereas English has only five and lacks accents. It would have been easier to romanise Korean in some ways if the accents of the French language had been adopted at the same time.

In this guide the McCune-Reischauer system is used to render Korean into English because it's simpler and doesn't involve cluttering words up with dubious diphthongs – Kyongju is far easier to read (and pronounce) than Gyeongju, for example. On the other hand, we'll also give you the Ministry of Education spelling in brackets because many maps, publications and even some bus stations still use this system.

Greetings & Civilities

Good morning/Good afternoon/Good evening.

annyong hasimnika (very formal)

안녕하십니까?

annyong haseyo (less formal)

안녕하세요?

What is your name?

irumi muosimnika?

이름이 무엇입니까?

My name is ....

nae irumun ....imnida

내 이름은……입니다

Hello.

yoboseyo

여보세요

Goodbye.

aniyong ikaseyo (if you are leaving) or

안녕히계세요

aniyong ikaseyo (if you are staying or if both parties are leaving)

안녕히 가세요

Small Talk

Korean grammar is very hard to understand without considerable study but two verbs you will hear constantly are *isimnida* and *isimnika*. The former is used for statements. For example, 'I have cigarettes' – *tambay isimnida*. The latter is the interrogative. For example, 'Do you have cigarettes?' – *tambay isimnika?* The affix *ka* indicates a question. Two other verbs you'll hear a lot of are *chuseyo* and *tuseyo*. The former means 'please give me' so 'please give me cigarettes' is *tambay chuseyo*. The latter means 'here you are' so 'here are cigarettes' is *tambay tuseyo*.

Yes.

ye

예

No.

anyo

아니오

Thank you.

kamsa hamnida

감사합니다

Excuse me.

sille hamnida

실례 합니다

I am sorry.

mian hamnida

미안 합니다

Never mind.

kokjong maseyo

걱정마세요

This is good.

cho sumnida

좋습니다

This is bad.

nappumnida

나쁩니다

Don't mention it.

chomaneyo

천만에요

Can you speak English?

yong-o halsu issumnika?

영어 할수 있읍니까?

Can you speak Korean?

hanguk-mal halsu issumnika?

한국말 할수있읍니까?

Do you understand me?

ihaehaseyo?

이해 하세요?

Accommodation

It's usually women who are in charge of renting out rooms to guests in traditional *yogwan* and *yoinsook*. You address the woman as *ajimah* unless she is old in which case the correct word is *haromoni*. If it's a man, you address him as *ajosi* unless he's old in which case the correct word is *haroboji*. The same words are used to address waiters and waitresses in restaurants and bars. One of your fondest memories of Korean hotels may well be the cries of, *ajimah! mool chuseyo!* (Madam, please bring me tea) echoing down the corridor or across the courtyard.

Do you have a room?

pang-ee isimnika?

방이 있읍니까?

How much does it cost?

olma imnika? or *olmayo?*

얼마 입니까? 얼마요?

Can I see it please?

poyo chuseyo?

보여 주세요

Is there hot water?
toe-oon mool-ee isimnika?
더운 물이 있읍니까?

It's too expensive.
nomu pisamnida
너무 비쌉니다

Can you bring tea please?
ajimah/haromoni mool chuseyo?
차를 주세요

I'll buy this.
i kos-ul sa gaysumnida
이것을 사겠읍니다

Can I have the bill?
kesanso-rul chuseyo?
계산서를 주세요

Getting Around

Two very useful words are: *yogi* (here) and *jogi* (there). Hence, *yogi isimnida* (here it is) and *jogi isimnida* (there it is).

Can you show me the way to ....?
.........un odiro gamnika?
...... 은어디로겁니까?

Where is ....?
........ee odi imnika
......이 어디입니까?

What is this place called?
yogi-nun odimnika?
여기는 어디입니까?

How many km is it from here?
yogi-eso myot kilomet imnika?
여기에서 몇 킬로 미터 입니까?

How long does it take to get there?
olmana kollimnika?
얼마나 걸립니까?

It takes 30 minutes (an hour).
samsip-pun (han si-kan) kollimnida
(삼십분) (한시간) 걸립니다

Stop here.
sewoe juseyo
세워 주세요

How much is the (fare/bill/etc)?
olma imnika?
얼마 입니까?
or *olmayo?*
얼마요

Around Town

airport
konghang 공항

bus station
chu chajang 주차장

bus stop
chong yujang 정류장

subway
jon choel 전철

railway station
yokjon 역전

train
kit-cha 기차

ferry terminal
pudu yoegek terminal or *hang* in combination with the town name (eg Pusan-hang)

post office
oo-chay guk 우체국

bank
un-heng 은행

city hall
si-chong 시청

toilet
hwajang-sil 화장실

market
si-jang 시장

supermarket – same in Korean

pharmacy
ya-guk 약국

bookshop
soe-jom 서점

restaurant
shiktang 식당

makkoli bar/beer bar
makkoli-jip/maekju-jip 막걸리집, 맥주집

general store
ka-gay 가게

Odds & Ends

bread
pang 빵

cigarettes
tambay 담배

matches
songyang 성냥

needle
pan-eul 바늘

thread
shil 실

writing paper
pyon-jiji 편지지

book
  chek 책
ballpoint pen
  ballpen 볼펜
envelope
  bong-too 봉투
string
  koon 끈
aerogramme
  hanggong soegang 항공서간
stamp
  oo-pyo 우표
toothbrush
  chi-sol 치솔
toothpaste
  chi-yak 치약
shampoo
  same in Korean 샴푸
soap
  bee-noo 비누
toilet paper
  hwajang-ji 화장지

Fruit
apple
  sagway 사과
pear
  bae 배
watermelon
  subak 수박
rock melon
  chamwhey 참외
mandarin
  kuel 귤
peach
  poksung-ah 복숭아
persimmon
  kam 감
pomegranate
  songryu 석류
grapes
  podo 포도
Orange 오랜지 , pineapple 파인애플 and banana 바나나 are the same in Korean since they are not indigenous fruits.

Vegetables
cabbage
  yang-betchu 양배추

Chinese cabbage
  betchu 배추
radish
  mu-oo 무우
carrot
  tangun 당근
potato
  kamja 감자
sweet potato
  ko-kuma 고구마
spinach
  sigumchi 시금치
chilli
  gochu 고추
onion
  yangpah 양파
spring onion
  paqh 파
garlic
  ma-nuel 마늘
lettuce
  sangchi 상치
cucumber
  oh-ee 오이
zucchini/pumpkin
  hobak 호박
beans
  kong 콩
peas
  wandu-kong 완두콩

Meat, Fish & Dairy Products
beef
  soggogi 소고기
pork
  tejji-gogi 돼지고기
chicken
  takgogi 닭고기
fish
  sengsong 생선
egg
  kae-ran 계란
boiled egg
  salmun kae-ran 삶은계란
milk
  ooyoo 우유
Cheese 치즈 and butter 버터 are the same word in Korean as they are not traditional foods. They're also very expensive.

Beverages

water 물
  mool (also means barley tea in a hotel,
  though strictly speaking, this is *bori-cha*)
  보리차
beer
  maekju 맥주
mineral water
  yaksu 약수

Rice

rice
  sal 쌀
cooked rice
  bap 밥

Condiments

cooking oil
  kirum (this usually means soy bean oil)
  기름
sesame oil
  cham kirum 참기름
soy sauce
  kanjang 간장
chilli sauce
  kochujang 고추장
ginger
  sengang 생강
soy bean paste
  tenjang 된장
vinegar
  sikcho 식초
salt
  sogum 소금

Time

second
  cho 초
minute
  poon 분
hour
  seekan 시간
day
  onool 일
week
  ju 주
month
  dal 달
year
  yon 년

today
  onool 오늘
yesterday
  ojay 어제
tomorrow
  nae-il 내일
day after tomorrow
  mo-rae 모레
weekend
  chu-mal 주말
morning
  achim 아침
afternoon
  chomsim 오후
evening
  chongok 저녁
night
  bam 밤
this evening
  onool chongok 오늘저녁

Days of the Week

Monday
  wo-ryo-il 월요일
Tuesday
  hwa-yo-il 화요일
Wednesday
  su-yo-il 수요일
Thursday
  mogyo-il 목요일
Friday
  kumyo-il 금요일
Saturday
  to-yo-il 토요일
Sunday
  i-ryo-il 일요일

Months

January
  i-rwol 일월
February
  i-wol 이월
March
  sam-wol 삼월
April
  sa-wol 사월
May
  o-wol 오월
June
  yu-wol 유월

July
  chi-rwol 칠월
August
  pa-rwol 팔월
September
  ku-wol 구월
October
  shi-wol 십월
November
  shi-bi-rwol 십일월
December
  shi-bi-wol 십이월

Seasons

winter
  kyo-ul 겨울
spring
  pom 봄
summer
  yo-rum 여름
autumn
  ka-ul 가을

Numbers

1	*il*
2	*ee*
3	*sam*
4	*sa*
5	*o*
6	*yuk*
7	*chill*
8	*pal*
9	*ku*
10	*sip*
11	*sip-il*
20	*ee-sip*
30	*sam-ip*
40	*sa-ip*
48	*sa-sip-pal*
50	*o-sip*

100	*paek*
200	*ee-paek*
300	*sam-paek*
846	*pal-paek-sa-sip-yuk*
1000	*chon*
2000	*ee-chon*
5729	*o-chon-chil-paek-ee-sip-ku*
10,000	*man*
20,000	*ee-man*

There are two different sets of words for numerals in Korean. The former are used when simply talking about numbers as such. When talking about objects (eg eggs, cabbages, tables, animals, people, etc) the other system is used. This other system is:

1	*hanna*
2	*dul*
3	*set*
4	*net*
5	*tasot*
6	*yosot*
7	*ilgop*
8	*yodol*
9	*a-hop*
10	*yol*
11	*yol-hanna*
12	*yol-dul*
20	*su-mool*
21	*su-mool-hanna*
30	*so-run*
40	*ma-hun*
50	*shi-hun*
60	*yes-hun*
70	*il-hun*
80	*yord-hun*
90	*a-hun*
100	*pek*

Facts for the Visitor

VISAS

Visas for South Korea are not required by nationals of western European nations except for the Irish Republic. If you fall into this category you'll be given a 30-day, 60-day or 90-day stay permit on arrival depending on the passport you're carrying – for most it will be 60 days. All other nationals including Australians, Canadians and New Zealanders require visas. US nationals also require visas, but they can get a transit visa on arrival by air, valid for 15 days, though this is not extendible. If you plan to stay longer than that, get a tourist visa before arrival. Onward tickets and/or proof of 'adequate funds' are not required as a rule.

Visa extensions are becoming quite difficult to get, and you may find that if you apply for one, they demand that you have a sponsor or letter of recommendation from a Korean company or from your own embassy. Apply at the Seoul immigration office opposite Chong Dong Church at the back of Toksu Palace. The office is open Monday to Friday from 9 am to 6 pm and on Saturdays until 1 pm. Extensions cost W500 and no photographs are necessary.

Do not overstay your visa. The fine for doing this varies between W50,000 and W200,000.

WORK

Officially you're not allowed to work if you come in on either a stay permit or a tourist visa, but many people do. There's plenty of work available teaching English – and other European languages – in Seoul. Few of the schools or institutes which offer work to foreign language teachers will ask for a work permit. However, if you're thinking of doing this you should first ask around at the main travellers' *yogwan* in Seoul to find out if any of the schools are currently exploiting this lack of legal status by paying low wages or, in one or two isolated cases, not paying at all.

CUSTOMS

South Korean customs can be pretty thorough, and if you bring in expensive watches, cameras or cassette players then the chances are that they'll be recorded in your passport, which means you have to take them out with you or pay the import duty. All these goods are considerably more expensive in Korea than they are in places like Singapore, Hong Kong and Japan. You're allowed to bring in 400 cigarettes and two bottles of spirits duty-free. The latter can be sold for about double the cost price without problem if you want to subsidise the cost of your stay. Instant coffee has much the same exchange value.

MONEY

The unit of currency in South Korea is the won (W). There are coins of W1, W5, W10, W50, W100, and W500 though it's unlikely you'll see a one won coin anywhere except at a bank. Notes are in denominations of W1000, W5000 and W10,000.

USA	US$1	=	W714
Australia	A$1	=	W825
UK	£1	=	W1400
Canada	C$1	=	W617
Denmark	Kr1	=	W120
France	Fr1	=	W136
Germany	DM1	=	W465
Italy	Lira 100	=	W61
New Zealand	NZ$1	=	W420
Netherlands	Guilder 1	=	W410
Hong Kong	HK$1	=	W91
Japan	Y100	=	W524
Singapore	S$1	=	W404
Switzerland	SwF1	=	W522

There is a street market for cash US dollars (and certain other hard currencies) which varies between 6% and 8% above the bank rate. Ask around in the travellers' *yogwan* or try some of the shops, particularly the electronic and camera shops, in the underground arcades around the GPO in Seoul.

Most banks these days can change cash or travellers' cheques so you don't have to go hunting for a branch of the Exchange Bank of Korea. Rates for travellers' cheques are generally slightly higher than for cash (a little over 1%) but since most banks charge 1% commission on travellers' cheques, it amounts to the same. Outside banking hours money can be changed at most of the larger hotels though their exchange rates are somewhat lower than at the banks. Money can be changed 24 hours a day at Seoul's Kimpo International Airport.

If you want cash dollars, the Exchange Bank of Korea will sell them to you at 2.2% commission provided you pay for them with hard currency travellers' cheques.

American Express cannot issue their own travellers' cheques against one of their credit cards plus a personal cheque drawn on your bank back home. If this is what you want to do at their main office in Seoul (Kyobo Building) they'll direct you to the Bank of California on a lower floor of the same building. You'll need your credit card, passport and either a personal cheque or one of their counter cheques. The transaction takes about 10 minutes and there's no fuss.

There is no bank on Ulleung-do Island so it's impossible to change travellers' cheques there. Make sure you take enough local currency with you from the mainland.

Major credit cards (Amex, Diners, Visa, Mastercard) are accepted at most large hotels and shops in the major cities.

You can reconvert up to the equivalent of US$500 into hard currency on leaving South Korea if you have receipts to prove you changed the money at a bank in the first place.

Inflation in South Korea has been considerably reduced and, according to the government, now stands at around 5%.

Airport departure tax on international flights is W5000.

CLIMATE

Korea has four distinct seasons which are influenced predominantly by winds from Siberia and the Gobi Desert, and by the East Asian monsoons.

Spring arrives in late March/early April with average temperatures of around 10°C to 12°C rising gradually through May and June to around 20°C. There is occasional light rain during these months.

July and August are not only the hottest months but also the monsoon season with average temperatures hovering between 20°C and 30°C. Humidity is high during these months – around 80% – and rain can be frequent and prolonged though it's often possible to avoid most of it by tuning in to the weather report in the evening and making appropriate travel plans. The monsoon generally comes to an end during September. Hurricanes are liable to devastate areas of the country at any time during the monsoon season. When this happens there is usually widespread flooding and disruption of communications, so it's a good idea to keep your eye on weather reports otherwise you could find yourself stuck for several days. In the major cities, umbrella vendors are always on hand to do a lively trade during downpours with those who have ventured out unprepared. The umbrellas which they sell are made of bamboo and plastic and are a bargain at around W500. They'll last several days.

Autumn, when Korea is at its most riotously colourful, comes in mid-October but the best time is late October and early November when temperatures average around 12°C. Very little rain falls at this time of year.

Winter arrives with a vengeance in November and continues through to late March. During this time freezing winds from Siberia can push the temperature down to -15°C at night, though during the day it generally hovers a few degrees on either side of freezing point. Winter is also characterised by a succession of three cold days followed by four milder days. Cheju-do's climate is naturally warmer all year than the mainland's and even in winter the temperature on the low-lying areas seldom drops below an average of 7°C.

The best times to visit Korea with regard to temperature, rainfall and natural beauty are April, May and June before the monsoon and September, October and early November after the rains. You should not be put off by the monsoon, however, as the country is incredibly green at that time of year.

TOURIST INFORMATION
Local Tourist Offices

The Korean National Tourism Corporation (KNTC) produces an extensive range of well-illustrated leaflets, booklets and maps with details of all the country's beauty spots, centres of interest and major cities. Many of these leaflets are available in Japanese, German and French as well as English. Almost all of them can be picked up at the major points of entry:

Kimpo International Airport, 1st Floor, Airport Terminal Building, Seoul (tel (02) 665-0086/8)

Kimhae International Airport, Pusan (tel (051) 98-1100)

Cheju International Airport, Cheju-do, (tel (064) 42-0032)

Apart from the three international airports there are also tourist information centres in Seoul and Pusan.

Seoul The headquarters of KNTC is in a high-rise building on Chonggyechon-ro near the junction with Namdaemun-ro, two blocks up from Ulchiro-1-ga subway station or one block down from Chonggak subway station. In the basement of this building is a huge tourist information hall with every conceivable publication put out by KNTC plus helpful and informative staff. There are also huge topographical models of both Korea and Seoul, videos and photographs of the various provinces and even a computer which the public can use to call up information on any topic they care to choose. If you're not familiar with Korea then it's worth spending an hour or so here. It's open daily from 9 am to 6 pm.

The other very useful tourist information centre is that at the back of City Hall right in the heart of Seoul. You can't miss it as there's a large sign in English. It's open Monday to Friday from 9 am to 6 pm and on Saturday from 9 am to 1 pm but closed Sundays. The staff are helpful and knowledgeable and there's a full range of leaflets, booklets and maps available.

Tours organised by KNTC, including those to Panmunjom, can be booked at either place.

There are also tourist information kiosks at Kangnum Express Bus Terminal (in front of the Kyobo Building on Sejong-ro), at Poshingak on Chongro (at the entrance to Myong-dong) and at Tongdaemun Market, but they are limited in the scope of what they offer.

Pusan There is a KNTC office in the Tourist Section, City Hall. Only a limited range of information is available here.

Overseas Tourist Offices

Outside the country the KNTC maintains offices in the following places:

Argentina
    Cuenca 445 Cap, Buenos Aires (tel (611) 9209)
Australia
    17th Floor, Tower Building, Australia Square, George St, Sydney 2000 (tel (02) 27 4132/3)
Austria
    Tomi Consult Trade & Tourism, Mayerhofgasse 2A/3, A-1040 Vienna (tel (0222) 5050250)
France
    Tour Maine Montparnasse Building, 4e Etage No 11, 33 Ave du Maine, B P 169, 75755 Paris Cedex 15 (tel (01) 45-38-71-23)
Germany
    Wiessenhüttenplatz 26, 6000 Frankfurt am Main (tel (069) 233226)
Hong Kong
    Room 506, Bank of America Tower, 12 Harcourt Rd, Hong Kong (tel 5-238065)
Japan
    Room 124 Sanshin Building, 4-1 1-chome, Yuraku-cho, Chiyoda-ku, Tokyo (tel (03) 580-3941/4, 508 2384). There are branch offices in Fukuoda (tel (092) 471-7174/5) and Osaka (tel (06) 266-0847/8)
Netherlands
    Leerdamhof 229, 1108 BV Amsterdam (tel 020-975182)

Sweden
    Västmannagatan 3 nb, 111 24 Stockholm (tel 08-206693)
Switzerland
    Postfach 343, CH-8126, Zumikon, Zurich (tel (01) 918-0882)
Singapore
    24 Raffles Place, 20-03 Clifford Centre, Singapore 0104 (tel 533-0441/2)
Taiwan
    Room 1813, 18th Floor, 333 Keelung Rd Sec 1, Taipei (tel 732-8281)
Thailand
    11th Floor, CCT Building, 109 Surawongse Rd, Bangkok 10500 (tel 236-2880, 233-1399)
UK
    2nd Floor, Vogue House, 1 Hanover Square, London W1R 9RD (tel (071) 409-2100)
USA
    205 North Michigan Ave, Suite 2212, Chicago, Ill 60601 (tel (312) 819-2560/2
    1188 Bishop St, Century Square, PH1, Honolulu, Hawaii 96813 (tel (808) 521-8066)
    Suite 323, 510 West Sixth St, Los Angeles, CA 90014 (tel (213) 623 1226/7)
    Suite 400, 460 Park Ave, New York, NY 10022 (tel (212) 688-7543/4)
    4th Vine Building, Seattle, Washington 98121 (tel (206) 441-6666)

Foreign Embassies

For foreign country embassies and consulates represented in South Korea see the Seoul chapter and Pusan section.

GENERAL INFORMATION
Post

South Korea has a very well-organised postal service and you shouldn't experience any great problems either sending or receiving mail. A poste restante service 유치우편물 is available at all main city post offices but only in Seoul and Pusan will you find a counter dealing exclusively with poste restante. Elsewhere you may well have difficulty making yourself understood. Indeed, a letter sent to you c/o poste restante might not even end up there. This is because most postal clerks speak very little, if any, English and it's unlikely that a sorter would know what to do with a letter addressed (in English) to poste restante. If you do want mail sent to you at post offices other than

Seoul and Pusan, make sure they bear the words 'poste restante' in Korean.

Most large post offices have a packing service available for parcels which relieves you of the bother of having to visit several different places to acquire boxes, polystyrene, tape and string. Their charges are very reasonable and they pack things very well. On the other hand, if you pack a parcel yourself you don't have to leave it open for customs inspection before mailing.

Time

The time in Korea is Greenwich Mean Time plus nine hours. When it is noon in Korea it is 2 pm in Sydney or Melbourne, 3 am in London, 10 pm the previous day in New York and 7 pm the previous day in Los Angeles or San Francisco.

MEDIA
Newspapers & Magazines

There are two English-language newspapers, the *Korea Herald* and the *Korea Times*. They are published daily except Mondays and cost W180. Like Korean-language

newspapers, both of these are subject to government censorship so they tend to keep a low political profile, though this is gradually changing in line with political liberalisation. These newspapers are only available in Seoul and Pusan.

The other English-language newspaper is the *Stars & Stripes*, published by the US military authorities, but it's only available on US bases or from the USO outside of the Yongsan base in Seoul. The only way of getting into a base is to have a contact escort you inside. You won't be allowed in on your own.

All the usual international newspapers and magazines (often printed regionally in Hong Kong) are available from large bookstores in Seoul and Pusan but not generally elsewhere. They include the *International Herald Tribune*, the *Asian Wall Street Journal*, *Time* and *Newsweek*. If you can't find them on the street or at a major bookshop, try one of the large hotels.

Radio

There are four major radio stations, three of which broadcast entirely in Korean. The government-run KBS, however, not only broadcasts in Korean but also airs programmes in English, French, German, Chinese, Spanish, Portuguese, Russian, Italian, Japanese, Indonesian and Arabic. In addition, the US armed forces operate eight transmitters, including two FM stations. Programmes are entirely in English and include hourly news broadcasts.

TV

There are two Korean-language TV networks, KBS (run by the government) and MBC (the commercial station), as well as the English-language AFKN-TV. The latter is run by the US military and can be picked up in most parts of Korea though it's decidedly biased in favour of American events and news as you might expect. For better coverage of South Korean events, it's better to tune in to either KBS or MBC even if you don't understand Korean. KBS naturally toes a

progovernment line but it's not as blatant as you might expect.

HEALTH

South Korea is a very healthy country to travel in and you are unlikely to encounter any of the things which might have you running for the nearest pharmacy in places further south like Thailand, the Philippines and Indonesia. Not only are the people very hygiene-conscious but the government fosters and funds many public health schemes. Malaria has been eliminated, cholera and typhoid are things of the past and you certainly won't come across fleas or lice. In fact, the only thing which is likely to disturb your sensibilities is the intangible clouds of garlic-tinged fumes which emanate from everyone's mouths first thing in the morning before a coffee dispels them. But then you're unlikely to even notice these since your own breath will be scented with the same essential elixir of Korean cuisine.

On the other hand, should you need medical advice or treatment for any reason, help is always close at hand and the standards are excellent.

Korea has two systems of medicine – Western and traditional medicine. The traditional system, known as *hanyak*, is based on Chinese herbal remedies and acupuncture.

Western Medical Treatment

Western medicine was introduced into Korea around 1880. Nowadays there are large hospitals in every city and in many of the smaller towns. Hospital treatment is, however, expensive and, in any case, many Koreans prefer to treat their aches and pains in the traditional manner.

Despite this, there are well-stocked pharmacies to be found along almost any shopping or commercial street and they are staffed by well-qualified people. You don't need a prescription to buy drugs from these places. Simply go along to any of them, tell the staff what's wrong with you and they'll fix you up with what you need. If you know the chemical or commercial trade name of the drug you specifically need, then just ask for it. Naturally, they won't supply you with narcotics, in case you were thinking this system is very lax compared with the West.

Tampons also have to be bought from a pharmacy. Only sanitary towels are available in supermarkets as a rule.

Herbal Medicine

The traditional system goes back almost 1500 years, when it was introduced to the Koguryo court from China. It spread from there to the Paekje and Silla kingdoms and across the sea to Japan. Gradually, more and more indigenous herbs found their way into the system and pharmacopoeia began to be published with remedies which combined knowledge from both the Chinese and Korean herbal systems. By the time Koryo was overthrown and the Yi Dynasty came to rule Korea, the art of herbalism was highly developed. This fact was not lost on the Japanese when they invaded Korea at the end of the 16th century. While they laid waste to the countryside and reduced many temples to ashes, they were careful that valuable loot was shipped back to Japan. One such item was the medical manual known as the *Uibang Nuchwi*, the most valuable of those produced during the Yi era.

The theory behind herbalism is that health is based on the maintenance of a physiological balance between positive and negative elements in the body. To the Chinese, these elements are known as *yin* and *yang* and to Koreans as *um* and *yang*. Illness indicates an imbalance and the use of various herbal concoctions is designed to correct this. Some herbs are strong in yin and others in yang. The most famous of all the herbs used is ginseng (*Panax ginseng*).

Ginseng Known to Koreans as *insam*, it is an essential ingredient in many herbal remedies, and its use goes back as far as 3000 BC. In those days it was easily found in the forests and ravines of northern China, Mongolia and Korea, but vigorous harvesting made it rare by the time of the Koryo Dynasty. In order to meet demand, cultiva-

tion of the herb was encouraged in the southern provinces and has continued to this day. Though it is also cultivated in the USSR and China, South Korea is the world's foremost supplier. In 1981 the export of ginseng brought in an estimated US$145 million.

Cultivation of the root is a carefully controlled and involved process, and it takes four to six years before it can be harvested. Seeds are planted in a mulch of chestnut and oak leaves and the plants are shielded from direct sunlight by thatched matting. You'll see row after row of these inclined mats on many hillsides around Korea. Once harvested, the roots are processed into two grades – the highly potent red (*hong*) variety and the more common and less potent white (*paek*) variety. The price difference is considerable. If buying by weight, the red variety commonly sells for four times the price of the white variety. Wild roots – and particularly very old wild roots – are extremely expensive since they are considered to be very potent. The oldest recorded root ever found was said to be 400 years old – reported in the *Russian Journal of Botany* in 1952.

All manner of virtues have been attributed to ginseng ranging from it being an aphrodisiac to a mental stimulant. A great deal of scientific research has been done in an attempt to discover which components are

Korean Ginseng

the active principles but it's generally accepted that it stimulates the central nervous system, counteracts hypotension and stimulates gastrointestinal activity.

Other Herbal Remedies Traditional herbal remedies are sold in specialised shops often clustered together along certain streets in every town and city. In Seoul they are concentrated around Jong-ro 5-ga and along the bottom side of Namdaemun Market. The displays in these shop windows are fascinating and often bizarre since they include not only herbal preparations but the more esoteric animal-based stimulants and remedies such as powdered deer antlers and snakes pickled in wine, sometimes with ginseng added. Most Westerners would recoil at the thought of drinking such wine followed by eating the pickled snake but to Koreans it is the food of the gods. Not only is it regarded as an aphrodisiac but certain varieties of snake are commonly prescribed for longevity and neuralgia and were, in the past, even regarded as a cure for tuberculosis.

Dog meat soup is highly regarded as a rejuvenator, though it's not sold in the medicine shops but in specialised restaurants. These are becoming rare in the areas where tourists normally go, as a result of government pressure. It's felt that Western tourists might be revolted by such practices.

· Other common roots and herbs used in traditional medicine include iris roots (to stimulate mental activity), chrysanthemum roots (to cure headaches) and snakeberry leaves (to regulate the menstrual cycle). Roasted barley tea (supplied free to every guest at a *yogwan*) is also widely used as a general pick-me-up.

If you've been brought up on antibiotics, vaccines and all the other pharmaceutical wonders of allopathic medicine, you might well feel that all these herbal remedies and snake wine concoctions are unscientific nonsense. Undoubtedly some of them are but these are the days when modern research is discovering that many traditional remedies do actually contain active constituents which are effective in curing certain illnesses,

though they are naturally in a less concentrated form.

Before you go to Korea, take a look at an average health food store in the West and compare what are listed as constituents on shelves full of remedies for all known ills with what are contained in remedies in *hanyak* shops in Korea. You'll be amazed by the similarity!

FILM & PHOTOGRAPHY

Those with an interest in photography are in for a treat. Not only does Korea have four radically different seasons but it's a very mountainous country and the views can be spectacular. Autumn in the mountains is a riot of colour which has to be seen to be believed. Taking a cue from nature, the women's national costume has to be one of the most colourful in the world yet it's never garish. (Harmonious but striking is the password in the rag trade.) Then there are faces ranging from the smooth olive skins of youngsters to the wrinkled leather of the old folks. And, of course, all those superbly crafted and intricately painted Buddhist temples hiding away in their landscaped Gardens of Eden.

South Koreans are well acquainted with photography, and even though cameras are expensive, few families are without one. It's very unlikely that you will encounter any adverse reaction to taking photographs but, with old people, it is a mark of respect to ask first. Some may refuse but most will gladly pose, particularly if you have something simple like a postcard of your own country to offer in exchange. Many of those who initially refuse do so because they think you are making fun of them. Age is always treated with great deference in Korea and if an old person says and means no, don't push the issue.

Taking photographs of military installations, airports, dams and the like should also be avoided. There are notices to this effect in many places. The South Korean authorities are rightly concerned about espionage and North Korean infiltrators. If you feel that this verges on paranoia then just remember that if you took similar photographs in many African countries you'd be jailed and your equipment confiscated.

One other situation where you are not allowed to take photographs is on internal flights. If you fly on one or other of the domestic airlines keep your camera in its bag or case.

It is advisable to bring all your film requirements with you rather than buy it in Korea. It's not that film is necessarily more expensive in Korea but rather a question of availability. Slide film can usually only be found in large department stores and specialist photography stores in the main cities. You won't find it in small towns or in the countryside. Colour negative film, on the other hand, is widely available in Kodak, Agfa and Fuji. A 24-frame film of 35 mm colour negative costs around W1800 (less than US$3). A 36-frame film would be around W2400 (less than US$4). Colour slide film costs around W5000 (about US$8) for a 24-frame film and around W7800 (about US$12) excluding processing. Developing facilities are of the highest standard so you need have no reservations about this. The smallest prints cost about W120 (about US$0.15) but the price rapidly escalates if you want larger sizes.

Warning

Korean houses and hotels use the underfloor method of heating known as *ondol* in the winter months which means that the floors can get quite hot. If you leave your equipment on the floor the film may get ruined.

ACCOMMODATION
Hotels

Like almost everywhere else in the world, high-rise, Western-style hotels (many of them part of international chains) providing all possible creature comforts, can be found in all the main cities and tourist spots. They're usually very expensive and, because of their nature, you could be almost anywhere in the world. They won't leave you with much feeling for the country though

most of them do offer Korean-style rooms in addition to Western-style rooms.

Yoinsook & Yogwan

Budget travellers and anyone with a yen to experience the real Korea will find themselves staying in traditional Korean inns known as *yogwan* 여관 and *yoinsook* 여인숙. These are government-classified according to the standard of accommodation which they offer. *Yogwan* are generally of a higher standard than *yoinsook* but this isn't always the case. Prices are government-controlled; there should be a posted price list in each room and you shouldn't have to pay more than this. Prices are generally on a 'per room' basis so it costs the same whether you are alone or there are two of you, though you may come across some places which have separate prices for single and double occupation. There is invariably a surcharge for a third person in the same room (except babies and children who are never charged for). Proprietors will expect you to want to see the room and the bathroom facilities before you decide to stay but note that very few will speak any English at all.

Never wear your shoes into the room – take them off and leave them outside. No-one will ever steal your shoes. In some *yogwan* shoes are removed at reception. If there's an obvious pile of shoes at this point, do likewise.

Basic accommodation in these inns consists of a room provided with a thin mattress, known as the *yo* 요, a top cover, called the *ibul* 이불, and a hard pillow. The bedding will always be freshly laundered except perhaps at one or two of the most basic *yoinsook*. If it's not, ask them to change it. They'll always do this without protest or even comment.

In winter the rooms are kept warm by underfloor heating (known as *ondol*). The most commonly used fuel for this is coal in the form of dust compacted into a cube with many holes through it to allow for ease of ignition and combustion. Until the 1980s, particularly in traditionally constructed houses with mud floors, this method of heating carried with it the danger of carbon monoxide poisoning. If there were any small cracks in the floor the gas could escape into the room, so during winter it was important to ensure that the room was adequately ventilated. It's very unlikely you will face this danger in most of the *yogwan* or *yoinsook* in which you stay as concrete will have replaced mud as a construction material. On the other hand, if you do stay in an old mud-floored traditional house in winter, make sure you leave a window open at night.

Underfloor heating in Korean inns is only provided from around dusk until breakfast time. If you wish to stay inside during the day and a cold room doesn't appeal, you'll have to go and seek heat elsewhere if there's no electric heater in your room. Some very cheap *yoinsook* are reluctant to stoke up a fire at all unless there are sufficient guests staying in the inn to warrant the expense.

If you have camera equipment, don't leave it on the floor of an *ondol* room. The floors of these rooms can get very warm – even hot – and you'll end up with spoiled film.

Yoinsook are the cheapest type of accommodation and will cost between W4000 and W6000 (occasionally more) depending on where they are and what facilities they offer. At the very bottom of the range what you will get is a room with bedding but no other furniture, and access to communal bathing and toilet facilities. Bathing facilities may not always be adequate to cope with demand, especially in the morning, and in some cheaper places will consist only of a tap in the courtyard surrounded by several plastic bowls and buckets. If this is the case you're advised to watch a local get washed first before you attempt it as there is usually a ritual attached to which bowl you use for what and if you don't do it properly you can easily offend. Always rinse out any bowls you use with clean water when you're finished. You'll quickly get used to the copious quantities of water which Koreans get through when they're washing though initially it can be mind-boggling! Cold water is usually the rule in *yoinsook*, even in winter,

though some offer buckets of hot water on request for a small extra charge.

Naturally, you can't strip off and have a complete shower in places like this and you'll have to make use of the public bathhouses known as *mok yok tang* 목욕탕 . They're easily identified with the symbol ♨ and there are plenty of them. At bathhouses you can rent towels and soap and bathe for as long as you like for around W800. Men and women have separate facilities. Many bathhouses also double as *yogwan*. Even if you do stay in places with attached bathrooms, don't miss out on a visit to a bathhouse. It's an experience you shouldn't miss and a very pleasant one too. Would you visit Turkey without, at least once, going to a Turkish bathhouse?

Yogwan generally offer a better standard of accommodation and are priced between W7000 and W12,000. At the lower end of the scale this will mean just a little extra furniture in the room, but by the time you get to W9000 you should expect an attached bathroom with hot water at least part of the day. At that price, too, you can expect a TV and fan. By the time you are paying W10,000 to W11,000 you will certainly expect to have an attached toilet and bathroom, constant hot water and a bedroom with a colour TV, fan, a wardrobe and table. At W13,000 to W14,000 you would expect air-conditioning as well. Many *yogwan* at the top end of the scale will have a choice of Korean and Western-style rooms. Basically, the only difference between them is the type of bed you get.

If the name of a *yogwan* contains the word *jang* 장 (eg Myong Jang Yogwan, Horim Jang Yogwan, Jongwon Jang Yogwan, etc), it's an indication that it is in the top price range for this type of accommodation. In line with Korea's increasing standard of living, many *yogwan* are undergoing renovation to bring them up to a higher standard so *yogwan jang* are becoming quite common and, in many places, outnumber ordinary *yogwan*. Almost without exception, all *yogwan* will provide hot water even where facilities are communal. The only respect in which they differ is when hot water is available. In the cheaper places it's usually only between evening and early morning. At the top end you can expect hot water 24 hours a day, as is the case if the *yogwan* is part of a bath-house.

Some *yoinsook* and *yogwan* may have cooking facilities in which case they'll be able to provide meals on request. If not, most can arrange to have meals brought to your room from an outside restaurant if you don't want to eat out.

The provision of free *mool* (roasted barley tea) 보리차 is taken for granted in *yoinsook* and *yogwan* and a pot of it will usually be placed in your room as soon as you move in. The strident calls of *Ajimah! Mool chuseyo!* echoing through the corridors will probably become one of your more prominent memories of Korea in the same way as the barking of *Chai! Chai! Garam chai!* by the *chai wallahs* is amongst those who have been on long railway journeys in India.

Many of the more basic *yoinsook* will not have lockable doors but this is of little consequence. Koreans are an exceptionally honest people and you'd be extremely unlucky to have anything stolen.

Minbak

The last form of traditional accommodation is the *minbak* 민박 . This is a room in a private house. Bathing and cooking facilities are shared with the family that lives there though occasionally you may find separate facilities for guests. In popular tourist areas these places will be signposted but elsewhere you'll have to ask around. Souvenir shops, teashops and restaurants can usually point you in the right direction and may actually have *minbak* themselves.

In many rural areas, *minbak* may be the only form of accommodation available. Prices are always on a 'per room' basis and should be in the W4000 to W6000 range. Meals can generally be provided on request.

Minbak offer considerable discounts if you plan to stay long-term (eg one month).

South Korea is beginning to experiment with 'home-stays' and you can make arrangements for this before you get there through any of their tourist offices outside of Korea. They're often not particularly cheap (US$25 a night is common) but there will generally be someone in the family who speaks a European language.

Long-Term Accommodation

If you're staying in the same area for a month or so it's well worth making inquiries about renting an apartment or a room in a private home, *hapsook* 합숙, as this is much cheaper than staying in a *yogwan* on a day-to-day basis. *Hapsook* are usually better value if you plan to stay longer than a month as the family will provide breakfast and dinner (included in the room price). Many students rent rooms in *hapsook*. You're looking at around US$100 per month including meals in such places. Self-contained apartments are much more expensive and you'll have to cook for yourself or eat out.

Other travellers have suggested patronising a particular *tabang* (tea or coffee shop) in the area where you want to stay and asking the staff about the quality of the nearby *yogwan*. Most *tabang* employ a girl to take coffee in a thermos and cups wrapped in large cloths to offices, shops and *yogwan* in the neighbourhood. As a result, they have an intimate knowledge of the *yogwan* in the area.

Youth Hostels

Like many countries, Korea has a network of youth hostels scattered around the country. These hostels bear little resemblance to their counterparts in Europe, USA and Australasia. They're usually huge, modern places resembling expensive hotels and conference centres for businesspeople. The facilities are of a similar standard. You can forget about spartan rooms, cleaning and cooking duties and all the other joys (?) associated with the sort of down-to-earth accommodation provided by youth hostels elsewhere in the world. Here it is luxury at a bargain price if you don't mind dormitory rooms.

Dormitories consist of four, six and eight-

Top: Korean children (CHP)
Left: Horseplay on Ulleung-do Island (CHP)
Right: Kyongju school children (GC)

Top: Changdok Palace, Seoul (GC)
Bottom: The Olympic Stadium (CHP)

bunk rooms, and the price for a bed varies between W4000 and W5000 depending on how many bunks there are to a room. They all offer private rooms in addition to the dormitories but these cost between US$25 and US$45 and some of them even offer suites which can cost as much as US$60! All the hostels have their own restaurants but the price of meals is pitched towards those who occupy the private rooms.

Outside of public holidays, the summer holiday season and Christmas/New Year, there's usually no need to book ahead for the hostels if you intend to stay in the dormitory rooms. During school holidays, however, you'll be extremely lucky to get a bed without advance booking and, even if you get one, you probably won't be able to sleep. School kids anywhere in the world are usually extremely boisterous.

The staff at hostels can usually speak English and Japanese.

For more information and reservations contact the Korea Youth Hostel Association, 27-1 Supyo-dong, Chung-gu, Seoul (tel (02) 266-2896). Some of the hostels have separate offices in Seoul where you can make bookings.

There are youth hostels at the following places:

Seoul
Bando Youth Hostel 679-3 Yoksam-dong, Kangnam-gu, Seoul (tel (02) 567-5033). Total of 100 bunk beds. The hostel is five minutes by bus from Kangnam Express Bus Terminal.
Academy House San 76, Suuy-dong, Tuboung-gu, Seoul (tel (02) 993-6181/5). Total of 16 bunk beds. The hostel is located in the resort area of Mt Tobong-san.

Pusan
Aerin Youth Hostel 41 1-ga, Posu-dong, Chung-gu, Pusan (tel (051) 27-2222/7). Total of 23 bunk beds. The hostel is in downtown Pusan. Seoul bookings office (tel (02) 735-5022).

Nak-san
30-1 Chonjin-ri, Kanghyon-myon, Yangyang-gun (tel (0396) 3416/8). Total of five dormitory rooms. The hostel is on the same hillock as the Naksan temple. Seoul booking office (tel (02) 313-2911/5.

Sorak-san
Sorak Youth Hostel 155 Tomun-dong, Sogcho,

Kangwon-do (tel (0392) 7-7540/50). Total of 73 bunk beds. The hostel is in the village of Sorak-dong. Seoul booking office (tel (02) 762-6425).

Puyo
Buyeo Youth Hostel 105-1 Kugyo-ri, Puyo-up, Puyo-gun, Chungchongnam-do (tel (0463) 2-3101/10). Total of 33 bunk beds. The hostel is at the foot of Mt Puyo-san very close to the centre of town. Seoul booking office (tel (02) 567-2055).

Kyongju
Kyongju Youth Hostel 145-1 Kujong-dong, Kyongju, Kyongsanbuk-do (tel (0561) 2-9991/6). Total of 47 bunk beds. The hostel is outside of town close to Pulguk-sa Temple. Seoul booking office (tel (02) 732-7140).

FOOD

There are four main types of food available in Korea – Korean, Chinese, Japanese and Western.

While Chinese and Japanese people eat their food exclusively with chopsticks, Koreans use both chopsticks and spoons so, if you haven't yet mastered the art of eating with sticks, you're in luck. Chopsticks are usually of the disposable type and brought to you half-split in a paper envelope.

Most of the cheaper restaurants consist of a dining hall with tables and chairs but the better ones will have a choice between tables and chairs and rooms where you sit on cushions on the floor at a low table. Footwear should always be removed before entering one of the latter.

Wherever you eat, do it heartily. You need never worry about the Western fetishes about slurping food, making a mess or belching.

An excellent book for absolute beginners in Korean cuisine and one which could be a very useful travelling companion is *All Purpose Guide to Korean Food*, Suh Hwan (Seoul International Publishing House, 1987). Written in English, it is a pictorial dictionary of virtually every Korean dish complete with a description of the ingredients and the method of preparation. It includes the *hangul* for each dish (making it easy for non-English-speaking Koreans to understand what exactly you want) as well as an estimated price.

Korean Food – han-shik 한식

Whatever Korean dish you order, regardless of the restaurant, it will always include a plate of *kimchi* 김치 – the national dish. The ingredients and taste of this vary from place to place and there are several distinct regional varieties. The most common is that made with Chinese cabbage, garlic, ginger and chilli. Grated vegetables such as carrot and radish are usually added. It's a labour-intensive process but when the preparation is finished the whole lot is placed into an earthenware pot and allowed to ferment. This process can take as little as one day in the height of summer, and weeks in winter. These earthenware *kimchi* pots can be seen cluttering the courtyards of all Korean houses and even the outside balconies of high-rise apartments. The length of the fermentation period, which allows the flavours of the seasonings to percolate through the cabbage, is crucial to the quality. There is an optimum before which and after which it doesn't taste as good.

At the beginning of winter, in every traditional household, the housewife will buy and prepare up to 100 head of cabbage, the same amount of radish, up to three kg of chillies, 40 roots of fresh ginger and plenty of garlic with which to put down the winter stash of *kimchi*. All over Korea at this time of year the streets will be jammed with vegetable carts selling the necessary ingredients.

If you've never tasted *kimchi* before, you may be in for a culinary shock. To Western palates it is fiery hot and pungent. Nothing you have ever tasted is comparable and it's probably true to say that it's an acquired taste. Once acquired, however, you may find, as most people do, that you can't eat enough of it. Whatever you may think of it, on the other hand, it is nutritionally excellent.

The *kimchi* prepared with Chinese cabbage is only one variety and there are others which usually accompany every meal. They include *mool kimchi* (sliced radish flavoured with garlic, but without chilli, which floats in the liquid in which it fermented) and *tongchimi* (much the same as *mool kimchi* but without the liquid).

The basic Korean meal is known as *pekpan* 백반 and consists of rice 쌀, soup 국, and side dishes. The number and variety of side dishes varies but at some restaurants you'll begin to wonder whether the table is large enough to hold them all! At one restaurant in Mogpo I was served with a total of 15 side dishes in addition to the main seafood dish, rice and soup! You can order *pekpan* for breakfast, lunch or dinner. The average price for this meal is W1500 depending on where you eat.

Three other cheap, filling dishes are *pindatok* 빈대떡 (a vegetarian pancake/omelette made with bean flour, eggs and chopped vegetables), *be bim bap* 비빔밥 (rice topped with parboiled fern bracken, soybean sprouts, spinach, red pepper sauce, sometimes broiled beef – though this costs more – and garnished with a fried egg) and *kimbap* 김밥. The latter is similar to the Japanese sushi and is made of sticky rice rolled up inside sheets of dried seaweed in the centre of which is grated carrot, spinach or other vegetables and cooked egg, meat or fish. After being rolled up it is sliced into approximately three-cm-thick cakes and generally eaten with soy sauce. *Kimbap* can be found in most Korean picnic baskets.

A variation of *pindatok* is *pa jon* 파전 (green onion pancakes). Other simple snack meals are *naeng myong* 냉면 (buckwheat noodles in chilled soup) and *bibim naeng myon* 비빔냉면 (buckwheat noodles with spicy sauce).

Cheap meals at simple restaurants generally contain little or no meat though the side dishes may include various types of seafood. The reason for this is that meat is expensive. Protein is derived mainly from various bean curds and vegetables. Indeed a substantial amount of Korean cuisine is basically vegetarian. This does not mean that Koreans don't eat meat or that they don't like it. They certainly do, and there are plenty of restaurants catering for meat eaters, but dishes where meat is the main ingredient are always more expensive than the others.

Most South Koreans on average wages would regard more than two meals a week in which meat was the main component as exceptional. On the other hand, there are two meat dishes which, like *kimchi*, can be regarded as national dishes. They are *pulgogi* 불고기 and *kalbi* 갈비.

Pulgogi is very thin strips of beef marinated in garlic, onions, soy sauce, sesame oil, black pepper and roasted sesame seeds. It is then grilled over a fire and most restaurants offering this dish will cook it in front of you. They have special cone-shaped grilling utensils and a burner (either a gas ring or coal briquette burner, which forms an integral part of the dining table.

Kalbi is beef or pork short ribs marinated in much the same way as *pulgogi* and then grilled over charcoal until tender. Both dishes come complete with rice and the usual side dishes.

Most restaurants serving *pulgogi* and *kalbi* also offer the cheaper, unmarinated meat dishes known as *gwee* 구이 (sliced beef) and *teji gwee* 돼지구이 (sliced pork). These are also cooked at your table but in the form of a barbecue. Instead of the usual side dishes, these are usually served with lettuce or *kenyip* 깻잎 leaves, *tenjang* paste (a soy bean paste) and *kimchi*. You may also come across *kalbi-chim* 갈비찜 which is beef rib stew made with short ribs, turnips, chestnuts and mushrooms and cooked slowly for a few hours.

For *pulgogi* and *kalbi* you can expect to pay W5000 to W6000 per person though somewhat less for the unmarinated varieties.

One other delicious meat dish which you can find in various restaurants is *mandu* 만두. This dish consists of meat, vegetables and sometimes soybean curd stuffed into dumplings. It comes in various forms which include *mandu guk* 만두국 (*mandu* soup), *kun mandu* 군만두 (fried *mandu*), *mool mandu* 물만두 (boiled *mandu*), and *jin mandu* 찐만두 (steamed *mandu*). It's a relatively cheap dish and shouldn't cost you more than W1500.

Chicken is usually only served in specialised restaurants and the most popular dish is *samgye-tang* 삼계탕 (ginseng chicken). Shredded ginseng root and gluti-

nous rice are stuffed into the chicken which is then boiled in an earthenware pot. The end product varies a lot depending on the skill of the cook. Personally, I find it tasteless in comparison to other meat dishes with their spicy marinades and sauces but many people like it.

With such an extensive coastline it is not surprising that Koreans also love their seafood. Many restaurants, especially in coastal towns and cities, cater exclusively for this, but since no part of the peninsula is more than a few hours drive from the sea you can also find it in inland towns and cities. Dishes run the whole gamut from cockles, mussels and oysters, to sea cucumbers, octopus, squid, crab, prawns and fish. Squid is particularly popular, either freshly cooked as calamari or dried and eaten as a snack with beer or *soju*. The words you need to know to order any of these are:

cockle – *soe-ra* 소라
cod/haddock/whiting – *taegu* 대구
crab – *kay* 개
fish – *sengson* 생선
herring – *chong-o* 청어
lobster – *tae-ha* 대하
mackerel – *kodung-o* 고등어
mussel – *honghap* 홍합
octopus – *moon-ah* 문어
oyster – *kul* 굴
plaice – *kaja-mi* 가자미
prawn – *say-oo* 새우
sardine – *chongo-ri* 정어리
sole – *hyo-gaja-mi* 해 가자미
squid – *ojing-or* 오징어
trout – *song-o* 송어
tuna – *cham-chi* 참치

Most seafood restaurants keep their seafood alive right up to the moment that a customer makes an order, so you can be sure it's fresh. Fish intended to be eaten raw are kept in huge aquariums in the dining area so you can choose a particular one. It's eaten thinly sliced with soy sauce or hot chilli sauce. Ask for *sengson-hae* 생선회. Unfortunately, there's a huge drawback to this even in places on the coast which have a substantial fishing fleet. And that is the cost. A raw fish meal sufficient for three to four people regularly comes to W30,000 (around US$47)! It's obviously not a dish which Koreans on average wages can afford let alone budget travellers.

But there's good news too. Shellfish soups are very cheap and not all fish is landed alive. The ones that are not are served up fried or barbecued. This sort of meal can be excellent value at around W3000 per person including side dishes. Ask for *sengson-gwee* 생선구이. Fried fish is fairly easy to find on street stalls but as there's obviously more money to be made from raw fish than fried fish, finding a restaurant which serves it is not always easy. Whether this is a function of the Korean conglomerates' grip on the trawling fleets is hard to determine but it certainly wasn't like that a few years ago. Perhaps the Koreans, despite their avowed antagonism to things Japanese, are beginning to emulate those people?

Eel (*pemjang-o* 뱀장어) is also popular, particularly with men, since it is regarded as an aphrodisiac. It is eaten either grilled or as a stew with *kimchi*. Sea cucumber (*hae-sam* 해삼) is regarded as having the same properties but is always eaten raw – and alive (remember it's an animal, not a plant, regardless of the name). It's very chewy indeed and somewhat tasteless so probably best left alone unless you're familiar with it. Many of the smaller crustaceans like shrimp (*chansae-o* 참새우) and the smaller fishes like anchovy (*me-ol-chi* 멸치) are dried and used to flavour other dishes though they're sometimes served on their own as a side dish – particularly dried anchovies. Likewise, crab is often served as a side dish liberally covered in spicy sauce.

One very tasty broth based on seafood is *chongol* 전골. This is a rich soup cooked in a pot with a variety of vegetables, fish and shellfish. Sliced meat is sometimes added.

The other main type of Korean dishes are various soups and broths (*ji-gay* 찌게). These include fish soup (*seng son ji-gay* 생선찌게), meat soup (*kogi ji-gay* 고기 찌게) with either beef or pork, bean curd soup (*too-boo ji-gay* 두부찌게) and fermented soy bean and vegetable soup (*tenjang ji-gay* 된장찌게). Unlike in the West, soups will be served at the same time as the other dishes.

The last category of Korean cuisine is various forms of mountain food – *chayon shikpoom* – consisting of nuts, roots, shoots, seeds and mushrooms, some of which are cultivated and others which grow wild. Most of the roots would be unfamiliar to Westerners, but pine kernels and pine mushrooms are familiar enough. This sort of food is only served in specialised restaurants and meals are relatively expensive.

Lastly, there are a couple of esoterica you should know about. One is *bondeggi* 번데기 which are steamed silkworm larvae sold on street stalls around the country, and *haejang-guk* 해장국 which is 'hangover soup'. The last is pork-blood and vegetable soup served in the mornings and it reputedly has the power to dispel cerebral cobwebs!

As elsewhere in the world, cheap restaurants cater for hungry people with limited finances so while the food may be very tasty, presentation is usually a low priority. At its best, however, Korean cuisine is meant to be more than just a taste sensation. Presentation is equally important and a lot of effort will be put into making sure that it is also a visual delight. It's worth splurging at a good restaurant from time to time just to see how well this can be done.

Chinese Food - *chungkuk um-shik*
중국음식

Chinese restaurants are identified by two black swinging signs in Chinese characters above the entrance which are flanked by red streamers on either side. The cheaper restaurants are primarily designed for quick meals and often used by people looking for a quick lunch or breakfast, but there are others which cater for lengthier meal times. The cheapest dishes (*om rice*, for example) will cost W1000 to W1500 but meat dishes (sweet and sour pork, etc) will be in the W3500 to W4000 range. Restaurants usually offer the following individual dishes:

Fried rice with egg
om rice 오므라이스
Hot spicy noodle soup with meat/seafood
cham pong 짬봉
Noodles with sauce
u-dong 우동
Deep fried wonton
yakimandu 야끼만두
Noodles with black bean sauce
cha ja myon 짜장면
(*Cha ja myon* is the favourite lunch of many Koreans and generally costs less than W1000.)

Dishes which you would share with others include:

Sweet and sour pork
tang su-yuk 탕수육
Deep fried battered pork with a spicy sauce
chajo-yuk 자조육
Mixed seafood in sauce
chap tang 잡탕
Fried noodles, meat and vegetables
chap che 잡채
Egg soup
keran kook 계란국

Japanese Food – *il-sik* 일식

Japanese restaurants have become almost as common as Chinese restaurants and can be found all over the country, but they invariably belong in the higher price range so treat them as a splurge. The cheaper, hot dishes at these restaurants include tempura (*teegim* 튀김) – battered, deep-fried dishes. The most usual are:

Shrimp tempura with vegetables
saoo teegim 새우 튀김
Fish tempura
sengson teegim 생선 튀김
Vegetable tempura
yache teegim 야채튀김

The main cold dishes include:

Sashimi – (*sengson hae*) 생선회 – raw fish with either soy or hot chilli sauce and rice

Kimbap 김밥 – the same as the Korean variety described earlier
Yubu chobap 유부초밥 – prepared in a similar way to *kimbap* except bean curd and rice mixed with vinegar are wrapped up into a roll with egg which has been fried as a very thin omelette

Western Food – *yang shik* 양식

Although most of the larger hotels have had separate Western-style restaurants for years, it was only recently that their fast food equivalents began to appear on the streets of Korea. The 1988 Seoul Olympics changed all that virtually overnight. These days Kentucky Fried Chicken, Pizza Hut and McDonald's (as well as their Korean equivalents) can be found on most city boulevards.

Another development has been the appearance of German-style beer halls offering German food. Many of these are excellent value, and although they describe their food as 'snacks', they're usually substantial enough to be regarded as a meal. Prices are very reasonable.

Other beer bars double as fried chicken outlets, Korean-style. The fried chicken is the same as what you would get elsewhere in the world except here it is served either with *kimchi* or grated cabbage salad. A portion usually costs around W1000.

Other Western-style restaurants offering a wider selection of food are popping up here and there in the larger cities.

Self-Catering

In every Korean town and city there will be one or more areas given over to either open-air or covered markets. You'll find every conceivable vegetable as well as meat, fish, eggs and dairy products. Most things, especially vegetables but not meat and cheese, are quite cheap – much cheaper than buying the cooked product from a restaurant – so self-caterers have no problems. In addition, there are many supermarkets where you'll find a whole range of Korean foods and drinks as well as many of the products which you'd take for granted in a Western supermarket. Bottles of beer bought in these places will have a small returnable deposit (about W30) on the bottle.

A list of Korean words for basic foodstuffs is to be found in the 'Language' section in the Facts about the Country chapter.

DRINKS
Alcoholic Beverages

Koreans love their booze like they do their *kimchi* and there is no shortage of drinking establishments to suit every pocket and every taste. The traditional drink is *makkoli* 막걸리, a beer made from rice, though in times of poor harvests wheat and corn may also be used. It's a thick, milky liquid which is not filtered like other fermented drinks, and the colour and quality vary widely from one place to the next. At its best, it's very tasty indeed, full of 'body' and almost fragrant but it does have a short optimum 'life' and begins to lose its taste after three days at room temperature. Home-brewed is always better than commercially brewed. It's also the cheapest alcoholic drink available so widely consumed in the countryside.

Apart from specialised restaurants, it's sold in places called *makkoli-jip* 막걸리집 which range from raucous beverage halls to more sedate but still informal establishments. They can be found all over Korea. What is not sedate about any of these establishments is the method of serving the *makkoli*. It's doled out of large vats or tubs into cheap and often battered teapots and drunk out of any convenient receptacle. *Makkoli-jip* are great places to visit if you're looking for a spit-and-sawdust binge and an easy introduction to the local people. Usually one group or another will break out into song as the evening wears on and sometimes there is live music.

Also served at *makkoli-jip*, as well as at almost all restaurants, is the much stronger *soju* 소주. This is a bottled liquor distilled from fermented grains and/or potatoes with an alcohol content of around 25%. Like *makkoli*, it's cheap and goes down very smoothly with various dishes. The taste of it falls somewhere between white Bacardi rum and furniture

polish remover. It's a common sight in restaurants to see groups of diners with glazed-over eyes chatting around a table groaning with empty *soju* bottles. After several sessions with various Korean hosts, I was left disoriented and hung-over for at least a day afterwards and I resolved never to touch the stuff again. But resolutions are made to be broken, I discovered. Maybe you'll find it to your liking.

Makkoli and *soju* are always drunk with various snacks which are known as *anju* 안주. These are often seafood, either fresh or dried, and include fresh oysters, dried squid, salted peanuts (*tang kong*) and *kim* (small sheets of lightly fried, salted seaweed). You'll be asked what *anju* you want when ordering your drink.

In addition to the more permanent *makkoli-jip* you'll come across collections of roadside carts in certain streets in most towns and cities of Korea which set up shop in the evenings. These are covered with waterproof canopies (often striped red and white) and enclose tables and chairs. Lighting is provided with kerosene pressure lanterns. These carts provide a gutsy, down-to-earth and convivial atmosphere where you can drink *soju* and enjoy good street meals in the form of snacks and soups made from seafood, chicken and meat, though the dishes made of the latter are usually things like trotters. Prices are very reasonable. The stalls tend to close by midnight but they'll usually have run out of food well before that.

The other main alcoholic beverage is beer (*maekju* 맥주). It's been popular for years and has replaced *makkoli* as the preferred drink among many city dwellers. There are two varieties – OB and Crown. As a connoisseur of the amber nectar I'd say OB was the better of the two. In the early 1980s, both the OB and Crown companies built stand-up bars all over the country. They were furnished with stools and chunky pine furniture and were good places to meet local people. Most of them laid on taped music. Some of these open-plan bars still survive but in most cases they've been divided up into private booths with curtains or hardboard partitions.

This has no doubt been welcomed by young lovers seeking privacy who want to look longingly into each others eyes or engage in more tactile pursuits, but it has meant that it's not as easy to meet local people in these bars as it used to be.

What have sprung up in their place are recreations of the classic German beer hall complete with photographic murals of the Oktoberfest, half-timbered walls and chunky glass beer jars. These places are almost always open-plan and can be very lively in the evenings.

Other types of beer bars are to be found everywhere and are easily recognisable by their OB or Crown logos. You'll often see the words, 'Stand Bar' (in English) outside these places but that doesn't necessarily mean you have to drink standing at the bar. There are always tables and chairs and some don't even have a stand bar at all despite the sign outside. They're not exclusively male bars by any means so women travellers need have no hesitation in using them.

Draught beer (*saeng-maekju*), where available, is sold in two sizes of glass – 500 ml and 1000 ml – and costs the same whether it's OB or Crown – W600 for the smaller glass and W1200 for the larger. The only difference in Korea is that you pay for the head as well as the liquid and the former takes up about one-third of the glass. You probably wouldn't go back to the same bar again if you were served beer like that in the West but here it's expected. Bottled beer (*pyong-maekju*) is generally more expensive than draught and a large bottle ordered in a bar usually costs W1400 to W1800 (the higher price in an air-conditioned place).

Bottled beer bought from a corner store or supermarket costs much less – W800 is the usual price – and you can expect it to come out of a refrigerator. A returnable deposit of around W30 is charged on the bottle when buying from a store but most travellers leave the empties at the *yogwan* for the *ajimah* to trade in with tinkers who collect them.

As in *makkoli-jip*, beer is always drunk with *anju* and you'll be asked which one you want when ordering a beer.

Whether you drink in a *makkoli-jip* or a beer bar it's unlikely you'll be there long without being drawn into a group of drinkers. Drinking is a gregarious activity and as soon as you sit down you'll quickly find yourself in conversation with someone who'll ask you what your name is, how old you are and where you come from. And, from that point on, you may well need to know what protocols are involved in drinking with friends. What generally happens is that one drinker will offer his empty glass to another. The recipient takes it and holds it while the giver fills it up. The recipient can then drink and, when he's finished, hand it back to the giver who will accept it and wait until it is refilled. All giving and receiving must be done with *both* hands. Variations on this involve the giver shouting *Kambay!* once he's filled his partner's glass or for several people to offer one person their glasses. *Kambay* is an invitation to skull the contents of your glass in one hit. You are at liberty to return the injunction. You can end up very drunk at sessions like this but if you do, it's more than likely that your partners will see you safely home. Drunkenness is not regarded with the same degree of disdain as it is in the West though you will be expected to hold whatever you drink.

The reason the male pronoun has been used exclusively in the last paragraph is because all this drinking protocol relates to all-male groups. Women and couples would not be expected to take part.

Other than the walk-in beer bars, there are plenty of other places where beer or spirits are the main social lubricants. Most of these are more like clubs than bars though generally open to the public. If you're on a strict budget you should be very wary of these places as a night out in one of them can turn out to be disastrously expensive. Almost all of them employ 'hostesses' who are there to cater for whatever proclivities the male clients may have and to ensure that the supply of alcohol keeps flowing. You pay for the hostesses' drinks even if your contact with them is only brief and purely verbal, unless you make it quite clear from the start that you don't require their 'services'. They will also expect a substantial tip at the end of the evening. Do not expect the same openly sexual behaviour at these places that you would in Bangkok or Manila. Koreans demand a certain degree of subtlety and decorum in this respect and it's likely to remain that way.

Nightclubs in large hotels and department stores are a different kettle of fish. They attract a wide variety of people, from students to rich businessmen. Most offer live music. To get in you pay a group rate (regardless of numbers) which varies between W10,000 and W30,000. That generally entitles you to three large bottles of beer and snacks. If you want more than that you can expect to pay through the nose for it. With these figures in mind, it's obviously an expensive night out if you're alone but relatively cheap if you're part of a group. If you're on a budget, make sure you know what the cover charge is.

Nonalcoholic Beverages

For nonalcoholic beverages the most popular places are the *tabang* or coffee shops which, like the bars, are found all over Korea. They are popular with everyone wanting somewhere to relax – from businesspeople wanting to talk, to young lovers looking for a quiet corner to exchange sweet nothings. During the day they're always very busy and at lunchtimes you may be hard-pressed to find a seat. A coffee averages around W500 to 600 but, having bought one, you can sit there as long as you like. Many *tabang* also offer ginseng tea (*insam-cha* 인삼차) which costs about the same.

Tabang are not licensed to sell food – they're strictly for drinking coffee or tea in a relaxing atmosphere. Likewise, restaurants are not licensed to sell coffee so you can't order this at the end of a meal.

Quite a few *tabang* cater for young people wanting to listen to the latest records and the waitresses may even bring you a record request slip with your coffee. Most DJs have extensive collections of American, British and Australian records as well as all the records of contemporary South Korean rock stars.

BOOKS
History
An Account of the Shipwreck of a Dutch Vessel on the Isle of Quelpaert, together with a Description of the Kingdom of Corea, by Hendrick Hamel (Reprint Amsterdam, 1920, B Hoetink), is a translation of the original book, published in 1668, which was the first account of Korea ever to reach Europe. The survivors of the *Sparrowhawk*, which was wrecked on the southern coast of Cheju-do Island in 1653, were taken to Seoul by orders of the king and forced to remain there for some 12 years until they were finally able to escape to Japan and make their way back to Europe. It was a best seller when first published but is hard to find these days. The book was the inspiration for Simon Winchester's book (see under Travel Guides).

A New History of Korea by Ki-baik Lee, translated by E W Wagner (Ilchokak Publishers, Seoul, Korea, 1984), 474 pages, W18,000. This is probably the best and most recent academic account of the history of Korea for those in search of accuracy and detail. It covers the entire span of Korean history up until 1960.

The Origins of the Korean War by Peter Lowe (Longman, New York, USA, 1986), 237 pages, W3200. This is a very readable account of the war which devastated the peninsula between 1950 and 1953. It concentrates particularly on the relationships between General MacArthur, the US President and other powerful members of his administration.

Religion
Korea Buddhism (Korea Buddhism Chogye Order, Seoul, Korea, 1986), W10,000, is a large-format paperback which is hard to find but worth searching for. The bulk of the book is taken up with stunning colour photographs of all the major temples in Korea, plus there are chapters on the history of Buddhism in Korea, an account of the daily life of the monks, and a section on Buddhist art. It's one of my most prized mementoes of Korea.

Shamanism – The Spirit World of Korea,

edited by Chai-shin Yu & R Guisso (Asian Humanities Press, Berkeley, USA, 1988), 190 pages, W11,900. This is a scholarly account of the belief systems and practices of Korea's original religion before the advent of Buddhism and Confucianism. Though still practised even today, it has been frowned upon by the adherents of the more sophisticated religions for centuries yet it still has its place in the Korean psyche. It's a book for those interested in the cult of nature spirits and Oriental witchcraft.

General

Korea's Kyongju – Cultural Spirit of Silla in Korea by Edward B Adams (Seoul International Publishing House, Seoul, Korea, 1986), 375 pages, W10,000. If you are planning to spend a lot of time in Korea and particularly in the Kyongju area then this beautifully illustrated book is well worth the price. The author has spent the best part of his life in Korea. It covers every known Silla site in and around Kyongju as well as many other points of interest. Good maps show the location of all the major sites.

The same author has also written: *Korea Guide – A Glimpse of Korea's Cultural*

Lonely Planet's Korean Phrasebook

Legacy (1983), 402 pages; *Palaces of Seoul* (1982), 218 pages; *Art Treasures of Seoul* (1980), 180 pages; *Through the Gates of Seoul* (1978), two volumes, 800 pages; and *Korean Folk Stories for Children* (1983), 32 pages.

Living in Korea by Richard B Rucci (Seoul International Publishing House/ American Chamber of Commerce in Korea, Seoul, 1987), 295 pages, W9000. Written by the principal of Seoul International School, this is mainly a book for people who are planning to live and work in South Korea and is packed with information. It includes chapters on moving preparations, housing and services, schools, health and medical care, shopping, transportation and doing business in Korea.

Korea by Jean-Claude & Roland Michaud (Thames & Hudson, London, UK, 1981). This large-format hardback, originally published in French, paints an unashamedly romantic view of Korea but the 85 full-page photographs are superb. It's definitely a collector's item and quite expensive.

Korean Cultural Potpourri by Jeon Kyu-tae (Seoul International Publishing House, Seoul, Korea, 1987), 116 pages, W4000. Superficially, this looks like an interesting book but after a third of the way into it, I threw it aside. It's legitimate to call for the preservation and even restoration of a culture but the text of this book is unbearably chauvinistic, even xenophobic in parts, and the English is not only pretentious but written by a person (the Dean of Cheonju University) who ought to have a better command of the grammar.

Korean Impact on Japanese Culture – Japan's Hidden History by Jon Carter & Alan Covell (Hollym, New Jersey, USA, 1984), 115 pages, W9500. Japanese historians have consistently ignored or only very grudgingly acknowledged Korea's contribution to Japanese culture although it has been extensive. This book is an excellent attempt to put the record straight. It's beautifully illustrated with colour photographs and maps.

All Purpose Guide to Korean Food by Suh Hwan (Seoul International Publishing House, Seoul, Korea, 1987), W3500. If you're unfamiliar with Korean cuisine then this handy little paperback is an ideal travelling companion. It shows 200 everyday dishes in full colour with the name of the dish in Korean and English, a description of the ingredients, the method of preparation, the estimated price range and suggestions about where to find the dish.

Korean for Travellers (Berlitz Guides, Lausanne, Switzerland, 1986), W4000. This is a very useful language guide for those who plan to stay in Korea for a while and/or explore the country. It covers just about every topic you're likely to need, in English, *hangul* (the Korean script) and a romanisation of the *hangul*.

An extremely handy and useful pocket-sized phrasebook for travellers is Lonely Planet's *Korean Phrasebook*. Hangul script is given for all the phrases.

Travel Guides

Korea (Insight Guides, Apa Productions, Hong Kong, 1983), 377 pages, is one of Apa's series of guides to various countries and regions around the world. Put together by a team of writers and photographers, it's a very comprehensive account of Korea and beautifully illustrated throughout with colour photographs. It includes separate sections on Korean history, art, religions, music and dance, cuisine and costume. It's an excellent book to read before you go in order to get an idea of the places you most want to visit.

Korea – A Walk through the Land of Miracles by Simon Winchester (Prentice Hall Press, 1988), 240 pages, US$17.95. This is definitely one of the best travel books ever written in terms of both content and style. The author literally walked from one end of South Korea to the other essentially following the route taken by the shipwrecked sailors of the Dutch ship *Sparrowhawk* in 1653. It's a matchless blend of history, character sketches, politics, customs, American military involvement, anecdotes and humour. It's a book you'll want to read many times and wish you'd never got to the end of. Thoroughly researched and very sensitively portrayed it's top reading.

THINGS TO BUY

Traditional craftwork and the arts are alive and well in Korea and even the impecunious traveller will have a wide range of things to choose from. Naturally, quality determines price, but even cheap souvenirs are generally well made. Few visitors return without at least bringing with them one of the ubiquitous lacquerware boxes inlaid with mother-of-pearl. These are definitely some of the best bargains to be found and they're unique to Korea. They range from tiny cigarette and jewellery boxes which cost just a few dollars to much larger and incredibly detailed items containing many internal subdivisions.

Lacquerwork is one of Korea's ancient crafts and these boxes are just one example of this tradition. It also encompasses furniture from tables and chairs to wardrobes and storage chests. The latter can be particularly stunning and a great deal of attention is also given to the brass fittings. Naturally, these larger items are bulky – and more expensive – so, if you were to buy them, you'd have to arrange for them to be shipped to your home country. Most retailers can make these arrangements for you.

In most of the shops which sell lacquerware there is usually a wide selection of brassware as well. Hand-hammered and moulded brassware is made into everything including paperweights, plates, goblets, lamps, vases and even beds. There's also much which draws its inspiration from Buddhist statuary. Prices are reasonable.

Ceramics are another Korean craft with a long pedigree going back to the days of the Koryo Dynasty when the pale blue-green, crackle-glazed celadon pottery was regarded as perfection itself. It was much sought after, even in China which had its own highly developed ceramics. The tradition of excellence has been maintained and there are many beautiful pieces to be found in specialist shops. It is, however, generally expensive so don't expect to pick up pieces for a song. Ceramics definitely fall into the realm of art rather than craftwork.

Much cheaper, and well within the range of a budget traveller's pocket, are the carved wooden masks which you'll come across in many a souvenir shop in country areas. Only rarely do these resemble the shamanistic spirit posts found at the entrance to rural villages. Instead they concentrate on exaggerated facial expressions and range from the grotesque to the humorous. They're easily carried in the average backpack and usually cost between US$5 and US$10 though the detail determines the price.

Hand-carved Wooden Mask

Visit any Korean home and you'll see scores of examples of embroidery. It's a national hobby among the women and highly regarded as a decorative art. Many fabric shops specialise in it along with incredibly ornate brocades and you can pick up everything from handkerchiefs and pillow cases to room-size screens. Many such shops do personalised embroidery either to their own or to the customer's designs. Another similar national hobby is macramé. Common items are colourful wall hangings and the long *no-ri-gae* tassles which adorn the front of every Korean woman's traditional costume. The latter always hang from a painted brass headpiece which itself is often very colourful.

Korea produces a wide range of precious and semiprecious stones including amethyst, smoky topaz, rubies, sapphires, emeralds and, of course, jade. Korean jade is lighter in colour than Chinese green jade and is often almost white, but it's a lot cheaper. You will find jewellery shops everywhere and at most of them you have a choice of mounted and unmounted stones. As with buying stones anywhere else in the world, you will need to have a good knowledge of current prices and know what to look for in order to find bargains.

Ordinary items of footwear and clothing can be picked up quite cheaply in Korean markets. In department stores, on the other hand, prices are often high since these places cater largely for the dictates of current fashion. Leatherware is a bargain – particularly in the shops of Itaewon in Seoul – but you need to do some shopping around before you buy. Prices vary widely as does quality and in the high season (late Spring to late Autumn) your bargaining powers are limited because there are so many other tourists and particularly Japanese tourists who flock here for a week or so of nonstop shopping and who will pay the first price asked. While that may seem silly, equivalent prices in Japan are up to four times greater. When business gets slack, on the other hand, it's a buyers' market.

Cheju-do Island specialises in reproductions of the famous *harubang*, or grandfather, figures. These are made out of pumice stone and range in size from just a few cm high to over two metres. They're one of the more attractive souvenirs and almost every traveller comes back with one or more of the smaller ones.

Last but not least, there is ginseng (*insam*). This is one of Korea's major exports and its sale is controlled by a government monopoly. The quality of Korea's product is world-renowned and you won't find it cheaper anywhere else in the world, though there is a limit to the amount which can be taken out of the country without an export licence. The average traveller is very unlikely to exceed this amount.

Ginseng can be bought from specialist shops or from herbal medicine stores and includes teas, powders, liquid extracts and capsules as well as whole roots.

There are two forms of ginseng. The cheapest is white ginseng (*paeksam*) which is grown for four years after which it is washed, sorted and graded. The most expensive is red ginseng (*hongsam*) which is grown for the same number of years but is then steamed, dried and returned to the earth where it is allowed to mature for another two years in a mulch of chestnut leaves. This maturation process concentrates the active ingredients. Anyone is allowed to process the white form but the red is all processed under strict government supervision at a factory just outside of Puyo. Here it's lovingly washed, dried, steamed and sorted into various grades by an army of women. Even the lowest grades are regarded as much superior to white ginseng but the top grade is pure gold and is priced accordingly.

If you're interested in seeing this process at the Puyo factory make enquiries at the tourist office in Seoul. They may be able to arrange a visit.

Wild ginseng is perhaps even more sought-after – and particularly the more its roots resemble the human body – but it's very rare these days. Most mountainsides in Korea have been scoured for generations and there's very little left.

Another popular ginseng product is ginseng wine. This is usually available in the same shops which sell dried ginseng but it can also be bought in many country restaurants. It is made by immersing a root of ginseng into a (usually sweet) wine and allowing it stand for a long period of time. The active constituents of the root are gradually leached out into the wine. In the countryside, this is a popular way to consume the root.

Getting There

You can get to South Korea by flying into one of the three international airports – Seoul (Kimpo), Pusan (Kimhae) and Cheju-do – from most of the capital cities of South and North-East Asia. The only major exceptions are the People's Republic of China and North Korea but negotiations are almost complete for a service to start between Seoul and Beijing. Likewise, there are air flights into South Korea from most of the capital cities of Europe and many of the larger cities of the USA. From Canada there are only flights from Vancouver. There are no direct flights from either Australia or New Zealand but that may soon change. Some travellers will want to fly via Tokyo.

Airlines which fly to Korea include Air France, All Nippon Airways, British Airways, Cathay Pacific, China Airlines, Delta Airlines, Japan Airlines, Japan Air System, KLM, Lufthansa, Malaysia Airlines, Northwest Airlines, Saudia, Singapore Airlines, Swissair, Thai International and United Airlines.

You can also get to Korea by ferry from either Shimonoseki or Osaka in Japan and recently a jetfoil service has started from Nagasaki. See the section on Ferries for details.

Overland entry into South Korea is not possible since the only land border is that with North Korea.

AIR

Assuming you are going to fly into South Korea, the first thing to do is equip yourself with as much information as possible and to be familiar with ticketing jargon. One of the best sources of information is the monthly magazine *Business Traveller* which is available in a British and Hong Kong version. They're available from newsstands in most developed countries, or direct from 60/61 Fleet St, London EC4Y 1LA, UK, and from 13th floor, 200 Lockhart Rd, Hong Kong.

Airline Tickets

Most travellers arrive in South Korea by plane. All manner of ticket deals are available and the ticketing jargon can be confusing so, to get the best deal, you need to do some research and planning before you buy. Which sort of ticket you opt for will largely depend on how much time you have available, how flexible you are about your departure and return dates and which other countries you wish to visit.

Normal Economy-Class Tickets Buying one of these is usually not the most economical way to go though they do give you maximum flexibility and the tickets are valid for 12 months. Also, if you don't use them they are fully refundable as are unused sectors of a multiple ticket.

APEX Tickets APEX stands for Advanced Purchase Excursion fare. These tickets are usually between 30% and 40% cheaper than the full economy fare but they have restrictions. You must purchase your ticket at least 21 days in advance (sometimes more) and you must stay away for a minimum period (usually 14 days) and return within a maximum period (often 180 days). Stopovers are not allowed and if you have to change your dates of travel or destination there will be extra charges to pay. If you have to cancel altogether they are not fully refundable and the refund is often considerably less than what you paid for the ticket. To avoid loss, take out travel insurance to cover you.

Round-The-World Tickets These are generally some of the best bargains available if you plan to travel for a long time. Tickets are valid for a year and may involve several airlines. You must keep going in the same direction all the way around – back-tracking and zigzagging are not possible. Stopovers are an integral part of these tickets but how many you are allowed depends on the price you pay. Those with five to seven stopovers are the cheapest. It doesn't cost that much extra, however, to have up to 14 and more stopovers.

Student Discounts Some airlines offer student discounts on their tickets of between 20% to 25% to student card holders. The same often applies to anyone under the age of 26. These discounts are generally only available on ordinary economy-class fares. You wouldn't get one, for instance, on an APEX or a Round-the-World ticket since these are already discounted.

Bucket Shop Tickets At certain times of year and/or on certain sectors, many airlines fly with empty seats. This isn't profitable. It's more cost-effective for them to fly full even if that means having to sell a certain number of tickets which have been drastically discounted. They do this by off-loading them onto certain agents which are commonly known as 'bucket shops'. The agents, in turn, sell them to the public at reduced prices. These tickets are often the cheapest you will find. You cannot buy them from the airlines themselves. Their availability varies widely and you not only have to be flexible in your travel plans but you have to be quick off the mark once the advertisements for them appear in the press.

Most of the bucket shops are reputable organisations but there will always be the occasional fly-by-night operator who sets up shop, takes your money and then either disappears or issues you with an invalid or unusable ticket. Be sure to check what you are buying before you hand over the money. Luckily, they are rare. I've used them for many years and never had problems even though some of the tickets occasionally looked a little dubious.

These agents advertise in newspapers and magazines and there's a lot of competition and different routes available so it's best to telephone first before rushing round there. Naturally, they'll advertise the cheapest available tickets but, by the time you get there, those may be sold for the date on which you want to leave and you might be looking at something slightly more expensive if you cannot wait.

Children's Fares Airlines usually carry babies up to two years of age at 10% of the relevant adult fare, a few may carry them free of charge. Reputable international airlines usually provide nappies (diapers), tissues, talcum and all the other paraphernalia needed to keep babies clean, dry and half-happy. For children between the ages of two and 12 the fare on international flights is usually 50% of the regular fare or 67% of a discounted fare. These days most fares are likely to be discounted.

To/From North America

In the USA, the best way to find cheap tickets is by checking the Sunday travel sections in major newspapers such as the *Los Angeles Times* or *San Francisco Examiner/Chronicle* on the west coast and the *New York Times* on the east coast. The student travel bureaus are also worth trying – STA Travel or Council Travel.

The cheapest tickets from the USA are invariably obtained in San Francisco, which has become America's bucket shop capital for the Orient. These bucket shops are almost entirely in the hands of ethnic travel agents who offer 'unofficially discounted' tickets on most major airlines. The reason for this is that the trans-Pacific is second only to the trans-Atlantic as an area of massive seat overcapacity.

The cheapest fares through these agents are on Korean Air (KAL), the Taiwanese China Airlines (CAL) and Philippine Airlines (PAL), which cut up to 30% on published APEX fares and 60% on full economy-class fares. One-way trips usually cost 35% less than a round trip. In some cases selected stopovers are permitted.

Usually, and not surprisingly, the cheapest fare to whatever country is offered by a bucket shop owned by someone of that particular ethnic origin.

Bucket shops in San Francisco can be found through the Yellow Pages or the major daily newspapers. Those listed in both Roman and Oriental scripts are invariably discounters. A more direct way is to wander around Chinatown where most of the shops are – especially in the Clay St and Waverly Place area. Many of these are staffed by recent arrivals from Hong Kong and Taiwan who speak little English. Enquiries are best made in person.

To Seoul, return prices from the west coast flying Korean Air start at US$889 in the low season and US$1039 in the high season. Flights to Tokyo from the west coast flying Korean Air start at US$559 (low season) and US$689 (high season).

From the east coast - New York or Boston - low season return prices start at US$1009, rising to US$1149 in the high season. To Tokyo, return prices start at US$759 (low season) and US$879 (high season).

In Canada Vancouver is the city for discounted tickets to Asia. The Canadian student travel organisation Travel Cuts has a variety of discounted fares.

To/From Europe

London and Amsterdam are the two major centres for unofficially discounted tickets although you can also find bucket shops in Paris, Brussels, Frankfurt and other places.

The London travel agent Trailfinders (tel 071-603 1515), 42- 48 Earls Court Rd, London W8 6EJ, which specialises in discounted tickets, publishes the quarterly magazine *Trailfinder* with a great deal of information about the fares they offer. It's free if you pick it up in London but if you want it mailed four issues costs £6 in the UK or Eire and £10 or the equivalent in Europe or elsewhere in the world (airmail). Trailfinders can fix you up with all your ticketing requirements, they've been in business for years and are highly recommended. Trailfinders now have a second branch at 194 Kensington High St, London W8 7RG (tel (071) 938-3444). STA Travel (tel (071) 937-9962) at 74 Old Brompton Rd, London SW7 or 117 Euston Rd, London NW1 are another reputable agent. FETC (Far East Travel Centre) (tel 071-734-9318) at 3 Lower John St, London W1A 4XE specialise in flights to Korea and east Asia.

If you live in the UK (or Europe for that matter) then the weekly publication *Time Out*, available from any newsstand or newsagent in London, contains what must be one of the world's best collection of discount ticket advertisements. *Time Out* (tel 071-836 4411) is London's weekly entertainment guide and the price is about £1. There are also a number of free magazines which you can pick up from central London's underground stations, and though the news sections cater mainly for Australians and New Zealanders living in the UK, they carry pages of travel advertising.

It's easier to find cheap fares to Tokyo or Hong Kong than to Seoul from London. Typically return flights to Tokyo start from as low as £700 or from £900 to £1000 with the more popular airlines or by more direct routes. You can probably get a Tokyo flight with a Seoul stopover for around £900. Return flights to Hong Kong cost from around £500 and a Hong Kong-Seoul return ticket bought in Hong Kong will cost from US$300.

To/From Australasia

Finding competitively priced tickets to Korea from Australia is unlikely to be easy. There are no direct flights yet although they may commence soon. The popular gateways to Korea are Japan and Hong Kong but nothing to Japan is cheap and although there is more competition to Hong Kong the flights tend to be heavily booked.

The weekend travel sections of papers like the *Age* (Melbourne) or the *Sydney Morning Herald* are good sources for travel information. STA Travel, the Australian based student travel organisation which now has offices worldwide, is an excellent place to look for discounted tickets. They have offices all around Australia (check your phone directory) and you definitely do not have to be a student to use them. Flight Centres International are another chain of agents specialising in discounted tickets and with offices all around the country.

Most of these deals will be for one-way or return flights to Japan (usually Tokyo or Osaka). They start at around A$1100 return from the east coast. If you want a Korean sector added to one of these tickets then you're looking at a further A$300 (Tokyo-Seoul return). If you're not interested in visiting Japan and want to save money go via Singapore, Bangkok, Hong Kong or Manila. From these cities you can fly direct to South Korea.

Regular return fares to Seoul from the east coast with reputable carriers like Thai International, Cathay Pacific or Singapore Airlines are around A$1500 or A$1700 during the 10 December to 10 January high season.

To/From Japan

There are many flights between Japan and South Korea, not only from Tokyo to Seoul but also from other cities in Japan including Fukuoka, Nagasaki, Nagoya, Osaka and Sapporo and to Pusan and Cheju-do in Korea. The daily flight between Fukuoka and Pusan is the cheapest way of flying between the two countries.

If you're on your way to Korea via Japan you are not going to save any money making your way right across Japan from Tokyo in order to take a cheaper flight from Fukuoka or the ferry service from Shimonoseki. By the time you add on food, accommodation and the flight or ferry cost it would still be cheaper to add the Tokyo-Seoul sector to your ticket in the first place.

To/From Other Places in Asia

There are also flights from Jakarta, Singapore, Bangkok, and Manila to Seoul. The cheapest places to buy airline tickets in Asia are Penang, Singapore and Hong Kong, the latter being the best as a rule.

FERRY

There are several ferry services from Japan to South Korea, one from Osaka to Pusan, one from Shimonoseki to Pusan and a recently introduced jetfoil from Nagasaki to Cheju-do.

Shimonoseki-Pusan This is the cheapest of the ferries. It departs daily at 5 pm from both Pusan and Shimonoseki and arrives the next day at 8.30 am. In Pusan the ferry leaves from the International Ferry Terminal. The fares are US$90 (1st class A), US$80 (1st class B), US$65 (2nd class A) and US$55 (2nd class B). There's a 20% discount for students but only in 2nd class B. The fares for children between six and 12 years old is 50% regardless of class. Infants under six years old travel free. Those with seamen's tickets are also entitled to a 20% discount. There is a departure tax of W1000 in Pusan. Facilities on board include a restaurant, bar, sauna, duty-free shop and tourist information counter.

Osaka-Pusan This ferry departs Osaka on Monday, Wednesday, Friday and Saturday at noon and arrives in Pusan the following day at 10.30 am. From Pusan it departs on Monday, Wednesday, Thursday and Saturday at 5 pm and arrives in Osaka the following day at 3.30 pm.

There are two boats, one Korean and the other Japanese. On the Japanese boat you cannot use Korean won to pay for anything so make sure you get rid of all this currency before boarding. The fares are US$200 (Special Suite), US$130 (1st class special), US$125 (1st class – two bunks), US$100 (2nd class – four bunks) and US$90 (2nd class – six, eight and 10 bunk cabins). Children under six years old travel free and those between the ages of six and 12 are entitled to a 50% discount on the above fares. Students are entitled to a 20% discount on the above fares.

Neither of these ferries are what you might call cheap. Even in 2nd class it's costing almost as much as it would to fly so if you don't care to spend all night on board a boat it's worth considering a flight instead.

Nagasaki-Cheju-do The jetfoil service whisks you across in four hours at a fare of about US$120.

Getting Around

AIR

There are two domestic carriers – Korean Air and Asiana Airlines. Both have a good network of flights connecting all the main cities and the principal tourist sites. Fares are very reasonable when compared to domestic flights in neighbouring countries and 20% discounts are available to those with student cards.

Fares are the same on either airline but Korean Air offers 35% discounts to students while Asiana Airlines offers only 20%. Children under six years old travel free and those between six and 12 years old travel at 50% of the adult fare on either airline.

You must have your passport handy before boarding a domestic flight – you won't be allowed on the plane unless you have it. You are not allowed to take photographs from a plane and, officially, you're supposed to remove all batteries from electronic equipment (including cameras) and arrange for them to be carried separately. In practice, this rule is rarely enforced.

Korean Air lays on a free shuttle bus between the domestic and international airports at Seoul.

Korean Air Flights

From Seoul To Cheju-do (12 flights daily plus three extra on Monday, six extra on Tuesday, Wednesday and Thursday, four extra on Friday, five extra on Saturday and Sunday); to Chinju (two flights daily); to Kangnung (two flights daily); to Kwangju (three flights daily); to Pusan (18 flights daily plus three extra on Monday, Tuesday, Wednesday, Thursday, Friday and Saturday); to Pohang (three flights daily); to Sogcho (two flights daily); to Taegu (three flights daily); to Ulsan (five flights daily plus one extra on Tuesday, Thursday, Saturday and Sunday); to Yeosu (five flights daily).

From Pusan To Cheju-do (three flights daily plus four extra on Monday, nine on Tuesday and Sunday, five extra on Wednesday and Saturday, eight extra on Thursday, three extra on Friday); to Seoul (18 flights daily plus three extra every day except Sunday).

From Cheju-do To Chinju (one flight daily); to Kwangju (three flights daily); to Pusan

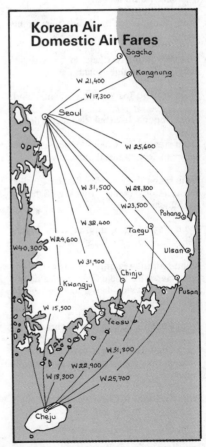

Korean Air Domestic Air Fares

Sogcho
Kangnung
W 21,400
W 17,300
Seoul
W 25,600
W 31,500   W 28,300
W23,500
Pohang
W 32,400
Taegu
W24,600
W40,300
Ulsan
W 31,900
Chinju
Kwangju
Pusan
W 15,500
Yeosu
W 31,800
W 22,900
W 18,300   W 25,700
Cheju

(four flights daily plus five extra Monday, Wednesday and Saturday, seven extra on Tuesday and Sunday, six extra on Thursday, four extra on Friday); to Kwangju (three flights daily); to Seoul (nine flights daily plus seven extra on Monday and Sunday, 10 extra on Tuesday, eight extra on Wednesday and Saturday, nine extra on Thursday, six extra on Friday); to Taegu (three flights daily); to Yeosu (two flights daily).

From Chinju To Cheju-do (one flight daily); to Seoul (two flights daily).

From Kangnung To Seoul (two flights daily).

From Kwangju To Cheju-do (three flights daily); to Seoul (three flights daily).

From Pohang To Seoul (three flights daily).

From Sogcho To Seoul (two flights daily).

From Taegu To Cheju-do (three flights daily); to Seoul (three flights daily).

From Ulsan To Seoul (five flights daily plus one extra on Tuesday, Thursday, Saturday and Sunday).

From Yeosu To Cheju-do (two flights daily); to Seoul (five flights daily).

Asiana Airlines Flights
From Seoul To Cheju (eight flights daily); to Kwangju (twice daily); to Pusan (eight flights daily).

From Pusan To Cheju (four flights daily).

From Cheju To Kwangju (two flights daily); to Pusan (four flights daily); to Seoul (eight flights daily).

From Kwangju To Cheju (two flights daily); to Seoul (two flights daily).

BUS
Travelling by bus in Korea is a dream come

true and even very minor rural roads are sealed. There's an excellent system of fast, safe and comfortable buses to almost everywhere. In addition, there's a whole network of expressways which have been built to link Seoul with all the major cities.

Only occasionally will you come across a minor country road which has not yet been sealed, but where this is the case, the gravel roads are usually well maintained.

There are several types of buses. The fastest and most luxurious are those which operate along the expressways to the country's major cities and tourist sites. These are the express (*kosok*) 고속 buses which offer a nonstop service (apart from occasional coffee stops on longer journeys), reserved seats and usually air-conditioning. These buses normally operate out of their own separate terminal though in smaller cities and towns they may share a terminal with the *chikheng* 직행, or limited express/stopping buses. It's not normally necessary to book a seat on *kosok* buses more than five or 10 minutes in advance unless there are only one or two per day or during holidays, weekends and the height of summer (July to mid-August). At those times, try to book a few hours in advance. Fares are very reasonable. Pusan to Seoul for instance, costs about US$9 for a journey of around 400 km.

The next type of bus is the *chikheng* 직행 bus which operates along provincial roads and the expressways. These are limited express buses which make scheduled stops at various towns along their route or at special shelters if travelling along the expressways. They vary considerably in the degree of speed and comfort which they offer. Some will only sell tickets for seated passengers and others accept standing passengers. Asking for the direct bus 버스 will normally get you a better bus which doesn't accept standing passengers. The ordinary *chikheng* buses will normally drop you anywhere you care to get off. The terminals for *chikheng* buses are usually separate from the *kosok* terminals though in smaller places they may share the same, in which case you should specify the type of bus you want to travel on. *Chikheng* buses often share a terminal with the local buses, known as *wanheng*.

Wanheng 완행 or local buses, are the last category of bus. They service rural areas, operate along set routes and will stop anytime someone wants to get off or on and accept all but the bulkiest of freight. There are two types – ordinary, cheaper buses which will take as many standing passengers as they can fit in, and *chaesok* 좌석 buses where you are guaranteed a seat and there are no standing passengers. *Chaesok* buses cost a little less than double the fare on a normal *wanheng* bus. *Chikheng* and *wanheng* buses often operate side-by-side out of the same terminal and have the same routes, so you need to make sure you're getting on the right type of bus.

A few years ago, bus schedules and ticket windows were entirely in Korean – even in Seoul – but this is changing rapidly. In most large cities these days both the schedules and the ticket windows will be in Korean and English so it's easy to find your way around. Nevertheless, there are still some places which have not got around to doing this. Cheju City bus terminal and Kyongju *chikheng* terminal are two which stand out which is quite remarkable considering how many foreign tourists go through those places. Schedules for *wanheng* buses are always entirely in Korean.

TRAIN

Korea has an excellent railway network which connects all the major cities. The railways operate four types of trains which are classified according to the degree of speed and comfort which they offer, whether seats can be booked and whether the trains are nonstop, limited stop or local stopping trains. The fastest, super-luxurious, air-conditioned, nonstop trains are called *saemaul-ho* 새마을호 and these are naturally the most expensive. Next comes the *mugung-hwa* 무궁화호 which is an air-conditioned, limited-stop train with dining car attached.

There is also a non-air-conditioned, limited-stop train sometimes with a dining car attached known as the *tongil-ho* 통일호 . All seats on the above trains can be booked but note that on the limited-stop trains there are two types of seat – the 1st class 일등칸 and the economy class 이등칸 – as well as standing tickets 표 . At the bottom of the list are the local trains known as *wanheng* 완행 which stop at all stations. Seats cannot be booked on the local trains and because of the frequent stops they are very slow.

Train schedules at stations on the main lines are now usually in both Korean and English so it's easy to find your way around, but the words for the various types of train will only be in Korean so you need to familiarise yourself with the Korean script for those words. Very few ticket clerks speak any English so if your Korean isn't up to much, write down the date you want to travel, the time of the train, the type and your destination.

If you're planning on using the railways extensively then it's well worthwhile buying a copy of the booklet called 시각표 which is published monthly, costs W1400 and is available from most booksellers and stationers. It contains the complete air, train, bus and boat schedules for the entire country. Most of it is entirely in Korean except for the rail schedules which are in Korean and English.

FERRY

Korea has an extensive network of ferries that service the islands off west and south coasts and Ulleung-do off the east coast. Cheju-do, Korea's largest island, can be reached by both car and passenger ferry from Mogpo, Wando and Pusan. There are daily departures and a wide choice of ferries from each of these towns. If you want to explore the smaller islands of the south-west then Mogpo and Wando are the main departure points. All of these ferries are dealt with in detail in the Getting There & Away sections of each town.

For all those seafaring souls who prefer

the rolling of the waves to the bumping of a bus, there is a ferry connecting the mainland towns of Wando and Mogpo (seven hours), and the *Angel* hydrofoil plies between Pusan and Yeosu. The latter is a popular trip as it goes through the beautiful Hallyo Waterway National Park and stops at the islands and main towns along the way. The journey takes only about three hours, though some trips only go between Pusan and Chungmu.

You can get ferries to Ulleung-do from Pohang, Hupo and Mukho but those from Hupo and Mukho only operate on a daily basis during the summer months. During rough weather the ferries can be cancelled, and it is wise to book in advance during the summer months.

As well as the sea ferries, there are boats that connect the towns on the northern lakes of Paro and Soyang and on Chungju Lake further south.

CAR

Renting a self-drive car in Korea isn't a cheap option unless there is a group of three to four of you to share the costs, but if there is then it's well worth considering. It natu-rally allows you the freedom to get to the more out-of-the-way places or simply to pack more into a day than would otherwise be possible if you were reliant on local trans-port.

Rental rates for 24 hours with unlimited mileage are typically around W31,000 for a small car up to W44,000 for a larger car including insurance but excluding fuel costs (roughly US$45 to US$67). Fuel costs are not a major consideration since Korea is quite a small country. Some rental companies even rent out cars for shorter periods such as six and 12 hours at propor-tionately lower rates – worth thinking about if you only want the car during daylight hours. To rent a car you need your passport and an international driving permit (or tem-porary Korean licence) and you must be over 21 years old.

For further details call any of the follow-ing:

Hertz Korean Rent-A-Car (tel (02) 585-0801), Seoul
Pusan Rent-A-Car (tel (051) 462-1400), Pusan
Hankook Rent-A-Car (tel (051) 754-2967), Pusan
Samjin Rent-A-Car (tel (0561) 42-3311), Kyongju
Yongil Rent-A-Car (tel (053) 952-1001), Taegu

Sangmu Rent-A-Car (tel (062) 55-0400), Kwangju
Cheju Rent-A-Car (tel (064) 42-3301), Cheju
Halla Rent-A-Car (tel (064) 62-3446), Cheju

Korean National Railways also offer car
rentals at the following stations: Seoul,
Pusan, Taegu, Taejon and Kwangju. Their
rates are comparable with the companies
listed above.

Driving in Korea

Some guide books on Korea suggest that
driving in this country is dangerous. That's
debatable. I'd say it's potentially hazardous
and even hair-raising especially in the larger
cities but that the risks are quite acceptable
for experienced drivers. Certainly the
expressways are no worse than in any other
country and driving in rural areas is pure
bliss since there's very little traffic and the
roads are excellent. On the other hand, there
are a few rules you must observe if you are
to avoid accidents.

The main rules are:

1. Always keep your distance from other
vehicles.
2. Never travel at speeds which will not
allow you to stop in an emergency – potentially every blind corner or crest of a hill.
3. Never expect any consideration from other
road users.

The main hazards are:

1. Parked vehicles pulling out into the traffic
flow without warning.
2. Vehicles ahead of you turning left or right
without warning.
3. Bus drivers. These are legitimately
described as certifiable whether they're travelling in the same or the opposite direction.
Expect and allow for insane risk-taking.
4. Drivers who stop anywhere, any time for
no apparent reason, park anywhere regardless of the dangers this might create, hurl tin
cans, bottles and fruit skins out of car
windows.
5. Pedestrians. Road sense is very poor

indeed. Expect people to walk out into the
middle of the road at any time without a care
in the world and particularly be prepared for
children running out after balls and the like.
Use that horn and use it frequently!

The speed limits vary considerably and there
are not that many signs indicating what it is.
In general, the limits are 100 km/h on
expressways, 80 km/h on main highways, 60
km/h on provincial roads, and 50/60 km/h in
urban areas. Speed cops make a small
fortune stopping offenders and they're out in
force at weekends and during the annual
summer holiday period (July to mid-
August). This doesn't stop drivers routinely
exceeding the limits by considerable
margins. Drivers coming in the opposite
direction will often indicate the presence of
a speed trap ahead of you by flashing their
lights.

There are both army and police checkpoints on many roads where you will have to
stop but they don't normally bother foreigners.

Other than the checkpoints, it's unlikely
you'll be stopped unless you're speeding but
if you are and there's evidence that you've
been drinking, they'll put the bag on you and
the fines are heavy. Nevertheless, many
people do drink and drive.

There appear to be no (enforced) rules for
parking. If there's a space, someone will park
there. The one thing which all drivers respect
are traffic lights. What they certainly don't
respect are pedestrian crossings which are
not light-controlled. The general rule here is
hand on horn and hit the gas.

A detailed road atlas is essential. Signposting inside cities and large towns is totally
inadequate especially if you're trying to find
your way out. Most of the signposting is for
the various *dong* (suburbs) and such things
as 'Railway Station', 'City Hall' or 'Express
Bus Terminal'. These signs are blue with
white lettering. Inter-city signs are green
with white lettering but they're few and far
between in the cities themselves. In the countryside only the next small town may be
indicated so you need to know your route

thoroughly or stop now and again to consult your atlas.

The best atlas is the *Korea Road Atlas* which splits the country up into 51 blocks on the scale 1:250,000, plus there are 49 detailed street maps of the major towns and cities. It costs W9000 and is available from major bookshops in Seoul.

Driving Licences

If you intend to rent a car in Korea make sure you bring an international driving permit with you. A national licence from your own country is not acceptable. It is possible to obtain a temporary Korean driving licence valid for three months against your national licence in Seoul but you'll waste a day doing so and it's not exactly cheap.

If you have to get one, here's the procedure.

There are several places in Seoul where you can get this licence but you must make sure that the address you are going to give is covered by the office where you apply. Make enquiries first at the tourist information centre behind City Hall. All the licensing centres have a counter which deals exclusively with the temporary licences for foreigners so you won't have to join the endless queues at the other counters.

You will need your passport plus photostats of the relevant front pages and your Korean visa page; your national driving licence plus a photostat of both sides; six photographs of a size suitable for the Korean licence (about half the size of a normal passport photograph); money to pay for the licence (varies between W6180 and W8000 depending on nationality and visitor status).

Photographs (W1500 for four), photostats (W200 each) and fiscal stamps can all be obtained at the licensing centres. The forms you will be given are entirely in Korean but the staff can usually help you fill them in. Once you've done this, obtained photographs, photostats and fiscal stamps, you must take a compulsory eye test (the chart has numbers on it, not Korean letters of the alphabet). Assuming you pass it, you can pick up your licence 24 hours later.

LOCAL TRANSPORT
Local Bus

Inside cities and their outlying suburbs, buses are classified the same as the inter-city buses – ordinary *wanheng* and *chaesok*. The former generally cost W130 regardless of distance (or W120 if you buy your ticket from a booth beforehand) but they get incredibly crowded at rush hours. A *chaesok* bus over the same route will cost about double, sometimes more. Don't be put off getting an ordinary *wanheng* bus, however, even if you have shopping bags or luggage. Most of the time, if you are laden down and have to stand, someone who is seated will offer to take your load off you. You'll find Koreans very polite and helpful in this respect but times are changing. Young people, for instance, rarely give up their seat for an older person these days whereas a few years ago they would invariably do this.

All city buses carry a route number and a destination on the front and the sides. Bus stops, likewise, carry panels on the post indicating the route served. None of these will be in English so you need to be able to recognise the name of your destination in Korean. There are no schedules available for city buses but there are for rural *wanheng* buses. The only trouble is they're often written in cursive Korean on a blackboard and, unless you're very proficient at reading Korean, they'll be almost indecipherable. When in doubt – ask. You'll almost always be able to find someone who can speak some English and, even if you can't, it doesn't matter too much. Just show them the Korean for where you want to go. Most people will direct you to the right bus but double check with the driver when boarding.

Subway

Both Seoul and Pusan have subways (underground railways). A phenomenal amount of money and building construction went into the creation of the Seoul subway system during the late '70s and early '80s so that it is now the world's 7th longest at 116.5 km. There are four separate lines and they're colour coded. Pusan presently has only one line. Both of these subways offer a very convenient and cheap way of getting around. All signs are in Korean and English. Tickets are bought at vending machines or at ticket windows and the fares depend on the distance travelled. Further details can be found in the appropriate chapters

Taxi

In the cities there are two types of taxi. The regular taxis (usually painted yellow) are the cheapest and are not air-conditioned. The basic fare is W600 for the first two km and W50 for each additional 400 metres. The larger air-conditioned taxis (often painted blue) cost W800 at flag fall plus W100 for each additional 400 metres. Both types of taxi are metered and you'll never have to remind the driver that it's there. A surcharge of 20% is added from midnight to 4 am. Tipping is not expected but much appreciated – most taxi drivers don't own their vehicles but work for a company and they have to work long hours before they start earning anything other than the basic wage.

If you find that empty taxis are not stopping to pick you up or refuse to take you after you've told them your destination, it usually means they're at the end of their shift and will only take you if where you want to go happens to be in the same direction.

You'll occasionally come across private cars which stop and announce that they're a private taxi. It's up to you whether you take them but Koreans strongly advise against it (there have been occasional horror stories). You'd naturally have to negotiate a fare if you did decide to take one of these.

If you take a metered taxi to a place where the driver won't necessarily get a return fare (to a temple outside of a town, for instance), he will usually demand you pay 1½ times what the meter says at the end of the journey. This can work in your favour if you didn't take a taxi out but want to take one for the return journey.

If you telephone for a taxi, the charge is W1000 at flag fall for the first two km plus W400 for each additional 400 metres.

SOUTH KOREAN RAILWAY TIMETABLES

Train Types
A = air-con luxury express　　　　B = air-con limited stop
C = air-con limited stop with dining car　　D = local train

Seoul-Taejon-Taegu-Pusan
Route: Seoul-Suweon-Chonan-Chochiwon-Taejon-Yongdong-Kimchon- Kumi-Taegu-Samnangjin-Pusan

Station	B	B	C	A	C	B	A	C	B	C	A
Seoul	0610	0700	0730	0800	0815	0830	0900	0915	0930	0945	1000
Suweon	0638	0728	0758		0843	0859		0943	0959	1013	
Chonan	0714	0804	0833		0916	0934		1016	1032	1046	
Taejon	0804	0855	0919	0933	1002	1023	1033	1102	1121	1136	1133
Kimchon	0910	1000	1017		1101	1132	1125	1201	1237	1234	
Taegu	1002	1053	1113	1104	1150	1224	1208	1250	1328	1321	1304
Pusan	1127	1220	1228	1210	1305	1345		1405	1448	1435	1410

Station	C	B	C	A	C	B	C	A	C	B	C
Seoul	1015	1030	1045	1100	1115	1130	1145	1200	1215	1230	1245
Suweon	1043	1101	1113		1143	1200	1213		1243	1259	1313
Chonan	1116	1134	1146		1216	1236	1246		1316	1332	1346
Taejon	1202	1223	1236	1233	1302	1324	1336	1333	1402	1421	1436
Kimchon	1301	1337	1334		1401	1438	1435		1501	1537	1534
Taegu	1350	1427	1421	1404	1450	1530	1522	1504	1550	1628	1622
Pusan	1505	1549	1536	1510	1605	1651	1639	1610	1705		1738

Station	A	C	B	C	A	C	C	C	A	C	B
Seoul	1300	1315	1330	1345	1400	1415	1430	1445	1500	1515	1530
Suweon		1343	1400	1413		1443	1458	1513	1543	1602	
Chonan		1416	1436	1446		1516	1531	1546	1616	1636	
Taejon	1433	1502	1524	1536	1533	1602	1617	1636	1633	1702	1724
Kimchon		1601	1637	1634		1701	1718	1734	1801	1837	
Taegu	1604	1650	1728	1722	1704	1750	1813	1822	1804	1850	1928
Pusan	1710	1805	1852	1838	1810		1928	1938	1910	2025	2049

Station	C	A	C	B	C	A	C	A	C	B	A
Seoul	1545	1600	1615	1630	1645	1700	1715	1730	1745	1815	1830
Suweon	1613		1643	·1659	1713		1743		1813	1844	
Chonan	1646		1718	1734	1746		1816		1846	1925	
Taejon	1736	1733	1806	1823	1836	1833	1907	1904	1930	2016	2003
Kimchon	1834		1904	1937	1934		2005	1956	2031	2124	
Taegu	1922	1904	1953	2028	2021	2004	2055	2039	2118	2216	2134
Pusan	2038	2010	2107	2148	2135	2112	2210		2233		2240

Station	C	A	C	B	C	B	C	A	C	C
Seoul	1845	1925	1930	2130	2200	2230	2300	2320	2340	2355
Suweon	1913		1959	2208	2234	2306	2335	2355	0015	0032
Chonan	1946		2035	2251	2312	2346	0014		0054	0113
Taejon	2032	2059	2128	2350	0008	0045	0113	0127	0153	0211
Kimchon	2131		2234	0101	0117	0156	0224		0304	0321
Taegu	2219	2232	2325	0206	0217	0300	0333	0325	0409	0424
Pusan	2336	2340		0345		0440	0510	0450	0545	0600

Pusan-Taegu-Taejon-Seoul

Station	B	B	C	A	C	B	C	B	C	A
Pusan	0600	0630	0730	0800	0815	0830	0915	0930	0945	1000
Taegu	0723	0752	0845	0909	0930	0952	1031	1050	1059	1106
Kimchon	0814	0843	0933		1019	1043	1120	1147	1154	
Taejon	0921	0949	1033	1039	1119	1155	1219	1257	1252	1237
Chonan	1009	1035	1124		1203	1241	1303	1342	1333	
Suweon	1045	1111	1156		1236	1315	1336	1418	1405	
Seoul	1115	1142	1226	1212	1305	1348	1405	1448	1435	1410

Station	C	C	A	C	B	C	A	C	B	C
Pusan	1015	1045	1100	1115	1130	1145	1200	1215	1230	1245
Taegu	1130	1159	1206	1230	1250	1258	1306	1330	1350	1358
Kimchon	1219	1254		1319	1347	1353		1419	1447	1454
Taejon	1319	1353	1337	1419	1457	1451	1437	1519	1557	1552
Chonan	1403	1437		1503	1542	1534		1603	1642	1633
Suweon	1436	1512		1557	1618	1608		1636	1718	1705
Seoul	1505	1542	1510	1605	1649	1638	1610	1705	1748	1735

Station	A	C	B	C	A	C	C	A	C	B
Pusan	1300	1315	1330	1345	1400	1430	1445	1500	1515	1530
Taegu	1406	1430	1451	1458	1506	1545	1558	1606	1630	1650
Kimchon		1519	1547	1554		1633	1654		1719	1747
Taejon	1537	1619	1657	1652	1637	1742	1752	1737	1819	1857
Chonan		1703	1742	1733		1826	1833		1903	1945
Suweon		1736	1818	1805		1859	1905		1936	2022
Seoul	1710	1805	1849	1835	1810	1929	1935	1910	2005	2054

Station	C	A	C	B	C	A	C	C	A	C
Pusan	1545	1600	1615	1630	1645	1700	1715	1745	1830	1845
Taegu	1658	1706	1730	1750	1759	1806	1830	1859	1936	2000
Kimchon	1754		1819	1847	1854		1919	1954		2049
Taejon	1852	1837	1919	1957	1952	1937	2019	2052	2107	2149
Chonan	1934		2003	2042	2033		2103	2133		2233
Suweon	2007		2036	2118	2105		2136	2205		2306
Seoul	2037	2010	2105	2148	2135	2110	2205	2235	2240	2335

Station	B	A	B	B	C	A	C	C		
Pusan	1900	1925	2130	2230	2300	2320	2340	2355		
Taegu	2041	2034	2309	0009	0038	0050	0118	0131		
Kimchon	2137		0010	0111	0146		0220	0233		
Taejon		2206	0123	0222	0258	0251	0333	0344		
Chonan			0218	0317	0352		0427	0438		
Suweon			0301	0401	0433	0415	0508	0518		
Seoul		2340	0340	0440	0510	0450	0545	0555		

Seoul-Sodaejon-Iri-Mogpo

Route: Seoul-Suweon-Chonan-Chochiwon-Sodaejon-Nonsan-Iri-Chongju- Yong San Po (change here for Kwangju)-Mogpo

Station	B	B	A	C	B	B	C	B
Seoul	0720	0820	0905	1105	1120	1220	1305	1420
Sodaejon	0917	1019	1040	1255	1319	1419	1455	1625
Nonsan	0953	1055	1112	1330	1356	1456	1531	1703
Iri	1026	1128	1138	1402	1430	1533	1604	1735
Yong San Po	1227	1542	1305	1544	1627	1728	1755	1920
Mogpo	1320				1719	1820	1845	

Station	A	B	B	C	B	B	C
Seoul	1605	1620	1805	2050	2215	2305	2330
Sodaejon	1741	1820	2002	2312	0038	0126	0146
Nonsan	1812	1857	2039	2355	0120	0209	0227
Iri	1839	1931	2112	0035	0200	0249	0306
Yong San Po	2008	2126	2257	0238	0406	0454	0455
Mogpo	2053	2218		0333	0500	0549	

Mogpo-Iri-Sodaejon-Seoul

Station	D	A	B	C	B	B	B	C	B	B
Mogpo	0650	0820	0930	1120	1210	1400	1505	2055	2150	2320
Yong San Po	0801	0905	1021	1209	1302	1451	1554	2147	2244	0015
Iri	1109	1035	1215	1359	1455	1647	1752	2346	0049	0223
Nonsan	1155	1100	1248	1430	1526	1720	1824	0020	0124	0258
Sodaejon	1306	1133	1327	1510	1604	1803	1902	0105	0210	0344
Seoul		1310	1529	1659	1800	1959	2100	0325	0430	0602

Seoul-Sodaejon-Chonju-Namwon-Yeosu

Route: Seoul-Suweon-Chonan-Sodaejon-Nonsan-Iri-Chonju-Namwon- Sunchon-Yeosu

Station	C	B	B	B	C	A	B	B	B
Seoul	0805	1020	1320	1505	1610	1800	2145	2245	2350
Sodaejon	0955	1217	1518	1659	1758	1942	0005	0107	0212
Nonsan	1028	1254	1554	1737	1832		0046	0150	0255
Iri	1059	1331	1630	1812	1904	2042	0125	0232	0335
Namwon	1221	1506	1814	1946	2021	2206	0258	0407	0509
Sunchon	1329	1622	1929	2100	2128	2308	0415	0528	0641
Yeosu	1405	1705	2008		2204	2345	0455	0613	0820

Yeosu-Namwon-Chonju-Sodaejon-Seoul

Station	C	A	B	B	D	C	D	B	B
Yeosu	0735	0840	1015	1330	1455	1630	1720	2010	2205
Sunchon	0813	0917	1057	1415	1559	1709	1822	2101	2251
Namwon	0919	1019	1209	1534	1756	1815	2021	2221	0018
Iri	1041	1139	1342	1705	2030	1936	2246	0005	0158
Nonsan	1111	1416	1738	2007	0042	0234			
Sodaejon	1149	1241	1457	1821	2045	0128	0319		
Seoul	1336	1425	1654	2022	2230	0350	0538		

Chongnyangni (Seoul)-Kapyong-Chuncheon

Station	B	C	B	B	C	B	C
Chongnyangni	0645	0830	0920	1030	1135	1230	1330
Chuncheon	0836	1005	1110	1224	1309	1428	1509

Station	B	B	C	B	C	B	C
Chongnyangni	1435	1550	1645	1735	1830	1950	2100
Chuncheon	1637	1746	1820	1934	2008	2158	2237

Chuncheon-Kapyong-Chongnyangni (Seoul)

Station	B	C	B	C	B	B	C
Chuncheon	0700	0840	0940	1100	1200	1300	1405
Chongniyangni	0854	1018	1138	1234	1402	1450	1546

Station	B	C	B	B	C	B	C
Chuncheon	1500	1555	1720	1820	1925	2010	2105
Chongniyangni	1658	1738	1922	2018	2102	2207	2249

Chongniyangni-Wonju-Yongju-Kyongju-Pusan

Route: Chongniyangni-Wonju-Chechon-Yongju-Andong-Yongchon- Kyongju-Ulsan-Pusan

Station	D	D	C	B	C	B	D	C	D	B
Chongniyangni	0600	0700	0900	1100	1300	1400	1525	1700	1900	2200
Wonju	0829	0933	1045	1254	1444	1555	1802	1846	2135	2355
Yongju	1217	1242	1503	1807	2044	1112	0215			
Kyongju	0946	1605	0525							
Ulsan	1040	1658	0605							
Pusan	1231	1857	0732							

Pusan-Kyongju-Yongju-Wonju-Chongnyangni

Station	D	D	D	D	C	D	D	D	D	B
Pusan	0400			0625	0915	0935	1250	1630	1845	2100
Ulsan	0547	0826	1035	1125	1439	1822	2042	2227		
Kyongju				0923	1115	1215	1539	1929	2140	2310
Yongju	0852	1037	1607	1312	1400					0220
Wonju	1100	1234	1803	1611						0433
Chongniyangni	1251	1420	1946	1848	0625					

Mogpo-Kwangju-Sunchon-Chinju-Masan-Pusan

Station	D	D	D	D	B	D	D	B
Mogpo	0955	1520	1245	1855	2230			
Kwangju	1204	1733	1440	2102	0009	0500	0635	1333
Sunchon	1502	2026	0830	0228	0752	0933	1542	
Chinju			1034		0408		1137	
Masan	0640		1227		0540		1336	1835
Pusan	0818		1420		0700		1523	2043

Pusan-Masan-Chinju-Sunchon-Kwangju-Mogpo

Station	D	D	D	D	B
Pusan	0605	0950	1140	1350	2105
Masan	0749	1203	1339	1557	2231
Chinju	0932	1352	1529	1745	2356
Sunchon		1555	1727	1954	0131
Kwangju		1851			0350
Mogpo					

Seoul 서울

The capital of South Korea with a population exceeding 10 million, Seoul is a city of incredible contrasts which, despite its immense size, make it one of the most fascinating cities in the world. It has risen from the dust and ashes of the Korean War, when it was flattened, to become a modern metropolis of high-rise buildings, 12-lane boulevards and nonstop traffic. Yet right beside this pulsing extravaganza of concrete, steel and glass, are centuries-old royal palaces, temples, pagodas and imposing stone gateways set in huge traditional gardens far removed from the bustle of the rest of the city. It's here that you can experience the timeless, eerie atmosphere, somehow Central Asian in origin, which endows this city with its unique character. This same feeling permeates the narrow alleys and back streets below the skyscrapers and the few remaining traditional areas of the city which escaped the destruction of the war and, later, the bulldozers of the developers.

Seoul hasn't always been the capital of Korea, indeed there have been several, the most famous being the Silla Dynasty capital at Kyongju in the south. Though Seoul was the original capital of the Paekje Kingdom some 1500 years ago, its modern origins as the nation's capital go back to 1392 with the establishment of the Yi Dynasty which ruled Korea until 1910. It was during these centuries, when Korea remained largely a closed country to the outside world, that the palaces, shrines and fortresses which still stand today were constructed. Naturally, some things have disappeared, such as the 10-mile wall which once surrounded the city, but five of the original nine gateways still remain and have been repaired by the government. This kind of funding for the repair and restoration of historic sites is one of Korea's outstanding features and explains why the very new and ancient continue to exist side by side in apparent harmony whereas in many other capitals around the world much of historic value has been swept aside to make way for new development.

It's more than likely you will enter Korea via Seoul and many travellers seem to go no further. The reasons for this are not hard to fathom. Seoul is a city which caters for every taste as well as being the cultural hub of the country. Public transport is excellent and it's easy to get around. You can still live very cheaply right in the centre of the city, and if you're short of money, you can even get a job teaching English (learning English could be classed as a national obsession). As long as you observe a few social rituals, people here can be disarmingly friendly and helpful. This is not a city where people, however busy, don't have the time of day to pass with you or, as in Japan and China, prefer to keep you at arm's length. Things are changing, of course, and the 1988 Olympics are largely responsible for that but this is still a society which respects its traditions.

It's worth staying in Seoul at least a week, but after that it's worth making the effort to get down to either Seoul Railway Station or the Kangnam Express Bus Terminal and seeing the rest of the country.

ORIENTATION

The main budget hotel areas, the ancient royal palaces, the National Museum, the GPO, the tourist offices, Seoul Railway Station, many of the embassies and airline offices, and the shopping and entertainment area of Myong-dong are all within walking distance of each other in the very heart of the city. Only Kangnam Express Bus Terminal is some considerable distance from the centre on the south side of the Han River but connected to the centre by subway.

INFORMATION
Tourist Office

The Korean National Tourism Corporation (KNTC) has its main information centre in the basement of its headquarters on

Chonggyechon-ro near the junction of Namdaemun-ro and just a few minutes' walk from City Hall. Here you can find the full range of well-produced booklets, leaflets, street plans and maps (all free of charge) in various languages, and the receptionists (who also speak a range of languages) can answer more specific inquiries. There are also large topographical models of Korea and Seoul which are useful for orienting yourself as well as a computer which you're free to use to call up any information you may be interested in. It's open daily from 9 am to 6 pm.

The other main tourist information centre (and the one which most travellers use) is that at the back of City Hall which itself is opposite the Plaza Hotel and the Toksu Palace. They have a similar range of literature, can book tours, answer specific inquiries and the staff speak a range of languages. It's open daily Monday to Friday from 9 am to 6 pm, on Saturdays from 9 am to 1 pm and closed on Sundays.

At both centres you can also pick up copies of the free weekly tourist newspapers, *Weekly Travel Korea* and *This Week in Seoul*.

There are also a number of tourist information kiosks, the most useful being those outside the Kyobo Building on Sejong-ro, Kangnam Express Bus Terminal, and Kimpo International Airport.

While the above tourist offices are good and probably more than adequate for most people's needs, it's useful to know that there's another source of information. This is the United Service Organisation (USO) (tel 792-3028/63), 104 Gal Wol-Dong, Yongsan-gu, just opposite Gate 21 of the Yongsan US Army Base down the road a few hundred metres past Seoul Railway Station. This, in case you're not American, is an information, entertainment and cultural centre which serves the US army bases in Korea though you don't have to be with the US forces to get in. The nearest subway station is Sookmyung Women's University, one stop beyond Seoul Railway Station on Line 4.

This organisation offers all kinds of tours to places near Seoul, including Panmunjom, and they are much cheaper than the national tourist organisation. You may hear it said that they will only accept US dollars in payment for these tours. That's not the case. They'll take won. Because they're cheap, however, they're heavily booked so reserve ahead as far as possible. There's also a restaurant here offering American-type meals.

Post

Seoul and Pusan are the only post offices in Korea which have a poste restante service 유치우편물 of the type you can find in other countries. It can be very difficult to locate letters addressed to poste restante at any other Korean post office even if the staff understand what you are talking about. The poste restante in Seoul is well organised and they keep a record of letters received. You have to sign for letters collected but the service is free.

The GPO offers a packing service for parcels which is excellent and quite cheap so there's no need to go chasing around for cardboard boxes and the like. This service is also available at Pusan GPO and many of the branch post offices around the perimeter of the Yongsan US military base in Seoul.

Foreign Embassies

Foreign embassies which are represented in Seoul include:

Australia
    11th Floor, Kyobo Building, 1-1 Chongno 1-ga, Chongno-gu (tel 730 6491)
Austria
    Room 1913, Kyobo Building, 1-1 Chongro 1-ga, Chongno-gu (tel 732 9071)
Bangladesh
    33-5 Hannamdong 1-ga, Yongsan-gu (tel 796 4056)
Belgium
    1-65 Tongbinggo-dong, Yongsan-gu (tel 793 9611)
Brazil
    Kum Jung Building, 192-11 Ulchiro 1-ga, Chung-gu (tel 720 4769)
Brunei
    1-94 Tongbinggo-dong, Yongsan-gu (tel 797 7679)

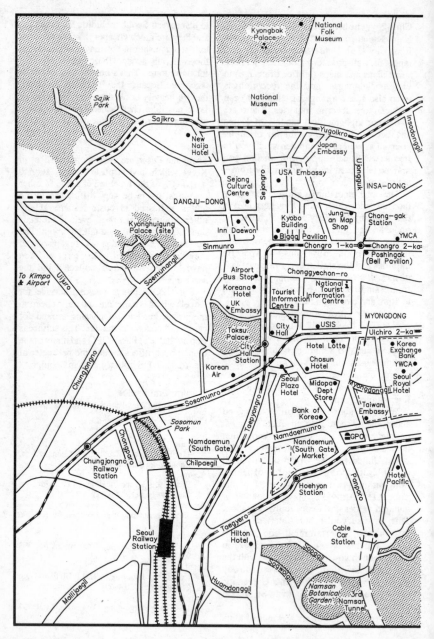

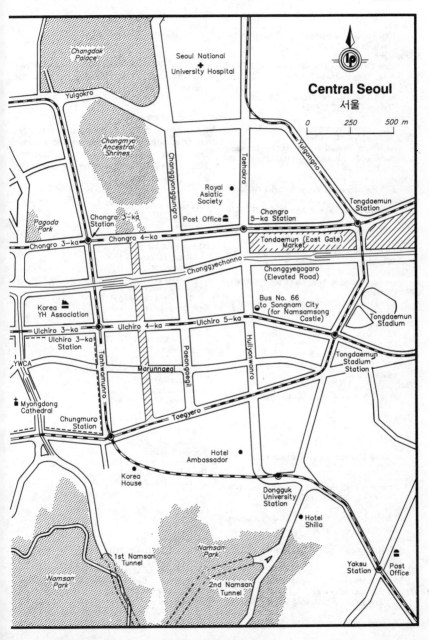

Central Seoul
서울

Canada
    10th Floor, Kolon Building, 45 Mugyo-dong,
    Chung-gu (tel 753 2605)
Denmark
    Suite 701, Namsong Building, 260-199 Itaewon-
    dong, Yongsan-gu (tel 795 4187)
Finland
    Room 1602, Kyobo Building, Chongno 1-ga,
    Chongno-gu (tel 732 6223)
France
    30 Hap-dong, Sodaemun-gu (tel 312 3272)
Federal Republic of Germany
    4th Floor, Daehan Fire & Marine Insurance
    Building, 51-1 Namchang-dong, Chung-gu (tel
    779 3272)
India
    37-3 Hannam-dong, Yongsan-gu (tel 798 4257)
Indonesia
    55 Youido-dong, Yongdungpo-gu (tel 782 5116)
Italy
    1-398 Hannam-dong, Yongsan-gu (tel 796 0491)
Japan
    18-11 Chunghak-dong, Chongno-gu (tel 733
    5626/8)
Malaysia
    4-1 Hannam-dong, Yongsan-gu (tel 795 9203)
Netherlands
    Room 1406 Kyobo Building, Chongno 1-ga,
    Chongno-gu (tel 737 9514)
New Zealand
    18th Floor, Kyobo Building, Chongno 1-ga,
    Chongno-gu (tel 730 7794)
Norway
    124-12 Itaewon-dong, Yongsan-gu (tel 795
    6850)
Pakistan
    58-1 Shinmunro 1-ga, Chongno-gu (tel 739
    4422)
Philippines
    559-510 Yoksam-dong, Kangnam-gu (tel 568
    9131)
Spain
    726-52 Hannam-dong, Yongsan-gu (tel 794
    3581)
Sri Lanka
    11th Floor, Kyobo Building, Chongno 1-ga,
    Chongno-gu (tel 735 2966)
Sweden
    8th Floor, Boyung Building, 108-2 Pyong-dong,
    Chongno-gu (tel 720 4767)
Switzerland
    32-10 Songwol-dong, Chongno-gu (tel 739
    9511)
Thailand
    653-7 Hannam-dong, Yongsan-gu (tel 795 3098)
Taiwan (Republic of China)
    83 Myong-dong 2-ga, Chung-gu (tel 776 2721)
UK
    4 Chong-dong, Chung-gu (tel 735 7341)

USA
    82 Sejong-ro, Chongno-gu (tel 732 2601)

There are also consulates of Taiwan, Japan
and the USA in Pusan (see the Pusan
section).

Airline Offices
Seoul has to be one of the most convenient
cities in which to organise airline tickets
since most of the offices are in the Chosun
Hotel right in the centre of the city near City
Hall. They include:

Air France
    Room 236 (tel 752 3921)
Air India
    Room 209 (tel 778 0064)
Alitalia/Gulf Air
    Room 111 (tel 779 1676)
American Airlines
    Room 108 (tel 755 3314)
British Airways
    Room 238 (tel 774 5511)
British Caledonian Airways
    Room 238 (tel 777 8131)
Canadian Pacific Airlines
    Room 205 (tel 753 8271)
China Airlines
    Room 211 (tel 755 1523)
Continental Airlines/LAN Chile/Sabena
    Room 206 (tel 778 0394)
Eastern Airlines
    Room 207 (tel 777 9786)
KLM
    Room 110 (tel 753 1093)
Scandinavian Airlines System
    Room 220 (tel 752 5123)
Singapore Airlines
    Room 202 (tel 755 1226)
Thai International Airways
    Room 218 (tel 779 2621)

Other airline offices are:

All Nippon Airways
    Room 1501, Center Building, 91-1 Sogong-
    dong, Chung-gu (tel 752 1160)
Cathay Pacific Airways
    Room 701, Kolon Building, 45 Mugyo-dong,
    Chung-gu (tel 779 0321)
Delta Airlines
    Room 1402 Dongbang Life Insurance Building,
    150 Taepyong-ro 2-ga, Chung-gu (tel 754 1921)

Top: The royal Yi tombs, Taenung near Seoul (CHP)
Bottom: Shamanist spirit posts, Folk Village, Suweon (CHP)

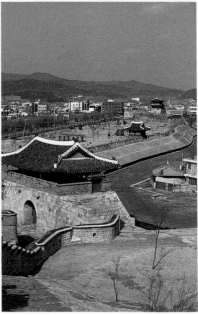

Top: Kyongbok Palace, Seoul (GC)
Left: Small pavilion of Kyongbok Palace, Seoul (HJMG)
Right: The old walls and gates of Suweon (GC)

El Al
Room 805, Center Building, 91-1 Sogong-dong, Chung-gu (tel 755 1345)
Garuda
Room 301, Dongmin Building, 95 Mugyo-dong, Chung-gu (tel 755 3183)
Iberia Airlines
Room 605, 100 Tangju-dong, Chongno-gu (tel 739 0941)
Japan Air System
Room 503, Paiknam Building, 188-3 Ulchiro 7-ga, Chung-gu (tel 752 9400)
JAL
Room 202, Paiknam Building, 188-3 Ulchiro 1-ga, Chung-gu (tel 757 1715)
Korean Air
KAL Building, 41-3 Sosomun-dong, Chung-gu (tel 755 2221)
Lufthansa
Room 601, Center Building, 91-1 Sogong-dong, Chung-gu (tel 777 9655)
Malaysian Airline System
14th Floor, Dongbang Life Insurance Building, 150 Taepyong-ro 2-ga, Chung-gu (tel 777 7761)
Northwest Airlines
7th/8th/9th Floors, In-joo Building, 111-1 Sorin-dong, Chongno-gu (tel 734 7800)
Pan Am
Room 1510, Anguk Insurance Building, 87 Ulchiro 1-ga, Chung-gu (tel 757 8916)
Qantas
Room 801, Dongmin Building, 95 Mugyo-dong, Chung-gu (tel 777 6871)
Saudi Arabian Airlines
Room 1301 Daeyeonkak Building, 24-5 Chungmuro 1-ga, Chung-gu (tel 755 5621)
Swissair
Room 301, Oriental Chemical Building, 50 Sogong-dong, Chung-gu (tel 757 8901)
TWA
1st Floor, You-one Building, 75-95 Sosomun-dong, Chung-gu (tel 777 4864)
United Airlines
Room 1503, Anguk Insurance Building, 87 Ulchiro 1-ga, Chung-gu (tel 757 1691)
Varig
Room 601, Kumjeong Building, 192-11 Ulchiro 1-ga, Chung-gu (tel 779 3877)

Bookshops

There are three excellent bookstores in the centre of Seoul where you can find books in English, French, German, Spanish and Japanese. The first is the Kyobo Book Center which takes up the entire basement of the Kyobo Building on the corner of Sejong-ro and Chongro. The second is the Chongro Book Center, 84-9 Chongro 2-ka, in the same block as Poshingak (the Bell Pavilion) and diagonally opposite the YMCA. Foreign language books are on the 4th floor whereas maps and guide books to Korea are on the 2nd floor. The third source is the Royal Asiatic Society, Room 611, Christian Broadcasting Building, 136-46 Yonji-dong, Chongno-gu. Many travellers consider this bookstore to have the best selection of books in English on Korean subjects.

Information and books on Korean Buddhism are available from the Lotus Lantern International Buddhist Center (tel 735 5347), down a small alley opposite the entrance to the Kyongbok Palace.

The bookshops lining the street outside Chogye-sa Temple and the bookshop in the temple grounds itself only stock books in the Korean language.

Maps

If you're going to hike in the mountains of the national parks then it's a good idea to pick up a selection of those maps available either at the KNTC office or the City Hall tourist office. They're usually adequate if you intend to keep to the well-marked trails but if you want to get off the beaten track then you'll need better maps. The best place to get these is the Jung-An Map & Chart Service (tel 720 9191/2/3), 125-1 Gongpyeong-dong, Chongno-gu. They have a vast range of maps in various scales as well as accurate 'tourist' maps of various sections of the country such as the East Coast, Cheju-do, South Coast, etc, which cost W2000 each and are quite adequate for trekking. They also have larger scale maps with contours which cost W300 each but you need your passport to get them (the government likes to keep a check on who buys them – you might be a Communist spy!). Another good place for maps recommended by other travellers is the Asia Map Centre (tel 717 7511/5), Head Office, Asia Aero Survey & Consulting Engineers Inc, 429 Shinsoo-dong, Mapo-gu, Seoul.

KYONGBOK (GYEONGBOG) PALACE
경복궁

This palace is at the back of the former Capitol Building at the end of Sejongro and was first built in 1392 by the founder of the Yi Dynasty, King Taejo. It was burnt down during the Japanese invasion of 1592 and thereafter left in ruins until it was rebuilt in 1867 when it became the residence of the 26th ruler. The walled grounds of this palace contain some exceptionally beautiful buildings and a collection of old stone pagodas from other parts of the country, many of which were brought here by the Japanese during their occupation of Korea. The superbly landscaped grounds, including formal ponds, are a haven of peace and tranquillity in comparison to the eight lanes of snarling traffic which lead up to it, so take your time here and soak up some of the atmosphere.

The Kyongbok Palace is open daily from 9 am to 6.30 pm (April to October) and 9 am to 6 pm (November to March) and costs W550 entry.

National Folk Museum

This museum is in the grounds of the Kyongbok Palace and contains full-scale recreations of traditional houses, festivals, costumes and agricultural implements. There's also a real surprise here in the form of a display of movable metal type which was invented and used in Korea around 1234 – 200 years before Gutenberg's 'invention' of movable type printing in Europe! This museum is one of the best in Korea and it's well worth spending a morning or an afternoon here.

The Folk Museum ·is open daily, except Tuesday, from 9 am to 5 pm and entry costs W150.

NATIONAL MUSEUM

The National Museum is housed in the former Capitol Building at the top of Sejongro on the bottom side of Kyongbok Palace. The collections are mainly of pottery and roofing tiles from the various Korean kingdoms but there's also an excellent section of stone and brass Buddhas and Bodhisattvas. Personally I found the displays a little pedantic and felt they needed some life breathed into them, though I dare say archaeologists and academics might disagree.

The museum is open daily, except Monday, from 9 am to 5 pm and costs W500 entry.

CHONGMYO (JONGMYO) ROYAL ANCESTRAL SHRINES 종묘

This forested park east of the Kyongbok Palace contains a collection of beautiful traditional Korean shrines which house the ancestral tablets of the 27 Yi Dynasty kings and queens. The two main shrines, however, are only opened to the public on certain ceremonial days. The main ceremony is on the first Sunday of May each year when the descendants of the royal family come here to honour the spirits of their ancestors in a very colourful Confucian ceremony which lasts six hours. On this day there's also traditional court dancing and music. It's something which shouldn't be missed if you're here at that time. Entry costs W1000 (W500 for children) and the park is open daily between 9 am and 6 pm.

CHANGDOK (CHANGDEOG) PALACE
창덕궁

Originally constructed in 1405 as an eastern detached palace, this is the best preserved of Seoul's five palaces and is still the residence of the remnants of the royal family. Like the other palaces in the capital it was burned down during the Japanese invasion of 1592 but rebuilt in 1611 and used as the official royal residence until 1867 when the king moved to Kyongbok Palace. The gateway to Changdok is a classic piece of traditional Korean architecture and the oldest original gate in the city.

Changdok is also the site of the enchanting Secret Garden (Piwon), a landscaped, wooded retreat which covers over 78 acres and was, during the days of the Yi Dynasty, reserved for members of the royal family and the king's concubines. This is Korean landscape gardening at its best. The garden contains over 40 pleasure pavilions as well as many ponds and stone bridges.

The palace and the Secret Garden are open daily but to see them you must join a tour group. These are fairly informal and it is possible to wander around on your own at various points. Each tour lasts about 1½ hours and costs W1800. Tickets go on sale half an hour before a tour starts. There are English-speaking tours at 11.30 am, 1.30 and 3.30 pm from April to November and at 10 am and 1 pm from November to March. Japanese-speaking tours are at 10.30 am, 12.30, 2.30 and 4.30 pm. Korean-speaking tours are at 9, 10 and 11 am, noon, 1, 2, 3, 4 and 5 pm plus there are additional tours during summer at 8 am, 6 and 7 pm. You don't have to speak any particular language to get on any of the tours.

CHANGGYONG PALACE 창경궁

Adjacent to Changdok Palace is another restored royal palace complex which was built in 1104 by the Koryo king, Sukjong, and later used by the first Yi Dynasty king while the Kyongbok Palace was being built. Most of the buildings here date from a reconstruction carried out in the 1830s. For most of the 20th century, this palace was the city's botanical gardens and zoo but the zoo was moved to Seoul Grand Park in 1983 when restoration began. Entry to this complex is through a large gateway on the eastern side of the wall which encloses it. It's open from 9 am to 6.30 pm from April to October and 9 am to 6 pm the rest of the year. Entry costs W550.

TOKSU (DEOGSU) PALACE 덕수궁

This palace is directly opposite Seoul Plaza Hotel right in the centre of the city and was originally built as a royal villa towards the end of the 15th century. It became the official residence of the last of the Yi Dynasty kings, King Kojong, in 1897 following his year-long asylum in the Russian Legation. Kojong abdicated in 1907 but continued to live here until his death in 1919. After that, the palace was left to deteriorate until 1933 when it was restored by the royal family. It's

much smaller than the Kyongbok and Changdok palaces but worth a visit. Entry costs W550 and the opening times are the same as for Kyongbok Palace.

POSHINGAK (BOSINGAG) 보신각

Poshingak, or Bell Pavilion, houses Seoul's city bell, used in former times to announce dawn and sunset when the city gates were opened or closed. The bell is 2½ metres high and was cast in 1468. The street on which it stands – Chongro (Chong-no) – translates as Bell Street. The pavilion is floodlit at night.

PAGODA PARK 파고다

Pagoda Park is on Chongro just east of Poshingak, and is famous for its 10-storey Koryo pagoda. Pagoda Park is also where the proclamation of independence against Japanese colonial rule was made on 1 March 1919 and it's one of the few parks in Seoul which remain open at night (up to 11 pm April to September and 10 pm for the rest of the year). It's a good place to sit and watch life go by and it's a popular meeting spot for old and young alike. Entry costs W200.

CHOGYE-SA TEMPLE 조계사

Very few Korean cities have Buddhist temples standing in their centres as a result of the Yi Dynasty's attempts to suppress the religion in favour of Confucianism. Indeed, Chogye-sa was founded only in 1910 but it's the largest of its kind in the city and the headquarters of the Chogye sect of Korean Buddhism. The sect is by far the largest in Korea with some 14 million adherents (70% of the total Buddhists), around 12,000 monks and over 1600 temples. Despite its recent foundation, it's a stunningly beautiful and colourful building and the golden Buddha must be one of the largest in the country.

The temple buildings are squeezed into a small but leafy courtyard containing a number of rare trees just below Yulgok-ro. Entry is via a narrow alleyway near the top end of Ujongguk-ro which itself is lined with shops selling Buddhist paraphernalia ranging from books and bells to monks'

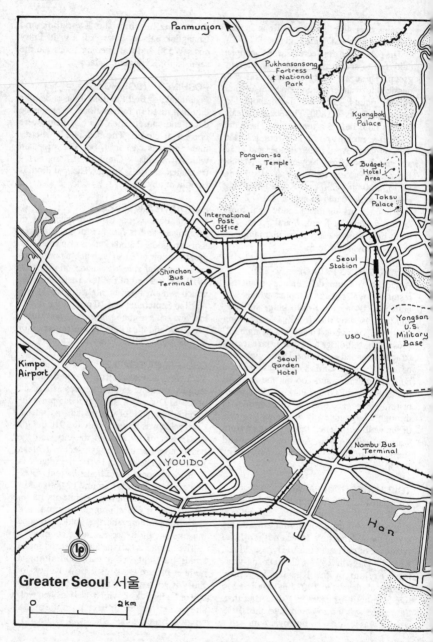

Panmunjon

Pukhansansong
Fortress
National Park

Kyongbok
Palace

Pongwon-sa
Temple

Budget
Hotel
Area

Toksu
Palace

International
Post
Office

Shinchon
Bus
Terminal

Seoul
Station

Yongsan
U.S.
Military
Base

USO

Seoul
Garden
Hotel

Kimpo
Airport

Nambu Bus
Terminal

YOUIDO

Han

Greater Seoul 서울

0   2 km

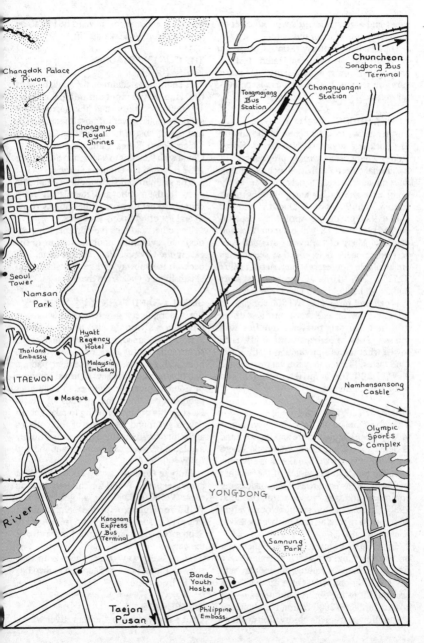

robes and altar statues. It's a good street to search for souvenirs of this nature.

On Buddha's birthday (May), Chogye-sa is where the city's largest lantern festival ends up so if you're around at that time make sure you see this. It's one of the most colourful events of the year.

KOREA HOUSE   한국의집

Further away from the centre of the city on the northern slopes of Namsan is Korea House which offers weekly programmes of traditional cultural activities such as dancing and music. There's a performance every night except Sundays and public holidays from 8.30 to 9.30 pm (7.20 to 8.20 pm and 8.40 to 9.40 pm during April, May, September and October). They also put on films and displays. Many of the events are well subscribed so check beforehand to see if seats are available (for reservations telephone 267 8752 or 266 9101). If you're on a strict budget you should also check the prices as you can end up paying W8800 for just an hour's performance. Korea House also offers gourmet Korean buffets, lunches and dinners. They're perhaps worth it just once to see what the full production really looks (and tastes) like but they are very expensive – W13,200 for a buffet or lunch and W14,300 for dinner.

NAMSAN TOWER   남산타워

This tower sits on the top of Namsan mountain between the city centre and Itaewon and is Seoul's most prominent landmark. There are superb views over Seoul and its environs from the top of this mountain if the weather is fine. The tower carries TV broadcasting equipment and was opened to the public in 1980. Up near the top are three observation decks and a revolving (but fairly expensive) restaurant.

To get up to the tower, you can either walk or take the cable car which operates every five to 10 minutes throughout the day and costs W1200 one way. Once up there, you take the lift to the observation decks which costs a further W2000 return. No photography is allowed from the observation decks of

the tower and cameras have to be left at the bottom before you take the lift.

THE OLYMPIC STADIUM
올림픽경기장

This enormous stadium on the south bank of the Han River accommodates around 100,000 spectators, and the surrounding sports complex covers almost three sq km. It first played host to the 1986 Asian Games, in which South Korea came second only to China with 93 golds to 94, then in September 1988 it hosted the Olympic Games.

The stadium and surrounding complex is open to the public and there's no entry charge. To get there, take the subway (Line 2) and get off at Sports Complex.

The other stadiums (velodrome, gymnastics) and swimming pool are further to the east in the Olympic Park. To get there, hop back on the subway and go two stations to Chamshil and walk from there.

SEOUL GRAND PARK   서울그란드공원

For a completely different perspective on this city, it's worth a visit to Seoul Grand Park. Aptly named, it takes in almost seven sq km and contains an artificial lake, the zoo, botanical gardens, an amusement park, a dolphinarium and the new National Museum of Contemporary Art (opened in 1988 after being moved from the grounds of Toksu Palace). It's obviously going to take you all day to get round just some of these places and a lot of walking, though there is a trolley available between the entrance and the zoo for W400.

Entry to the park costs W1000 (W800 for adolescents and W500 for children) plus an extra W300 (W200 for adolescents and W100 for children) for the dolphin show. The park is open 9 am to 7 pm from April to September and 9 am to 6 pm for the rest of the year.

The easiest way to get there is to take subway Lines 2 or 4 to Sadang and then bus No 16 from there.

RIVERBOATS
Until a few years ago, the Han River wasn't

a particularly attractive waterway with its raggy banks and pollutants. That's now all changed following a massive effort to clean it up, construction of levees and landscaping of recreational areas and even the dredging of parts of the river. In line with this there are now shallow-draught, open-sided pleasure boats on which you can go for a cruise along the river. There are two routes you can take, the longest being the one hour trip between Yoido and Chamshil (Olympic Complex) or vice versa. On weekdays there are boats every two hours from 11.30 am to 7.30 pm plus another two at 8 and 9 pm from Yoido and at 10.30 am, 2.30, 6.30, 7.40 and 9 pm from Chamshil. On holidays and weekends there are boats every 1½ hours from 11 am to 8 pm plus another two at 8.20 and 9.10 pm in either direction. The fare is W3500 (W1800 for children).

The shorter boat trip starts and finishes at Yoido and takes you on a loop downstream and back up again. The fare is W3000 (W1500 for children).

PLACES TO STAY

Seoul seems hellbent on continuing to do what many other large cities around the world are now having second thoughts about, namely, tearing down the old and even the not-so-old and replacing it with high-rise. As a result, there's an excellent choice of expensive hotels and restaurants but a serious lack of cheap places to stay. Only in Insa-dong does there seem to have been any attempt to preserve and restore traditional-style housing. Elsewhere, the one-storied timber houses with their red-tiled roofs and verandahs surrounding shady courtyards are being swept away by the bulldozers and replaced with the anonymity of concrete, steel and glass. Perhaps it's inevitable given the value of real estate in the central business district.

Meanwhile, there are still a few travellers' hotels clinging on tenaciously in between the high-rise down narrow alleyways at the back of the Sejong Cultural Centre, Insa-dong and there's even one within a stone's throw of the huge Lotte Hotel although the owners talk resignedly of numbered days. Some of these hotels, like others in various cities in India, Athens, Cairo, Nairobi, Bangkok and Bali to name a few, have become legends in their own time among travellers. It will be a sad day if or when they disappear. With them will go the friendly, down-to-earth informality which has drawn travellers to this area for so long.

Enjoy them while they're still there!

Places to Stay – bottom end

One of the main budget hotel areas is at the back of the Sejong Cultural Centre which is on Sejong-ro near the junction with Chongro. If you arrive by airport shuttle bus (No 601), get off at the Koreana Hotel, walk up to the junction and cross the road via the subway.

Arriving by rail all trains except those from Chuncheon terminate at Seoul Railway Station. From there to the budget hotel area, take the subway one stop to City Hall and walk towards the Koreana Hotel from there.

If you arrive at Kangnam Express Bus Terminal on the other side of the Han River, take the subway to City Hall. There is one other possible entry into the city which you will come across if you have taken either the train or bus from Chuncheon, north-east of Seoul. The former terminates at Chongnyangni (pronounced 'chong-nang-ni') Station, east of the city centre. From here, take the subway and go six stops to Chonggak. By bus, you will arrive at Songbong Bus Terminal even further east than the railway station. From here, take the bus to Chongnyangni/Mammoth Hotel and take the subway from there to Chonggak.

In this area the most popular place to stay and one which has become a legend in its time is the *Daewon Yogwan* (more usually known as the *Inn Daewon*) (tel 735 7891) 대원, Dangju-dong, Chongno-gu 종로구. This *yogwan* is always overflowing with travellers so, depending on the season, you may have to wait a day or two before you can get a bed. It's a very friendly and informal place to stay and has

Sejong Cultural Centre Area

0   25   50 m

서울 문화 회관 지역

Naija & New Naija Hotels

Japanese Embassy

Taesin Jang Yogwan

US Embassy

Sam Song Yogwan

Sung Do Yogwan

U–Jong Yogwan

Kyong–do Jang Yogwan

Royal Building

Sejong Cultural Centre

Kyobo Building

Inn Daewon

Wendy's

Bigag Pavilion

Sinmun–ro

Chong–ro

Kentucky Fried Chicken

Subway

managed to preserve its traditional Korean character with the rooms arranged around a central courtyard in which there's never a dull moment. Some travellers seem to become semipermanent residents. These days the facilities are much improved and include 24-hour hot water, clean toilets, a washing machine and cooking facilities. A bed (usually in a shared room) costs W6000 plus they have double rooms for W7000 all with shared bathroom facilities. This is definitely one of the best places to stay if you're searching for language teaching jobs (officially illegal without a work

permit) but also the best place to find out all manner of things from where to sell your duty-free whisky to the best places to stay from Tokyo to Timbuktu.

If it's full or you don't like the facilities, another popular place to stay is the *Sung Do Yogwan* 성도여관 (tel 738 8226, 737 1056), 120 Nae Su-dong, Chongro-gu 종로구 , There are a total of 15 rooms here which cost W6000 for a small room, W7000 to W8000 for a standard size room without bath and W10,000 for a double room with bath. Constant hot water is available in both the private and communal showers.

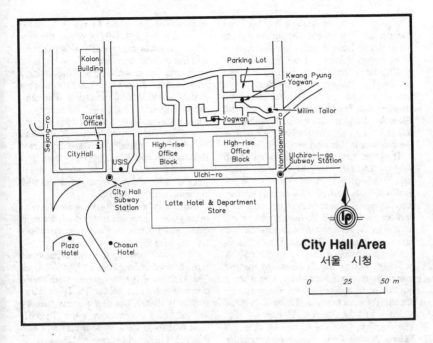

City Hall Area
서울 시청

It's a very friendly place and often full in the spring and autumn times. The only minor drawback here is that there's no courtyard.

If both of these are full there are several similarly priced *yogwan* in the same area. They include the *U-Jong Yogwan* 유정여관 and the *Sam Song Yogwan* 삼성여관, both very close to the Sung Do Yogwan, and the *Kyong-do Jang Yogwan* 경도장여관, though this is more expensive.

Away from this area, my own particular favourite and one which I'd rate even higher than the Inn Daewon is the *Kwang Pyung Yogwan* 광평여관 (tel 778 0104), 123-1 Da-dong, Chung-gu 대동 종로구. The owners of this *yogwan*, Mr & Mrs Lee, are extremely friendly, very helpful and speak Japanese as well as some English. The rooms are arranged around a traditional courtyard where there's always a gaggle of travellers in the mornings and evenings – usually about equal numbers of Japanese and Westerners. It's spotlessly clean, totally safe (as far as

your gear goes) and hot water is available in both the private and communal bathrooms. Rooms cost W9000 to W10,000 without bath and W11,000 with bath.

To get to the Kwang Pyung, take the subway to Ulchiro 1-ga on Line 2. As you emerge from the tracks you come to a large hall full of shops and a complicated system of exits. The exit you want is the one diagonally opposite that leading directly to the Lotte Department Store. Assuming you take the right one, you'll find yourself on the north-west corner of the road junction with the Lotte Hotel across the other side of Ulchiro and the high-rise Hanil Building beside you. Head north from here and cross over a street which goes alongside the back of the Hanil Building. Shortly after this you come to a narrow alleyway on the left hand side next to a shop called 'Milim Tailor' (sign in English). Here there's also a sign in Chinese and English for the Kwang Pyung. Go down the alleyway and follow the signs.

If arriving from Kimpo International Airport, take the No 601 airport bus and get off at the Koreana Hotel. From there, walk to the tourist information center at the back of City Hall. Right opposite here is a road lined with restaurants and other shops. Walk down it until you get almost to the end where an alleyway branches off to the left (the alleyway doubles as a car park during the day). There's a sign for the Kwang Pyung at the entrance to this alleyway.

The other main area in which to find cheap *yogwan* and the more expensive *yogwan jang* is Insa-dong (formerly known to Westerners as Mary's Alley). The nearest subway stations to this area are Chonggak on Line 1 and Anguk on Line 3. Assuming you get off at Chonggak, head east towards Pagoda Park on the north side of Chongro. The first landmark you come to is the large YMCA building. Taking the first road to the left immediately after the YMCA, you'll see a number of signposts for various *yogwan* up ahead. They include the *Young-il Yogwan* 영일여관 and the *Taewon Yogwan* 대원여관. The Taewon (like its namesake near the Sejong Cultural Centre) has become popular with travellers over the last few years though it's nothing special. You can get a room here with common bath for W8000.

Turning left up this same road beside the YMCA but then taking the first alleyway on the right hand side, you'll find another selection of *yogwan*. They include the *Won-kam Yogwan* 원감여관, the *Chongno Mogyoktang* 목욕탕 which is a combined bathhouse and *yogwan* with a sign in English saying 'Hotel', the *So-bok Yogwan* 수복여관, the *Unjong Jang Yogwan* 운종장여관 and the *Insong Yogwan* 인성여관. Take your pick but remember that the *jang* will be more expensive.

Instead of turning left immediately after the YMCA, continue on to the next major road junction opposite Pagoda Park. This is the junction of Insadonggil and Chongro. Turn left here and bear left where the road forks. This is Mary's Alley. About 100 metres up here off to the left is an alleyway down which there's a choice of three places

to stay. The first is the *Kangwon Yoinsook* 강원여인숙 (tel 734 2992) – one of the very few *yoinsook* in this area. It's fairly primitive and has a Dickensian atmosphere but it's a traditional house with rooms surrounding a courtyard and it costs just W5000 for a single or double and W6000 for a triple. The communal bathrooms have cold water only. A little further on is the *Kumcha Jang Yogwan* 금자장여관 (tel 732 3047) which is a modern building with friendly staff and hot water. Rooms here cost W11,000 with bath. Just opposite is the *Dongsan Yogwan* 동산여관 (tel 732 6358) where you can get a room with common bath for W8000.

Further up Insadonggil, there are plenty of other places to choose from which are indicated on the street map but it depends how far you want to walk with a rucksack.

Very good value up this end of the street is the *Young Bin Jang Yogwan* 영빈장여관 (tel 732 4731) which offers rooms with bath, constant hot water, colour TV, fan and aircon for W11,000. The staff are very friendly and the place is spotlessly clean. Turn off right when you see a sign for the San Chon Restaurant (sign in Chinese and English).

Continuing on up Insadonggil, you'll see signs for the *Changmi Yogwan* 장미여관 and the *Pyuk-o Jang Yogwan* 벽오장여관 (tel 734 3353). The latter is at the end of an alleyway off to the right and is a modernised traditional-style house surrounding a courtyard. Unfortunately, whoever undertook the modernisation ruined the place by sealing in the verandahs and putting windows in the rooms which are so high and so small that they resemble police cells! Other than this, it's a very well-maintained *yogwan* with small rooms for W12,000 and larger rooms for W20,000 all with bath, constant hot water, colour TV, fan and air-con.

There's better value further up Insadonggil down the next alley to the right. Here you'll find the *Han Hung Jang Yogwan* 한흥장여관 (tel 734 4265) which is popular with Western tourists. It's a modern building and offers rooms for W11,000 with bath, constant hot water and air-con.

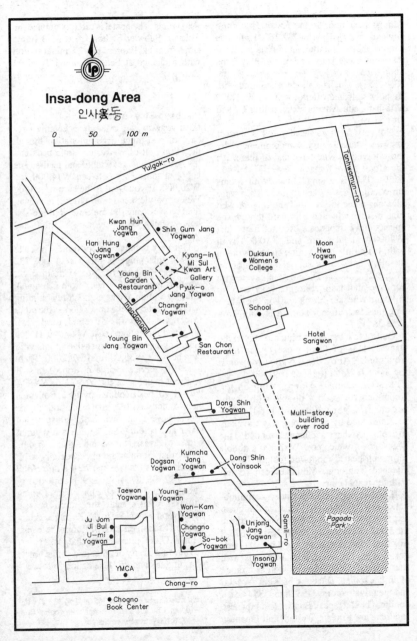

Insa-dong Area
인사동동

0   50   100 m

Yulgok-ro

Tanhwamun-ro

Kwan Hun Jang Yogwan
Shin Gum Jang Yogwan
Han Hung Jang Yogwan
Moon Hwa Yogwan
Kyong-in Mi Sul Kwan Art Gallery
Duksun Women's College
Young Bin Garden Restaurant
Pyuk-o Jang Yogwan
Changmi Yogwan
School
Insadong-gil
Young Bin Jang Yogwan
San Chon Restaurant
Hotel Sangwon
Dong Shin Yogwan
Multi-storey building over road
Dogsan Yogwan
Kumcha Jang Yogwan
Dong Shin Yoinsook
Taewon Yogwan
Young-il Yogwan
Won-Kam Yogwan
Ju Jom Ji Bul
U-mi Yogwan
Chongno Yogwan
So-bok Yogwan
Unjong Jang Yogwan
Pagoda Park
Samil-ro
YMCA
Insong Yogwan
Chong-ro
Chogno Book Center

Almost next door is the *Kwan Hun Jang Yogwan* 관흥장여관 (tel 732 1682) which is similar, though smaller, and offers rooms at the same price. At the end of this alley is the *Shin Gum Jang Yogwan* 신흥장 여관 (tel 733 1355). This is a modern building with friendly staff and offers rooms at W11,000 with bath, constant hot water, colour TV and air-con.

Not very far from Insadonggil is another *yogwan* which is highly recommended by those travellers who have stayed there. It's the *Moon Hwa Yogwan* 문화여관 (tel 765 4659). This is a small place with rooms surrounding a leafy courtyard. It's a very pleasant place to stay and the *ajimah* who runs it is friendly and tries hard though she speaks only Japanese. Rooms here cost W7000 without bath and W10,000 with bath. It's a little hard to find since it's down an alley between a school and Duksung Women's College. The alley is paved with concrete and has a concrete wall on one side and a besser-block wall on the other. The nearest subway station is Anguk on Line 3.

Quite a few travellers prefer to stay in the Itaewon area of town close to the huge Yongsan US Army Base. A good *yogwan* is the *Sung Ji Hotel* (tel 792 1691) 성지여관 , 211 30 Itaewon-2 Dong, Yongsan-gu. Rooms cost W9000 a double with bathroom. It's very clean, friendly and recommended by many long stay travellers in Seoul. Another traveller recommended the *O-bok Hotel* which cost W12,000 a double for a well-heated room with colour TV and attached bathroom. Valuables can be left with the management.

If you don't mind dormitory accommodation or you want to stay near the Kangnam Express Bus Terminal then you could stay at the *Bando Youth Hostel* (tel 567 5033), 679-3 Yoksam-dong, Kangnam-gu. This is a large hostel with 100 bunk beds in rooms with four, six and eight bunks as well as a range of private rooms. The bunk beds cost W4400 and the private rooms US$28 to US$44.50 a double. The staff speak English and Japanese and there are Korean, Western and Japanese

restaurants. The hostel is directly outside the Yoksam Subway Station on Line 2 (three stops from the Express Bus Terminal station with a change at Seoul National Teachers College).

Places to Stay – middle

Most *yogwan jang* offer an acceptable standard of mid-range accommodation though they don't all offer Western-style beds and it's rare that you get a table and chairs. The better of these vary between W14,000 and W20,000. If you want to be sure of getting Western-style accommodation, however, then you're mostly looking at three-star hotels which cost between W25,000 and W40,000.

One very popular and convenient place to stay in this range is the *YMCA* (tel 732 8291/8), 9 Chongro 2-ga, Chongro-gu, which is two minutes' walk from Chonggak Subway Station. It's an eight-storey building with the rooms on the upper floors (the other floors are used for different purposes). Singles/doubles here cost W24,000/31,000 plus they have more expensive rooms with twin beds for W38,000 and W43,000. There is a 10% service charge on top of this. If you're a member of the YMCA or YWCA the bill will be discounted by 10%. Both men and women can use this place and all the rooms have their own bath, constant hot water and colour TV. There is a restaurant with Western-style food and a games room.

Another popular hotel, especially with Americans, is the two-star *New Naija Hotel* (tel 737 9011/5), 201-9 Naeja-dong, Chongro-gu. This is at the back of the Sejong Cultural Centre near the junction with Sajikro and very close to the Kyongbokkung Subway Station on Line 3. Rooms here cost from W37,000 plus service charges.

There are plenty of other mid-range hotels of a similar standard. A selection follows:

Sang Won Tourist Hotel (tel 765 0441/9) 33 Nakwon-dong, Chongro-gu. Two-star with rooms from W38,100 plus service charges.

Eastern Hotel (tel 764 4101/9) 444-14 Changshin-dong, Chongro-gu. Two-star with rooms from W24,200.

Daehwa Tourist Hotel (tel 265 9181/9) 18-21 Ulchiro 6-ga, Chung-gu. Two-star with rooms from W30,000.

Chon Ji Tourist Hotel (tel 265 6131/3) 133-1 Ulchiro 5-ga, Chung-gu. Two-star with rooms from W31,500 to W34,200.

Central Tourist Hotel (tel 265 4120/9) 227-1, Changsa-dong, Chongro-gu. Two-star with rooms from W31,000.

Places to Stay – top end

Seoul is awash with multistar accommodation so, if money is no object, you'll be spoilt for choice. Three-star hotels range from W38,000 to W53,000; four-star hotels from W50,000 to W110,000 and deluxe hotels from W95,000 to W200,000. Anyone who's got this sort of money available will not be in need of even a selected list of hotels since they'll probably have made a booking from overseas and, if they haven't, all this can be done from Kimpo International Airport on arrival before they even take a taxi into the centre. At the airport, bookings will be made free of charge at the relevant counters where the staff speak a variety of European languages as well as Japanese. The only decisions you will have to make are price range and location.

In the absolute heart of the city and within a stone's throw of City Hall are the *Hotel Lotte* (tel 771 10) at W113,000 to W127,000, the *Seoul Plaza Hotel* (tel 771 22) at W104,000 to W113,000, the *Chosun Hotel* (tel 771 05) at W122,500 to W135,000, and the *Hotel President* (tel 753 3131) at W88,000 to W93,000.

There are similar hotels scattered all over Seoul both on the north and south side of the Han River.

Those looking for this kind of accommodation in Itaewon should try the new four-star *Hamilton Hotel* (tel 794 0171) which has rooms from W49,000.

PLACES TO EAT

There are literally a million restaurants, snack bars and bars in the centre of Seoul where you can find a good meal without burning a hole in your pocket. Most restaurants specialise in a particular type of food whether it be Korean, Japanese, Chinese or Western. It's usually obvious which are likely to be cheap and which expensive and, if you're not sure, then simply ask to have a look at the menu. At most of the cheaper restaurants, the menu will be entirely in Korean so you're going to need a working knowledge of the more common Korean dishes but you'll certainly be able to read the prices.

For those on a budget, the best areas are those at the back of the Sejong Cultural Centre; the street at the back of the Kyobo Building/US Embassy; the area between City Hall and the Kwang Pyung Yogwan; Insa-dong; and Myong-dong between Ulchiro and the GPO. The best of these are between City Hall and the Kwang Pyung Yogwan (Ta-dong and Mugyo-dong), and Insa-dong, though many of the restaurants in the otherwise ritzy area of Myong-dong are remarkably cheap.

It's often the case that certain streets – or sections of streets – cater exclusively for particular types of food and this is particularly true of Ta-dong and Mugyo-dong. The narrow alleyways in this part of town are replete with restaurants standing cheek by jowl all the way down their length. Here there are streets specialising in *pulgogi* and *kalbi*, others in fried fish, and, in between, there are a plethora of bars, nightclubs and restaurants offering simpler, less expensive, Korean dishes. This area is quite small (though the profusion of neon signs makes it look otherwise at night) so the best way to get to grips with it is to walk around and decide what you'd like to eat and where. It won't take you more than 20 minutes to walk around. It's very popular with Koreans as well as travellers especially in the evenings. I've eaten well in many of these restaurants and so it would be unfair to single out individual places for special mention nor would it help to name names since most are in Korean in any case.

Restaurants in the Insa-dong area are generally a little more expensive than those in Ta-dong and Mugyo-dong since there is a greater proportion of foreign tourists in this area but, even here, there are plenty of cheap restaurants. Most of these are in the alley immediately north of Chongro at the back of the YMCA. There's a similar collection in the street one block back from Chongro going south. The restaurants and bars here are popular with students and other young people.

On Insadonggil itself there are two restaurants which are worth considering for a splurge. The first is the *San Chon Restaurant* 산초 (tel 735 0312). Owned by a former Buddhist monk, this restaurant offers traditional vegetarian meals. The main ingredients are drawn from the mountains of Korea, though not exclusively. The number of dishes which are placed before you here is truly staggering but then perhaps it should be since the average price of a meal is W13,000. Even if you consider that to be expensive, what makes it worth while is the nightly floor show of traditional music and dancing in the central courtyard which starts about 8 pm and goes on for about 45 minutes. The design of the restaurant is also beautifully conceived. Apart from the food itself, there's a wide choice of country wines and delicious home-made *makkoli* (W4000). It's worth reserving a table at this restaurant if you intend to eat there as it's a popular place to go for a night out. The menu is in both English and Korean and there's a sign (in Chinese and English) for the restaurant on Insadonggil.

The other restaurant which is worth a splurge is the *Young Bin Garden Restaurant* 영빈 식당 which, as its name suggests, is arranged around a traditional garden. It's just a little further up Insadonggil from the San Chon. This place is big on atmosphere but not especially good value as far as the amount of food provided goes, though it is very tasty. The restaurant specialises in meat dishes and there are facsimile meals on display at the entrance. Plan on spending W6000 to W7000 per person.

Those in need of a break from Korean food should head for Itaewon where there are a large number of restaurants offering Western food at very reasonable prices. One such place which is popular and where you have the choice of sitting inside or out is *Popeye House*.

Another good place to find typical American food where the prices won't make you wince is the restaurant at the USO on Hangang-ro just opposite Gate 21 of Yongsan US Army Base. The nearest subway station is Sookmyung Women's University, one stop beyond Seoul Station. A huge chicken dinner with French fries, vegetables, salad and rolls will cost about W2500. It's a bargain.

Further afield, the Shinchon district west of the city centre is worth exploring. There are no less than six different universities as well as the huge Severance Hospital in this area. That adds up to a lot of students looking for cheap restaurants and entertainment. To get there from the centre, take the Line 2 subway from City Hall and get off at Shinchon Station (don't confuse this with the other Shinchon Subway Station, also on Line 2, south of the river near the Olympic Complex). Ask around when you get off the subway – many students will be able to speak passable English.

Over the last few years a lot of construction has taken place on the south side of the Han River which ranges from shiny office towers to funky little village-type neighbourhoods. Many of these 'villages' are happy hunting grounds for lively night life with all manner of little shops, restaurants and bars. They've become very popular with Koreans but you'll rarely see another Westerner here. One such area is just south-west of the Shinchon Subway Station on Line 2, one stop before the Sports Complex. One of the largest areas, however, is north and west of the Kangnam Subway Station (also on Line 2).

A long-term resident recommends a restaurant not too far from this area. It's called the *Namgang Garden* 남강가든 . It serves excellent *pulgogi* and *kalbi* and, although slightly more expensive than the average *pulgogi* house, the food is excellent and the waitresses will bring you endless refills of the side dishes. The tables and chairs are arranged around a picturesque artificial waterfall. To get there, take the subway to Sonnung Station (Line 2) and when you come out of the station head north on the main road opposite (Sonnung-no). The restaurant is on the right hand side a short distance up here.

Lastly, a very mellow place in which to have tea and snacks is the *Kyong-in Mi Sul Kwan* 경인미술관 off Insadonggil and close to the Young Bin Garden Restaurant. This is a combined art gallery and teahouse housed in traditional buildings inside a walled courtyard. It's a very mellow and peaceful place and there can be few like it left in Seoul.

ENTERTAINMENT
Itaewon

Between Namsan Mountain and the River Han is probably the most popular entertainment and shopping area of Seoul – at least for Westerners, Japanese and US army personnel. It's an area of bars, music and dancing clubs (there's no entry fee as a rule), restaurants, brothels, footwear, clothing and furniture shops, etc. Many embassies are also in this area, as well as the Seoul Mosque. The price of a drink in these clubs varies a great deal and depends on the standard of entertainment available. Even at the cheaper clubs you should expect to pay up to W2000 for a beer. Different clubs cater for different expectations and tastes in music. Just wander around and hop into any which take your fancy.

Itaewon is usually thronged with travellers, tourists and American GIs any day of the week and particularly at weekends but the flesh trade has definitely diminished considerably since the advent of AIDS. The disease is nowhere near as widespread in Korea as it is in many other countries but few would want to take the risk. As a result, it's probably true to say that some of the steam has gone out of Itaewon.

Most of the clubs are clustered together up near the far end of Itaewon-ro opposite the Hamilton Hotel but there is one, *All That Jazz*, which is further down towards the Yongsan US Army Base on the northern side of Itaewon-ro. Even if you're not normally a jazz fan this club is excellent, but best on Sunday nights when black American GI's usually jam together. Most of the clubs tend to close around midnight.

To get to Itaewon from the budget hotel area you can take bus No 23 or 72 from outside the Sejong Cultural Centre (fare W130 or W120 if you buy a token beforehand) and get off anywhere on the main street of Itaewon. You can also take bus No 79 which is more frequent and goes over Namsan, or No 710 from in front of the Lotte Department Store which goes through the 3rd Namsan Tunnel. If you take a taxi from the Sejong Cultural Centre it will cost around W1200. There are no convenient subway stations close to Itaewon.

Bars

Seoul is awash with bars of all shapes and sizes though many cater for young couples and small groups of businessmen so they're divided up into curtained cubicles and aren't particularly good places to meet other people. Luckily there are plenty of others which aren't like this and which attract lively crowds. Some of the best are to be found in the alleyways of Mugyo-dong and Ta-dong (between City Hall and the Kwang Pyung Yogwan), and in Insa-dong. Some are piano bars, others attempt to recreate the atmosphere of a German beer hall, while others spill out onto the pavements and are good places for street watching. Wander around and take your pick. At a cheap place you'll be paying around W1200 for a bottle of beer and W1800 at the ritzier places. There is one bar, however, which deserves special mention and that is the *Ju Jom Ji Bul* 주점지불 in Insa-dong at the back of the YMCA. This bar could be straight out of Big Sur on the Californian coast or a transplant from a Cornish fishing village. It's an incredibly ornate, cluttered wooden building which is jam-packed with bric-a-brac and chunky

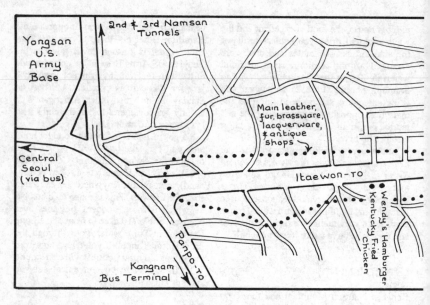

little tables and benches. It's divided into two floors with low ceilings connected by an almost impossibly narrow staircase. Whoever created this gem of pure intimacy must have had an inspired imagination. Despite this, it's actually cheaper than most bars (W1200 for a bottle of beer) and it has an excellent sound system. Go along and see it – it's better than the Folk Museum!

A traveller has recommended the *Banana* disco in Yongdong off the main street to Kangnam. There are nightly traditional dances interspersed with what he described as 'sexy dance shows'. He commented that the place was popular with 'local computer types'.

THINGS TO BUY

Seoul has many colourful markets and these are the place to go for a bargain. They stock everything from fruit and vegetables to clothes and calculator watches, as well as the more traditional handicrafts of Korea.

If you're thinking of stocking up on ginseng whilst in Korea, you're in luck.

Korea has to be the cheapest country in which to purchase this elixir.

Namdaemun (South Gate Market)
남대문시장

This is probably the best of the markets and the one where you're most likely to find bargains. This market spreads over many streets off the south side of Namdaemun-ro which is the road running from the GPO to Namdaemun, one of Seoul's ancient gateways, about halfway between City Hall and Seoul Railway Station.

There's an incredible variety of goods for sale here from bedrolls to turtles, lacquer boxes inlaid with mother-of-pearl to cushion covers, clothes, brassware, ceramics, bambooware and exotic tropical fish. On some side streets there are even shops selling snakes pickled in *soju* – regarded by Korean men as an aphrodisiac – though the government seems to be very sensitive about this and has been pressuring such shops to move to less high-profile areas.

Bargaining is *de rigueur*, of course, and if

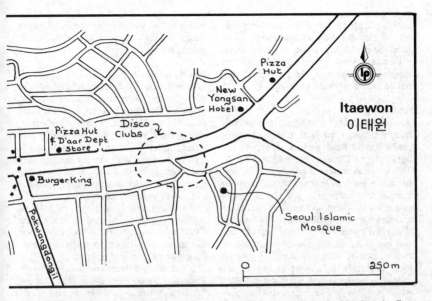

you're in no hurry you should be able to knock up to 20% off the marked prices (though many things have no marked price). I personally felt that the lacquered boxes inlaid with mother-of-pearl and the brocades were some of the best things on offer but there's something for everyone. It's a very lively area and a photographer's paradise.

Namdaemun Market is closed on Sundays.

Tongdaemun (East Gate Market)
동대문시장

Just as well known and even larger than Namdaemun, this market occupies two full city blocks between Chongro and Chonggyechonro and the surrounding streets. It has no less than four storeys and therefore thousands of different shops and stalls. If you can't find what you're looking for here then you probably won't find it elsewhere and, because there are far fewer Westerners here than Namdaemun, prices are lower for items such as craftware. To get here, take the subway to either Tongdaemun or Tongdaemun Stadium.

Tongdaemun Market is closed on the first and third Sundays of each month.

Itaewon

Outside of the city centre, the main shopping area is Itaewon and it's here that many visitors come to make their purchases. Itaewon isn't actually a market as such; it's just a long street full of small shops which spill off into the side streets. You can find most of the things here which are to be found at both Namdaemun and Tongdaemun markets with the added advantage that most of the shop-keepers will speak English (and maybe even French and German).

The only trouble with Itaewon is that the shops are inundated with well-heeled tourists during the summer months (many of the large five-star hotels actually lay on free buses for their guests) and prices naturally reflect what people are willing to pay. Not only that, but many of the things you find in the shops here will have been bought originally from Tongdaemun Market, so it's impossible to get better prices than at Tongdaemun. There are, however, some things which are worth coming for and that includes leather goods, shoes and some articles of clothing. Few shoppers walk away from the the leather boutiques here without a purchase since prices are some of the lowest in the Far East. Have a look around but be prepared for the hard sell!

Insa-dong

Anyone searching for antiques, tasty 'repro', quality ceramics, art of all kinds and handicrafts should head for Insa-dong, on the north side of Chongro behind the YMCA. This area has been well known to travellers for many years as Mary's Alley though no Korean will understand you if that's what you ask for. There are certainly plenty of antiques for sale at galleries in this area but if you don't want a hassle at customs on your way out of Korea and possible confiscation then be careful what you buy. The government prohibits the export of any object judged to have value as a cultural property, which, in general terms, means anything predating 1910. If that's the case you will need an export licence. Vendors can generally help out with paperwork and permits. Genuine antiques are, naturally, very expensive but don't let the fact that this is the best area for antiques put you off wandering around here. There are hundreds of other shops offering inlaid lacquerwork, brassware, sculpture, brushes and inkstones for calligraphy, wood carvings, paintings and quality cabinetwork. In many of the shops you can actually watch the articles being made. The other plus about Insa-dong in comparison with Itaewon is that it's unlikely you'll be subjected to the hard sell. Shop proprietors here are usually very polite and

laid-back but then they're generally selling things of a higher quality than what's available in Itaewon.

Myong-dong

This is the Oxford St of Seoul and right in the heart of the central business district. Many of the shops here are very ritzy and cater for the latest fashions but not exclusively so. It's also peppered with chain stores, coffee shops and restaurants and is always thronged with sharply dressed men and elegantly dressed women, students, and well-heeled tourists who might consider Itaewon to be a little gauche.

It's also a traditional centre of political protest centred on Myong-dong Catholic Cathedral. This is where sit-ins, rallies and spirited speeches take place under the watchful eye of bus-loads of riot police.

It's certainly a lively area and well worth a wander around even if you don't have a fistful of dollars to spend on the latest fashions.

Chongryangri Market

This market is some considerable way from the centre of the city but some travellers have recommended it highly. 'The largest pure local market we saw', was one comment. It's very unlikely you'll see another foreigner here.

GETTING THERE & AWAY
Air

Seoul is the main international arrival point in Korea with flight connections to cities all over the world.

Long-Distance Bus

The main bus terminal in Seoul is the Kangnam (Gangnam) Express Bus Terminal 강남고속터미널 on the south side of the Han River. There is a subway station right at the terminal called 'Express Bus Terminal'. There's everything here you could possibly want – restaurants, snack bars, coffee houses, pharmacies, bookstalls, even

religious newsletter stalls! There is also an advance sales office 예매소 which is open daily from 9 am to 6 pm though it's most unlikely you'll ever have to use this facility – there are plenty of buses to just about everywhere every day. The terminal is very well organised with signs in English and Korean at both the ticket offices and bus bays so you can't go wrong as long as you don't confuse places like Kongju, Kwangju and Kyongju.

In addition to this terminal there are a further six local bus terminals. The most important of these is the Songbong Local Bus Terminal 상봉버스터미널 in the eastern suburbs. This is the terminal for buses to/from Chuncheon. It is connected by bus with Chongnyangni/Mammoth Hotel where you can get the subway into central Seoul. There are buses to Chuncheon from this terminal every 10 minutes daily from 5.15 am to 9.30 pm. The fare is W1540 and the journey takes about two hours.

Another terminal you may find yourself at is the Nambu Local Bus Terminal 남부버스터미널 on the south-west corner of the US Yongsan Army Base, close to the Han River. The nearest subway station is Shinyongsan on Line 4. This is where direct buses from Songni-san National Park often arrive in Seoul (though not always). There are buses to Songni-san 12 times daily from 7.20 am to 6.40 pm. The fare is W3390 and the journey takes 3½ hours.

The other terminals are the Shinchon Local Bus Terminal 신촌버스 터미널, west of the city centre for buses to Kanghwa-do (Shinchon Subway Station, Line 2), Sobu Local Bus Terminal 서부버스 터미널 north-west of the centre (Pulgwang/Yonshinnae Subway Terminal, Line 3), the Tongmajang Local Bus Terminal 동마장버스 터미널, east of the city centre, and the Pukpu Local Bus Terminal 북부버스 터미널, north north-east of the city centre (Miasamgori Subway Station, Line 4).

A selected list of buses from Kangnam Express Bus Terminal follows:

To Chonan There are buses every 15 minutes from 6.30 am to 9 pm. The fare is W1250 and the journey takes one hour.

To Kangnung There are buses every 10 to 20 minutes from 6 am to 7.40 pm. The fare is W3530 and the journey takes about 3¾ hours.

To Kongju There are buses every 40 minutes from 7 am to 7 pm. The fare is W2240 and the journey takes 2½ hours.

To Kwangju There are buses every five to 10 minutes from 5.30 am to 8 pm. The fare is W4530 and the journey takes about four hours.

To Kyongju There are buses every 35 minutes from 7 am to 6.10 pm. The fare is W5090 and the journey takes 4¼ hours.

To Mogpo There are buses every 30 minutes from 6 am to 6.30 pm. The fare is W5520 and the journey takes nearly five hours.

To Nonsan There are buses about every hour from 6.30 am to 7.50 pm. The fare is W2990 and the journey takes 2¾ hours.

To Pusan There are buses every five or 10 minutes from 6 am to 6.40 pm. The fare is W5970 and the journey takes 5½ hours.

To Sogcho There are buses every 40 minutes or so from 6.30 am to 6.40 pm. The fare is W4460 and the journey takes 5¼ hours.

To Taejon There are buses every five to 10 minutes from 6 am to 7.40 pm. The fare is W2240 and the journey takes two hours.

To Taegu There are buses every five to 10 minutes from 6 am to 8 pm. The fare is W4220 and the journey takes four hours.

Train
Korea has an efficient, comfortable rail system that connects all the major cities with

Seoul. For full information on connections and timetables see the Getting Around chapter.

GETTING AROUND
Airport Transport
Most travellers arrive in Seoul via Kimpo International Airport which is a considerable distance west of the city. Two airport shuttle buses connect Kimpo with the city centre. Bus No 601 links Kimpo with the Sheraton Walker Hotel via the Seoul Garden Hotel, Koreana Hotel, Plaza Hotel, Korean Air City Terminal, Tokyu Hotel, Hyatt Hotel, and the Silla Hotel among others and is the one to take if you're heading for the budget hotel area.

The other, bus No 600, connects Kimpo with Chamshil via the Palace Hotel, Kangnam Express Bus Terminal, Riverside Hotel, Nam Seoul Hotel, Korea Exhibition Center and the Olympic Sports Complex. Both buses run every 10 minutes from 5.30 am to 9.30 pm (from the city to the airport they run from 6 am to 8.10 pm). The fare is W500 and the journey takes about half an hour.

A taxi will cost about W4500. If you don't mind taking somewhat slower local buses then catch No 41 (fare W130) or a *chaesok* bus No 63 or 68 (fare W350).

City Bus
There are city buses to the furthest corners of Seoul but, unfortunately, no routing guides or timetables are available. That's usually no problem since there are so many of them and, as far as travellers are concerned, only a few of them are of interest. Most of the areas of interest are more easily reached by subway. Itaewon is an exception.

There are two types of city buses – ordinary buses which take both sitting and standing passengers (and which get incredibly crowded around rush hours) and *chaesok* buses which are much the same except that you are guaranteed a seat – no standing passengers. Ordinary buses cost W130 (right change please!) or W120 with a token (same word in Korean) bought from a bus token booth of which there is usually one at most busy bus stops. Tokens are put into a machine as you board the bus.

Minibuses cost more and the fare depends on the distance you travel.

Subway
The Seoul subway is one of the most modern, fast, comfortable and cheap systems in the world. It's an excellent method of getting from one place to another. A vast amount of construction work went on for years during the 1980s during which many of Seoul's main boulevards were transformed into cavernous pits but that has all gone now with the completion of the system. The length of the entire system is about 116 km – the world's 7th longest.

There are four lines in total, all of them colour coded. The lines not only connect with each other (via transfer stations) but also with the national rail network. You can get to all of the bus terminals using the subway except for Songbong Local Bus Terminal out in the north-eastern suburbs. Fares are based on the distance travelled – W200 for Zone 1 and W300 for Zone 2. Tickets are bought at either ticket windows or from vending machines (correct change). Subway trains have their destination in Korean and English on the front of the engines and all stations have their name in the same two languages at frequent intervals along the platforms so you can't get lost. In addition, each station has a number. As with other subways around the world, the line is only underground in the city centre.

The only confusing thing for foreigners as far as the subway goes is that in the city centre many of the underground entry/exit halls double as shopping arcades and it can be difficult to select the right exit. You'll just have to wear this one and, if you find yourself on the wrong side of the road when you emerge, then it's back down into the hall and take a different exit!

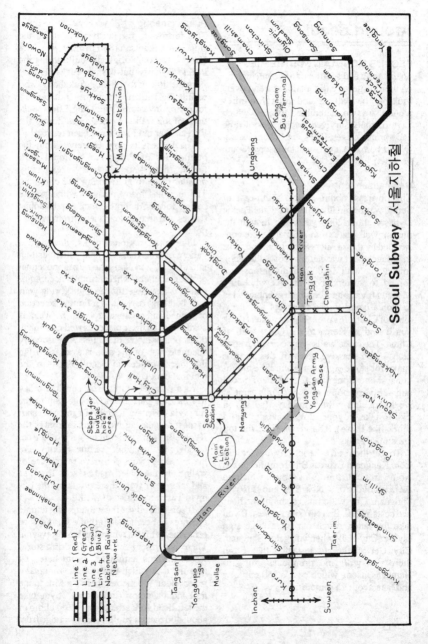

Seoul Subway 서울지하철

Around Seoul

SEOUL'S MOUNTAIN FORTRESSES

To the north and south-east of Seoul, high up on their respective mountain tops and over-looking the valleys and hills for miles around, are two incredible fortresses which have partially survived the ravages of time and various sieges. They are Pukansansong (North Fortress) and Namhansansong (South Fortress).

Namhansansong 남한산성

This fortress, about 30 km south-east of Seoul, was originally built during the Paekje Dynasty about 2000 years ago though the present walls date from 1626 and were constructed by the Yi rulers as protection against the Manchus. It was here, in 1637, that King Injo along with 14,000 of his troops was forced to surrender to an overwhelming Manchu invasion force which eventually led to Korea being forced to accept the suzerainty of China. It's probably the nearest thing you'll find in Korea to the Great Wall of China. The stone walls – up to seven metres high – and massive gates of this fortress snake for some eight km around the mountains above Songnam City east of Seoul and are very popular as a picnic spot at weekends and public holidays (so if you like to take in your ruins in peace, avoid times like these). The views from the top are stupendous.

To get there take Seoul city bus No 36 from Kangnam Express Bus Terminal or bus No 66 from Ulchiro 5-ka (others which go there include bus Nos 239 and 570) to Songnam City which takes about one hour and costs W210. Bus No 66 is the best. If you take the latter, watch out for a large sign saying 'City Hall' when you get to Songnam City. Get off the bus just after that. From there you will find minibuses going to Namhansansong which cost W350 one way and take about 15 minutes.

Pukansansong 북한산성

This fortress to the north of Seoul on the slopes of Pukan-san (836 metres), was, like Namhansansong, originally built during the Paekje Dynasty but the present walls date from the time of the Yi king, Sukchong, who rebuilt the battlements in the 16th century following invasions from Qing China. Sections of the wall were destroyed during the Korean War but have since been restored.

The fortress is now entirely within the boundaries of Pukansan National Park (about 78 sq km) which is an extremely popular place to go trekking and climbing. The area has many massive white granite peaks, forests, temples, rock-cut Buddhist statues and tremendous views from various points.

Like other national parks, there are a variety of well-marked trails which lead up into the park and along the ridges and a total of four shelters where simple accommodation is available for the night (bring your own bedding) as well as a limited selection of canned and packaged foodstuffs. Water is available at all these places as well as at many other points along the trails. A reasonably adequate map of the area is available from the tourist offices in Seoul. Entry to the national park costs W400.

As a sampler to this area, consider a day trip into the park from Uijongbu up to the ridge via Toson-sa Temple. To get to the start of the trail, take bus No 6 from in front of the Kyobo Building in Seoul or bus No 23 from Chongro to the end of the line. From where the bus drops you, you have the choice of walking up the sealed road as far as Toson-sa and taking off from there or taking the bus up to Toson-sa initially (W100).

Toson-sa isn't the most interesting temple in Korea but perhaps worth the short detour off to the left from where the bus drops you. There is a restaurant and cold drink stores where the bus terminates. From here you take the trail which leads up the mountain. After about 300 metres there's a fork in the trail and a signpost (in Korean). If you take the left-hand fork after a very steep climb of about 400 metres you'll come to a ridge from which there are superb views of Seoul all the way down to the Han River. At the back of this ridge is the spectacular granite peak of Insubong.

THE YI DYNASTY ROYAL TOMBS

Of the 115 Yi Dynasty tombs (105 of them in South Korea and the rest in North Korea), most are within easy reach of the centre of Seoul. All of these consist of the traditional earthen burial mound (similar to those of the Silla kings in Kyongju) but most of them are guarded by beautifully carved granite sentries and real or mythical animals. The similarities with the Ming tombs outside of Beijing are unmistakable though here they are on a somewhat smaller scale. All the Yi kings have been buried at one or other of these sites from the first, King Taejo in 1408, to the last crown prince, Yongchinwang, in 1970.

The five most interesting sites are Taenung 태능 , Tonggu-nung 동구능 , Kumgok-nung 금곡능 and Kwang-nung 광능 east and north-east of Seoul and Honin-nung 허니능 south of Seoul. Tae-nung and Honin-nung are perhaps the most well known and the easiest to get to though Tonggu-nung is the largest site with nine tombs in all, including that of Taejo and Honjong (the last Yi Dynasty king). All the tombs are open to the public between 9 am and 6.30 pm. Entry costs W340 (W170 for children).

Some of the burial sites may be closed to the public from time to time (to allow archaeological excavations, for instance) so it might be a good idea to check with the tourist office in Seoul before you set off.

Getting There & Away

The national tourist organisation, USO and other private touring companies generally offer organised trips to one or other of these burial sites but you can also get there individually by local buses.

The following local buses will take you to the various sites:

To Tae-nung: bus No 10 or 215 from Tongdaemun or No 45 from Seoul Railway Station.

Kumgok-nung: bus No 165 or 765 from Chongryangri.

Tonggun-nung: bus No 55 from Chongryangri or No 755 from Seoul Railway Station.

Kwang-nung: bus No 7 from Chongryangri or No 21 from Uijongbu.

Honin-nung: bus No 36 from in front of Kangnam Express Bus Terminal.

Traditional Tomb Site Guard

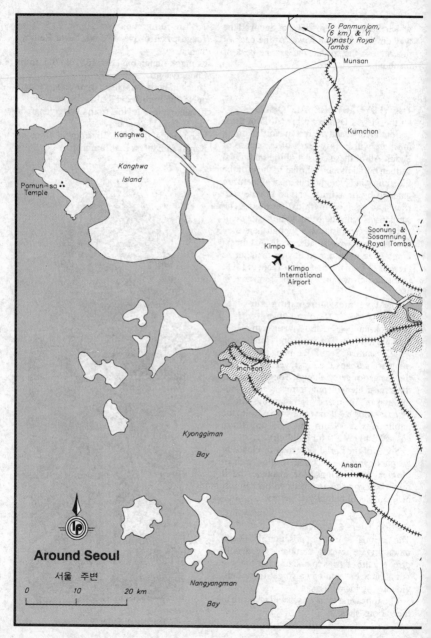

To Panmunjom,
(6 km) & Yi
Dynasty Royal
Tombs

Munsan

Kanghwa

Kumchon

Kanghwa
Island

Pomun-sa
Temple

Soonung &
Sosamnung
Royal Tombs

Kimpo

Kimpo
International
Airport

Incheon

Kyonggiman
Bay

Ansan

Around Seoul

서울 주변

0   10   20 km

Nangyangman

Bay

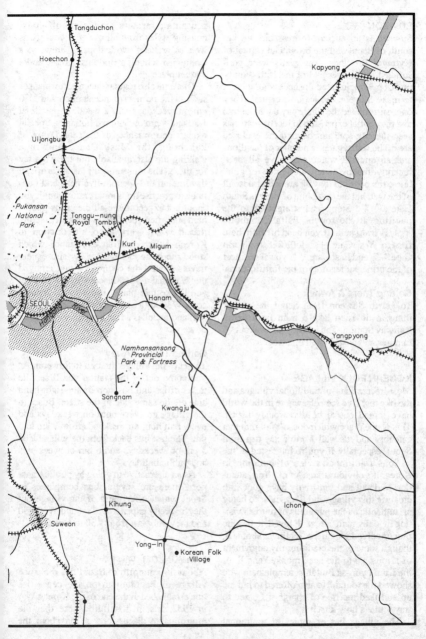

SUWEON 수원

Suweon is an ancient fortress city 48 km south of Seoul and the provincial capital of Kyonggi Province. The walls were constructed in the later part of the 18th century by King Kongjo in an unsuccessful attempt to make Suweon the nation's capital. They once surrounded the whole city but industrial and residential expansion in recent years has seen the city spill out beyond the enclosed area. The walls, gates, a number of pavilions and an unusual water gate have all been recently reconstructed along the original lines. It's possible to walk around almost all of the wall but the best point of entry is South Gate 남문 . Steps lead straight up to the pavilion at the top of Paltal Mountain 팔달산 from here. If you head off from here first to West Gate 서문 followed by North Gate 북문 and East Gate 동문 you'll see most of the principal features of the fortifications.

Getting There & Away

To get to Suweon from Seoul the easiest thing to do is to take a train from Seoul Railway Station. The journey takes about 45 minutes and costs W360 one way.

KOREAN FOLK VILLAGE

Most 'recreations' of traditional villages and the like that I've seen elsewhere in the world have turned out to be disastrously kitsch. This is one place which doesn't fall into that category and it's well worth a day trip from Seoul, especially if you're interested in the various traditional styles of building in Korea. It's obvious that a lot of effort, attention to detail and sensitivity have gone into creating this village and it's as near to being as authentic as the hundreds of tourists visiting it daily will allow. I loved it despite preconceived negative feelings about it, though some of the credit for my enjoyment of it must go to the head monk, Yang Il, of the Kum Lyun-sa Buddhist temple here who showed me round. He also offered to put me up and feed me free of charge if I cared to stay – that's how kitsch it is.

The village has examples of traditional peasants', farmers' and civil officials' housing styles from all over the country as well as artisans' workshops, a brewery, a Confucian school, a Buddhist temple and a market place.

There are also regular dance performances such as the farmers' dance at noon and 3.30 pm on weekdays and a wedding parade at 1.30 and 4 pm on national holidays. Special request performances of the Lion Dance of Pukchong, the Mask Dance and rope walking are also available but there's a fee for these. The museum isn't just an artificial daytime affair – people live here and continue to practise traditional crafts though you shouldn't expect to see all the crafts-people hard at it when you visit. I went away feeling that it was a very good introduction to Korean culture and an experience which stood me in good stead for my subsequent travels around the country. If you enjoyed the National Folk Museum in Seoul then you'll like this place. Entry to the village costs W3000 (less for those under 24 years old) and includes a free bus ride to and from Suweon.

Getting There & Away

To get to the village, first go to Suweon. As you come out of the station you'll see the ticket office and bus stop on the right-hand side on the same side of the street. Buses to the village go every hour on weekdays and every half hour on weekends from 9 am to 5 pm. The last bus back from the village is at 5 pm on weekdays and 6 pm on weekends and public holidays.

As an alternative to going by public transport, there are several bus companies in Seoul which offer tours of the village but they're pretty expensive at around W30,000 and they only last from 1.30 to 6 pm.

PANMUNJOM 판문점

About 56 km north of Seoul lies the truce village of Panmunjom on the cease-fire line established at the end of the Korean War in 1953. It's in a building here that the interminable discussions go on about the

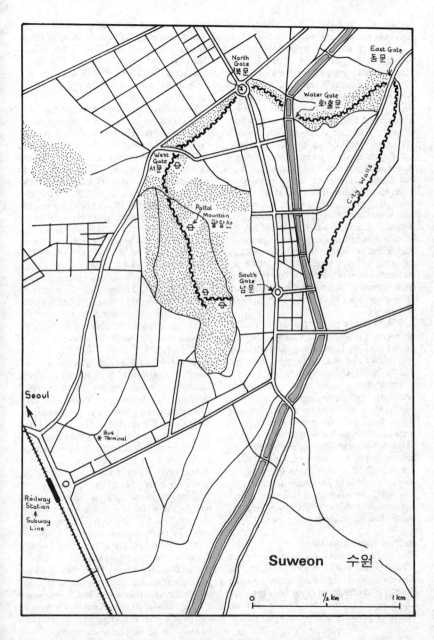

North Gate 북문

East Gate 동문

Water Gate 화홍문

West Gate 서문

Paltal Mountain 팔달산

City Walls

South Gate 남문

Seoul

Bus Terminal

Railway Station

Subway Line

Suweon 수원

0 ½ km 1 km

reunification of Korea and the violations of the cease-fire agreements.

There's nowhere else in South Korea where you can get quite so close to North Korea without being arrested or shot and the tension is palpable. It was here in 1976 that two American servicemen were hacked to death with axes by the North Koreans. It was also through here in mid-1989 that Lim Soo-kyong, a Seoul university student, and the Reverend Moon Gyu-hyon, a Catholic priest, were finally allowed to return to South Korea after protracted negotiations following Lim's visit to the Youth Festival in Pyongyang earlier in the year. Both were promptly arrested, whisked off to Seoul by helicopter and charged with violating the national security laws. Lim, a radical fervently committed to the reunification of Korea, had previously attempted to make the crossing several weeks before with the encouragement of the North Korean authorities but had been refused. The event made front-page news at the time both in Korea and elsewhere.

It's perhaps overrated as a 'tourist attraction' but that doesn't seem to stop the hordes flocking here to gawp at a continuation of the same geography, the propaganda and the North Korean soldiers.

There are a number of government-enforced regulations regarding a visit to Panmunjom and there's no way around them. First and foremost, you must be respectably dressed – definitely no T-shirts, singlets, blue jeans or running shoes. Long hair on men is not permitted. No-one under the age of 10 is allowed to go there and you're supposedly prohibited from making any gesture whatsoever to the North Koreans. If you can't meet these requirements then forget about going there.

Getting There & Away

The cheapest tours to Panmunjom are offered by the USO (tel 795 3028), the US Army's cultural and social centre opposite Gate 21 of the Yongsan Army Base in Seoul. They have one tour weekly, usually on Friday or Saturday, and it costs just US$10

but doesn't include lunch or a visit to the 'Third Tunnel of Aggression' (one of three tunnels dug under the DMZ by the North Koreans, all of which were large enough to take tanks). This tour is very heavily subscribed and you have to book weeks in advance.

Various other commercial enterprises offer similar tours but they're considerably more expensive. The best of them is probably that run by the Korea Travel Bureau (tel 585 1191) which takes you to all the areas of interest including the 'Third Tunnel of Aggression'. They go daily except Saturday and Sunday and the cost is W26,000 including lunch. The tour takes seven hours and you must have your passport with you. Departure is from the Lotte Hotel on Ulchiro. Bookings can be made through the tourist offices in Seoul but you need to book well in advance as the tours are heavily subscribed.

If you go through any other tour company then make sure that they are going to take you all the way to Panmunjom and not just to the Military Checkpoint on the southern side of the Imjin River. This can cost almost the same but it's essentially a rip-off.

KANGHWA ISLAND 강화도

Kanghwa Island, west of Seoul and north of Incheon, is where the Koryo court took refuge during the Mongol invasions of the 13th century and where the Koreans resisted American and French troops in the late 19th century. It is also where the second set of the 80,000 woodblocks of the Tripitaka Koreana were carved in the 14th century – later moved to Haein-sa Temple outside Taegu during the early years of the Yi Dynasty.

Being an island fortress, Kanghwa has seen its fair share of fortifications, palaces and the like but, although it occupies an important place in Korean history, it's overrated as a tourist attraction. The tourist literature and some guide books to Korea rave on about Kanghwa's 'attractions' giving you the impression that the island is littered with fascinating ruins and relics. To a degree it is, but they're so spread out that it would take days to see them, using local buses, and it's questionable whether they're worth the effort. One of the few redeeming features of a trip here is the temple of Pomun-sa but this is actually on a smaller island off the west coast of Kanghwa.

Kanghwa City

Despite all the hype, this city is a profound disappointment. True, the city gates still stand but the enclosing wall has disappeared. Likewise, the site of the Koryo court has a couple of traditional buildings of slight interest but that's all and you'll have to pay W330 to see it. If your time is limited you can skip all this and miss nothing.

Pomun-sa Temple 보문사

This important temple sits high up in the mountains on the island of Songmo-do off the western coast of Kanghwa. The compound is relatively small but there is some superb and very ornate painting on the eaves of the various buildings and especially those of the bell pavilion. The famous grotto here is quite plain and uninteresting though it is cool in there on a hot summer's day. One of the most interesting sights here is the 10-metre-high rock carving of Kwanseum Posal, the Goddess of Mercy, which stands below a granite overhang high above the temple compound. The carving was completed about 60 years ago and is quite unlike statues of the goddess to be seen elsewhere in Korea.

It's a steep walk up to the temple from where the bus drops you and there's a small tourist village with souvenir shops and restaurants at the bottom of the hill.

Getting There & Away

Buses to Kanghwa leave from the Shinchon Local Bus Terminal 신촌버스터미널 in the western part of Seoul. Take Line No 2 on the subway to Shinchon Station and ask directions from there. It's a five-minute walk.

Buses leave every 10 minutes from 5.40 am to 9.30 pm, take one hour and cost W1000. The

buses drop you at Kanghwa City Bus Station. All buses have to stop at the bridge which connects Kanghwa with the mainland for an army check.

To get to Pomun-sa from Kanghwa, take a bus from the same bus station to Oe-po-ri 외포리 . These are frequent, take 25 minutes and cost W260. The bus will drop you in front of the main ferry terminal but this caters only for long-distance ferries and is not the one you want. Walk through to the front of the terminal, turn right and continue down the waterfront for about 100 metres. You'll see a concrete ramp going down to the water and another ferry terminal on the right. From here ferries run daily to Sok-po-ri on Songmo-do approximately every hour from 8 am to 6.30 pm (8 am to 7 pm during the summer months) and they take both people and vehicles. It costs W200 and takes 10 to 15 minutes to cross the straits. Before buying a ticket you have to fill in a form (available in the ticket hall) stating your name, address and passport number (Kanghwa is very close to North Korea). The form is collected before you board the ferry.

On the opposite side there are buses to Pomun-sa which cost W300 and take about half an hour.

SOYO-SAN 소요산

This is another pleasant day-trip which one traveller suggested. Soyo-san is north of Seoul near Tongduchon 동두촌 . There are hiking trails, picnic spots, a Buddhist temple, camp site and an attractive mountain stream. To get there, take the subway to Chongryangri and then a train from there to Soyo-san (W360). The train takes about 40 minutes and runs on an hourly schedule. When you get off the train turn right and then follow the signs on the left. Entry to Soyo-san costs W600 (W350 for student card holders). It's two km from the station and a further two km to the temple – more walking if you want to visit the hermitages or climb to the peak of the mountain.

North-East Korea

Chuncheon 춘천

Chuncheon is the provincial capital of Kangwon-do Province and the urban centre of Korea's northern lake district, which includes lakes Soyang and Paro. It's a very beautiful mountainous area and popular with weekenders from Seoul. The principal attractions here are, of course, boat trips on the lakes. The town itself is fairly pleasant and is a major educational centre as well as host to a huge American military base – Camp Page – which takes up a good quarter of the town.

It's unlikely you'd come to Chuncheon just for the sake of the city itself, but it makes a good stopover en route to Sorak-san National Park if you'd prefer the bus and boat combination rather than taking a bus all the way. The express buses from Seoul to Sorak-san do not take the scenic route through the park from Inje to Yang-yang. Instead, they use the Seoul to Kangnung (Yongdong) Expressway.

You may well come across a lot of South Korean army activity outside of Chuncheon. The area is, after all, quite close to the border with North Korea.

CHUNCHEON LAKE

For some rest and relaxation you could do worse than spend a lazy afternoon rowing around Chuncheon Lake. Boats can be hired down by Ethiopia House which is under the railway bridge from the bus terminal. They cost W2000 to W3000 per hour. Bear in mind, however, that this lake can stink at certain times of year. It seems a lot of rubbish finds its way into the lake.

KUGOK POKPO (KUGOK WATERFALL) 구곡폭포

This is also a popular place to visit from Chuncheon. The waterfall is about 20 km south-west of the city, and though it's at its best during and just after the monsoon, it's worth visiting at any time of year. Entry costs W300. There are cafes and snack bars at the waterfall.

The best way to get there is to take the *chaesok* bus No 50 from the bus stop on the main street near the post office. They go every 40 minutes from 6.45 am to 6.15 pm and take about 20 minutes. The fare is W300. The last bus back from the waterfall is at 6.50 pm. After that you will have to take a taxi. The waterfall is the last stop for the No 50 bus so you can't go wrong. From where it drops you, it's a 10 to 15-minute walk to the waterfall.

West of Chuncheon on the other side of the lake is another waterfall – Tungson Pokpo 등선폭포 – which is said to be even more beautiful.

MT SAMAK

For a panoramic view of Chuncheon and the lake, you can make the steep climb up Samak Mountain. Take bus No 81 from near Ethiopia House in the direction of Seoul. After 15 minutes the bus crosses a bridge and turns right – the entrance to Samak is 50 metres down the road. It's a steep climb up past a small temple but well worth it for the views. Down the other side you pass another temple and enter a beautiful narrow gorge. Follow it down to the road and catch a local bus (any will do) back upstream to Chuncheon.

If you stay on the No 81 bus past Samak and get off at the last stop you'll find the huge grave site of General Shin off to the right. About a thousand years ago, this general disguised himself as the king and as a consequence was killed by the enemy. The king had the tomb built out of gratitude for this act of sacrifice and loyalty.

TEMPLES

If you take the road north from Camp Page, cross the bridge and continue on along the

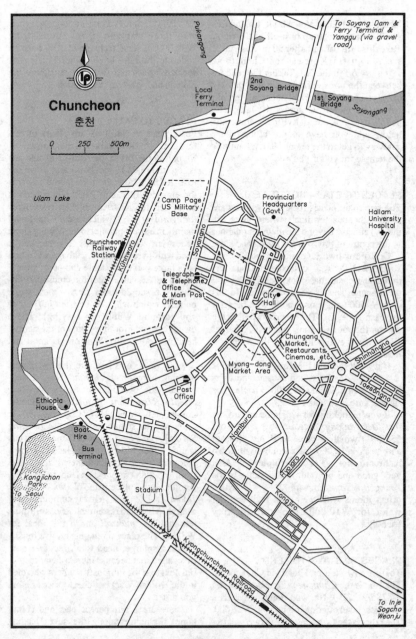

lakeside road then after about 150 metres you'll come to a sharp turn-off to the right. Take this turn off and after 50 metres you'll see a sign (in Korean) for Chongto-sa 경주여인숙 off to the left. Taking the road up between the houses from here will quickly bring you to this delightful but small temple with good views out across the lake. The people who look after it live in the house just below and you have to go through their gateway to get to the temple. They'll unlock the temple for you if you ask.

PLACES TO STAY – BOTTOM END

The two main places for cheap *yogwan* are around the bus terminal (where there are plenty) and just beyond the main roundabout in the centre of town on the right hand side.

One of my own favourites is the *Kyongju Yoinsook* 경주여인숙 opposite the bus terminal. It's clean, has cooking facilities and the manager speaks good Japanese. Rooms cost W4500 (single or double) with fans – if there isn't one, ask. The best room here is the one on the roof – a most unusual A-frame! Hot water is available only in the winter on request.

If it's full then try the *Kangnam Yoinsook* 강남여인숙 nearby which is basic and costs W4500 a double and W5400 a triple. The showers are cold water only.

If you're looking for a higher standard, try the *Taekwanjang Yogwan* 대광장여관 (tel 53-7891) which is clean and very pleasant and costs W10,000 for a double with own bathroom, hot water and colour TV. Also very good and pleasant in this range is the *Young Bin Jang Yogwan* 영빈장여관 which offers rooms with their own bath and hot water for W10,000. The staff are very friendly.

PLACES TO STAY – TOP END

There are two top-end hotels in Chuncheon. The first is the *Chuncheon Tourist Hotel* (tel 3-8285/9), 30-1 Nagwon-dong, which is a three-star hotel offering rooms from W31,000. The other is the *Chuncheon Sejong Hotel* (tel 52-1191/5), San 1, Pong-ui-dong, which is also three-star and offers rooms from W32,000. A service charge of 10% must be added to the rates at either hotel. The staff speak English and Japanese and there are Korean and Western restaurants.

PLACES TO EAT

For a place to eat, there are plenty of restaurants in the market area known as Myong-dong (off to the right-hand side just before the main roundabout) and down the road leading from the roundabout towards the entrance of Camp Page. Chuncheon is renowned for its fried chicken restaurants (*daggalbi* 닭갈비) which are to be found mainly in a street parallel to the Myong-dong pedestrian zone going east. The chicken is fried with sweet potatoes, cabbage and onion on a large pan at the table and costs around W800 per serving. After the chicken is finished you should order *sarri* – thick white noodles which will also be fried in front of you (around W300 per serving). These dishes are great for those tired of the normal healthy Korean diet. This one is good and greasy!

Also very good here are the restaurants offering home-made *mandu*. They're supposedly the best in Korea. Try the *King Mandu Restaurant* opposite the cinema immediately to the east of City Hall.

In the bus station area, try the *Jungang Shiktang* 중앙식당 right in front of the bus station which is a fairly big place offering a whole range of Korean dishes. Prices range from W1200 (for *pekpan*) up to W3000. Another good place is the *Noolbom Minsok Jujom* 늘봄민속주점 , a lively combination of a *makkoli* hall and restaurant. Prices are quite reasonable – *makkoli* and a full meal for W3000. The place often puts on live music.

For a splurge, head for *Ethiopia House* (it's called that because there's a war memorial next to it for Ethiopian soldiers who died in the Korean War) but check prices before you order.

There are a number of bars and (fairly tame) nightclubs along the street leading

Top left: Wolchong-sa temple, Odae-san (CHP)
Top right: The fish market, Jinbu, Odae-san (CHP)
Bottom left: Pavilion overlooking the East Sea, Naksan-sa temple, NE coast (CHP)
Bottom right: Entrance to Naksan-sa temple, NE coast (GC)

Top: Sorak-san National Park (GC)
Left: Sorak-san National Park (CHP)
Right: The Unjin Miruk stone Buddha at Kwanchuk-sa temple, near Nonsan (GC)

down to the main entrance of Camp Page if you're in search of a place to drink a few beers in the evening. They're largely patronised by personnel from the US base.

GETTING THERE & AWAY
Bus
There's only one bus terminal at Chuncheon for both express and *chikheng* buses.

To Kangnung Buses every hour from 6.40 am to 6.20 pm. The fare is W3300 and the journey takes just over four hours.

To Seoul There are buses every 10 minutes from 5.15 am to 9.30 pm. The fare is W1540 and the journey takes just less than two hours. These buses terminate at Sangbong Bus Terminal in Seoul which is near Chongryang-ri.

To Sogcho There are buses every hour from 6 am to 5.45 pm. The fare is W3250 and the journey takes four hours. The buses go via Inje 인제 , Wontong 원통 (a few km past Inje) and then take the Hangye-ryong road 한계령 which passes through the southern part of Sorak-san National Park. It's a very spectacular and beautiful road.

There are other buses from Chuncheon to Cheongju 청주 and Weonju 원주 among other places.

If you have your own transport and you're heading from Chuncheon to Sorak-san National Park, you have a choice of two routes both of which pass through Inje. The south-eastern route via Hongchon is paved all the way. The north-eastern route via Yanggu is a gravel road for most of its course and it's very winding.

Ferry
East and north-east of Chuncheon are the two huge artificial lakes of Soyang and Paro. Lake Soyang is a favourite recreation area for local people as well as tourists from elsewhere and along it there are ferries to Shinnam (throughout the year) and to Inje (when the level of water in the lake allows). The level of water in Lake Soyang is lowered before the monsoons to accommodate the extra water which will flow into it, so for part of the year the ferries only run from Chuncheon to Shinnam. The boat-bus combination from Chuncheon to Inje and the east coast via Shinnam is a popular way of travelling this part of Korea.

It's also possible to take these ferries if you're heading for Yanggu but they will drop you at the Yanggu wharf and from there you must take a bus the remaining 13 km into Yanggu.

Ferries leave from Lake Soyang dam wall and to get there from Chuncheon you must take bus No 11 or 12 from the city centre (it's much too far to walk). The buses will drop you at the top of the dam wall and from there it's a short walk down to the ferry piers. Only buses are allowed up to the top of the dam wall, so if you have your own transport you have to leave it in the car park at the checkpoint and take a bus from there (W100 each way).

There are also speed boats for hire at the dam wall to take you to Chongpyong-sa 청평사, a Buddhist temple up in the hills north of the lake. These are six-seaters and cost W10,000 (shared by the number of people in the boat). From where the boat drops you it's a four km hike to the temple, so make sure you're wearing suitable footwear.

To Yanggu There are slow ferries to Yanggu wharf at 9 and 11 am and 4 pm in the low season and every hour from 8 am to 6 pm in the high season. In the opposite direction, they leave Yanggu wharf at 10.20 am, 12.20 and 5.20 pm in the low season and every hour from 8 am to 6.20 pm in the high season. The fare is W1500 (W750 for children).

There are also fast boats to Yanggu wharf which leave at 9 and 11 am, 1 and 4 pm. In the opposite direction they leave at 10.20 am, 12.20, 2.20 and 5.20 pm. The fare is W2310 (W1210 for children).

To Shinnam Ferries to Shinnam leave at 11 am, 1 and 3 pm and return from Shinnam at 1.20, 2.30 and 4.30 pm. The fare is W4670 (half price for children).

Sorak-san (Seolag) National Park
설악산국립공원

This is one of the most beautiful areas in Korea with high craggy peaks, pine and mixed hardwood forests, tremendous waterfalls, boulder-strewn rivers with crystal-clear water, old temples and hermitages whose roots go back to the Silla era. It's at its best from mid to late autumn, when the leaves begin to change hue and the mountainsides are transformed into a riot of colour, but worth a visit at any time of the year. Nearby, on the coast, are some of Korea's most popular beaches.

Sorak-san is the most popular of the two parks and an excellent place to go walking for a few days or even longer if you have camping equipment with you. Pick up a good map of the area in Seoul from Jung-Ang Map & Chart Service, the Kyobo Book Center or the Chongno Book Center (see Seoul chapter for details) before you come here. The most useful is the *Tourist Map of the East Coast*. Though most of the trails are well marked you'll need a map if you intend to head out into the real wilderness beyond the more popular tourist areas. And head out there you'll have to, if you want to avoid the hordes.

Outer Sorak and particularly the area around Sorak-dong 설악동, the sprawling tourist village at the end of the road into Outer Sorak, is extremely popular throughout the summer and autumn. Two hundred bus loads of holiday-makers (not to mention thousands of private cars) on any one day is not unusual and you will literally have to queue to get on the various trails leading to the waterfalls and peaks. If you prefer to take in nature in more tranquil conditions then

you have little choice but to head into Inner Sorak 내설악. For some idea of what to expect during the holiday season, the newspapers reported over one million tourists visiting the Sorak-san/Sogcho area during one weekend in July 1989. Traffic jams along the coast road and at Sorak-dong and buses packed like sardine cans are all part of this massive annual influx.

The other drawback to visiting Sorak-san during the peak season (July to mid-August) is that the cost of accommodation skyrockets and you'll find yourself having to pay up to three times the normal rates. Even a simple room in a *minbak* will cost you W15,000 to W18,000. Officially this is illegal since room rates are government-controlled, but it happens every year. Only in Sogcho will you be able to find a room at the normal price and even then only at a few places.

Entry to Sorak-san National Park costs W1200 (less for students and anyone under 24 years old).

KWONGKUMSONG 권금성
Almost everyone takes the 1100-metre cable car to Kwongkumsong. It's good value at W1000 one way and W1900 return and you'll be rewarded with absolutely spectacular views. Cars go every 20 to 30 minutes. From where the cable car drops you, it's a 10-minute walk to the summit of the mountain. Unless the weather is clear, expect mist to shroud the summit for much of the day. This cable car gives immediate access to the trails which lead to Inner Sorak though you can of course walk up there if you prefer.

HUNDULBAWI ROCK 흔들바위
This famous rock is another spot which everyone seems to visit. It is right next to Sinhung-sa Temple 신흥사. You'll see photographs of this huge rock in just about all the tourist literature for this region. It's famous because it can be rocked to and fro by just one person. In fact, I'm surprised it hasn't been completely rocked off its base by now since half the population of Korea must have had a go! There can't be a single family in the whole of Korea that has visited this place

and not had their photograph taken pushing this rock. The adjacent temple was first constructed in 653 but later burnt to the ground and was only rebuilt in 1645.

The climb up to the rock from Sorak-dong takes 45 to 60 minutes.

YUGDAM, BIRYONG & TOWANGSONG WATERFALLS

Another short trip in the immediate vicinity is to the waterfalls. These are all along the same trail and the Towangsong falls are particularly spectacular. The trail is well marked and involves crossing many suspension bridges and climbing flights of steel stairs. There are various soft drink and snack stalls along the way. The most convenient entrance to this trail is across the bridge which spans the river a few hundred metres before you get to the cable car station.

TREKS

There's no point in describing all the various treks which are possible into Inner Sorak but the accompanying map should give you a good idea of the scope. Since we are limited to black and white, you shouldn't take the map as anything other than a rough guide though it was based on the *Tourist Map of the East Coast*. There are a total of seven shelters at various points along the hiking trails where you can stay overnight but only two of them are open year-round. The others are open during the fine weather months. Accommodation is on bare boards at W1000 per night and you must have your own sleeping bag and do your own cooking. A limited range of canned, bottled and packeted goods are for sale but at higher than normal prices. Plenty of water is available at all the huts – either pump-fed or spring-fed. The shelters are marked on the tourist maps of the area.

Campers can erect tents wherever they like but should dispose of litter sensibly. Garbage is rapidly becoming a major problem in the national parks.

PLACES TO STAY – BOTTOM END

Most budget travellers stay in a *minbak* and there are plenty of these. You won't have any problem finding one as most of the buses into Sorak-dong are met by a gaggle of *ajimahs* offering rooms at their houses. Most of these are very clean and pleasant and some even provide cooking facilities. Expect to pay around W5000 per room on average out of season but three times that amount during July/August. If you're not met at the bus, just look for the signs which are everywhere.

A cheap alternative to a *minbak* is to stay at the *Sorak Youth Hostel* 설악유스호스텔 (tel (0392) 7-7540/50), 155 Tomun-dong, about half way between Sorak-dong and the coast road. It has 73 bunk beds (eight beds to a room) which cost W5000 minus 10% for holders of youth hostel membership cards. As at other youth hostels, there are also much more expensive single and double rooms. The staff speak English and Japanese and there are Korean and Western restaurants with average meal prices of W1600 to W8000 depending on what you eat and which meal of the day it is. Don't expect to find accommodation here without prior booking during July/August. The only disadvantage of staying at this youth hostel is that it is about 4½ km from the park entrance so you'll have to catch a bus into Sorak-dong (W120).

For those with camping equipment, there's a huge camp site on the opposite side of the river beyond the Youth Hostel. It has good facilities and costs W1000 per site but, in the high season, it's like a rock festival site with not much more than a metre between tents.

Instead of staying at Sorak-dong you can use the Youth Hotel or beach houses at Naksan 낙산 nearby on the coast, or a *yogwan* or *yoinsook* in Sogcho. Frequent local buses connect Naksan and Sogcho with Sorak-dong.

PLACES TO STAY – MIDDLE

There's plenty of mid-range accommodation in Sorak-dong because of the large number of visitors, but it's a hotelier's market so prices are high. Expect to pay W15,000 minimum in the low season though possibly less if you can find an empty hotel among the scores available and haggle them down. You

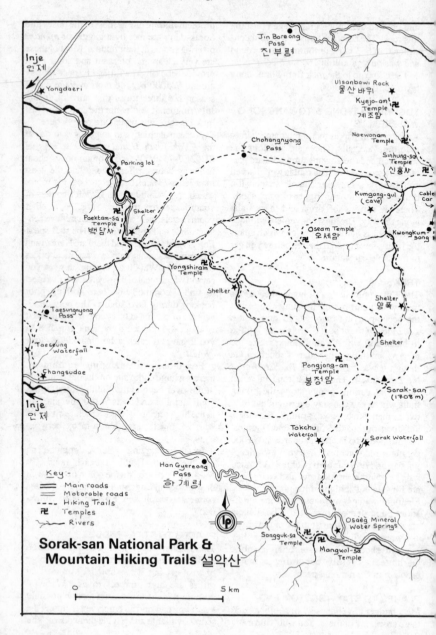

Jin Boreong
Pass
진부령

Inje
인제

★ Yongdaeri

Ulsanbawi Rock
울산 바위

Kyejo-am
Temple
계조암

Naewonam
Temple

Parking lot

Chohangnyong
Pass

Sinhung-sa
Temple
신흥사

Shelter

Kumgang-gul
(cave)

Cable
Car

Paektam-sa
Temple
백담사

Shelter

Oseam Temple
오세암

Kwongkum-
song

Yongshiram
Temple

Shelter

Shelter
양폭

Taesungnyong
Pass

Shelter

Taesung
Waterfall

Pongjong-am
Temple
봉정암

Changsudae

Sorak-san
(1708 m)

Inje
인제

Tokchu
Waterfall

Sorak Waterfall

Key :-
━━━ Main roads
═══ Motorable roads
---- Hiking Trails
卍 Temples
～ Rivers

Han Gyereong
Pass
한계령

Osaeg Mineral
Water Springs

**Sorak-san National Park &
Mountain Hiking Trails 설악산**

Songguk-sa
Temple

Mangwol-sa
Temple

0   5 km

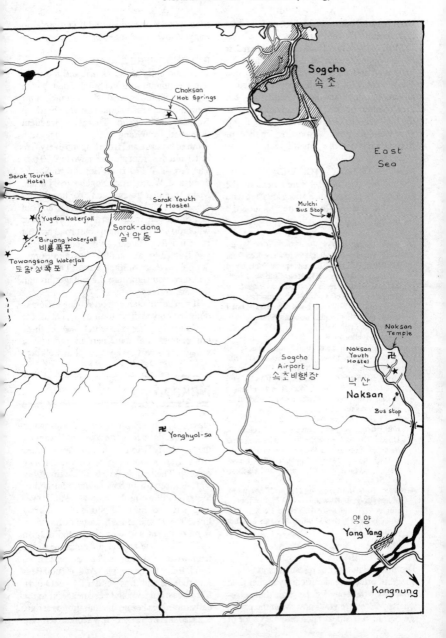

would expect your own bathroom, hot water and a colour TV for that price.

Most of these hotels are clustered together on the opposite side of the river from the main road and are adjacent to the camp site. There's not a lot to choose between them – all are of much the same standard – but they're often booked out in advance during the high season. Get there early in the day if you want to have a sporting chance of finding a room at that time of year.

PLACES TO STAY – TOP END

Except for one hotel located next to the Osaek hot springs, all Sorak-san's top end hotels are at Sorak-dong. They include the following:

Hotel New Sorak (tel (0392) 34-5304/5) 106-1 Sorak-dong, Sogcho. Five-star, 108 rooms priced from US$96 to US$106. The staff speak English and Japanese and there are Korean, Chinese, Japanese and Western restaurants with average meal prices of US$3.60 to US$4.30 (breakfast) and US$5 to US$17.50 (lunch and dinner). The hotel has a coffee shop, nightclub and swimming pool.

Hotel Sorak Park (tel (0392) 34-7711/24) 74-3 Sorak-dong, Sogcho. Five-star, 121 rooms priced at US$96. The staff speak English and Japanese and there are Korean and Western restaurants with average meal prices of US$4.60 to US$6 (breakfast), US$9.50 to US$12.50 (lunch) and US$12.50 to US$20 (dinner). The hotel has a coffee shop, bar, cocktail lounge, nightclub, casino and game room.

Sorak-san Tourist Hotel (tel (0392) 34-7101/5) 170 Sorak-dong, Sogcho. Three-star, 59 rooms at US$38. The staff speak English and Japanese and there are Korean and Western restaurants with average meal prices of US$3.50 to US$7 (breakfast), US$3.50 to US$8.30 (lunch) and US$3.50 to US$17.50 (dinner).

Nam Solag Hotel (tel Yangyang 2131/4) 507 Somyon, Yangyang-gun, Kwangwon-do. Eighty rooms, singles & doubles for US$20 to US$25. This hotel is at the Osaek mineral water and hot springs.

PLACES TO EAT

There are all manner of restaurants in Sorak-dong but prices are significantly higher than what you would pay for the same thing elsewhere. Make sure you know what the prices are before you order. There are also a lot of food stores scattered around if you prefer to put your own food together.

GETTING THERE & AWAY

The main entry to Sorak-san and the trails into the mountains is via Sorak-dong, which is at the end of the road which branches off from the coast road about half way between Naksan and Sogcho. There are frequent buses both from Yang Yang 양양 , a few km south of Naksan, and from Sogcho every five to 10 minutes from around dawn to 9.30 pm. The fare is W120 from Sogcho to Sorak-dong and W200 from Sogcho to Naksan. Make sure that the bus you take has Sorak-dong 설악동 on the direction sign and not just Sorak-san Ipku 설악산입구 . The latter will drop you on the main coast road at what is called the Mulchi 음치 bus stop and you'll have to take another bus into Sorak-dong from there or hitch a ride. The former will take you right into the village through the park entrance gate.

If you're not planning on staying in Sorak-dong but only visiting for the day, get off the bus at the very last stop which is about three km beyond the main part of the tourist village. This will save you a lot of walking.

Naksan 낙산

Naksan is famous for its temple, Naksan-sa 낙산사 and its huge white statue of Kwanum, the Goddess of Mercy, which looks out to sea from atop a small, pine-covered rocky outcrop. The temple was built originally in 671 AD, rebuilt in 858 AD and burned to the ground during the Korean War. It was reconstructed in 1953 along the original lines. The 15-metre-high statue of Kwanum is more recent and was completed only in 1977. The stone arch at the entrance to the temple with a pavilion built on top dates from 1465. Entry to the temple costs W1660 (less for students and those under 24 years old). It's a beautiful spot and very peaceful in the early mornings before the tour groups arrive. It's also one of the very few Korean temples which overlooks the sea. Don't forget to visit the Uisang Pavilion which sits right on top of a cliff next to the ocean shaded by an old (and ailing) pine tree. It's an excellent spot to watch the sunrise.

Down below the temple is Naksan Beach, one of the best in the area, but unbelievably crowded during July and August.

PLACES TO STAY & EAT

There's plenty of accommodation at Naksan ranging from simple *minbak* to more expensive *yogwan* and you should expect to pay W4000 to W5000 for the cheapest rooms in the low season. As elsewhere around Soraksan, however, prices triple in the high season and you can expect to pay W15,000 minimum at that time. Don't expect constant water at the simpler places as it has to be pumped up from wells. Meals can be arranged at most of them but agree on a price beforehand.

An excellent alternative here is the *Naksan Youth Hostel* 낙산유스호스텔 (tel (0396) 3416/8). This is situated on the same hillock as Naksan-sa and there's a large sign on the coast road in English and Korean at the turn-off. Like other youth hostels in Korea this is a huge, plush place with its own restaurant, coffee shop, etc. There are five dormitory rooms here with varying numbers of beds which cost W5000 per bed. They also have more expensive private rooms for US$18 to US$24 a single and US$29 to US$41 a double. It's a beautifully furnished place, spotless and well maintained. The bathrooms have hot and cold running water. This place is excellent value and the cheapest place to use as a base for Sorak-san other than the Sorak Youth Hostel itself but you need to book in advance in the high season. English is spoken and cheap meals are available.

There's also the five-star *Hotel Naksan Beach* (tel (0396) 672 4000/3), 3-2 Chonjin-ri, Kanghyon-myon, Yangyang-gun, which has rooms available for US$85 to US$95.

GETTING THERE & AWAY

All the local buses plying between Sogcho

and Yang Yang pass by Naksan and since there's one every 10 to 15 minutes you'll have no problems getting to Naksan. Buses from either place to Naksan cost W200 and take about 25 minutes.

Sogcho 속초

Sogcho is a sprawling fishing town north of Sorak-san almost entirely enclosing a lagoon which is connected to the sea. It is the last major centre of population before the border with North Korea. There's not much of interest here for the traveller but it does have a lot of seafood restaurants and *yogwan* and it can be used as a base for exploring Sorak-san.

There are two bus terminals in Sogcho. The local bus terminal which takes care of *chikheng* and *wanheng* buses is right in the centre of town but the express bus terminal is a long way from the centre on the south side of the lagoon. Local bus No 2 connects the two terminals. Buses to Sorak-dong and Naksan start from the local bus terminal but can also be caught outside the express terminal.

PLACES TO STAY

Most of the cheap *yogwan* and *yoinsook* are to be found along or just off the main street and in the side streets around the market area.

At the cheaper end of the scale, the *Ulsan Yoinsook* 울산 여인숙 is worth checking out. It's reasonable value at W5000 per room but there's no hot water and the toilets tend to be smelly. Of a similar standard but better value is the *Tong Ah Yogwan* 동아여관 near the local bus terminal which is clean and pleasant and costs W6000 per room but has cold water only.

Going up in price, the *Sorak Yogwan* 설악여관 is a good choice at W12,000 a double with own bathroom, colour TV and fan, plus they have cheaper rooms without their own bathroom. It's a new place and very clean and both the private and communal bathrooms have hot water. This is one of

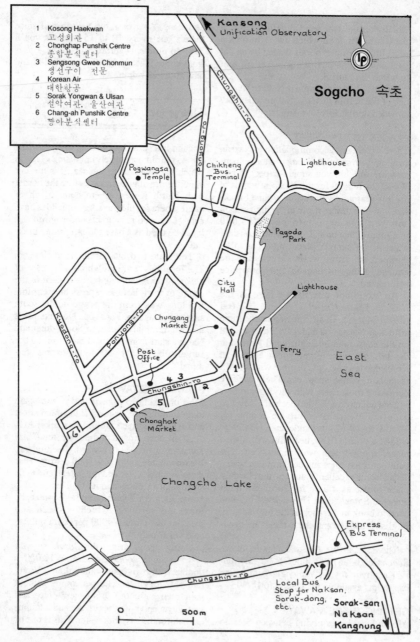

1 Kosong Haekwan
  고성회관
2 Chonghap Punshik Centre
  종합분식센터
3 Sengsong Gwee Chonmun
  생선구이 전문
4 Korean Air
  대한항공
5 Sorak Yongwan & Ulsan
  설악여관, 울산여관
6 Chang-ah Punshik Centre
  창아분식센터

Kansong
Unification Observatory

Sogcho 속초

Chungshin-ro

Ponyong-ro

Pogwangsa Temple

Chikheng Bus Terminal

Lighthouse

Pagoda Park

City Hall

Lighthouse

Chungang Market

ferry

East Sea

Kyodong-ro

Ponyong-ro

Post Office

4 3
Chungshin-ro
5   2
1

Chonghak Market

Chongcho Lake

Express Bus Terminal

Chungshin-ro

Local Bus Stop for Naksan, Sorak-dong, etc.

Sorak-san Naksan Kangnung

0   500 m

the very few *yogwan* which doesn't triple its prices in the holiday season.

Also recommended is the *Taesongjang Yogwan* 대성장여관 (tel 33-5361) which is very clean and friendly and costs W12,000 a double with own bath, hot water, colour TV and fan. An extra person in a double room costs W2000.

Several years ago we recommended the *Tonghae Yogwan* 동해여관 which used to be almost next door to the local bus terminal. Since then we've heard from several irate travellers that no such place exists. Not true! But it's no longer next to the bus terminal. There is indeed a *yogwan* of that name but it's now in a side street on the opposite side of the main street from the market area. The correspondent who located it didn't say what they charged but she did say it was good value.

PLACES TO EAT

With a fishing fleet stationed at Sogcho you would expect an excellent range of seafood restaurants. There are indeed a lot of them, most tucked into the short streets between the main road and the lagoon off to the right between the post office and the Chungang Market. You can't miss them as they all have huge aquariums as well as a plethora of maroon plastic buckets full of live fish and various crustaceans. The only problem is the price of a meal. The majority only offer raw seafood and the average price of a meal is an incredible W30,000 – spread between however many people eat at the same table. How Koreans afford this sort of meal given current wage levels is a mystery but the restaurants don't seem to suffer from a lack of custom.

The only way round this is to eat standard (non-seafood) meals or to find a restaurant which offers cooked seafood. There are very few of the latter but there is one which is not only very popular but excellent value. This is the *Gu Jip* 구집 (tel 33 1140). Here you'll be served a huge plateful of three or four different kinds of fried fish with all the trimmings for W3000 per person. They also offer

raw seafood dishes but at the usual high prices.

For a very cheap meal, there's a choice of two excellent restaurants. The first is the *Chonghap Punshik Centre* 종합분식센터. *Chonghap* means 'all foods' and this restaurant offers Korean, Chinese and Japanese dishes for just W400 to W1000 per plate. It's run by young people and is a friendly place to eat. The second restaurant is the *Chang-ah Punshik Centre* 짱아분식센터, a small restaurant which offers *kimbap* for W500, hamburgers for W500 and the equivalent of Japanese *yakimando* for W500 per 10 pieces.

GETTING THERE & AWAY

Remember that there are two bus stations in Sogcho – the local bus terminal in the centre of town (which handles *wanheng* (local) and *chikheng* buses) and the express bus terminal a long way from the centre on the south-eastern side of the lagoon. It's unlikely you'll use the latter unless you're coming from or going to Seoul by express bus.

From the express bus terminal there are buses to Seoul every 40 to 60 minutes from 6.30 am to 6.40 pm which cost W4460 and take 5¼ hours. These buses use the expressway.

At the local bus terminal are the following buses:

To Chuncheon

There are 13 buses per day, the first at 6.40 am and the last at 5.30 pm. The fare is W3250 and the journey takes four hours. These buses are the ones which take the Hangyreong 한계령 scenic route through the southern part of Sorak-san and on to Inje. It's a spectacular route and well worth your time rather than taking an express bus direct to Seoul. All express buses use the Kangnung-Seoul (Yongdong) Expressway via Weonju, and although there's one point on this route which offers panoramic views across to Odae-san National Park and the coast it's not as spectacular as the Hangyreong route.

If you choose the Hangyreong route you have, of course, the option of getting off the bus at either Inje (water level permitting) or Shinnam and taking the fast launch to Chuncheon via Lake Soyang. See the Chuncheon section for details of this boat service.

Another route is possible between Sogcho and Chuncheon via a road which skirts the northern side of Sorak-san. This is known as the Jinbiryong 진부령 route and goes via Yongdae. It joins the Hangyreyong road at Wontong north of Inje. Buses along this route are hard to find and you may have to do the trip in stages.

To Kangnung
There are buses every 10 minutes from 5.30 am to 9.10 pm which cost W1370 and take 1¾ hours.

To Seoul
There are 18 buses per day from 6 am to 6 pm. The fare is W4490 and the journey takes 5½ hours.

All the buses which depart from the local bus terminal can also be picked up at Yang Yang 양양 south of Naksan. Local buses to Sorak-dong and Naksan also start from this same terminal but you can pick them up anywhere along their route including outside the express bus terminal.

North of Sogcho

BEACHES
There are a number of sheltered sandy coves and beaches north of Sogcho and they're far less crowded than those to the south, though you're only allowed onto them at certain points and only at certain times of year. In the low season that endless razor-wire fence which stretches along the whole of the eastern coast of Korea is firmly sealed and you'll be arrested (or, worse, shot at) if you venture onto the beaches.

The best of the coves are to be found at Taejin 대진 north of Kansong 간성. Taejin is a small fishing village which also doubles as a

small, laid-back resort during the summer months. You can either camp on the beaches at certain points or rent a room at a *minbak*, plus there are a few relatively cheap *yogwan* with the usual facilities. Taejin can be reached by *chikheng* bus from Sogcho via Kansong. These leave every half hour from 6.30 am to 7.20 pm, cost W800 and take 70 minutes.

THE NORTH/SOUTH KOREA BORDER AREA
A visit to the Unification Observatory (Tongil Chunmangdae 통일전망대) close to the DMZ north of Taejin has become almost as popular these days as a trip to Panmunjom north of Seoul. Tourists by the bus load turn up here daily throughout the summer months and you don't have to book weeks in advance like you often do for Panmunjom. It isn't quite the same as going to Panmunjom, however. There's little of the palpable tension evident at Panmunjom since the Unification Observatory isn't actually in the DMZ but a few km away, so if you want to see anything at all (such as the UN post, the North Korean post - only just - and the North's propaganda signs) then you have to use the telescopes – at W500 a pop for two minutes' viewing. It's essentially a non-event but it's a pleasant day out, there are no dress or age regulations, it's much cheaper than going to Panmunjom and the government lays on a free propaganda slide show. The only drawback is that you have to join a tour bus group or have your own transport since Taejin is the last town that foreigners are allowed to travel to by local bus.

Getting There & Away
If you don't have your own transport then you'll either have to take an organised bus tour or hitchhike. In either case you'll need your passport handy but the red tape will be taken care of by the tour company or the person who gives you a lift. A number of commercial tour companies in Sogcho and Sorak-dong put on coaches to the Observa-

tory including Sorak Tourist Co (tel 32-8989). The round trip costs W5000 and takes about five hours.

With your own transport you head first for Taejin. About one km north of Taejin you'll find the Unification Hall to your left surrounded by a sort of tourist village (souvenir shops, restaurants and the like) and vast car parks. This is where you complete the necessary formalities. First you have to fill in a form which is entirely in Korean stating names, addresses, passport numbers, nationalities and the vehicle registration number. One form is sufficient for everyone in the vehicle. When you hand this in, you'll be given a numbered identification card. Next you line up for the slide show which takes place every half hour or so and lasts about 20 minutes. There's no point in trying to miss this show as you have to allow sufficient time to elapse for the form you filled in to reach the first checkpoint – right outside the Hall.

The numbered identification card has to be surrendered at the first checkpoint and then you'll be allowed to drive to the next checkpoint where you have to leave one passport per car. After that you can drive to the Observatory without further ado. On the way back, you collect your passport at the same checkpoint. It's all very efficient and there's no charge for anything. The roads are excellent and the various obstacles designed to bring to a rapid halt any attempt at an invasion by North Korea are formidable. Not only that, but the guards will salute you as you pass through the last checkpoint!

Odae-san National Park
오대산 국립공원

Like Sorak-san, Odae-san is another mountain massif where nature reigns supreme. There are excellent hiking possibilities and superb views. It also hosts one of Korea's foremost winter skiing resorts – known as the Alpine Ski Run – though the main two

centres for this, at Yongpyong 양평 and Taekwanryeong 대관령, are actually south of the park on the other side of the Seoul-Kangnung (Yongdong) Expressway. Deep inside the western section of the park are two of the most famous Buddhist temples in Korea – Wolchong-sa and Sangwon-sa.

As with Sorak-san, the best times to visit are early spring and late autumn when the colours of the landscape are at their best. Entry to Odae-san National Park costs W1200 (less for students and those under 24 years old).

WOLCHONG-SA TEMPLE 월정사

Although there are numerous hiking possibilities from various points around the perimeter of the park, most visitors begin their tour of Odae-san with a visit to Wolchong-sa. This temple was founded in 654 AD by the Zen Master Chajangyulsa during the reign of Queen Sondok of the Silla Dynasty in order to enshrine relics of Sakyamuni (the historical Buddha). Over the next 1300 years or so, it went through various trials and tribulations and was destroyed by fire on at least three occasions, notably in 1307 during the Koryo Dynasty and again during the Korean War in 1950. Yet today you would hardly suspect these disasters had ever happened. The 1969 reconstruction is simply magnificent and the internal painting of the main hall containing the Buddha image is a masterpiece of religious art. Not even in Tibet will you find anything quite as intricate, well-balanced and spellbinding as this.

Luckily, not everything was destroyed in the various disasters which have befallen this temple over the centuries. Prominent remains from the Koryo era include a kneeling – and smiling! – stone Bodhisattva and a number of interesting stone stupas. There's also a unique, octagonal nine-storied pagoda dating from the same period which is classified as a national treasure. There's no entry charge as such for Wolchong-sa – it's included in the national park entry fee.

The road is sealed as far as the temple.

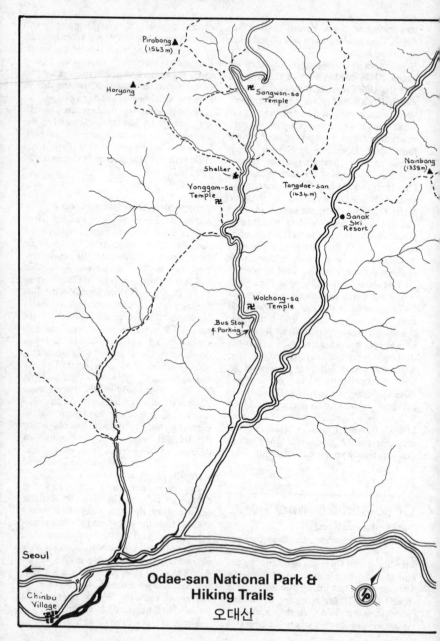

Pirobong ▲
(1563 m)

Horyang

Sangwon-sa
Temple

Noinbong ▲
(1338 m)

Shelter

Yonggam-sa
Temple

Tongdae-san
(1434 m)

Sanak
Ski
Resort

Wolchong-sa
Temple

Bus Stop
& Parking

Seoul

Chinbu
Village

**Odae-san National Park &
Hiking Trails**
오대산

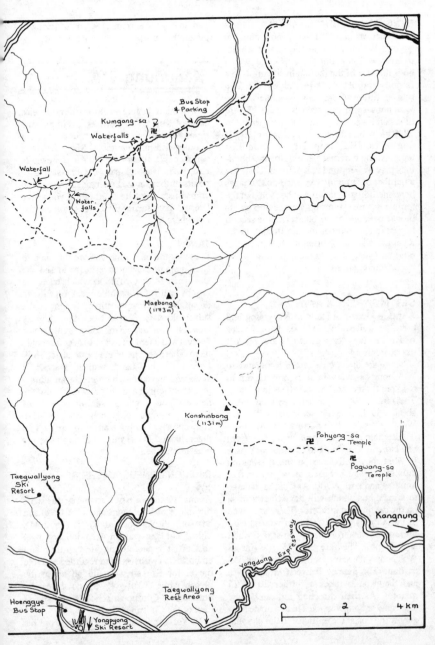

SANGWON-SA TEMPLE 상원사

Much deeper into Odae-san, some nine km beyond Wolchong-sa at the end of a relatively well-maintained gravel road which hugs the side of the mountain stream, is this famous temple constructed by the Zen master after whom it was named. Like Wolchong-sa, it has seen its share of hard times and was last burned to the ground in 1949 but reconstructed the following year. If you're familiar with Tibetan Buddhist temples, the external painting of the buildings may well remind you of them. There are a number of superbly executed gold images here, including Mansuri and her son, but the temple's most famous possession is its bronze bell, one of the oldest and the second largest in Korea (after the Emille Bell in the Kyongju National Museum). It was cast in 663, one year after the construction of the temple commenced.

GETTING THERE & AWAY

A trip to Odae-san starts in Kangnung and there's a choice of direct buses or local buses which involve a change at Chinbu, just off the expressway.

There are direct buses from Kangnung to Wolchong-sa every hour from 6.10 am to 6.45 pm for most of the year (less in winter). The fare is W1040 and the journey takes about 1½ hours. These buses will have Wolchong-sa on their destination indicator.

Alternatively, take a *chikheng* bus from bay No 2 in Kangnung to Chinbu 진부 (this is what they will have on the destination indicator). These buses leave every five minutes and cost W700. At Chinbu, change to a local bus which will have Sangwon-sa on the destination indicator. There are seven of these buses per day (less in winter) with the last bus back from Sangwon-sa to Chinbu at 5.30 pm. The fare is W250 (as far as Wolchong-sa) and the journey takes about half an hour. The journey between Wolchong-sa and Sangwon-sa takes a further 20 to 25 minutes. As their direction indicates, they terminate at Sangwon-sa. There's no need to get off the bus at the entrance to the national

park to pay the entrance fee – an official will get on the bus to sell you a ticket.

Kangnung 강릉

Kangnung is the largest city on the north-east coast of Korea, and worth an overnight stay if you have an interest in Confucianism, but is otherwise unremarkable. Most travellers simply pass through it en route to somewhere else, such as Sorak-san or Odae-san or to points further south. You may, however, find yourself staying here overnight if you arrive late and there are no suitable bus connections elsewhere.

TANO FESTIVAL

Probably the only time you would come to Kangnung for its own sake is to see the shamanist festival of Tano which takes the city by storm for a whole week on the 5th day of the 5th lunar month (early June on the solar calendar). People flock into the city from all over the surrounding area for this festival and a tent city rises to accommodate them. There are circus and carnival acts, folk operas, farmers' bands and all manner of stalls and hawkers which create an atmosphere redolent of a medieval fair. It's also the nearest you'll get to seeing aspects of Korea's original religion unless you have contacts who can put you in touch with its practitioners. Don't miss it if you're in the area at the time.

OJUK'ON CONFUCIAN SHRINE
오죽헌

About 3½ km north of Kangnung, this is the birthplace of Shin Saimdang (1504-51) and her son, Yi Yul-gok (or Yi-yi) (1536-84). Shin Saimdang was an accomplished poet and artist (specialising in painting and embroidery) who has been regarded as a role model for Korean womanhood up to the present while Yi Yul-gok was one of the most outstanding Confucian scholars and statesmen of the Chosun period.

Yi Yul-gok learned the classics from his

mother at a very young age and subsequently won first prize in the state examinations for prospective government officials in 1564. After that he served in various government posts such as Governor of Hwanghae-do Province, Inspector General, and Minister of Personnel, Punishment and Military Affairs. Along with his contemporary, Yi Toegye, another famous Confucian scholar, he wielded great influence among the various political factions at the royal court and was instrumental in advising the king to raise an army of 100,000 men to prepare for a possible invasion by Japan. His advice was tragically ignored, since only eight years after he died, the Japanese did indeed invade and the peninsula was devastated.

The actual buildings at Ojuk'on were erected by another Confucian scholar, Choe Chi-un (1390-1440), and eventually passed on to the father of Shin Saimdang who left it to his son-in-law, Kwon Hwa. The house remained in the possession of the Kwon family until 1975 when it was given to the nation and extensively renovated by order of the then President, Park Chung-hee.

The Yulgok-jae Festival is held annually here on 26 October when traditional rituals are enacted and classical Korean music is played.

A small museum forms part of the complex and houses examples of painting, calligraphy and embroidery executed by Shin Saimdang and Yi Yul-gok. Entry to the shrine costs W400 (W200 for those under 24 years old) and it's open daily from 9 am to 5 pm.

Local buses (No 1, 2 and 3) will take you to the shrine from Kangnung city centre.

KAEKSA-MUN

This national treasure stands at the back of the main post office and close to the telephone and telegraph office. The gateway is all that remains of an official government inn which was first built in 936 during the reign of King Taejo of the Koryo Dynasty. Known as Imyonggwan, the inn was eventually converted into an elementary school in 1929 and later demolished by the Japanese occupation authorities. The gateway is a fine example of Koryo architecture with tapered wooden columns and an unusual gabled roof instead of the normal hipped roof. It's also one of the few such structures from that period which was never painted.

PLACES TO STAY

The majority of *yogwan* and *yoinsook* are to be found in the streets opposite the express and *chikheng* bus terminals and there's an excellent choice available.

At the cheap end of the scale the *Hengun Yoinsook* 행운여인숙 is good value. It's clean and friendly though a little noisy from time to time due to the proximity of the railway station. Rooms cost W5000 and include a fan and a black and white TV. The *Kyongpo Yoinsook* 경포여인숙 is similar and has rooms for the same price. Better than either of these and excellent value for the price is the *Mi-chong Yoinsook* 미정여인숙 which costs W6000 to 7000 (depending on the season). None of the rooms at the above have their own bathroom or hot water.

Many of the *yogwan* in Kangnung are

Traditional Korean Musician

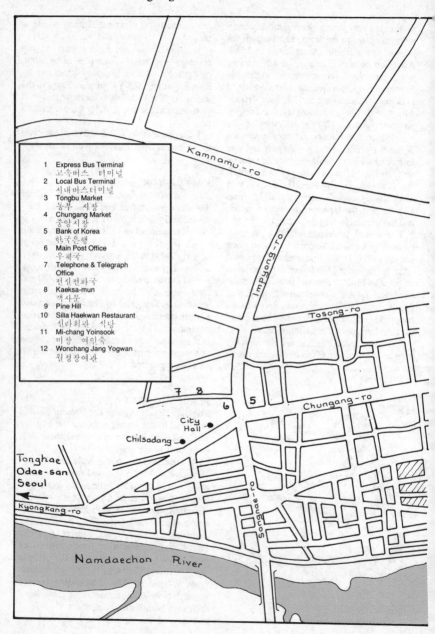

1 Express Bus Terminal
   고속버스 터미널
2 Local Bus Terminal
   시내버스터미널
3 Tongbu Market
   동부 시장
4 Chungang Market
   중앙시장
5 Bank of Korea
   한국은행
6 Main Post Office
   우체국
7 Telephone & Telegraph
   Office
   전신전화국
8 Kaeksa-mun
   객사문
9 Pine Hill
10 Silla Haekwan Restaurant
   신라회관 식당
11 Mi-chang Yoinsook
   미창 여인숙
12 Wonchang Jang Yogwan
   원정장여관

Kamnamu - ro

Impyong - ro

Tosong - ro

Chungang - ro

Songnae - ro

7 8
6   5

City Hall

Chilsadang

Tonghae
Odae-san
Seoul

Kyongkang - ro

Namdaechon   River

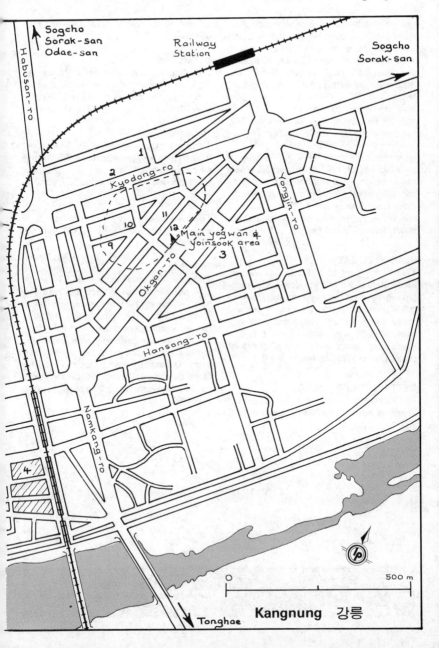

Kangnung 강릉

going through what appears to be a country-wide transition into *yogwan-jang* so expect a considerable price hike if you want a room with its own bathroom. Typical of these is the *Wonchang-jang Yogwan* 월정장여관 , diagonally opposite the Mi-chong Yoinsook, which costs W15,000 for a room with own bath, hot water, fan and TV. The staff are friendly and the rooms are pleasant. Also recommended is the *Oorijang Yogwan* 우리장여관 which offers rooms with own shower and hot water for W10,000 (Korean style) and W12,000 (Western style) plus a few cheaper rooms without their own bathroom. Also fairly cheap in this category is the *Pandojang Yogwan* (tel 2-2087) 반도장여관 which has rooms with own bathroom, hot water, colour TV and fan.

PLACES TO EAT

There are plenty of restaurants of various kinds around the bus stations and particularly in the street right opposite the *chikheng* bus station, but if you want to eat seafood check prices before you order. One restaurant which stands out as being excellent value and which never lacks plenty of custom is the *Silla Haekwan* 신라회관.

GETTING THERE & AWAY
To Chuncheon

There are buses every 30 minutes from 6.30 am to 5.50 pm which cost W3300 and take 4½ hours.

To Odae-san

These buses terminate at Wolchong-sa Temple. There are buses every hour, the first at 6.10 am and the last at 6.45 pm. The fare is W1040 and the journey takes 1½ hours.

To Seoul

There are express buses every 30 minutes from 6 am to 6.40 pm which cost W3530 and take four hours. There are also *chikheng* buses every hour from 6 am to 7.20 pm.

To Sogcho

There are buses every 10 minutes from 5.30 am to 9.10 pm which cost W1370 and take 1½ hours.

To Pusan

There are five buses daily from 8.10 am to 2.30 pm which cost W6320 and take 5½ hours – these are the non stop express buses. There are also *chikheng* buses which do this run and which you can use to get to various towns along the east coast such as Ulchin, Pohang and Kyongju. These buses leave every 40 minutes from 5.23 am to 3 pm. The fare is the same as the express buses to Pusan but they take eight hours. To Pohang the fare is W4600.

West-Central Korea

Taejon (Daejon) 대전

In line with Taejon's growing importance as a major industrial and commercial centre, its status was recently raised to that of a city province like Seoul and Taegu, but it also still remains the provincial headquarters of Chung Cheong Nam Province. For the traveller, there's little of interest in the city itself – though this may all change as Taejon gears up to host World Expo following that due to be held at Osaka. There are certainly ambitious plans for it, some of which rival those for the 1988 Olympics, and already major construction works are in progress along some of the main boulevards. For the present, however, it's an excellent base from which to explore nearby temples and national parks since transportation facilities from here are very good. You'll also come here if you're heading south to Mogpo 목포 by rail and from there to Cheju-do 제주도.

INFORMATION

There is a tourist office in a kiosk in the forecourt of Taejon Railway Station which has a reasonable selection of literature about the province, and the staff speak English.

PLACES TO STAY – BOTTOM END

A cheap place to stay and one which is very clean and friendly is the *Yong-il Yoinsook* (tel 23 2035) 영일여인숙 which has rooms for W3000 a single, W4000 a double and W5000 a triple all without bathroom. The communal showers have cold water only. Many travellers stay here and it's very close to the market, post office and other facilities.

Directly opposite is the *Yongsong Yogwan* (tel 282 9060) 영성여관, which is good value at W6000 a single and W7000 a double for a spotlessly clean, well-furnished room with bathroom (hot water in the winter only), TV and fan. The best rooms are on the 2nd floor at the back. Both floors of the *yogwan* have rooms in the centre of the building which have no windows so make sure you get a side room – they cost the same. The staff are very friendly and you can dry clothes on the roof.

Also good value and popular with travellers is the *Songji Yogwan* (tel 256 6388) 성지여관, close to the junction between Inhyo-ro and Taehung-ro. It's on the 3rd floor and shares its entrance with a pool hall which itself is on the 2nd floor – look for the crossed cues and ball sign. The staff are friendly and it offers ordinary rooms for W8000 plus air-con rooms for W10,000. There are also air-con triple rooms for W12,000. All the rooms have a bathroom, constant hot water, colour TV and fan.

More expensive but a beautiful place to stay if you're looking for something out of the ordinary is the *Sorinjang Yogwan* (tel 283 6221) 서린장여관 in the block next to the Yongsong Yogwan. Rooms here cost W13,000 complete with bathroom, constant hot water, air-con and colour TV. There's a choice of Korean or Western-style rooms and a cocktail bar in the basement.

There are several other, somewhat cheaper, *yogwan* up this same street which include the *In Hung Yogwan* (tel 283 5019) 인흥여관, the *Nam Gwan Yogwan* (tel 282 7487) 남광여관, and the *In Song Yogwan* 인성여관.

If you'd like a room overlooking the river then try either the *Il Shin Jang Yogwan* 일신장여관 or the *Pyong Hwa Jang Yogwan*. They're situated next to each other and have room rates similar to the Sorinjang.

There's another collection of *yoinsook* and *yogwan* of various categories on the top side of Chungang-ro between the river and Taejon Railway Station.

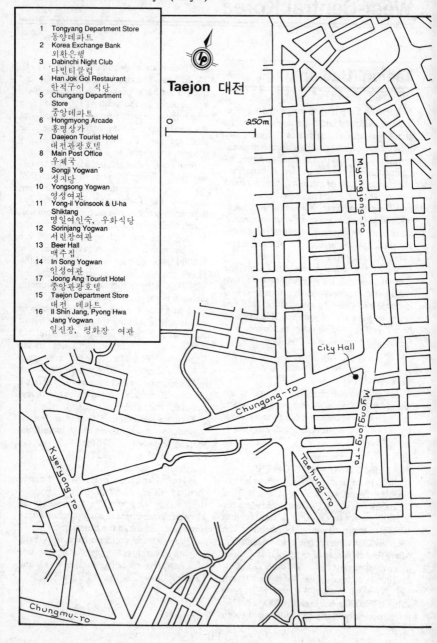

1   Tongyang Department Store
    동양데파트
2   Korea Exchange Bank
    외환은행
3   Dabinchi Night Club
    다빈티클럽
4   Han Jok Gol Restaurant
    한적구이 식당
5   Chungang Department
    Store
    중앙데파트
6   Hongmyong Arcade
    홍명상가
7   Daejeon Tourist Hotel
    대전관광호텔
8   Main Post Office
    우체국
9   Songji Yogwan
    성지당
10 Yongsong Yogwan
    영성여관
11 Yong-il Yoinsook & U-ha
    Shiktang
    명일여인숙, 우화식당
12 Sorinjang Yogwan
    서린장여관
13 Beer Hall
    맥주집
14 In Song Yogwan
    인성여관
17 Joong Ang Tourist Hotel
    중앙관광호텔
15 Taejon Department Store
    대전 데파트
16 Il Shin Jang, Pyong Hwa
    Jang Yogwan
    일신장, 평화장 여관

Taejon 대전

0   250m

Myongjong-ro

City Hall

Chungang-ro

Kyeryong-ro

Taehung-ro

Chungmu-ro

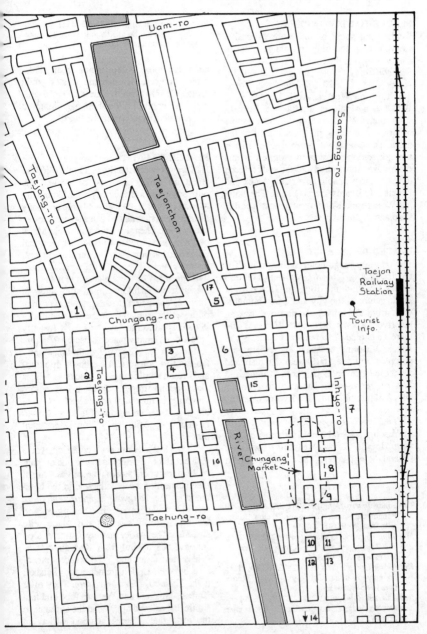

PLACES TO STAY – MIDDLE

Discounting some of the more expensive *yogwan jang*, the only mid-range hotel in Taejon – right in the centre of the city – is the *Daejeon Tourist Hotel* (tel (042) 253 8131) 대전 관광호텔, 20-16 Won-dong, Tong-gu, Taejon. Western-style rooms cost W31,180 a single or double and Korean-style rooms W19,800 to W23,760 a double or single depending on the standard of the room. These rates will probably soon rise as a major renovation was in progress as this edition was researched and the staff refused to quote the probable new rates. Amex and Diners Club cards are accepted. The hotel has Western and Korean restaurants, a coffee shop and nightclub.

PLACES TO STAY – TOP END

The only top range hotel in Taejon itself is the *Joong Ang Tourist Hotel* (tel (042) 253 8801), Chung-dong, Tong-gu, Taejon, right in the centre of the city and a few minutes' walk from the railway station overlooking the river. Rooms here cost W36,000 and there's a choice of Korean or Western-style. Amex, Visa and Master Charge cards are accepted and the staff speak English and Japanese. The hotel has both Korean and Western restaurants. There's also a coffee shop, nightclub and laundry/dry-cleaning service.

Outside of Taejon at the hot springs resort of Yusong 유성 (about 15 minutes by taxi from Taejon Railway Station) there are several top-end hotels. The cheapest of them are:

You Soung Tourist Hotel (tel (042) 822 0611), 480 Pongmyong-dong, Chung-gu, Taejon. Room rates from W40,000.
Mu Gung Hwa Tourist Hotel (tel (042) 822 1234), 213-2 Pongmyong-dong, Chung-gu, Taejon. Room rates from W28,000.
Hot Spring Tourist Hotel (tel (042) 822 8220), 211-1 Pongmyong-dong, Chung-gu, Taejon. Room rates from W25,000.
Royal Tourist Hotel (tel (042) 822 0720), 202-5 Pongmyong-dong, Chung-gu, Taejon. Room rates from W24,000.

Hotel Riviera Yusung (tel (042) 823 2111), 478 Pongmyong-dong, So-gu, Taejon. Super luxurious. Room rates from W100,000.

All these hotels accept major credit cards, offer a choice of Korean and Western-style rooms, have Korean, Japanese and Western-style restaurants, coffee shop, bar, nightclub and laundry/dry-cleaning services.

PLACES TO EAT

Half way between the river and Inhyo-ro (the street on which the post office and the railway station are situated) is the Chungang Market 중앙시장. All around here are many different restaurants and cafes where you can eat well and cheaply. Take your pick. Many of them have food on display so you can point to what you want if your Korean isn't up to scratch. There are no worries about hygiene at any of these places and it's one of the most colourful and interesting areas in Taejon. People flock to this market every day of the week from all over the city and outlying areas but as the day starts early (usually before 6 am) many places close by 9.30 pm.

The *soju* tents don't close quite so early (so long as you're still eating or drinking) and offer a whole range of snacks as well as alcoholic beverages. Check prices before you order as they vary considerably. One of the largest concentrations of these stalls is to be found opposite the Taejon Department Store.

Those less adventurous could do worse than eat at the restaurants inside one or other of the department stores themselves. One of the cheapest of these is the one in the basement of the *Tongyang Department Store* 중앙데파트, corner of Taejong-ro and Chungang-ro. It's a popular place with students. They offer mainly Chinese food (noodle-based) but also Korean dishes. Prices start at around W800. More expensive, but with a much greater range of dishes, is the *Taejon Department Store*. They offer Korean, Japanese and Western food and facsimile dishes are displayed at the entrance to the restaurant. There's a good variety of dishes available for between W2500 and W4500 all the way up to a huge 'door-step' steak for W8300.

If you're staying at either the Yongsong Yogwan or the Yong-il Yoinsook then try the *U-ha Shiktang* 우화식당 right next door. They offer a wide variety of Korean dishes which are good value at around W1000 per dish (without meat) though they'll also cook you up *pulgogi* if you want to splurge.

For a restaurant which specialises in *pulgogi*, try the *Han Jok Gol* 한적골 close to the Yurak Department Store on the opposite side of the river. It's a good restaurant and isn't too expensive at W4000 per person.

ENTERTAINMENT

Like all Korean cities, the centre of Taejon is peppered with beer bars and cocktail bars but most of them are a poor choice for meeting local people as they're broken up into a series of curtained partitions to give couples or small groups of friends a degree of privacy.

Far better is to spend the evening doing the Korean light fandango joining the *makkoli* and *soju* hordes on the benches in the sea of tents around the Hongmyong Arcade, 홍명상가 by the river and opposite the Taejon Department Store. This is an extremely popular spot (even in the depths of winter!) and by the time you leave you'll have met half of Taejon. They stay open until around midnight.

If you want to party-on then head for the *Dabinchi* 다빈치 nightclub just off Chungang-ro (third street on the left hand side after you cross the river coming from the railway station) but make sure there's a group of you together because, regardless of group size, it will cost you W9500 per group to get in. For this you get three large bottled beers and snacks. Additional beers cost W2000 each, Coca-Colas W1500 but additional snacks (not obligatory) cost W5000! It's a large place and popular especially with young people. The music is a mixture of contemporary Korean and Western but they often have live rock bands. It closes about 2 am.

A more up-market nightclub which frequently puts on top Korean chartbusters is that on the top floor of the *Tongyang Department Store* but, again, you need to be part of a fairly substantial group if you're on a budget since the group entry price is W28,000 to W30,000. Another place in this bracket is the *Casablanca* nightclub on the 9th floor of the Daejeon Tourist Hotel which runs from 7.30 pm to 3 am. Group entry rates here are W28,000 which buys you three large bottles of beer with snacks. There's a live band on every night plus frequent Korean singers. There's also a similar nightclub at the *Joong Ang Tourist Hotel* where the cover charge is W32,000.

GETTING THERE & AWAY
Bus

There are three bus terminals in Taejon – the West (Sobu) Chikheng Bus Terminal 서부버스터미널 , the East (Tongbu) Chikheng Bus Terminal 동부터미널 and the Express (Kosok) Bus Terminal 고속버스터미널 . The latter two are located side by side on the eastern outskirts of town.

Buses from the Express (Kosok) Bus Terminal:

To Taegu Buses every 20 minutes from 6.30 am to 8 pm. The fare is W2170 and the journey takes two hours.

To Kwangju Buses every 40 minutes from 6.40 am to 7.10 pm. The fare is W2700 and the journey takes nearly three hours.

To Kyongju Four buses per day, the first at 8.20 am and the last at 6 pm. The fare is W3110 and the journey takes two hours and 40 minutes.

To Pohang Buses once every two hours from 7 am to 6.10 pm. The fare is W3600 and the journey takes three hours and 20 minutes.

To Pusan Buses every 50 minutes from 6.30 am to 6.30 pm. The fare is W4030 and the journey takes 3½ hours.

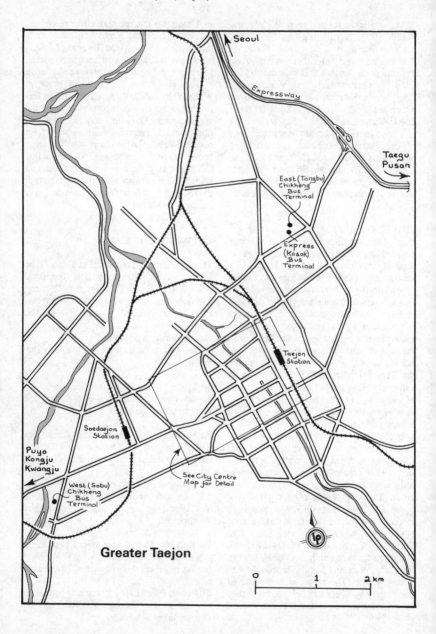

Greater Taejon

To Seoul Up to 12 buses per hour, the first at 6 am and the last at 9.40 pm. The fare is W2240 and the journey takes two hours.

Buses from the East Chikheng Bus Terminal:

There are frequent buses from this terminal to Cheonan, Cheongju, Chungju and Kimchon, but the main interest for travellers is that it's here you get buses to the famous temples of Popju-sa 법주사 in Songni-san National Park 속리산 and Mujuguncheondong 무주구천동 in Togyu National Park 덕유국립공원 Details of these are included under Around Taejon.

Buses from the West Chikheng Bus Terminal:

To Puyo Buses every five minutes from 6 am to 9.35 pm. The fare is W1160 and the journey takes one hour and 20 minutes. All of these buses stop briefly at Nonsan so they can be used as the first leg of the journey to Gwanchuk-sa temple (Unjin Miruk) 은진미륵. There are many other buses scheduled for Nonsan. The fare as far as Nonsan is W740.

To Kongju Buses every five minutes from 6.30 am to 10.30 pm. The fare is W710 and the journey takes one hour.

To Kap-sa Temple Direct buses seven times daily, the first at 7.30 am and the last at 5.50 pm. The fare is W1010 and the journey takes one hour.

To Seoul Buses every 30 minutes, the first at 8 am and the last at 7 pm. The fare is W2240 and the journey takes two hours and 10 minutes.

Train

There are two railway stations in Taejon. Taejon Railway Station in the centre of the city serves the main line between Seoul and Pusan and all trains en route to either of those cities stop here. The other station on the west of town is Seodaejon Railway Station. This station serves the line to Mogpo via Nonsan,

Iri and Kwangju though if you're heading for Kwangju you must change at Yeong San Po.

GETTING AROUND

The most important local bus as far as travellers are concerned is the No 841 which connects the East Chikheng/Express Bus terminals with the West Chikheng Bus Terminal via Taejon Railway Station and the city centre. Bus No 851 also connects Taejon Railway Station with the East Chikheng/Express Bus terminals and No 714 connects Taejon Railway Station with the West Chikheng Bus Terminal. The fare is the same on all city buses – W120 or W110 if you buy the ticket from a booth.

Around Taejon

GWANCHUK-SA TEMPLE (UNJIN MIRUK) 관촉사

This old Buddhist temple just outside Nonsan is famous throughout Korea for possessing the largest stone Buddha in the country. It has some features unique in Korea, and is well worth a visit. The Unjin Miruk statue was built in 968 AD during the Koryo Dynasty and stands 18 metres high. It's made out of three massive pieces of granite – one piece for the head and body and two pieces for the arms – and must have presented some interesting construction problems. The courtyard in which it stands is surrounded by typical Korean temple buildings as well as a five-storey pagoda, and stone lanterns. If you're lucky, you may come across a small festival going on here. Admission costs W600 (W500 for students and those under 24 years old).

Places to Stay

If you'd like to stay at the temple overnight, there's a small *yogwan* just below the temple entrance.

Getting There & Away

To get to Gwanchuk-sa, take a bus from Taejon to Nonsan (W740, 45 minutes).

When you arrive there you will find yourself at the *chikheng* bus terminal. Walk out of the bus terminal onto the main street and turn right. Continue up the street for about 500 metres and then take the road which forks to the right. A little way down this road you'll see a signposted bus stop for Gwanchuk-sa. Wait here for the local bus which will take you direct to the temple. The buses also have the same destination sign on the front and they run every 15 to 20 minutes. The fare is W120 and the journey takes about eight minutes.

TAEDUN-SAN PROVINCIAL PARK
대둔산 공립공원

Being a very mountainous country, there are many craggy peaks in Korea which offer spectacular views over the surrounding countryside, but this one ranks among the best. Not only that, but the climb to the top along steep, stony tracks is an adventure in itself. Calm nerves are required here since the ascent involves crossing a hair-raising steel rope bridge stretched precariously between two rock pinnacles followed by an incredibly steep and long steel stairway. Those in search of a thrill have struck gold. Vertigo sufferers should go somewhere else for the day. It's a very popular place on weekends with local people as well as others from further afield and you'll even meet wrinkled old grandfathers (*haroboji*) and grandmothers (*halmoni*) huffing and puffing their way to the summit loaded with goodies for the inevitable picnic.

The ascent will take between two and 2½ hours for any reasonably fit person and about one hour for the descent. There are soft drink stalls at various places on the climb but prices tend to be about double what you would pay elsewhere – not that that's going to deter you from digging deep if you go up there in the summer – though fresh water (free) is available at certain points. Entry to the park costs W300.

Places to Stay

If you want to stay overnight in the area, there are a number of *minbak* available at the

entrance to the park where the buses drop you. Most of these are souvenir shops with one or two rooms to let. Recommended is the *San Ullim Souvenir Shop* 산울림 , run by Choe Kil Ung, which has a few rooms to rent for W5000 irrespective of the number of people per room. Facilities are basic and there are no hot showers (except by request in winter time) but there are flush toilets. Meals can be provided on request and the proprietor speaks a little English. The other *minbak* are similarly priced.

Getting There & Away

To get to Taedun-san, take a bus from either the East Chikheng Bus Terminal or the West Chikheng Bus Terminal in Taejon. The buses have the name of the park but they don't have numbers. There are buses every hour (every 20 minutes at weekends) from 7.30 am to 6.20 pm. The fare is W610 (50 minutes) from the West Terminal and W750 (one hour) from the East Terminal.

POPJU-SA TEMPLE 법주사 & SONGNI-SAN NATIONAL PARK
속리산 국립공원

Popju-sa is one of the largest and most famous temple sites in Korea and an absolute must for all travellers. It's also very popular as a weekend picnic destination with Koreans, so if you're not keen on hordes of people and prefer to enjoy your temples in relative peace and quiet then go during the week. Entry to the national park (including the temple) costs W1300 (W750 for students and those under 24 years old).

The temple was begun as early as 553 AD during the Silla Dynasty which was when the Daeongbo-jeon Hall with its enormous golden Buddhas and the five-roofed Palsang-jeon Hall were constructed. At the time it was one of the largest sanctuaries in Korea. Repairs were undertaken in 776 AD but in 1592 it was burned to the ground during the Japanese invasion. Reconstruction began in 1624 and it's from this time that the present Palsang-jeon Hall dates, making it one of the few wooden structures at Popju-sa to survive since the 17th century. Most of the others were constructed or reconstructed towards the end of the Yi Dynasty.

Popju-sa is, however, famous for yet another reason. Until 1986, it had the largest Buddha statue in Korea – possibly in the whole of North-East Asia – and the 27-metre-high, concrete statue of the Maitraya Buddha dominated the temple compound. It took 30 years to build and was completed only in 1968. It featured prominently in all the tourist literature of this area. Unfortunately, by the 1980s the statue had begun to crack so, in late 1986, it was demolished. In its place has risen a new statue, 33 metres in height, only this time made out of 160 tons of brass which sits on top of a massive white stone base containing a ground-level shrine. This gigantic project, which cost about US$4 million, was completed in late 1989.

There are many other interesting features at Popju-sa including stone lanterns, a rock-cut seated Buddha, a huge bell and an enormous iron cauldron cast in 720 AD which was used to cook rice for the 3000 monks who lived here during its heyday.

As though the magnificence of the temple buildings themselves were not enough, Popju-sa is surrounded by the luxuriously forested mountains of Songni-san National Park which, although at its best in the autumn, is beautiful at any time of the year. There are many hiking trails in the mountains above the temple – all well marked – and several hermitages where you may be able to stay for the night. If you have the time, several days' hiking is highly recommended.

Places to Stay & Eat

Like all important temple complexes in Korea, Popju-sa has its own tourist village (called Songni-dong) before the entrance to the national park except that here it's more like a small town. Songni-dong has expanded by leaps and bounds over the last 10 years and there's a wide choice of places to stay though most of them are *yogwan jang* and so fairly expensive (W8000 to W14,000). There are not many *yoinsook* or

ordinary *yogwan* to be found – and even those that are left are being upgraded. So, if you want a cheap place to stay, especially in the summer holiday season, you'll have to do some asking around. There are also *minbak* available and some of the owners of spare rooms go down to the bus terminal to meet incoming buses.

For campers, there's a free camp site (signposted 'Camping Ground' in English) on the opposite side of the river from the village which usually isn't crowded. Facilities are good and include clean toilets and wash basins.

As with places to stay, there are any number of restaurants in Songni-dong, most of them along the main road to the park entrance. You can get virtually any Korean dish at one or other of these restaurants (except fresh seafood) and a few of them specialise in 'mountain food'. Expect to pay more for a meal at any of these restaurants than you normally would elsewhere.

Getting There & Away

Direct buses to Popju-sa from Taejon depart from the East Chikheng Bus Terminal. There are buses every 20 minutes, the first at 6.22 am and the last at 8.10 pm. The fare is W1260 and the journey, over an exceptionally scenic route, takes 1¾ hours. Buses depart from bay No 12 – look for the Songni-san 속리산 and Poeun 보은 destination sign in the front window. The buses terminate at Songni-san Village about one km before the temple.

From Songni-san Village, there are buses to Taejon every 20 minutes or so, the first at 6.30 am and the last at 7.56 pm. To Seoul, there are buses approximately every hour, the first at 6.10 am and the last at 6.35 pm. The fare is W3390 and the journey takes three hours and 20 minutes. These buses to Seoul sometimes go to the Nambu Local Bus Terminal at the south-west end of Yongsan rather than the Kangnam Express Bus Terminal. If so, bus No 25 or 35 from in front of the terminal will take you to the city centre.

There are six buses to Taegu daily, the first at 9.35 am and the last at 6.26 pm. The journey costs W2950 and takes three hours. To Cheongju there are buses every 10 minutes, the first at 6.10 am and the last at 7.40 pm. The trip costs W1310 and takes 1½ hours. There are also buses to Suweon.

TOGYU-SAN NATIONAL PARK
덕유산 국립공원
If Popju-sa whets your appetite for magnificent old temples set in beautiful surroundings then you might also like to visit the temples here and, because this park is not as famous as Songni-san, it tends not to get so crowded on weekends. The two main temples in this park are Anguk-sa 안국사 and Songgye-sa 상계사.

Getting There & Away
To get to this national park take a bus from Taejon's East Chikheng Bus Terminal to Muju (otherwise known as Mujugunchong-dong 무주구천동).

They leave every 30 minutes from 6.20 am to 6.20 pm. The fare is W2140 and the journey takes about 2¼ hours.

KAP-SA TEMPLE 갑사 & TONG HAK-SA TEMPLE 동학사
If you haven't yet visited one or other of these two tranquil and very old temples in Kyeryong-san National Park west of Taejon then remember that they're well worth it.

Getting There & Away
Access to Kap-sa is probably easiest from Kongju though you can also get there direct from Taejon (see page 137 for buses and times). However, you can't get from Kongju to Tong Hak-sa by bus. The only way to get there by bus is from Taejon and you will have to take a local or *chaesok* bus from the main street in front of Taejon Railway Station. These buses run every 20 minutes or so, cost W120 and W200 respectively and take about 40 minutes.

Puyo (Buyeo) 부여

Standing to the south of a wooded hill (Puso-san) around which the Paengma River makes a wide sweep, Puyo is the site of the last capital of the Paekje Kingdom. The capital was moved here from Kongju in 538 AD and flourished until destroyed by the combined forces of Silla and the Tang Dynasty of China in 660 AD. Today it's a quiet provincial town surrounded by wooded hills and paddy fields with a friendly and very traditionally minded people. Of the Paekje ruins, not a great deal remains save for the kings' burial mounds a little way out of town, a few foundation stones of the army's arsenal and foodstore on Puso-san and a five-storey stone pagoda – one of only three surviving from the Three Kingdoms period. The main point of interest here is the museum, opened in 1971, which has one of the best collections of artefacts from the Paekje Kingdom you will find in Korea as well as other exhibits from later periods in the country's history.

INFORMATION
If you need any help in Puyo there's an 'information centre for foreign tourists' right next to the police station and close to the Chikheng Bus Terminal on the main street. Mr Chai Keong Suk who runs this place is very friendly and helpful and also runs a foreign language school in town. He speaks Japanese, English, Filipino and Spanish as well as Korean.

PUYO NATIONAL MUSEUM 박물관
The museum houses bronze spearheads, daggers, pottery and musical instruments from the 5th to 4th centuries BC, Paekje Dynasty jars, Buddha images and examples of roof tiles embossed with various designs, as well as a collection of celadon vases, funeral urns and bronze bells dating from the 6th to 14th centuries. There is also a number of interesting stone objects – baths, lanterns, Buddha images, etc – in the gardens in front of the museum. Unfortunately, there's very

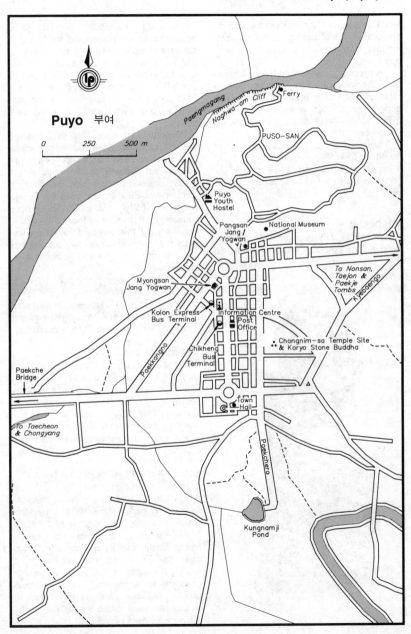

Puyo 부여

0   250   500 m

Paengmagang

Naghwa-am Cliff

Ferry

PUSO-SAN

Puyo Youth Hostel

Pangsan Jang Yogwan

National Museum

Myongsan Jang Yogwan

To Nonsan, Taejon & Paekje Tombs

Kyeoraengo

Kolon Express Bus Terminal

Information Centre

Post Office

Chikheng Bus Terminal

Chongnim-sa Temple Site & Koryo Stone Buddha

Paekche Bridge

Paekkanano

Town Hall

To Taecheon & Chongyang

Paekcheno

Kungnamji Pond

little explanation of the various objects in the museum so it's of limited interest to those without a knowledge of Korean archaeology.

Also recently moved into the grounds of the museum are three Puyo county government offices dating from the late Chosun period. They include the county magistrate's office, his residence and a guest house for government officials.

The museum is open daily, except Mondays, from 9 am to 6 pm in summer and 9 am to 5 pm in winter. Entry costs W110 (W50 for students and those under 24 years old).

PUSO-SAN 부소산

Rising up behind the museum is the pine-forested hill of Puso-san which is where the royal palace and fortress of the Paekje kings

once stood. It's now a popular park honeycombed with paths and roads and it contains a number of very attractive temples and pavilions with some excellent views over the surrounding countryside. Also on this hill are the ruins of the Paekje army's food store where it's said that it is still possible to find carbonised rice, beans and barley.

Puso-san is associated with the legend of the 3000 court ladies who threw themselves onto the rocks from a high cliff – known as Naghwa-am – above the Paengma River, preferring death to capture by the invading Chinese and Silla armies when the Paekje Kingdom finally came to an end. People come from all over Korea to see this spot. A stroll around this peaceful hillside, combined with a visit to the museum, is a pleasant and relaxing way to spend a morning or afternoon.

The park is open every day and costs W600 entry (W500 for students and those under 24 years old). There is a detailed map of the hill at the entrance though all the points of interest are marked in Chinese characters.

CHONGNIM-SA 정림사

The small Chongnim-sa temple site near the centre of town contains a five-storey pagoda dating from the Paekje period and a weather-beaten, seated stone Buddha from the Koryo Dynasty. This latter is one of the strangest Buddhas you're ever likely to see and bears an uncanny resemblance to the Easter Island statues.

GUNGNAM JI POND & PAVILION
궁남지

About one km past Chongnim-sa and surrounded by paddy fields stands a pavilion which was originally constructed by King Mu of the Paekje Kingdom as a pleasure garden for the court ladies. Until a few years ago it stood in virtual ruins but restoration was then undertaken and the bridge which takes you across the pond to the pavilion is now in good repair. It's a beautiful place to sit and relax and watch the activity in the surrounding paddy fields.

ROYAL PAEKJE TOMBS 왕능

About two km from Puyo along the road to Nonsan stands an extensive collection of Paekje royal tombs dating from 538 to 660 AD which are similar to those at Kongju. Most of them have been excavated and are open for viewing though all the contents have been removed so they're of limited interest and the wall painting in the 'painted tomb' is actually a modern reconstruction. What is worth seeing here is the museum, which has been designed to resemble a tomb. Inside is a number of scaled-down reproductions of the various tombs showing their manner of construction as well as a burial urn.

The area around the tombs has been landscaped and is a popular picnic spot.

The tombs are open daily and entry costs W350. To get there, take a local Puyo-Nonsan bus or hire a taxi (W1500). You can't miss the site as it's right next to the road on the left hand side.

PLACES TO STAY

One of the cheapest places to stay is the *Kyongbuk Yoinsook* 경북여인숙 where you can find a room for just W4000 a single and W5000 a double without bathroom. There's only cold water in the showers. They also have a so-called 'special' room which is basically just a Western-style bedroom and at W7000 hardly worth the extra. There's also a very pleasant *minbak* (no sign) on the left-hand side of the road leading to the Youth Hostel. It is run by a very friendly woman and costs W4000 with *ondol* and a communal bathroom with hot water. It's just past the sign for the Youth Hostel (on the right hand side) and a small shop (on the left hand side).

More expensive but a very pleasant place to stay is the *Myongsong Jang Yogwan* 명성장여관 , which has *ondol* rooms circling a leafy and well-maintained rock garden. The management are very friendly (but speak no English) and the rooms are very clean. Rooms around the garden cost W7000 for a single or double without bathroom plus there are more luxurious rooms on the upper floor of the main building with bathroom, hot water and colour TV for W13,000. It's a good place to stay and is popular with Japanese budget travellers as a result of appearing in their main guide book to Korea.

Similar is the *Pang San Jang Yogwan* 방산장여관 (tel 2-2154, 32-9977) close to the Puyo National Museum. There are several storeys to this modern hotel and a choice of Korean or Western-style rooms all with bathroom, hot water and colour TV. The ordinary rooms cost W10,000, rooms with air-con cost W12,000 and there's one room with a water bed for W13,000. The staff are very pleasant.

Also recommended is the *Purimjang Yogwan* (tel 2855) 부림장여관 , which is similar in standard and price to the Pang San Jang. It's a fairly small place with 18 rooms all with bathroom, constant hot water, colour TV and fan. There's a choice of Korean or Western-style rooms.

If you're happy with dormitory accommodation then check out the *Puyo Youth Hostel* (tel (0463) 2-3101) 부여유스호스텔 , 105-1 Kugyo-ri, Puyo-eup. It's not at all cheap at W6000 for a bed, though the facilities are excellent and include a bar, coffee shop, restaurant, laundry service and souvenir shop. The showers have hot water. As with other youth hostels in Korea, there are also much more expensive private rooms available but the price of these is considerably higher than what you would pay for the same thing in a *yogwan*.

PLACES TO EAT

There's a reasonable selection of restaurants in the cross streets which connect Puyo's two main streets. For a no-frills snack-type meal there are a few cafes around the bus compound where you can eat reasonably well for around W1000.

A good middle choice is the *Chungnam Shiktang* 충남식당 , which has a range of dishes from W1500 to W4000. A simple meal of omelette, rice, *kimchi*, soup and raw turnip costs around W2000. For a more substantial meal of *pulgogi* or *kalbi* you should expect to pay the usual W5000. Another place where you can get a good meal is the *Changsu Kalbi* 장수갈비 , a large restaurant with an extensive menu. They offer ordinary meals for W1500 to W2000 and their speciality, *pulkalbi*, for W5000, plus they also do raw fish but this is expensive.

GETTING THERE & AWAY
There are two bus stations in Puyo, both close to one another. The Express Bus Terminal is, in fact, just a patch of dirt and it only serves buses belonging to the Kolon Express bus company. The only time you'll use it is if you want an express bus to Seoul. All other buses use the Chikheng Bus Terminal opposite the post office.

The following buses leave from the Chikheng Bus Terminal:

To Seoul & Kongju
There are buses every 20 minutes from 6.55 am to 6.30 pm. The fare is W2910 and the journey takes three hours and 20 minutes. This bus goes via Kongju so you can use it to get there too. The fare to Kongju is W660 and the journey takes about 45 minutes.

To Taejon & Nonsan
There are buses every 10 minutes from 6.15 am to 9.40 pm. The fare is W1960 and the journey takes one hour and 20 minutes. All these buses go via Nonsan so you can use them to get there too (eg for Gwanchuk-sa Temple). The fare to Nonsan is W420 and the journey takes about 20 minutes.

To Daecheon
There are buses every 40 minutes from 6.55 am to 8.40 pm. The fare is W820 and the journey takes one hour and 40 minutes.

To Taedun-san Provincial Park
There are buses once every three hours from 7.27 am to 3.50 pm. The fare is W1220 and the journey takes 1½ hours.

Kongju (Gongju) 공주

Kongju was the second capital of the Paekje Kingdom established in 475 AD after its first capital south of the Han River near Seoul was abandoned. Nothing remains of that first capital today except for a few artefacts preserved in the National Museum at Seoul. At Kongju, however, there are far more tangible remains in the form of a whole collection of tombs of the Paekje kings.

The tombs are clustered together on a wooded hillside outside of Kongju. Inevitably, most of them were looted of their treasures over the centuries and nothing was done to preserve what remained until the Japanese carried out excavations there in 1907 and 1933. Even these excavations were marred by the looting which went on once the tombs were opened up, but in 1971, while work was in progress to repair some of the known tombs, archaeologists came across the undisturbed tomb of King Muryeong (501-523 AD), one of the last monarchs to reign here. The find was one of 20th-century Korea's greatest archaeological discoveries, and hundreds of priceless artefacts, which form the basis of the collection at the National Museum in Kongju, were unearthed.

Kongju is today a fairly small provincial market town and educational centre but its Paekje origins are celebrated with an annual festival held in mid-October which lasts for three to four days. It includes a large parade down the main street, fireworks, traditional dancing on the sands of the Kumgang River, traditional games and sports and various other events at local sites. If you're around at that time go to the Kongju Cultural Centre for full details.

KONGJU NATIONAL MUSEUM 박물관
The museum, opened in 1972, was built to resemble the inside of King Muryeong's tomb. It houses the finest collection of Paekje artefacts in Korea including two golden crowns, part of a coffin, gold, jade

Top left: The concrete Buddha, Popju-sa temple, in earlier days (GC)
Top right: The last haul, Taedun-san, south of Taejon (CHP)
Bottom left: Entrance to Tonghak-sa temple (CHP)
Bottom right: Pavilion on Puso-san, Puyo, former capital of the Paekje Kingdom (GC)

Top: Mogok-sa temple, near Kongju (CHP)
Bottom: Kap-sa temple, outside Kongju (CHP)

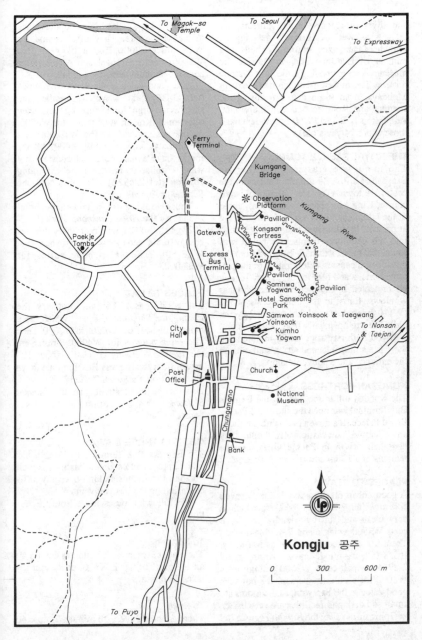

Kongju 공주

0   300   600 m

and silver ornaments, bronze mirrors and utensils as well as Bronze Age daggers, arrowheads and axes, an Iron Age bell and a number of Buddhist images. Outside the museum is an interesting collection of stone images. The museum is open daily, except Mondays, from 9 am to 6 pm during the summer and 9 am to 5 pm in the winter. Admission is W110 (W50 for students and those under 24 years old).

THE ROYAL PAEKJE TOMBS 무열왕능

The tombs are clustered together on Sangsan-ri hill, a 20-minute walk from the centre of town. The star attraction is, of course, King Muryeong's tomb. Only three of the burial chambers are open for viewing at present. Previously it was possible to go into the chambers themselves but it was found that moist warm air entering from the outside was causing deterioration of the patterned bricks and tiles inside so they're now all protected by hermetically sealed glass windows. Entry to the tombs costs W330 (W110 for students and those under 24 years old). They're open daily from 9 am to 6 pm.

If you're thirsty after the 20-minute walk there is a soft drinks and snack stall outside the entrance and a souvenir shop.

KONGSAN FORTRESS 공산산성

The wooded hill at the back of the Express Bus Terminal was once the site of the Paekje Royal Palace. It's now a park with pavilions and a temple. The castle walls, though they had their origin in Paekje times, are the remains of a 17th-century reconstruction.

PLACES TO STAY

A good cheap place·to stay is the *Samwon Yoinsook* (tel 2-2496) 삼원여인숙, which is very clean and run by friendly people. It costs W3500 a single and W4500 a double. There's a shady courtyard but no hot water. If it's full, try the *Taegwang Yoinsook* (tel 2-2964), which costs W3500 a single plus W1000 for each extra person. It's not such good value as the Samwon, as the rooms are small and dark and facilities are very basic.

Going up in price, the *Kumho Yogwan* (tel

2-5305) 금호여관 has been a popular place to stay for years. They offer rooms for W10,000 (W9000 if you haggle) plus W3000 extra for a third person. All the rooms have a bath, hot water, TV and fan.

Also good value is the *Samhwa Yogwan* (tel 2-3836) 삼화여관 which is up the same street as the large Hotel Sanseong Park. They offer small, Korean-style rooms for W8000, ordinary sized rooms for W10,000 and Western-style rooms for W13,000. All the rooms have a bathroom and constant hot water. Similar in price are the *Yurimjang Yogwan* (tel 2-4922) 유림장여관 and the *Sinpaekje Yogwan* 신백제여관.

Those looking for a mid-range hotel should try the *Hotel Sanseong Park* (tel 2-4023) 산성파크호텔 where ordinary doubles cost W16,500 and rooms with twin beds cost W18,500. They also have suites for W23,000.

PLACES TO EAT

For good, basic Korean food, try the *Hwanggum Shiktang* 황금식당 which has a range of dishes from W1200 to W2000. They also serve *pulgogi* for W4000. Similar are the *Taewoo Shiktang* 대우식당, about 100 metres from the Express Bus Terminal down the main street, the *Sonmi Shiktang* 선미식당, also on the main street, and the *Semmul Shiktang* 새물식당 opposite the Hotel Sanseong Park.

GETTING THERE & AWAY

The Express Bus Terminal in Kongju has both express and *chikheng* buses. It is well organised and you shouldn't have any difficulty finding the bus you want.

The following buses leave from the terminal:

To Nonsan

There are buses every 20 minutes from 6.40 am to 9 pm. The fare is W690 and the journey takes 45 minutes.

To Puyo

There are buses every 10 minutes from 6.40

am to 9.40 pm. The fare is W660 and the journey takes about 45 minutes.

To Seoul

There are express buses every 40 minutes from 7 am to 7 pm. The fare is W2240 and the journey takes two hours. There are also *chikheng* buses every 10 minutes from 6.50 am to 7.30 pm. The fare is the same but the journey takes 2½ hours. These buses go via Cheonan so you can use them to get there as well.

To Taejon

There are two types of *chikheng* bus which cover this route. One goes via Yusong and costs W710 and takes one hour. The other doesn't go via Yusong, costs the same but takes only 45 minutes. The latter run every five minutes from 6.55 am to 9.25 pm.

Around Kongju

KYERYONG-SAN NATIONAL PARK
계룡산 국립공원

This stunningly beautiful area of forested mountains and crystal clear streams between Kongju and Taejon is a popular hiking spot and also contains within its boundaries two of Korea's most famous temples, Kap-sa and Tonghak-sa. The best way to see the two temples is to set off early in the day and walk from one to the other. This takes about four hours at a comfortable pace. The trails are well marked and signposted but, other than a number of hermitages scattered over the mountain and the tourist villages at the temples themselves, there are no facilities so bring food and drink with you.

Entry to the national park costs W900 (less for students and those under 24 years old).

Kap-sa Temple 갑사

At the western end of the park stands Kap-sa, one of the oldest Buddhist temples in Korea dating back to the Unified Silla period (8th to 10th centuries AD). Unlike many of the temples in Korea which have been either restored or completely rebuilt from time to time, some of the buildings here are original. Times are obviously changing, however, as there's now even a souvenir stall in the temple compound itself. Usually these things are found only in the tourist villages. The monks at this temple are not keen on people photographing the Buddhas in the main hall even when no-one is praying so ask first if that's what you want to do.

There's a small tourist village down the road from the temple with a selection of *minbak*, *yogwan* and restaurants as a well as a camp site just inside the national park entry gate. It's possible you may be offered somewhere to stay at the temple itself if you meet the right person or have an interest in what goes on at the temple. *Yogwan* in the village tend to be expensive so, if you're trying to conserve funds, look for a *minbak*.

Tonghak-sa Temple 동학사

This temple stands at the eastern end of the park and although the buildings here are nowhere near as old as those at Kap-sa, the complex is a large one and the setting is stunning. As at Kap-sa, there's a small tourist village down the road from the temple with the usual facilities.

Getting There & Away

Bus There are direct buses from the Express/Chikheng Bus Terminal in Kongju. These buses run every 40 minutes, the first at 6.40 am and the last at 6.10 pm. The fare is W360 and the journey takes about 25 to 30 minutes. Buses go from bay No 3 – look for the sign: 갑사 . There are also slightly cheaper *wanheng* buses but they're not easy to track down and they take longer. The buses terminate at the tourist village which is about one km below the actual temple. You can also get to Kap-sa direct from Taejon (see Around Taejon for details).

Tong Hak-sa is best approached from Taejon. There are no buses from Kongju. See under Around Taejon for details.

Taxi If you take a taxi to either of these temples the drivers will demand that you pay around one-and-a-half to double what the meter would indicate. The reason for this is that they can't be sure of getting a return fare. On the other hand, if you're coming back from either of the temples then you can often get a taxi for much less than the normal meter fare for the same reason so it's worth considering if you can fill the taxi.

MAGOK-SA TEMPLE 마곡사

Another fairly remote and beautiful temple north-west of Kongju off the main road to Onyang is Magok-sa. Until a few years ago very few foreigners ever got to see this temple but it's well worth the effort. It was first constructed by the Zen Master Chajangyulsa during the reign of the first Silla queen, Son-dok (632-647 AD), a major patron of Buddhism who introduced Chinese Tang culture into Korea. The temple was reconstructed during the middle years of the Koryo Dynasty but since then, apart from additional structures erected during the middle of the Yi Dynasty, precious little has changed so you're in for a real treat of genuine Koryo religious art. The Chonbul-jon hall, with its three huge golden Buddhas is simply incredible both in size and execution. That beams of this size were lifted into place in the days before cranes is almost beyond belief. Another gem at this temple is the Yongsan-jon hall with its three golden Buddhas flanked by four smaller Boddhisatvas and backed by a thousand pint-sized white-painted devotees – all of them slightly different from each other.

Entry to the temple costs W550.

There's a small tourist village alongside the river before the temple entrance gate but not many places to stay as such. Most of the structures are souvenir shops and restaurants but, of the latter, some are attractively placed overlooking the river. You can eat well and fairly cheaply at these or sit and relax with a cold beer. If you want to stay overnight then the best place is the *minbak* across the other side of the river from the restaurants and reached by a footbridge. Make arrangements early in the day as it only has a few rooms.

Getting There & Away
There are eight buses daily direct to Magok-sa from the Express Bus Terminal in Kongju, the first at 7.50 am and the last at 6 pm. The fare is W490 and the journey takes 45 minutes.

GWANCHUK-SA TEMPLE 관촉사
You can also visit this temple with its famous granite statue of the Buddha (the Unjin Miruk) from Kongju by taking a bus to Nonsan 논산 and then transferring to a local bus which will take you direct to the temple. For details of transport from Nonsan, see the Taejon section.

Chonan 천안

Probably the only reason you would come to Chonan is to visit the Independence Hall of Korea, about 10 km south-east of the city, and the temple of Kagwon-sa, to the north-east where the largest copper statue of the Buddha in Asia stands. The city itself is of limited interest.

THE INDEPENDENCE HALL OF KOREA
독립기념관
Most nations which were at one time or another colonised and have since attained independence seem to have celebrated the event by simply taking over the bricks and mortar of the colonial authorities, renaming streets in the capital, and constructing stadiums where an extravaganza is staged every year on the anniversary of their independence. Some, it is true, have embarked on mega-dollar new capitals carved out of the bush, but very few of these have been successful and some have been the ruination of the national economy.

Korea has avoided these pitfalls, yet it has created a vast modern edifice eulogising its integrity as a nation and the coherence and uniqueness of its culture and has created an uncompromising yet superb display of its artistic talent and civil engineering skills.

The main hall of this totem to national sovereignty has to be one of the Seven Wonders of the modern world. It is enormous! – yet perfectly balanced. While built entirely out of concrete and tiles, it epitomises the apogee of Korean architecture. Kim Il-sung, eat your heart out! Your monolithic and egotistical statues of the so-called 'Great Leader' are fit for nothing but roadbase in comparison to this work of sublime perfection. Sydney is famous for its Opera House, India for the Taj Mahal and Paris for the Eiffel Tower, yet Korea will one day be famous for this incredible piece of modern engineering and construction. You have to see this place to believe it.

At the back of this hall is a whole complex of seven air-conditioned exhibition halls cataloguing the course of Korean history from the earliest recorded times up until the present. It's possibly the best museum in Korea – or rather it is if you can read Korean. Unfortunately for foreign visitors, most of the explanations which accompany the exhibits are in Korean and there's very little English. There's obviously a high propaganda content to much of the exhibits which chart the course of late-19th-century/20th-century Korean history, and the Japanese and North Koreans come in for some particularly virulent condemnation which isn't matched by an honest assessment of the effeteness of the Rhee years and the excesses of the Park and Chun regimes. Nevertheless, it's remarkably toned-down in comparison to similar nationalist exhibitions elsewhere, particularly that at the Chiang Kai-shek memorial in Taipei. Also, the penultimate exhibition purporting to show the improvement in living standards from 1950 to 1980 is definitely tongue-in-cheek. Few Koreans would have the wealth to support the kind of living standards portrayed by the 1980 diorama and there's naturally no mention of the lack of unemployment benefits, old age pensions and subsidised medical services.

Despite such reservations, and what some travellers regard as outright chauvinism, it's worth spending at least half a day here and possibly a whole day. There's also the Circle Vision Theatre which presents a 15-minute film on Korea's scenic beauty, its traditions, customs and development using the latest audio-visual techniques and equipment.

Entry to the Independence Hall costs W1000 (W800 for those under 24 years old). Entry to the Circle Vision Theatre is an extra W1000 (W800 for those under 24 years old). The Hall is open daily March to October from 9 am to 6.30 pm (admission ends at 5.30 pm) and November to February from 9 am to 5.30 pm (admission ends at 4.30 pm). Strollers for babies can be rented at the entrance for W1000 but the lack of ramps makes them only partially useful.

The complex includes several restaurants, a bookshop, post office, souvenir shops and even a bank where you can change travellers' cheques. A large-format booklet is available (in English) with coloured photographs describing the many features of the complex including the theme of each of the various exhibition halls. The booklet is free and is also available from the main tourist offices in Seoul.

Getting There & Away

The easiest way to get to the Independence Hall is to take a train or bus to Chonan followed by a local bus to the Hall (about 20 minutes from Chonan). If you have your own transport then take the Seoul-Pusan Expressway and turn off at the interchange south of Chonan which is signposted for the Hall.

If you visit the Hall on a holiday weekend and don't want to stay in Chonan for the night then make absolutely sure you have a train or bus ticket for the return journey to wherever else you are staying. If you don't, the chances are that all transport will be fully booked.

KAGWON-SA TEMPLE 각원사

Some seven km north-east of Chonan on the slopes of Mt Taejo 대조 stands Kagwonsa Temple which has the largest bronze statue of the Buddha in Asia. It was erected in 1977 as a kind of plea for the reunification of Korea and is over 14 metres tall. It's well worth combining a trip here with one to the Independence Hall.

Local bus No 46 from Chonan will take you there. From where this bus drops you it's a steep walk up just over 200 steps to the temple precincts.

East-Central Korea

Kimchon 김천

The Chikchi-sa Temple is the main reason for visiting Kimchon. There's little of interest in the town itself since it was completely destroyed during the Korean War and is totally modern, but if you find yourself having to stay the night there are a number of good places to stay.

PLACES TO STAY
One of the cheapest is the *Chon-il Yoinsook* 천일여인숙, which is good value at W4000 per room. It's clean and there's hot water in the communal showers. More expensive but still good value and very friendly is the *Chung-ang Yogwan* (tel 23061) 중앙여관 in front of the railway station which has rooms without bathroom for W6000 and rooms with bathroom, colour TV and fan for W8000. If it's full, try the *Myongbo Yogwan* 명보여관, also in front of the railway station, which has small, dark rooms without bathroom for W5500 and rooms with bathroom, colour TV and fan for W8000. The *yogwan* is on the 1st floor and there's a coffee shop on the ground floor. The *Kumho Yogwan* 금호여관 has also been recommended at W8000 a double with bathroom. It's halfway between the railway station and the bus terminal and within walking distance of both.

GETTING THERE & AWAY
Bus
There's only one bus terminal in Kimchon, which serves both express and *chikheng* buses.

To Taejon There are *chikheng* buses every 20 minutes from 7.08 am to 6.48 pm. The fare is W1770 and the journey takes just over one hour. These buses terminate at Taejon's East Chikheng Bus Terminal.

To Taegu There are *chikheng* buses every seven minutes from 6.30 am to 9.40 pm. The fare is W1040 and the journey takes just over one hour.

To Kimchon There are also buses to Haein-sa Temple from Kimchon three times daily, the first at 7.50 am and the last at 3.05 pm. The fare is W1930 and the journey takes 2½ hours.

CHIKCHI-SA TEMPLE 직지사
Chikchi-sa Temple is one of Korea's largest and most famous temples. Situated in the foothills of Hwangak Mountain west of Kimchon, it was first constructed during the reign of the 19th Silla king, Nul-ji (417-458 AD), which makes it one of the very first Buddhist temples built in Korea. It was rebuilt in 645 AD by priest Chajang who had spent many years studying in China and brought back to Korea the first complete set of the Tripitaka Buddhist scriptures. Further reconstruction was done in the 10th century but the temple was completely destroyed during the Japanese invasion of 1592. Though there were originally over 40 buildings at Chikchi-sa, only some 20 or so remain, the oldest of which date from the reconstruction of 1602.

Chikchi-sa's most famous son is priest Sa-myong or Songun, a militant monk, who spent many years in the Diamond Mountains (these days over the border in North Korea). He organised troops to fight against the Japanese in 1592 and later became the chief Korean delegate to the Japanese court when a peace treaty was negotiated in 1604. Following the completion of the treaty, Sa-myong returned to Korea with over 3000 released prisoners of war.

Entry to the temple costs W1000. It's a

very popular temple to visit especially at weekends so if you don't like crowds then go there during the week.

The actual temple compound is quite a walk from where the buses stop – about 1½ km – so in summertime it's a good idea to get an early start to avoid the midday heat.

Places to Stay & Eat

There's a well-established tourist village down where the buses stop with a range of *minbak*, *yogwan* and restaurants, so if you don't want to stay in Kimchon you can stay close to the temple. As with most of the tourist villages next to temples, the *yogwan* here tend to be relatively expensive so it's worth inquiring about *minbak*. Expect to pay around W4000 for a room but don't expect hot water for that. Both the *Seoul Minbak* 서울민박 (signposted as such) and the *Kyongnam Shiktang* 경남식당, a restaurant which also doubles as a *minbak*, are recommended.

For food, there's a small but good selection of restaurants with the usual range of Korean dishes but the speciality here is mountain vegetarian food (*sanchay namool*) which, if you haven't already tried it, is worth a spin. One of the best places to eat this is the *Kyongnam Shiktang*. Expect to pay around W4000 for such a meal. Like all restaurants of this type, it also offers a range of home-brewed country wines and liqueurs which are definitely worth investigating even if you don't have a particular yen for mountain food.

Getting There & Away

There are local buses from Kimchon to Chikchi-sa every 15 to 30 minutes from 6.20 am to 10.40 pm which cost W210 and take about 20 minutes. If you arrive in Kimchon by train, walk out of the train station, turn right and head up the main road for a further 25 metres or so. You'll find the bus stop there. These buses also pass by the Express/Chikheng Bus Terminal, so you can pick them up from there.

Kyongju (Gyeongju)
경주

For almost 1000 years Kyongju was the capital of the Silla Dynasty and for nearly 300 years of that period, following Silla's conquest of the neighbouring kingdoms of Koguryo and Paekje, the capital of the whole peninsula. It had its origins way back in 57 BC at a time when Julius Caesar was laying the foundations of the Roman Empire, and survived until the 10th century AD when it fell victim to division from within and invasion from without. A time span like that is rare for any dynasty anywhere in the world.

Following its conquest by Koryo in 918 when the capital of Korea was moved far to the north, Kyongju fell into a prolonged period of obscurity during which time it was pillaged and ransacked by the Mongols in the early 13th century and by the Japanese in the late 16th century. Yet, despite these ravages and the neglect of centuries, the city survived to experience a cultural revival which began early in this century and continues today. A great deal of restoration work has been accomplished, all of it to original specifications, and almost every year archaeologists uncover yet another treasure trove of precious relics which help throw more light on what life was like during Silla times. Today, Kyongju is an expanding but still relatively small provincial town with friendly, easygoing people, but its major draw is that it's literally an open-air museum. In whatever direction you care to walk you will come across tombs, temples, shrines, the remains of palaces, pleasure gardens, castles, Buddhist statuary and even an observatory. It's an incredible place but these examples of Silla artistry down in the valley bottom are only the most conspicuous and accessible of the sights which Kyongju has to offer. Up in the forested mountains which surround the city are thousands of Buddhist shrines, temples, inscriptions, rock carvings, pagodas and statues. You could spend weeks wandering around these places and never grow tired of it. Needless to say, the views from many of these places high up in the mountains are incomparable. This is definitely one of the most interesting places in the whole of North-East Asia.

Try to spend as much time as possible in Kyongju. Trying to rush round this area in just a few days will leave you breathless and saturated and you'll have to forgo virtually all the more remote but extremely worthwhile sites. A week would allow a more leisurely pace and a couple of trips into the mountains.

INFORMATION

If you're going to spend a lot of time exploring Kyongju and the surrounding area and are interested in the legends, the detailed history and current archaeological debate of the Silla remains, then it's worth getting hold of a copy of *Korea's Kyongju – Cultural Spirit of Silla in Korea* by Edward B Adams, (Seoul International Publishing House, 1986). This is a beautifully illustrated guide to all known Silla sites written by a man who was born in Korea and who has spent most of his life there. It also contains many detailed and invaluable maps and is a bargain at W10,000. Pick up a copy at one of the large bookshops in Seoul.

There is a tourist information kiosk outside the Express Bus Terminal but it's of marginal use since they only have a list of entry fees to the various sites (in Korean) and a map of Kyongju and district. They have no bus timetables and scant details of how to get to the more remote places of interest. It's easy to get the impression that they're only here to direct well-heeled tourists to the resort complex at Bomun Lake outside of town. There's a similar information kiosk outside the railway station.

There is an entry fee to most of the sites (which goes towards maintenance, reconstruction and archaeological research) and if you pay separately at each site it will burn a hole in your pocket. You can partially avoid this by buying a combination ticket at the entrance to Tumuli Park for just W2000 (W1000 for students) which gets you into the

park itself and a number of other sites including Taenung, Anapji Pond, King Muyol Tomb, Posokjong, Kim Yu Shin Tomb, Onung and Chomsongdae. It's worth buying but you'll still have to pay separately at many of the sites outside the central area.

CENTRAL AREA
Tumuli Park 천마총

Right in the heart of Kyongju City is a huge walled area containing 20 tombs of the Silla monarchs and members of their families. Many of them have been excavated in recent years to yield fabulous treasures which are on display at the National Museum. One of the tombs, the Chonmachong (Heavenly Horse Tomb), is now open in cross-section to show the method of construction. This huge tomb, 13 metres high and 47 metres in diameter, built around the end of the 5th century AD, is the only one so far excavated which contains a wooden burial chamber. Facsimiles of the golden crown, bracelets, jade ornaments, weapons and pottery found here are displayed in glass cases around the inside of the tomb.

Tumuli Park is open daily from 8.30 am to 6.30 pm (1 April to 31 October) and 8.30 am to 5 pm (1 November to 31 March). Entry costs W700 (W350 for students).

Noso-ri & Nodong-ri Tombs
노소리, 노동리, 능

Across the other side of the main road and closer to the city centre are two other collections of Silla tombs for which there is no entry fee, since the area has been set aside as a public park. The Noso-ri Tombs were built between the 5th and 4th centuries AD and were excavated between 1921 and 1946. The finds included two gold crowns. Across the road are the Nodong-ri Tombs which include the largest extant Silla tomb – Ponghwangdae at 22 metres high and 250 metres circumference. Houses covered much of this area until 1984 when they were removed. It's tempting to climb to the top of one or other of these tombs, but if you do you'll have park guardians chasing you and blowing whistles! And that's despite the fact that hundreds of similarly minded people have done just that,

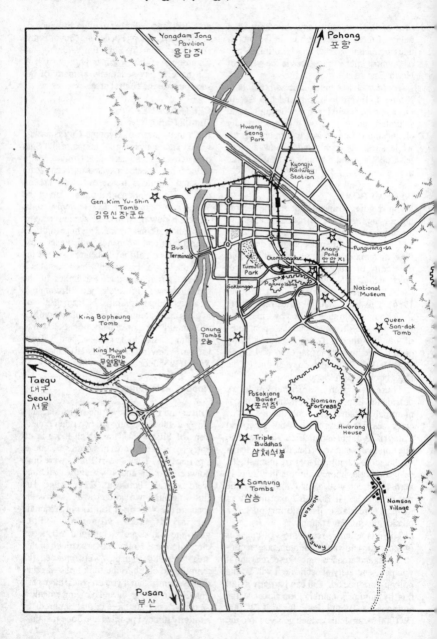

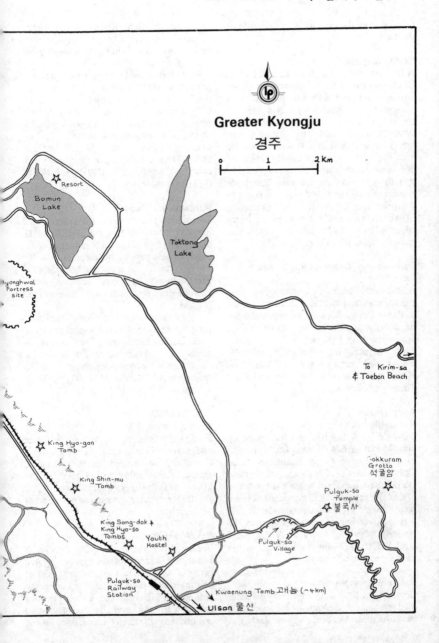

Greater Kyongju

경주

0   1   2 km

Resort

Bomun Lake

Toktong Lake

yonghwal Fortress site

To Kirim-sa & Taebon Beach

King Hyo-gon Tomb

King Shin-mu Tomb

Sokkuram Grotto 석굴암

Pulguk-sa Temple 불국사

King Song-dok & King Hyo-so Tombs

Youth Hostel

Pulguk-sa Village

Pulguk-sa Railway Station

Kwaenung Tomb 괘능 (~4km)

Ulsan 울산

judging from the bare tracks up the side of the tombs.

Chomsongdae 첨성대

A few hundred metres from Tumuli Park is Chomsongdae, a stone observatory constructed between 632 and 646 AD. Its apparently simple design conceals an amazing subtlety. The 12 stones of its base symbolise the months of the year and, from top to bottom, there are 30 layers – one for each day of the month. Altogether there are 366 stones used in its construction, roughly one for each day of the year. There are numerous other technical details relating to the tower's position, angles and the direction of its corners in relation to certain stars. Entry costs W150 (W70 for students) unless you have a combination ticket.

Panwolsong (Castle of the Crescent Moon) 반월성

A little further on from Chomsongdae on the right side at the junction with the main road is Panwolsong. Panwolsong was once the royal castle and the site of a fabled palace which dominated the whole area. There's hardly anything left of this fortress today except Sokbinggo 석빙고 or 'Stone Ice House' which was once used as a food store. There's no entry charge.

Anapji Pond 안압지

Across the other side of the road (on the left hand side) is Anapji Pond, constructed by King Munmu in 674 AD as a pleasure garden to commemorate the unification of Silla. Only remnants of the palace which once stood here remain, but when the pond was drained for repair in 1975 thousands of relics were dredged up, including a perfectly preserved royal barge now displayed in the National Museum. Entry to Anapji Pond costs W550 (W270 for students) unless you have a combination ticket.

National Museum 박물관

Continuing a little further up along the main road you come to the National Museum. This beautiful new building, whose design is based on classical Korean architecture, houses the best collection of historical artefacts of any museum in Korea, including the National Museum in Seoul.

Outside the main building in its own pavilion hangs the Emille Bell 에밀레종, one of the largest and most beautifully resonant bells ever made in Asia. It's said that its ringing can be heard over a three-km radius when struck only lightly with the fist. Unfortunately, you won't be allowed to test this claim! The museum is open during the same hours as Tumuli Park. Entry costs W200 (W110 for students).

Punhwangsa Pagoda 분황사

Completing this circuit is the Punhwangsa Pagoda. It was built in the mid 600s AD during the reign of Queen Sondok and is the oldest datable pagoda in Korea. It originally had nine storeys but only three are left today. The magnificently carved Buddhist guardians and stone lions are a major feature of the pagoda.

To get there follow the willow-lined road across from the National Museum until you reach the first intersection. Turn right at the intersection and then take the first lane on the right. The walk will take about 20 to 25 minutes in all. Entry costs W600 (W300 for students).

SOUTH AREA

Onung Tombs 오릉

Going south from the city over the first river bridge you will come to the Onung Tombs, five of the most ancient tombs in the area, including the 2000-year-old tomb of the kingdom's founder. Entry costs W200 (W100 for students) unless you have a combination ticket.

Posokjong Bower 포석정

Further down the road (quite a walk) is Posokjong Bower, a banquet garden set in a glade of shade trees (not the originals, of course) where there remains a fascinating reminder of Silla elegance. This is a curious granite waterway carved in the shape of an abalone through which a stream once flowed (the stream is still there but its course is now too low to feed the granite waterway).

Legend has it that the king, in the company of concubines and courtiers, would sit beside the waterway while dancers performed in the centre. One of the favourite games played here was for the king to recite a line of poetry and command one of his guests to respond with a matching line, at the same time placing a cup of wine on the water. If the guest couldn't come up with a matching line by the time the cup reached him then he was required to drain it to the last drop. Though there are records of similar entertainment in imperial China, Posokjong is the only banquet garden left in the world. Entry costs W300 (W150 for students) unless you have a combination ticket.

Triple Buddhas 삼체석불
Less than one km down the road from Posokjong on the left hand side are three mysterious statues known as the Triple Buddhas. Discovered only in 1923, it's not known how they came to arrive here since they are not of Silla origin but display the massive boldness characteristic of the Koguryo style.

Samnung Tombs 삼능
Last on this circuit, just a few minutes walk past the Triple Buddhas, are a group of four tombs known as the Samnung Tombs. The one which stands separate from the rest is the burial place of King Kyongae who was killed when a band of robbers raided Posokjong during an elaborate banquet. Nearly 1000 years separates these tombs from those in the Onung compound.

Local bus No 23 will get you to any of these sites.

WEST AREA
Muyol Tombs 무렬왕능
The main tomb of the Muyol group is that of King Muyol who, in the mid-7th century, paved the way for the unification of Korea by conquering the rival Paekje Kingdom. Just as you enter the tomb compound there is an interesting monument to his exploits in the form of a tortoise carrying a capstone

finely carved with intertwined dragons symbolising the power of his position. Entry to the tombs costs W300 (W150 for students) unless you have a combination ticket.

Tomb of General Kim Yu Shin
김유신 장군묘
Back towards town and along a branch road which initially follows the river is the tomb of General Kim Yu Shin. He was one of Korea's greatest military heroes who led the armies of both Muyol and his successor, Munmu, in the 7th-century campaigns which resulted in the unification of the country. Though smaller in scale than the tomb of King Muyol, the tomb of General Kim is much more elaborate and surrounded by finely carved figures of the zodiac. The tomb stands on a wooded bluff overlooking the city. Entry costs W300 (W150 for students) unless you have a combination ticket.

SOUTH-EAST AREA
Pulguk-sa Temple 불국사
Built on a series of stone terraces about 16 km south-east of Kyongju is Pulguk-sa Temple, the crowning glory of Silla temple architecture and probably Korea's most famous temple. It really is magnificent. Korea has never gone in for huge, monolithic (though magnificent) temples like the Potala Palace in Lhasa; instead it concentrates on the excellence of its carpentry, the incredible skill of its painters and the subtlety of its landscapes.

Originally built in 528 AD during the reign of King Pob-hung and enlarged in 751, it survived intact until destroyed by the Japanese in 1593. From then until the recent past it languished in ruin and though a few structures were rebuilt it never regained its former glory until 1970, when the late President Park Chee Hung ordered its reconstruction along the original lines. Work was completed in 1972.

Standing on the highest level and looking down you are presented with a rolling sea of tiles formed by one sloping roof after the next. The painting of the internal woodwork and of the eaves of the roofs should be one of the Seven Wonders of the World. Down in the courtyard of the first set of buildings are two pagodas which survived the Japanese vandalism and which stand in complete contrast to each other. The first, Tabotap Pagoda, is of plain design and typical of Silla artistry while the other, Sokkatap Pagoda, is much more ornate and typical of those constructed in the neighbouring Paekje Kingdom. Copies of these two pagodas stand outside the main building of the Kyongju National Museum. Entry to the temple costs W1500 (W750 for students).

Getting There & Away To get to Pulguk-sa from the city take bus Nos 11, 12, 101 or 102. Bus No 12 and 102 go via Bomun Lake on the way out and via Namsan Village on the way back. Bus No 11 and 101 do the opposite. The fare on bus No 11 and 12 is W120. On bus No 101 and 102 it is W300 since these are express buses. The buses drop you at Pulguk Village just below the temple.

Sokkuram Grotto 석굴암

High up in the mountains above Pulguk-sa, reached by a long, winding sealed road, is the famous Sokkuram Grotto, where a seated image of the Sakyamuni Buddha looks out over the spectacular landscape towards the distant East Sea. Constructed in the mid-8th century out of huge blocks of granite – quarried far to the north at a time when the only access was a narrow mountain path – it bears striking resemblance to similar figures found in China and India (especially those at Badami, north of Mysore). As a result of its simplicity and perfection, it is regarded by scholars as one of the greatest works of Buddhist art in the whole of North-East Asia.

It's certainly very impressive, yet when the Koryo Dynasty was overthrown and Buddhism suppressed during the Yi Dynasty, the Sokkuram fell into disrepair and was forgotten until accidentally rediscovered in 1909. This was the time of the Japanese occupation and, had the regional governor had his way, it might very well have ended up in a Japanese museum. Luckily the local Korean authorities refused to cooperate in its

removal and in 1913 a two-year restoration was undertaken. Unfortunately, incompetence resulted in the destruction of much of the superstructure at this time but in 1961 another, more thorough, restoration under the auspices of UNESCO was begun. It was completed three years later.

The one disappointing thing about Sokkuram Grotto is that the Buddha is encased in a shiny, reflective glass case and photographs are not permitted. Entry to the grotto costs W1500 (W740 for students).

Both Pulguk-sa and Sokkuram Grotto literally crawl with tourists every day of the week during the summer months and the place can take on the air of a mass picnic, so be prepared.

Getting There & Away To get to the grotto from Pulguk-sa, take one of the frequent minibuses which leave from the tourist information pavilion in the car park below the temple. The return fare is W950. The minibuses terminate at a car park and from there it's a 400-metre walk along a shaded gravel track to the grotto. You get about one hour to visit the grotto before the buses return. Alternatively, there's a well-marked hiking trail from Pulguk-sa to the grotto

Buddha at Sokkurum Grotto, Kyongju

(about 3½- km long) which you may prefer to take.

Kwaenung Tomb 괘능

Several km further off to the south-east along the main road is Kwaenung Tomb. It is worth visiting for its unusual carved figures which line the approach to the tomb – military guards, civil officials, lions and monkeys. The military figures are quite unlike any others in the Kyongju area with their wavy hair, heavy beards and prominent noses. It's said they may represent the Persian mercenaries who are known to have served the court of Silla. The tomb itself is decorated with carved reliefs of the 12 animals of the zodiac. This tomb compound is rarely visited. Entry costs W200 (W100 for students).

Getting There & Away From Pulguk-sa take bus No 12 which will take you down the road past the Kyongju Youth Hostel to the junction with the main road where the Pulguk Railway Station is. Change here for a bus going along the main road and tell the driver where you are heading. It's usually four or five stops from here depending on who wants to get off or on. The fare is W120. Where you get off there is a billboard at the side of the road with an illustration of Kwaenung Tomb on it. Take the tarmac road on the left hand side and follow it for about one km. It takes you directly to the tomb.

There are frequent buses back into Kyongju from the main road which go via the National Museum and the railway station – bus No 15 and 35 are two which cover this route. Simply flag them down. The fare is W130.

PLACES TO STAY – BOTTOM END

The most popular travellers' hotel – and one which well deserves its reputation – is the *Han Jin Hostel* (tel 2-4097, 2-9679) 한진호스텔, 173-1 Rose-dong. Here you can be guaranteed to run into many other travellers from all over the world so it's a good place to compare notes. The driving force behind it all is the energetic and disarming Mr Kwon

Young Joung. As well as making you welcome he's also a walking enthusiast and he knows the mountains around Kyongju like the back of his hand. Depending on his commitments, he may be willing to take you on walks to fascinating places which you would never have known existed. He speaks English and Japanese as well as his native Korean and is also a master of calligraphy and a yoga aficionado.

The rooms are spotlessly clean, the hotel well-maintained and there's constant hot water (oil-fired system). Singles/doubles without bath cost W7000/10,000 and rooms with bath, fan and colour TV cost W12,000 regardless of whether one or two people occupy the room. A third person occupying a room puts the price up by 30%. Towels and toothbrushes are provided. Limited cooking facilities are available in the proprietor's kitchen but please remember not to abuse this service and bring your own supplies. There's a leafy central courtyard on the ground floor where travellers gather in the mornings and evenings.

Some travellers have complained that this place is expensive (which it conceivably is for the rooms without bathroom) and that Mr Kwon isn't always the raconteur that he's made out to be. I asked him about this last time I was there and he explained that some travellers take too much for granted and that he gets annoyed. There's nothing unreasonable about that. What amazes me is that, after more than a decade of making travellers from all over the world welcome, he and his wife are still as fresh and energetic as they are about keeping the place running. There are plenty of other hotel proprietors, given the same pressures, who would have sold up and moved on years ago. It's still one of the best hotels in Korea. If the Han Jin is full or too expensive for you then another excellent place to stay is the *Tongsan Yoinsook* 동산여인숙 which is a traditional Korean style house surrounding a quiet courtyard with a small rock garden. It's spotlessly clean, has hot water (oil-fired), and the management are very friendly. Washing can be dried on the roof. Rooms without bathroom cost W6000 (negotiable down to W5000 if you're tight on funds).

If neither of these two places appeals, there are any number of *yoinsook, yogwan* and *yogwan jang* in the streets at the back of the bus terminals. Take your pick but don't expect to meet any other travellers or to find a lively courtyard where you can hang out in the evenings.

Outside of Kyongju between Pulguk-sa Temple and the main road to Ulsan is the *Kyongju Youth Hostel* (tel 2-9991/6), 145-1 Kujong-dong, Kyongju. This is a huge building with room for 600 guests. Like other youth hostels, it offers a range of accommodation from dormitory beds to private rooms and suites but the dormitory beds are no longer cheap at W5000 for members and W6000 for nonmembers! The private rooms are much more expensive. The staff speak English and Japanese and there are Korean, Japanese and Western restaurants, a coffee shop and money changing facilities. To get there from Kyongju take bus Nos 11, 12, 101 or 102 which go right past the front entrance.

PLACES TO STAY – MIDDLE

Other than the more expensive *yogwan jang* there are only two mid-range hotels in Kyongju itself. The first is the *Hyubsung Tourist Hotel* (tel 3-7771/5), 130-6 Noso-dong, Kyongju. This somewhat plain two-star concrete box has 30 rooms priced from W16,000 plus service charges and taxes. The staff speak English and Japanese and there is a Western-style restaurant, bar, coffee shop and nightclub. The other is *Kungjeon Tourist Hotel* (tel 42-8804), 170-1 Noso-dong, Kyongju. The rooms here start at W24,000.

Heading up the top end of this category is the three-star *Pul Guk Sa Hotel* (tel 41-1911/20), 648-1 Chinhyon-dong, Kyongju, close to Pulguk-sa Temple. Built to resemble, as closely as possible, the traditional architectural style in order to harmonise with the nearby temple, the hotel offers Western and Korean-style rooms from W34,000. Visa and Master Charge cards are accepted and the staff speak English and Japanese. There

are Korean and Western restaurants, a coffee shop, nightclub and sporting facilities.

Outside of Kyongju at Bomun Lake is the two-star *Pomun Lake Hotel* (tel 43-4245), 645 Shinpyong-dong, Kyongju, which has rooms from W20,000 to W30,000.

PLACES TO STAY – TOP END

Kyongju's top hotels are all outside the city either along the shores of Lake Bomun or close to Pulguk-sa Temple.

The most expensive is the five-star *Kolon Hotel* (tel 42-9001/14), 111-1 Ma-dong, Kyongju, close to Pulguk-sa Temple. Rooms here cost from W49,000 to W80,000. All major credit cards are accepted and the staff speak English and Japanese. There are Korean, Western and Japanese restaurants, bars, a nightclub, casino and many sporting facilities.

The other two top-range hotels are on the shore of Bomun Lake. The five-star *Kyongju Chosun Hotel* (tel 42-9601/19), 410 Shinpyong-dong, Kyongju, has 302 rooms priced from W75,000. All major credit cards are accepted and the staff speak English and Japanese. There are Korean, Western and Japanese restaurants, a coffee shop, cocktail lounge, nightclub and sporting facilities.

Similar is the five-star *Kyongju Tokyu Hotel* (tel 42-9901/16) 410 Shinpyong-dong, Kyongju, which has 303 rooms priced from W75,000. Credit cards are not accepted. The staff speak English and Japanese. There are Korean, Chinese, Western and Japanese restaurants, a bar, coffee shop and many sporting facilities.

PLACES TO EAT

There's an excellent choice of restaurants in Kyongju including Korean, Chinese, Japanese, Western and seafood, but the seafood restaurants, as elsewhere in Korea, tend to be very expensive. The best collection of them is to be found along Tongsong-ro though there are plenty of others scattered between Sosong-ro and the bus stations. Many are marked on the street map handed out by the Han Jin Hostel.

A good place to try for breakfast is the

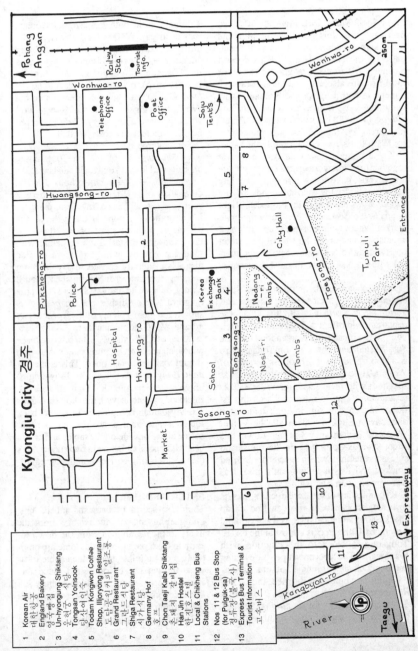

Kyongju City 경주

1 Korean Air
   대한항공
2 England Bakery
   영국빵집
3 Un-hyongung Shiktang
   은현궁 식당
4 Tongsan Yoinsook
   당산여인숙
5 Todam Kongwon Coffee
   도담공원커피 일군로룸
   Shop, Illjoryong Restaurant
6 Grand Restaurant
   그랜드식당
7 Shiga Restaurant
   시가식당
8 Germany Hof
   홍프
9 Chon Taeji Kalbi Shiktang
   춘태지 갈비집
10 Han Jin Hostel
   한진호스텔
11 Local & Chikheng Bus
   Stations
12 Nos 11 & 12 Bus Stop
   (for Pulguk-sa)
   불국장 (불국사)
13 Express Bus Terminal &
   Tourist Information
   고속버스

Chon Taeji Kalbi Shiktang 촌돼지갈비식당. You can't miss this place, as the blue and white sign outside says, 'Restaurant designated by the Hanjin Hostel'! This doesn't mean that it's a travellers' ghetto, as a lot of local Koreans also eat here, but it does have a menu in both English and Korean. As its name suggests, it specialises in *kalbi* and *pulgogi* (W4000) but it also offers an 'American Breakfast' (eggs, toast, jam and coffee) for W1500. *Pekpan* costs roughly the same.

If you prefer to put your own breakfast together (and many travellers do) then there are several bakeries where you can buy bread, notably the two branches of the *England Bakery* (sign in English). Right opposite the Sosong-ro branch is the main market where you can pick up fruit and vegetables, and on the far side of the market on Hwarang-ro is a well-stocked supermarket with canned goods, biscuits, beverages, etc.

For a cheap lunch or dinner, the *Silla-banjum* 신라반점 , close to the Express Bus Terminal, is worth a visit. It's a Chinese restaurant and offers dishes from W1000. If you'd like a break from Korean food then the *Siga Restaurant* 시계식당 on Tongsong-ro is a good place to go. It offers a range of Western-style food including such things as spaghetti with meat sauce for W2500. This restaurant is easy to miss as it's on the 1st floor and there's no sign in English though it does say in English underneath the *hangul* 'Western Restaurant'. Further down this street towards Sosong-ro on the right hand side is a restaurant which specialises in fried chicken and the like. You can't miss it as there are signs in English.

Kyongju, like other Korean cities, has its *soju* tent street where you can find cheap snacks, soup and the like as well as alcoholic beverages. This street is almost at the end of Tongsong-ro close to the junction with Wanhwa-ro. The tents open up in the evening and begin closing around 11.30 pm.

Going up somewhat in price, the *Grand Restaurant* 그란드식당 enjoys a well-deserved reputation for its *pulgogi*, though they also serve a good range of other dishes.

The menu is in both English and Korean. Expect to pay W4000 for *pulgogi*, a little more for *kalbi*. Similar is the *Taesong Shiktang* 대성식당 on Sosong-ro (marked as the 'Daesun Shikdang' on the Han Jin Hostel's map). It's a popular restaurant, the food is good and the prices reasonable but avoid their ginseng chicken (*samgetang*) which is bland and watery. *Pulgogi* served here is excellent and costs W4000.

For a splurge, it's hard to beat the *Un-hyon-gung Shiktang* 운현궁식당 on Tongsong-ro opposite the Noso-ri Tombs and adjacent to the large school. The restaurant is housed in traditional-style buildings surrounding a courtyard and set back a little from the road. It's an extremely popular place to eat, the cuisine is nothing short of excellent and there's an army of staff. Tables groaning with food and covered with a plethora of side dishes are literally carried into your room and, by the time you've finished, you'll hardly be able to move! There's a whole range of Korean dishes but the *pulgogi* is superb and there's plenty of it. Expect to pay around W5000 for a meal here.

As far as coffee shops go, there's one place which stands out as pure magic and you should visit it at least once. This is the *To-dam Kong-won* 도담공원 on Tongsong-ro diagonally opposite the Siga Restaurant. Enclosed by a stone wall, the shop surrounds a shady garden complete with waterwheel, fountain and a small pond. You can take your coffee either outside on the tables and chairs beside the pond or inside in pure luxury. It's the most relaxing coffee shop in Kyongju.

ENTERTAINMENT

There are scores of bars and music halls lining Tongsong-ro which range from the lively to the deadly and from the down-to-earth to the more up-market. Some are obviously pick-up joints, and indeed some of us were thrown out of one such place one evening because the *ajimah* apparently felt that the women of our group were too much competition for her 'girls'!

Less flesh-oriented are the two large 1st

floor bars, the *Germany Hof* and the *Munich Hof* beyond the Siga Restaurant. As you might expect from the names, they've both been done out to resemble German beer halls. Draught beer is available in 500 ml and one-litre glasses plus there's a range of 'snacks' (more accurately described as small meals). They're both popular watering holes and good places to meet local people and other tourists.

Along this same street are a few basement music halls of the 'karaoke' variety, usually with live music. Like all such places in Korea (and Japan), members of the audience are pressed into service at the microphone regardless of whether their voice resembles a spring chicken or a frog on heat. Assuming there's a lively crowd, it can be excruciatingly funny. These places are easy to spot even if you can't read Korean.

Going up-market, some of the larger *yogwan jang* in the area behind the bus terminals have nightclubs, again usually with live music. Before you head into one of these places, make sure you know what the cover charge is if there is one.

GETTING THERE & AWAY
Air
There is no airport at Kyongju. The nearest airports are at Taegu, Pohang, Ulsan and Pusan. Tickets for both Korean Air and Asiana Airlines can be booked at one of the two agencies in town. The first of these is at the back of the Express Bus Terminal and has a large Korean Air sign prominently displayed. The other is the Han Jin Tourist Agency on Hwarang-ro (no connection with the Han Jin Hostel).

There's one bus daily from Kyongju to Pusan's Kimhae International Airport which leaves the Express Bus Terminal at 9.40 am and costs W1520.

Bus
There are two bus terminals in Kyongju. The first one nearest the bridge across the river is the Express (*kosok*) Bus Terminal. Next to that is the local and Chikheng Bus Terminal. It's easy to find the right ticket booth and bus

at the Express Terminal as there are both English and Korean signs. At the Chikheng Terminal it's a different matter. Here it's relatively easy to find tickets and buses to the large towns but very difficult to work out which go to the more rural areas. Not only that, but the people who staff the ticket booths can be very off-hand about answering queries and they certainly speak no English. The posted timetables are a mess and, in part, illegible. Considering how many foreign tourists visit Kyongju, this is inexcusable and it's high time an effort was made to sort it out.

The following buses leave from the Express Bus Terminal:

To Pusan There are buses every 30 minutes from 7 am to 7.30 pm which cost W1150 and take one hour. This bus is of no use if you want to visit Tongdo-sa Temple halfway between Kyongju and Pusan as it doesn't stop. You need the *chikheng* bus for this.

To Seoul There are buses every 35 minutes from 7 am to 6 pm which cost W5090 and take 4¼ hours.

To Taegu There are buses every 20 minutes from 6.50 am to 9.10 pm which cost W970 and take about 50 minutes.

To Taejon There are buses four times a day, the first at 8.20 am and the last at 6 pm. The fare is W3110 and the journey takes two hours 50 minutes.

The following buses leave from the local and Chikheng Bus Terminal:

To Andong There are 11 buses daily from 6.20 am to 5.20 pm from bay No 7. The fare is W3040 and the journey takes 3½ hours.

To Hupo There are no direct buses to Hupo (for the ferry to Ulleung-do) from Kyongju. If this is where you want to take the ferry from then you must go first to Pohang and then take another bus from there to Hupo. There are seven buses daily from Pohang to

Hupo, the first at 10.36 am and the last at 7.20 pm. The combined fare from Kyongju to Hupo would be W2380 and the journey would take around three hours assuming bus connections were right.

To Pohang There are buses every five minutes from 5.25 am to 10.50 pm. The fare is W540 and the journey takes about half an hour.

To Pusan This is the bus you want if you intend to visit Tongdo-sa Temple halfway between Kyongju and Pusan. There are buses every 10 minutes from 5.40 am to 9.40 pm. The fare is W1180 and the journey takes about 1¼ hours.

To Taegu There are buses every 10 minutes from 6.10 am to 10.35 pm. The fare is W970 and the journey takes 50 minutes.

To Chikchi-sa Temple There's also a bus from the Chikheng Terminal direct to Chikchi-sa Temple near Kimchon if that's your next port of call. Buses run four times daily, the first at 9.30 am and the last at 5.20 pm. The fare is W2280 and the journey takes 2½ hours.

GETTING AROUND
Bicycle

Hiring a bicycle for a day or two is an excellent way of getting around the sites in the immediate vicinity of Kyongju. It also means you won't have to waste time waiting around for local buses from one site to the next. There are two places that bicycles can be rented from but the most convenient is probably the one along Taejong-ro. The cost is W4000 per day. None of these bicycles have gears so going uphill can be hard work.

Bus

Many local buses terminate in the road outside the Chikheng Bus Terminal alongside the river but these are mostly relatively long-distance local buses. For the shorter routes (eg to Pulguk-sa), buses can be picked up along Sosong-ro and Taejong-ro.

Four of the most important buses as far as travellers go are Nos 11, 12, 101 and 102. These are the buses you need for Bomun Lake, Pulguk-sa and Namsan Village. Bus Nos 12 and 102 go Kyongju, Bomun Lake, Pulguk-sa, Namsan Village, Kyongju. Bus Nos 11 and 101 go Kyongju, Namsan Village, Pulguk-sa, Bomun Lake, Kyongju. Bus Nos 11 and 12 are *wanheng* buses and the fare is W120. Bus Nos 101 and 102 are *chaesok* buses and the fare is W300. All four buses pass the National Museum on their way out and on their way back.

Around Kyongju

There are literally thousands of other relics from the Silla Kingdom scattered over the mountains all the way from Kyongju to Pohang on the eastern seaboard, to Taegu in the west and to Pusan in the south. There are also many other places of interest dating from the Chosun period as well as places of spectacular geographical beauty.

NAMSAN MOUNTAIN 남산

One of the most rewarding areas to explore within easy reach of Kyongju is Namsan Mountain, south of the city. Not only is it worth hiking around this area purely for its scenic beauty but the mountain is strewn with royal tombs, pagodas, rock-cut figures, pavilions and the remains of fortresses, temples and palaces. There are hundreds of paths which you can follow alongside the streams which come tumbling down the mountain as well as the 'Namsan Skyway' which is a winding gravel road which starts out close to Posokjong Bower, skirts the ridges of Namsan and ends up at Namsan Village near Unification Hall. The paths and tracks are all well-trodden and you cannot get lost, though at times you will need to scout around for relics which are not immediately visible since few of them are not signposted. Whichever point you decide to take-off from you're in for an exhilarating experience.

If your time is limited then two suggested daylong trips are:

Trip No 1

Take local bus No 23 from the local bus and Chikheng Terminal and get off at Posokjong Bower on the west side of Namsan (or at the Samnung Tombs if you've already visited Posokjong). From Posokjong walk to the Samnung Tombs (about one km) via the Sambul-sa triad. From the Samnung Tombs take the track which follows the stream up the side of Namsan to the crest of the mountain. On the way up there you will pass many freestanding and rock-cut images and a small hermitage near the summit where an old bearded monk lives. Follow the trail along the saddle until it joins the Namsan Skyway – the views from the saddle are incredible!

Carry on south along the Skyway towards Namsan Village for about half a km until the road makes a sharp turn to the left. A detour straight on from this point will bring you to two pagodas. Neither of these are visible from the road and the trail leading to them is somewhat indistinct. Also, the pagoda furthest from the road is not visible until you are just past the first so it's easy to miss. From here, backtrack to the Skyway and continue on down to Namsan Village, where you should visit the twin pagodas and Sochul-ji Pavilion & Pond. The latter is an idyllic little spot described in legends going back to the early days of Silla. If you've had enough for one day at this point you can catch local bus No 12 or 102 back to Kyongju from Unification Hall. If not, you could carry on south past Namsan Village to the seven Buddha reliefs of Chilbul-am. From there you would have to return to Namsan Village and take a bus back to Kyongju.

Trip No 2

Take local bus No 11 and get off as soon as the bus crosses the river about 2½ km past the National Museum. From here you can visit Pori-sa Temple in the Miruk Valley – a beautifully reconstructed nunnery set amidst old conifer trees with a number of ancient freestanding images. It is possible to make your way over the hill at the back of this temple to Pagoda Valley but it's a rough climb. If you don't have the right footwear it's perhaps easier to backtrack down to the bridge over the river and turn left there. Take the track along the west side of the river for several hundred metres until you come to a small village. Turn left here and head up Pagoda Valley. The first place you come to is Okryong-sa Temple. Just beyond it you will find the greatest collection of relief carvings anywhere in Korea, as well as a pagoda.

Returning to the river bridge and looking across to the main road to Ulsan you will see two stone pillars standing in a thicket of trees in the middle of paddy fields. These pillars are all that remain standing of what was once a huge temple complex during Silla times. If you like fossicking for ancient reliefs then this is the spot to do it. If that doesn't particularly interest you then head off down to Namsan Village and take any of the trails which lead up into the mountains.

EAST OF KYONGJU

There are a number of interesting places to visit along or not far off the road between Kyongju and Taebon on the east coast, and the road which takes you there passes through a beautiful and thickly forested section of Kyongju National Park.

Kirim-sa Temple 기림사

This is the first place of interest once you've descended from the pass which takes you through Kyongju National Park. The temple was one of the largest complexes near the Silla capital and its size (14 buildings in all) compares with that of Pulguk-sa, yet it is rarely visited by foreigners. You can enjoy this temple in peace and quiet as you will certainly never come across the picnic multitudes common at Pulguk-sa.

The temple has its origins back in early Silla times when a monk named Kwangyu arrived from India and acquired a following of some 500 devotees. Known originally as Imjong-sa, its name was changed to the

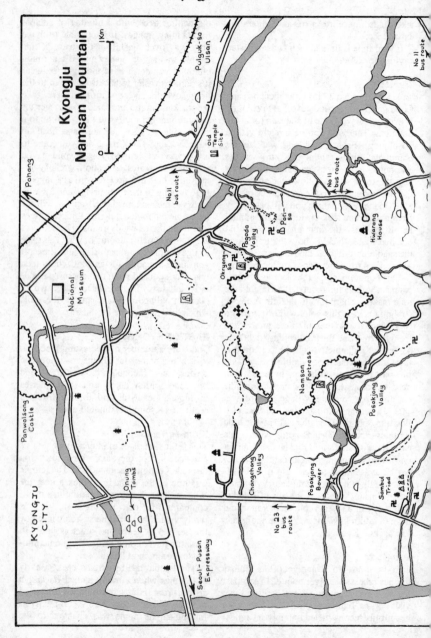

Kyongju
Namsan Mountain

1 Km

Pohang

Pulguk-sa
Ulsan

No 11 bus route

No 11 bus route

No 11 bus route

old Temple Site

Pagoda Valley

Pori-sa

Okyong-sa

Hwarang House

National Museum

Namsan Fortress

Posokjong Valley

Panwolsong Castle

Changchong Valley

Posokjong Bower

Sambul Triad

KYONGJU CITY

Onung Tombs

No 23 bus route

Seoul-Pusan Expressway

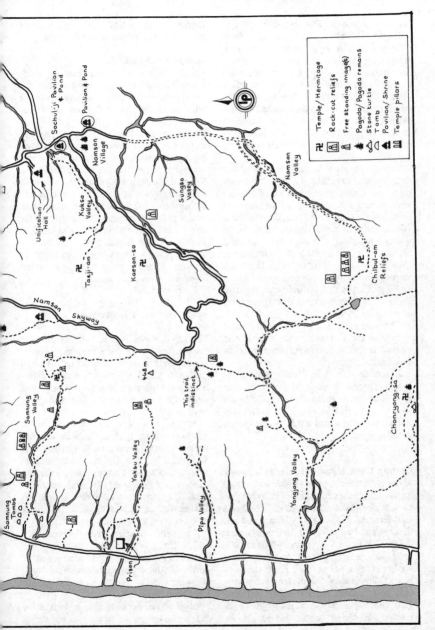

present one in 643 AD when the temple was enlarged. The present buildings date from 1786 when Kirim-sa was rebuilt. It's a very interesting temple with a number of impressive statues including a large Pirochana Buddha with attendants in the main hall, a Yaksa Yorae (Buddha of Medicine) in the adjacent hall and a gold-lacquered Bodhisattva of Mercy in the hall behind. The latter is said to date from 1501. The walls and beams of the various halls are superbly painted.

Perhaps the most amazing feature of this temple is the very unusual gold Buddha with eight main arms and hundreds of smaller arms radiating from the body plus a number of smaller heads in the hair of the main statue. The arms hold all manner of symbolic objects including a Tibetan-style *dorjes*, a Shiva trident and a bunch of grapes among other things. There's no other Buddha image vaguely similar to it anywhere else in Korea and it has a decidedly Hindu feel about it. Entry to the temple costs W700 (less for those under 24 years old).

There are the beginnings of a small tourist village at the entrance to the temple and *minbak* rooms are available if you want to stay for the night.

If you have the time, it's also worth visiting the rock-cut image of the Buddha at Kolgul-am off to the west along a footpath (two km) closer to the turn-off from the main road. It will take you about 25 minutes to get to the image.

Getting There & Away Getting to Kirim-sa requires a degree of perseverance since there are no direct buses from Kyongju. What you have to do is take a bus from the Chikheng Bus Terminal in Kyongju to Taebon and ask the driver to drop you off at Andong-ri where the turn-off to the temple goes off on the left hand side. From here to the temple it's about six km along a paved road. There are local buses from Andong-ri to the temple but they only go four times daily at 6.20, 10.10 am, 1.10 and 6 pm. These buses originate in Kampo about eight km up the coast from

Taebon. For the rest of the day you'll either have to walk, hitch a ride or take a taxi.

Kamun-sa Temple 가문사

About one km back from Taebon Beach along the main road to Kyongju stand the remains of what was once a large temple in Silla times. All that is left are two three-storied pagodas – among the largest in Korea – and a few foundation stones. The pagodas are prototypes of those constructed following the unification of Silla. A huge bell, some four times larger than the Emille bell in the National Museum at Kyongju, once hung in Kamun-sa but was stolen by the Japanese during their 1592 invasion, who tried to take it back to their homeland. They didn't get far and the bell was lost in the ocean close to Taebon. A search was made for the bell several years ago by a team from Kyongju National Museum but it was unsuccessful. There are plans to try again.

Entry to the site is free.

Taebon Beach & Taewang-am
대본, 대왕암

The small, rocky islet just off the coast at Taebon Beach is the site of the famous underwater tomb of the Silla king, Munmu (661-681 AD). It's perhaps the only underwater tomb in the world and at low tide it can be seen through the clear water of the pool in the centre of the islet.

Munmu had made it known that on his death, he wished his body to be burned and the ashes buried at sea close to the Kamun-sa Temple. The idea behind these unusual funeral rites was that his spirit would become a dragon and protect the eastern shores of the Silla Kingdom from Japanese pirates. His wishes were carried out by his son, Shinmu, who became the next Silla king.

The tomb was not rediscovered until 1967. There is speculation that the rock visible in the centre pool is actually a stone coffin but most experts dismiss this as a flight of fantasy though no investigations have been carried out.

It used to be possible to hire boats at the beach to take you out to the islet but access is now restricted and you need special permission from the police. Even if you're successful, it's questionable whether it's worth paying W5000 just to see a stone slab in the middle of a rock pool.

Taebon Beach itself is quite popular with Koreans especially during the summer holiday period but there's nothing special about it and there's garbage strewn everywhere. Like the rest of the east coast, too, the inevitable razor wire fence lines the beach.

Places to Stay Camping along the beach is prohibited but you can set up your tent along the banks of the river back from the town where the bridge crosses it. The only drawback to camping here is that there's garbage strewn everywhere.

Taebon itself has a number of *minbak* where you can stay for the night. Highly recommended is *Chingujip* 친구집 where a room costs W4000 regardless of numbers. The family who run it are very friendly and helpful.

There are a number of restaurants along the beach at Taebon which specialise in seafood but they're ridiculously expensive at W20,000 for a meal! Stay away from seafood here unless you want a large hole in your pocket.

Getting There & Away To get to Taebon Beach from Kyongju you need to take a bus going to Kampo 감포. These leave from the Chikheng Bus Terminal (bay No 2). There are buses every 30 minutes from 8.20 am to 8.30 pm daily, the first at 6.50 am and the last at 7.50 pm. The fare is W710 and the journey takes about one hour.

NORTH OF KYONGJU

The places of interest north of Kyongju are perhaps best seen as two separate day trips, though it's just possible to see them all in a single day so long as you make an early start.

Yang-dong Village 양동

Having steeped yourself in Silla history it's now time to immerse yourself in a different period of Korea's past which has escaped the ravages of modernisation. Yang-dong fits the bill perfectly. Here is a beautiful and peaceful Yi Dynasty village full of superb traditional wooden houses and mansions. It's been designated as a preservation area, like Hahae outside of Andong and Song Eup on Cheju-do, so it's an excellent opportunity to soak up the atmosphere of what life was like in most Korean villages before the advent of concrete and corrugated iron.

The village was established in the 15th and 16th centuries and consists of around 150 large and small houses typical of the *yangbang* class – a largely hereditary class based on scholarship and official position as opposed to wealth. It was the birthplace of Son-so (1433-84), a scholar-official who was one of the key figures involved in quashing the revolt against King Sejo in 1467. It was also the birthplace of Son Chung-ton (1463-1529), otherwise known as Ujae, and of Yi On-jok (1491-1553), a famous Confucian scholar during the early years of the Yi era but more widely known by his pen name of Hoejae.

Most of the houses here are still lived in so you need to observe the usual courtesies when looking around but the larger mansions stand empty and are open to the public. There's a plaque outside the more important structures on which you'll find the name of the building and an account of who built it and in what year. Most of these mansions are left open but there may be one or two which are locked. If that's the case, ask for the key at the nearest house. There are no entry fees to any of the buildings.

Of the larger buildings, make sure you see the Yi Hui-tae House, Shimsujong and Hyangdam House. There's a booklet for sale with a map and coloured photographs (entirely in Korean) at the general store at the entrance to the village for W1500. It's worth picking up even if you can't read Korean as it gives you a good idea of the lay-out of the village. A half hour's walk from the village stands Korea's second largest Confucian study hall which was built in honour of Yi On-jok and completed in 1575.

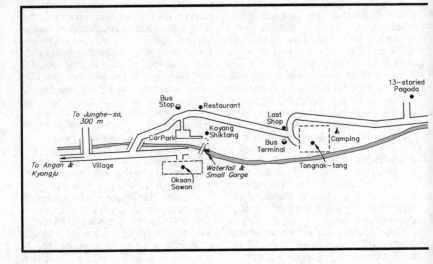

You're very unlikely to come across any other tourists in this village as it rarely features in any of the tourist literature. Possibly as a result of that, the people who live here are very friendly and it's easy to strike up a conversation and be invited to take tea and snacks. You should plan on spending several hours here.

There are no restaurants in Yang-dong but there are two general stores where you can buy packeted snacks, cold drinks and the like.

Getting There & Away From Kyongju, bus Nos 1, 2, 18, 55, 57 and 88 will all get you to within 1½ km of Yang-dong. These local buses go down the Kyongju-Pohang main road and then turn around after they've crossed the large river bridge. They then turn off to the right just before the bridge and head for Angang. A little way down this road is another fork to the right and this is where the buses will drop you. From here it's 1½ km to Yang-dong initially following the railway line and then going under it. You can't get lost as there's only the one road into the village.

There are no local buses which go directly into Yang-dong from Kyongju but bus No 1 from Angang (not the same as the No 1 from Kyongju) goes there three times daily. This bus returns to Angang from Yang-dong at around 11 am, 5 and 7.50 pm.

To get back to Kyongju from Yang-dong simply walk back to the turn-off where the bus originally dropped you. There are plenty of buses from there back to Kyongju. The fare is W430. Alternatively, if it's early enough in the day, take a bus to Angang from the turn-off and another bus from there to Oksan Sowon (see below), west of Angang.

Oksan Sowon 옥산서원

Oksan Sowon was once one of the two most important Confucian schools in Korea and like its counterpart, Tosan Sowon outside of Andong, one of the few such scholarly institutes to escape the destruction wrought on them by the father of King Kojong in the 1860s. It was established in 1572 in honour of Yi On-jok (1491-1553) by another famous Confucian scholar, Yi Toegye, and enlarged in 1772. A fire accidentally destroyed some

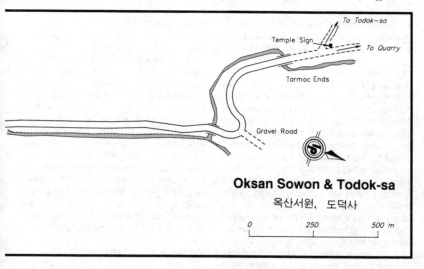

Oksan Sowon & Todok-sa
옥산서원, 도덕사

of the buildings here early this century so that today only 14 structures remain.

When first established in the 1500s, these *sowon* quickly became the centres of learning as well as of political intrigue and their alumni were numbered in the thousands. Indeed, they rapidly became so powerful that the Yi kings lost their supremacy over the Confucian scholars who thenceforth effectively controlled the entire country's economy and its political direction. Were a scholar to commit a crime, he was tried not by the state but by the Confucian college. The Korean kings were not to regain their supremacy until several centuries later.

These days, although they no longer function, the *sowon* are regarded as an important part of the country's cultural heritage since it was at these schools that most of the calligraphy and paintings of the Yi dynasty's last three centuries were produced.

Oksan Sowon has a sublime setting surrounded by shade trees and overlooking a stream with a waterfall and rock pools – an ideal place for contemplation and study. The main gate is usually unlocked so you can wander at will through the walled compound. Only one building is presently occupied by the family which looks after the place. There's no entry fee.

During the summer holiday period, the banks of the stream are a popular camping spot and swimming is possible in the rock pools below the waterfall.

Tongnak-tang 동해사
A 10-minute walk beyond Oksan Sowon along the main road up the valley will bring you to Tongnak-tang which was built in 1516 as the residence of Yi On-jok after he left the government service. Like the *sowon*, it has a timeless and relaxing atmosphere to it, as well as a beautiful pavilion which overlooks the stream. The walled compound is partly occupied by a family which looks after the place but you can wander at will through the rest of it. The main entrance gate is usually unlocked and there's no entry fee.

Chonghye-sa 청해사
Beyond Tongnak-tang and off to the left surrounded by rice fields is the unusual 13-storied stone pagoda of Chonghye-sa. It's a huge structure and the only one of its type in Korea. It's origins are somewhat obscure but it's generally agreed that it dates from the

unified Silla period. The temple of which the pagoda once formed part was destroyed during the Japanese invasion of 1592.

Todok-sa 도덕사

About 2¼ km beyond the pagoda of Chonghye-sa, high up in the forested mountains near the end of the valley, is the small temple of Todok-sa. It's a beautiful little place perched on a rock outcrop from which two springs emerge, and the views are magnificent. There are five buildings in all including a tiny hermitage above the temple itself but complete with its own *ondol* heating system. It's a steep walk up from the main road along a well-worn path but definitely worth the effort. It's about as far as you can get from the madding crowd and hardly anyone ever comes up here except the monks and the family who look after the cooking and cleaning. If male travellers were to bring their own food and drink, the monks would undoubtedly offer them somewhere to sleep.

To get to Todok-sa, take the main tarmac road up the valley past Tongnak-tang, ignoring the gravel road which forks off to the right just after you cross the first bridge. Several hundred metres beyond this you come to a second bridge where the tarmac ends. A little further on from here you'll see a rusty sign on the left hand side with a painting of a temple on it and a zigzag path leading up to it. This is where you turn off and head up the mountain. It's about 900 metres from here to the temple. Don't be put off by the steepness of the path as it gets gentler further up. You'll know you're on the right track when you come across a rock in the middle of the track saying (in Korean), 'Todok-sa 700 m'. There's a similar sign at the 500-metre point. For most of the way the path is shaded by trees so you can come up here even on a hot day. It's possible to hitch a ride with trucks along the main tarmac road as there's a rock quarry up near the end of the valley – you may hear the occasional explosion when blasting is in progress.

Places to Stay & Eat

You can camp alongside the stream either at Oksan Sowon or at Tongnak-tang, plus there's a signposted camp site adjacent to Tongnak-tang with basic facilities.

On the opposite side of the stream from Oksan Sowon there's a tiny tourist complex consisting of two restaurants and a souvenir/cold drinks shop. Of the two restaurants, the *Ko-yang Shiktang* 고향식당 is excellent value. The food here is tasty, only lightly seasoned (ideal for those not keen on hot food) and very moderately priced. *Pekpan*, for instance costs just W1500. They now have an English translation of the menu following our visit there. You can rent rooms here for W6000 to W7000 if you don't have camping gear. There's a third restaurant/yogwan nearby on the top side of the tarmac road – look for the Crown beer signs.

Getting There & Away

The most convenient way of getting to Oksan Sowon from Kyongju is to take bus No 57 which goes all the way. It leaves Kyongju at 6.30, 8.52, 11.52 am, 2.22, 4.37 and 6.54 pm. In the opposite direction, it leaves Oksan Sowon at 7.10, 10 am, 1, 3.30, 5.45 and 8 pm. The fare is W600 and the journey takes 35 to 40 minutes. Since this bus goes via Angang, you can also catch it from there (if coming from Yang-dong, for instance).

If the timings of the No 57 are inconvenient for you then take any bus from Kyongju going to Angang and change buses there. There are local buses between Angang and Oksan Sowon other than the No 57 from Kyongju. The stop for these buses in Angang is close to the post office and opposite a supermarket on the road to Yongchon. It's about seven km from Angang to Oksan Sowon. A taxi from Angang to Oksan Sowon will cost about W3000.

WEST OF KYONGJU

A number of interesting day-trips are possible to the west of Kyongju and include Buddhist temples, hermitages, the headquarters of a unique Korean religion known as Chundo-kyo, the remains of fortresses and a special vegetarian village.

Yongdam-jong Temple 용담정
Along a minor road in the heart of the countryside stands the temple complex of the Chundo-kyo (Heavenly Way) religion. This unique Korean religion was founded by Choe Che-woo in 1860. The religion incorporates aspects of Confucianism, Buddhism and Taoism. Choe was regarded by the Yi dynasty authorities as a troublesome subversive at a time when Korea was attempting to shut out foreign influences and he was martyred in Taegu in 1864. At the same time the original buildings of this temple were burned to the ground. His followers were a determined bunch, however, and, despite further repression, rebuilt the temple only to have it burned yet again. The most recent reconstruction was in 1960, this time with government assistance after the area had been made part of the Kyongju National Park. It's a beautiful, tranquil area of wooded mountains and terraced rice fields where farmers continue to cultivate the land in the traditional manner.

Getting There & Away To get there take bus No 5 from the Chikheng Bus Terminal in Kyongju and ask the driver to drop you at the turn-off for the temple. It's a short walk from where the bus drops you.

Pokdu-am 복두암
This is another interesting day trip not far from Konchon 건천 which involves a steep walk up almost to the top of a thickly forested mountainside. Close to the top is Pokdu-am Hermitage where you will find a huge rock-face out of which 19 niches have been carved. The three central niches hold a figure of the historical Buddha flanked by two bodhisattvas (Munsu and Pohyon) while the remainder house the 16 arhat. The carving is of recent age and, although there's an unoccupied house up here, the actual hermitage which used to stand here was burned down in 1988 after an electrical fault started a blaze. There's also a recently erected statue of Kwanseum, the Goddess of Mercy, just beyond the rock-face. The old couple who used to live up here and maintain the hermit-age have since moved down to the small temple off to the right at the start of the trail.

While unique to Korea, the rock-face niches of Pokdu-am are only part of the reason why it's worth coming out here. The climb itself would be ample justification since there are spectacular views over the surrounding countryside from various points along the trail. The trail is well maintained and easy to follow but bring your own liquid refreshments as there are no springs along the way. The walk up there will take around 1½ hours, less coming back down.

Some maps printed of this area (including the one handed out by the Han Jin Hostel) suggest that the trail continues on past Pokdu-am, along the saddle, and across to Chusa-am 주사암 and Mankyo-am 만교암. There is indeed a trail which once allowed you to do this but it's now thoroughly overgrown and you'd need a mattock to chop your way through. The rock-cut image of the

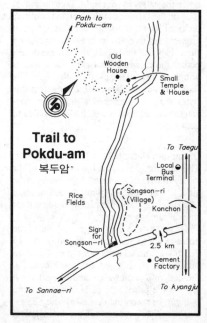

Path to
Pokdu-am

Old
Wooden
House

Small
Temple
& House

**Trail to
Pokdu-am**
복두암

To Taegu

Local
Bus
Terminal

Rice
Fields

Songson–ri
(Village)

Konchon

Sign
for
Songson–ri

2.5 km

Cement
Factory

To Sannae–ri

To kyongju

Buddha of Mankyo-am, on the other hand, can be seen across the valley from just above the Kwanseum statue if you look hard.

Getting There & Away Bus No 28 from Kyongju will take you direct to the village of Songson-ri 송산리 which is where the trail starts up the mountain. There are buses at 9.15, 10 and 11.27 am in the mornings and the buses will have Sannae-ri 산내리 in the front window.

If you can't find one of these buses, then take any *chikheng* bus along the old highway to Taegu and get off at the bus station in Konchon 건천 . These buses are very frequent and the fare to Konchon is W230. From the bus station in Konchon take one of the frequent local buses to Songson-ri Village (about 2½ km, W140).

Where the bus drops you, you'll see a blue and white sign saying 'Songson-ri' and a pedestrian crossing painted across the road. A few metres up from these a river comes down the valley to your right. Take the gravel road on the far side of this river and continue on until you get to the point at which it crosses the river by a concrete causeway (less than one km). Take the left hand fork before the causeway and after a few metres you'll see a small temple off to the right. The trail to Pokdu-am bears off to the left at this point and is well marked with Korean characters painted onto rocks. It's impossible to get lost.

Chusa-am Hermitage 주사암
This hermitage is on the opposite side of the valley from Pokdu-am and is the oldest in the area. It was founded by monk Uisang some 1300 years ago and has provided a home for several famous monks.

To get to this hermitage, use the same buses to get to Songson-ri as you would for Pokdu-am and take the same gravel road up into the valley, but instead of turning off at the concrete causeway, continue on over it and up the other side of the valley. About halfway between the causeway and Chusa-am, some 200 metres off the main gravel

road, is Mankyo-am, the area's third hermitage.

Ura Village 우라마을
Also west of Kyongju is the special vegetarian village of Ura. The inhabitants of this village consist of some 30 unmarried women and two or three old men, all of them Christians of a fundamentalist bent who eat only raw vegetarian foods such as pine needles, wild herbs, weeds and roots. In summer they drink a juice made from mountain grasses and in winter from pine needles. It's possible to visit this village and to sample a meal here if you make prior arrangements. Mr Kwon at the Han Jin Hostel can make arrangements if you get a small group together.

SOUTH OF KYONGJU
The main places of interest south of Kyongju are the temples of Tongdo-sa and Naewon-sa on either side of the expressway about halfway to Pusan. They are dealt with in the 'Around Pusan' section.

Andong 안동

Andong is a small town in Kyongsangbuk-do Province north of Taegu and Kyongju. It's well off the main tourist routes and has preserved much of its traditional character, as have many of the villages in the vicinity. Though it's not a particularly interesting town in itself, there are many interesting places to visit in the vicinity.

Most of Andong's sights are outside the city – some of them a considerable distance away – and getting to them requires a series of bus rides, but whilst you're in the city it's worth visiting the Folk Village.

FOLK VILLAGE 민속촌
The Folk Village here has been under construction for some time and is nearing completion, but until it is, entry is free of charge. It's nowhere near as large as its cousin outside of Suweon, south of Seoul, but it is well worth visiting. Here you'll find

a series of relocated and partially reconstructed traditional-style buildings ranging from simple thatched peasants' farmhouses to the more elaborate mansions of government officials and the like with their multiple courtyards. Where this village differs from the one at Suweon is that many of the houses are also restaurants, and for atmosphere and quality of food it cannot be beaten. Koreans have already discovered this and it's a very popular place to go for lunch or dinner. You'll find both the people who run the restaurants and their guests to be very friendly indeed. It has to be *the* place to meet people in Andong. Not only that, but the prices of meals here are very reasonable with the two simpler restaurants near the top of the hill being the cheapest.

The village is situated about three km to the east of Andong close to the dam wall on the opposite side of the river from the road which runs alongside the railway track. A concrete bridge connects the two sides at this point. (Note this is not the first bridge across the river at the smaller dam on the outskirts of Andong but the one beyond it.) Local bus No 3 from the city centre will get you here.

PLACES TO STAY

There is a good selection of *yogwan* and *yoinsook* close to the Express/Chikheng Bus Terminal on Hwarang-no. Two of the cheapest are the *Yonga Yoinsook* (tel 27165) 영가여인숙, and the *Posong Yoinsook* 보성여인숙 . Both cost W5000 per room without bathroom. They're clean but have only cold showers.

More expensive but excellent value is the *Chonggung Jang Yogwan* (tel 32336) 천궁장여관, which has rooms at W11,000 for a single or double plus W2000 for a third person. All the rooms have a bathroom with constant hot water, colour TV and fan. Similar is the *Sanho Jang Yogwan* 산호장여관 which has singles/ doubles without toilet and shower for W5000 and singles/doubles with bathroom for W11,000 The latter rooms have colour TV, fans and telephone but hot water only in the winter season. The staff are friendly. On the ground floor there is a bar (open evenings only).

PLACES TO EAT

A good cheap place to eat is the *Kukto Shiktang* 국도식당 where dishes cost W1500 on average so long as you don't order meat. They also have *pulgogi* but this will cost considerably more. Another good place for either *pulgogi* or *kalbi* is the *Insong Kalbi* 인성갈비 where you can get either of these dishes for W4000.

GETTING THERE & AWAY

There's only one bus terminal in Andong, which serves both express and *chikheng* buses.

To Pusan & Kyongju

There are 19 buses per day from 7 am to 7 pm. Ten of these buses go via Kyongju and Pohang, cost W4220 and take 4½ hours. The rest go via Taegu, cost W4040 and take 3¼ hours. If you're heading for Kyongju rather than Pusan, make sure you get on the right bus. The fare to Kyongju is W3040 and the journey takes about 3½ hours.

To Seoul

There are nonstop *chikheng* buses to Seoul every 25 minutes from 7 am to 6.45 pm. The fare is W4900 and the journey takes nearly five hours.

To Taegu

There are buses every 20 minutes from 5.35 am to 10.25 pm. The fare is W1920 and the journey takes about two hours.

To Taejon

There are buses approximately hourly from 7.25 am to 3.50 pm. The fare is W3590 and the journey takes about 4½ hours.

To Tanyang

There are 10 buses daily from 8.15 am to 7 pm. The fare is W1700 and the journey takes about two hours.

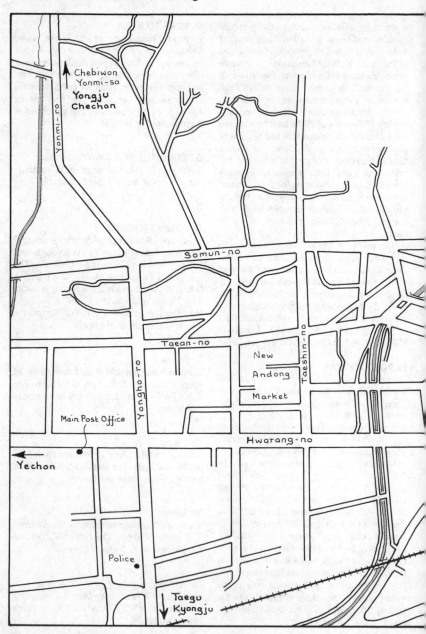

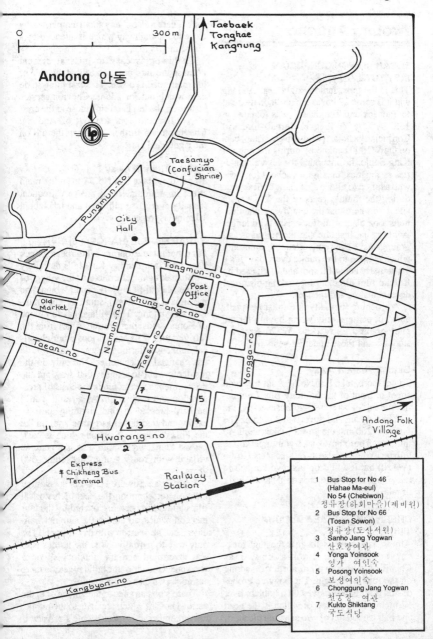

0   300 m

Andong 안동

Taebaek
Tonghae
Kangnung

Taesamyo
(Confucian Shrine)

Pungmun-no

City Hall

Tongmun-no

Post Office

Chung-ang-no

Old Market

Namun-no

Taesa-ro

Taean-no

Yongga-ro

Andong Folk Village

Hwarang-no

Express Chikheng Bus Terminal

Railway Station

Kangbyon-no

1   Bus Stop for No 46
    (Hahae Ma-eul)
    No 54 (Chebiwon)
    정류장(하회마을)(제비원)
2   Bus Stop for No 66
    (Tosan Sowon)
    정류장(도산서원)
3   Sanho Jang Yogwan
    산호장여관
4   Yonga Yoinsook
    용가 여인숙
5   Posong Yoinsook
    보성여인숙
6   Chonggung Jang Yogwan
    천궁장 여관
7   Kukto Shiktang
    국도식당

Around Andong

TOSAN SOWON CONFUCIAN INSTITUTE 도산서원

This is the most famous sight near Andong and it is some 28 km to the north on the road to Taebaek and Tonghae. It was founded in 1557 AD by Yi Toegye, Korea's foremost Confucian scholar (whose portrait appears on the W1000 banknote), during the reign of King Sonjo. It functioned for several centuries as the most prestigious school for those who aspired to high office in the civil service during the middle years of the Yi Dynasty and it was here that the qualifying examinations took place. Confucianism is no longer taught at the Institute and the buildings and grounds have been converted into a museum which is open to the public every day. It's a particularly beautiful spot and often used by Korean film directors for making historical documentaries and the like.

A brochure (partially in English) is available but perhaps only worth buying for the photographs. Entry costs W270 (less for students and those under 24 years old).

Getting There & Away

To get there, take bus No 67 from the main street in front of the Intercity Bus Terminal in Andong. There are five buses daily, the first at 6.40 am and the last at 3.40 pm. The fare is W200 and the journey takes about 40 minutes. These buses take you direct to the village. You can also take local bus No 66 (W120) but it will drop you two km before the village and from there you'll have to walk or take a taxi.

CHEBIWON (AMITABA BUDDHA) 제비원

Almost as famous as Tosan is the huge rock-carved Amitaba Buddha known as Chebiwon, some five km north of Andong on the road to Yongju. The body and robes of this Buddha are carved on a boulder over 12 metres high on top of which is the head and hair carved out of two separate pieces of rock. There's also a very small temple nearby close to the highway which is attended by a nun. Entry is free.

Chebiwon is easy to miss at present because the sign pointing to it at the side of the main road is down. The best thing to do is to watch out for a large Chevron service station on the left hand side close to the crest of a hill about four km out of Andong. Chebiwon is a further km down the hill on the right hand side.

Getting There & Away

To get there take bus No 54 from the main street in Andong. Buses are very frequent (usually every five minutes) and take about 10 minutes to get there.

HAHAE MA-EUL (HAHOE) 하회마을

For a memorable journey off the beaten track back into 16th-century Korea it's definitely worth making the effort to visit the village of Hahae Ma-eul (though it's spelt 'Hahoe' on the sign at the village), some 24 km southwest of Andong. This village has to be one of Korea's most picturesque. Apart from the refrigerators, TVs and various other electrical appliances in the houses, precious little has changed for centuries. Not only do the residents want to keep it that way but the government actually funds the costs of preservation and restoration. As a result, you'll be hard pressed to find anything quite as earthy and traditional as Hahae and, unlike the Folk Village at Suweon which is basically a tourist production, this is a genuine village with roots going back some 600 years.

Like Tosan Sowon, Hahae is a favoured location for shooting the sets of historical films and it has been discovered by the tour bus companies, so during the summer holidays it can be overrun with day-trippers. The only way to partially avoid the hordes is to stay overnight and try not to visit on a weekend. Outside of the holiday season there are no drawbacks of this nature.

There's no entry fee to the village or to the various houses which are open to the public, but remember to respect people's privacy if you step beyond the entrance gates. These are their homes, after all. The most important of the houses usually have a sign outside describing the history of the place.

Places to Stay & Eat

There are a number of *minbak* available in Hahae – most of them around where the buses stop – which cost W5000 per room on average. Some have signs (and there's even one in English saying 'Welcome Foreign Visitors'!) but if you're not sure then ask around. Dinner can usually be provided on request.

There's also a restaurant of sorts down by the river. It's a family house and there's no sign but everyone knows where it is. If you can't find it, ask at the fairly large general store down by the river. It's about 60 metres from there. They have quite an extensive menu, the food is good and the people who run it are friendly. Meals cost from W1000 to W1500 per dish and there's a choice of Korean and Chinese food. No English is spoken.

The general store at the bus stop also does a brisk trade in snacks and cold drinks but they don't offer full meals.

Getting There & Away

To get to Hahae take bus No 46 from the main street of Andong. There are six buses daily at 6.40, 8.40 and 11.25 am, and at 2.05, 4 and 6 pm. They return from Hahae at 7.10 and 9.50 am, and at 12.50, 3, 5 and 7 pm. The fare is W500 and the journey takes 50 minutes. If you miss the bus or you're in a hurry then a taxi costs W6000 one way. The last part of the journey is along a fairly rough gravel road.

If you have your own transport then you have to keep your wits about you as there are no signs for Hahae on the main roads, so it's easy to get lost. Take route No 34 out of Andong towards Yechon and turn off left along the 916 just past Pungsan. From there you drive a further five to six km and again turn off left. The sealed road continues for another km or so and then turns into gravel.

PUSOK-SA 부석사

Another very much out-of-the-way place that's worth visiting is Pusok-sa about 60 km north of Andong between Yongju and Taebaek. This temple was established in 676 AD by monk Uisang after he had returned to Korea from China bringing with him the teachings of Hwaom Buddhism. Though burnt to the ground in the early 14th century by invaders, it was reconstructed in 1358 and escaped destruction during the Japanese invasions under Hideyoshi at the end of the 16th century.

This stroke of good fortune has resulted in the preservation of the beautiful main hall (Muryangsu-jon) to this day, making it the oldest wooden structure in Korea. It also has what are considered to be the oldest Buddhist wall paintings in the country as well as a unique gilded-clay sitting Buddha.

Getting There & Away

Pusok-sa isn't easy to get to and requires a degree of perseverance. Once off the main highway, the road is dusty (or muddy depending on the season) and poorly maintained. Take a bus or a train first to Yongju and then ask around for transport to the temple, or walk/hitch the rest of the way.

Tanyang 단양

Tanyang is an up and coming resort town nestled between the mountains halfway across the peninsula, close to the eastern end of an artificial lake, in Chungchongbuk-do Province south of Wonju and north of Songni-san National Park. It's very popular with Koreans but hardly ever visited by foreign tourists, yet it's a very relaxing place to spend a few days and there are plenty of interesting things to see and do in the area.

The town itself is a recent creation and completely modern, since the old town of the same name was drowned by the waters of the dam, which stretch almost all the way to Chungju further west. Like Lake Soyang, east of Chuncheon, there are boats along the lake. There's also a very attractive bridge which connects the town to the eastern shore of the lake where one of Korea's most famous limestone caves stands and where a very scenic highway (No 595) branches off to Yong-wol and the east coast.

INFORMATION

There's a tourist information kiosk on the eastern side of the bridge into town, on which quite a lot of money has obviously been spent but they have precious little information other than a booklet (in Korean) containing coloured photographs of places of tourist interest in the area.

The Ferry Terminal for boats to Chungju is on the lake shore in the centre of town. It deals only with boats going to the dam wall (near Chungju). You cannot pick up sightseeing boats here. These go only from Todamsambong, a few km north of Tanyang.

The railway station is on the opposite side of the lake over the road bridge about four km west of Tanyang (this is a different bridge from the one in the centre of town) where the old town used to stand. Local buses run to the station from Tanyang at 8.05, 9, 10.15 am, noon, 2.15, 3.45, 4.30, 5.20 and 8.30 pm. The buses have 단양역 in the window.

KOSU-DONGGUL CAVES 고수동굴

Just across the bridge from the centre of Tanyang is one of Korea's most famous limestone caves, and Koreans flock here by the thousand during the summer holiday period. At that time of year you literally cannot move for people and it will take you an excruciating hour or more to walk round the system.

The caves are certainly spectacular and extensive – or rather they must have been before the catwalks and miasmic spiral steel staircases were installed up the main vertical galleries, but these aids to access (or was it commercial exploitation?) have been thoroughly over-done. Indeed, the grandeur of the caves has been destroyed irrevocably. A considerable amount of vandalism is also apparent on the tips of stalactites and stalagmites within reach of eager souvenir hunters.

Nevertheless, it's perhaps worth visiting the caves if the crowds are not too great.

Entry costs W1320 (W1100 for those under 24 years old). You should allow about one hour to get through the caves which are about 1300 metres long.

Just outside the caves is an extensive tourist complex with *yogwan*, restaurants and souvenir shops which completely obscure the entrance to the caves. Prices of everything here are well above average.

CHONDONG-DONGGUL CAVE 청동동굴

About four km beyond Kosu-donggul Cave, keeping left at the only road junction, is the smaller cave of Chondong-donggul which is some 300 metres long and was discovered only in 1977. Unlike its larger cousin which has both vertical and horizontal galleries, this cave is essentially just a vertical drop. Entry costs W990 (less for those under 24 years old).

There's the inevitable tourist village below the caves with *yogwan*, restaurants and a camp site.

There are local buses from Tanyang to Chondong-donggul at 7.05, 8.30, 10.30, and 11.40 am, and at 12.30, 1, 1.50, 3, 3.50, 4.40, 5.40, 7 and 8 pm.

NODONG-DONGGUL CAVE 노동동굴

If, instead of keeping to the left at the road junction, you turned right across the concrete bridge, continued on up the hill and then down the other side, you would arrive at the third set of caves. Nodong-donggul was the most recently discovered cave and is every bit as spectacular as Kosu-donggul with a length of around one km. There are the usual steel staircases and catwalks to make access possible but nowhere near the same number of people visit this cave so you don't get that feeling of claustrophobia that is possible in Kosu-donggul.

There are local buses from Tanyang to Nodong-donggul at 6.40, 8.50, 11 am, 1.40, 3.40, 5.45 and 8 pm.

BOATING ON THE LAKE

All the pleasure craft are moored at Todam

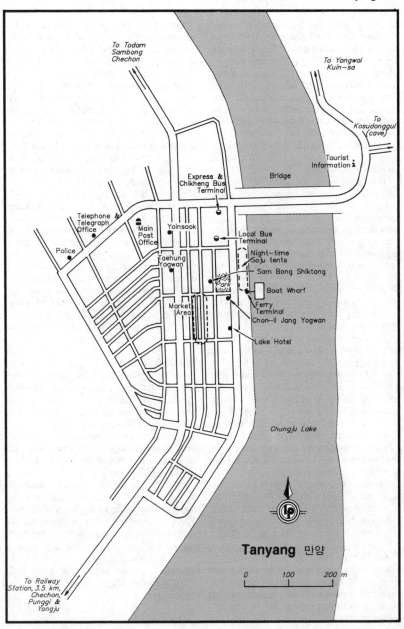

To Todam
Sambong
Chechon

To Yongwol
Kuin-sa

To Kosudonggul
(cave)

Tourist
Information **i**

Bridge

Express &
Chikheng Bus Terminal

Telephone &
Telegraph Office

Police

Main
Post
Office

Yoinsook

Local Bus
Terminal

Night-time
Soju tents

Taehung
Yogwan

Sam Bong Shiktang

Park

Boat Wharf

Ferry
Terminal

Market
Area

Chon-il Jang Yogwan

Lake Hotel

Chungju Lake

Tanyang 만양

0   100   200 m

To Railway
Station, 3.5 km,
Chechon,
Punggi &
Yongju

Sambong 도담삼봉 about three km north of Tanyang via the lakeside road. You cannot board them at Tanyang itself despite what the signs outside the Ferry Terminal suggest. There are local buses to Todam Sambong from Tanyang at 7.50, 10 am, 12.10, 1.30, 2.30, 5.10 and 7.40 pm. The buses will have Todam Sambong (in Korean) in the window and the journey takes about 10 minutes.

There are two varieties of boat which you can hire: speed boats taking up to six passengers; and slower open-decked boats which take many passengers.

The speed boats are good fun and the drivers really take them through their paces but it doesn't give you much time to take in the sights. They go when full and operate between 9.30 am and 5.10 pm and there are two options available. The first is a short eight-minute trip essentially just to the natural arch (Song-mun 석문) and around the island of Todam Sambong and costs W2000 per person. The second is an 18-minute trip which goes down the lake as far as Tanyang and then returns, and costs W4000 per person.

The slow boats are perhaps preferable as they are more mellow and you see far more of the sights along the lake. They go when full and operate between 9 am and 5 pm. There are two options available. The first is an 18-km round trip taking 50 to 60 minutes and costing W1500 per person. The second is a 40-km round trip taking 2½ to three hours and costing W4500 per person.

The ticket office for the slow boats is on the top side of the car park and that for the speed boats is down at the jetty.

There are a number of lakeside restaurants here, two of them with large PA systems so you can expect live music or disco in the evenings. If you stay until late, however, you'll have to take a taxi back to Tanyang.

PLACES TO STAY

There's a good selection of *yogwan*, *yogwan jang* and up-market hotels in Tanyang but very few *yoinsook*. There's also plenty of building work in progress but mostly for top-range hotels.

One of the cheapest places to stay is the *yoinsook* on the top side of the main street near the junction with the road which crosses the bridge. You can get a room here for W7000 without a bathroom.

There are scores of *yogwan* along the main street all the way down towards the bridge which leads to the railway station, but the most convenient places to stay are the *yogwan* between the main street and the lakeside in the centre of town. Most of them are *yogwan jang* so expect to pay between W12,000 and W15,000 for a room. Many of these *yogwan* have rooms looking out over the lake so they're very pleasant.

One of the cheapest places is the *Taehung Yogwan* 대흥여관 on the main street which offers rooms without bath for W11,000. For a room with a view, try the *Chon-il Jang Yogwan* 천일장여관 right in front of the Ferry Terminal on the 3rd floor. A room with a bathroom, constant hot water, fan and air-con costs W15,000. Similar in standard but somewhat cheaper is the *Palkark Jang Yogwan* 팔각장여관 (tel 22-2012) close to the Chikheng Bus Terminal. It, too, has rooms overlooking the lake.

PLACES TO EAT

As with *yogwan*, there are scores of restaurants, coffee shops and bars scattered around the central area, so take your pick, but one of the best and most reasonably priced is the *Sam Bong Shiktang & Yogwan* 삼봉식당 . The food here is excellent value and the staff very friendly. *Pulgogi* and a vast array of side dishes plus two beers cost three of us just W10,000.

An excellent alternative to the restaurants in the evenings are the *soju* tents on the lakeside road close to the Ferry Terminal. There's a variety of cheap snacks available at any of these or you can simply sit there and enjoy a cold beer or *soju* at the usual price.

For those who prefer to put their own food together, there's a market area with the usual range of foodstuffs.

GETTING THERE & AROUND

Bus

The Chikheng Bus Terminal and local bus terminal are next to each other facing the bridge across the lake in the centre of town.

The local bus terminal here is remarkably well organised and they even have a printed schedule of local buses. If you can read Korean and are planning on spending some time here then it's worth asking for a copy of this.

The following buses leave from the Chikheng Terminal:

To Seoul There are buses four times an hour between 7.10 am to 7.15 pm. The fare is W3030 and the journey takes nearly four hours. These buses stop in Wonju and Chechon so you can use them to get to these towns too.

To Andong There are 15 buses daily between 7.05 am to 7.53 pm which cost W1700 and take 2½ hours.

To Taegu There are eight buses daily between 7 am to 3.30 pm which cost W2620 and take four hours. These buses stop in Andong so you can use them to get to this city too.

To Samchok There are two buses daily at 11.45 am and 1.45 pm which cost W4320 and take six hours. This journey to the east coast goes through some of the most spectacular countryside in Korea and is well worth the effort if it coincides with your travel plans.

Lake Ferry

Ferries connect Tanyang with Chungju (617) at the western end of the lake (the dam wall is actually outside Chungju but local buses connect the ferry pier to the centre of town).

There are two types of ferry available:

Fast Boat During the summer months these leave Tanyang daily at 11 am, noon, 1, 1.30, 2.30, 3, 4, 5 and 6 pm, cost W5460 and take one hour and 40 minutes. In the winter months the boats leave less often. This might seem an attractive way to get down the lake and see the sights but the passenger area is completely enclosed behind windows and there's only a small area at the back of the boat which is open. There is no food and drink available on these boats and in the ferry terminal there's a notice warning passengers (in English and Korean) that, 'Drinking, dancing, disturbances and demoralisation are not allowed on board'!

Slow Boat The slow boats leave once daily at 3.30 pm, cost W5460 and take two hours and 10 minutes. These boats are far preferable since they are large with two open-sided lower decks and a completely open top deck and prow. This is definitely the way to see the lake. Meals and drinks are available on these boats.

Around Tanyang

KUIN-SA TEMPLE 구인사

About 20 km north-east of Tanyang off the No 595 road to Yongwol and deep into the mountains stands the headquarters of the Chontae sect of Korean Buddhism. The order was re-established only in 1945 by monk Sangwol Wongak after centuries of nonexistence and its precepts are based on an interpretation of the Lotus Sutra made by an ancient Chinese monk named Chijang Taesa. Entirely modern the temple may be (it's built in traditional Korean style but using concrete instead of wood), but it has a vast and obviously highly motivated following as well as being conspicuously mega-rich. This is real cult territory of the born-again kind. Devotees with name cards clipped to their shirts and dresses are very much in evidence, and that disgusting habit of smoking within temple precincts which occurs elsewhere is totally prohibited here.

There are some 38 buildings at this temple consisting of gateways, dormitories, administration blocks, halls dedicated to various bodhisattvas and an enormous five-storey main hall which it is claimed can accommodate up to 10,000 people. There's even a post office and bookshop! All these buildings are crammed into a steep, narrow and thickly wooded valley and wherever it's been necessary to contain water run-off or to landscape you'll see beautiful examples of dry-stone walling where it's obvious that no effort has been spared to create the best. Indeed, no effort has been spared anywhere in this temple to produce what is undeniably a masterpiece of civil engineering, sculpture, traditional painting and landscaping. The only thing they don't seem to have quite come to grips with yet are the septic tanks but then perhaps that's just a deliberate reminder of the transitory nature of the material world? Either way, they could hardly be blamed for having difficulty coping with the human waste produced by the many thousands of devotees who were there when I last visited.

This temple is an absolute *must* if you are passing through Tanyang. There's no entry charge.

Just below the temple is a small tourist village with a number of souvenir shops (mostly religious paraphernalia), restaurants, a couple of *yoinsook* and a public toilet which you won't want to use.

There are local buses from Tanyang to Kuin-sa which leave approximately every hour from 6.50 am to 8.10 pm.

Taegu 대구

Taegu, although the third largest city in South Korea, is usually just an overnight stop for travellers. Most use it as a convenient place from which to visit one of the country's most famous temples and one of its largest monasteries – Haein-sa Temple.

HAEIN-SA TEMPLE 해인사

The temple is some considerable distance from Taegu high up on the steep, forested slopes of Kaya-san National Park 가야산 국립공원 and is the repository of the Tripitaka Koreana – more than 80,000 carved wood blocks on which are the complete Buddhist scriptures as well as many illustrations remarkably similar to those you're likely to encounter in Nepal. The blocks are housed in two enormous buildings complete with a simple but effective ventilation system to prevent their deterioration.

The buildings are normally locked, and although it's possible to see the blocks through the slatted windows one of the friendly monks may open them up for you if you show an interest. Even if you don't manage to get into the library there's plenty of interest in the other buildings of the complex.

The wood blocks which you see today are actually the second set and they were carved during the 14th century when the Koryo Dynasty king, Kojong, was forced to take refuge on Kanghwa Island during the Mongol invasion of the mainland. The first set, completed in 1251 after 20 years work, was destroyed by these invaders. The Tripitaka was moved from Kanghwa Island to Haein-sa in the early years of the Yi Dynasty.

Haein-sa itself has origins going back to the beginning of the 9th century when it was founded by two monks, Sunung and Ijong, following many years of study in China. It was not until the early days of the Koryo Dynasty in the mid-10th century that it attained its present size.

The main hall, Taejkwangjon 대적광전 was burnt down during the Japanese invasion of 1592 and again (accidentally) in 1817, though miraculously the Tripitaka escaped destruction. The hall was reconstructed again in 1971. Other reconstruction has been undertaken since then, principally on the monks' quarters, and all of it, naturally, along traditional lines.

Haein-sa is one of the most beautiful temples in Korea but part of its beauty lies in its natural setting of mixed deciduous and coniferous forest. It's a romantic's paradise in wet weather when wisps of cloud drift at various levels through the forest.

Entry to the temple costs W600 plus, and you have to pay W400 entry to the national park. The temple is about 20 minutes walk from where the bus drops you.

Accommodation (*minbak*) is available in the tourist village below the temple, but unless you're planning to hike through Mt Kaya or explore the many hermitages scattered through the mountains above the main temple complex then it's likely you'll return to Taegu the same day.

Getting There & Away
The West Chikheng Bus Terminal is where the buses to Haein-sa Temple leave from. There are express buses 15 times daily from 8.55 am to 4.55 pm. The fare is W960 and the journey takes one hour and 20 minutes. There are also *chikheng* buses every 20 minutes from 6.30 am to 7 pm. The fare is W960 and the journey takes 1½ hours. Buy your ticket at booth No 4.

PLACES TO STAY – BOTTOM END
There are plenty of cheap and mid-range *yogwan* around the bus terminals and Dong Taegu Railway Station (the main station as opposed to Taegu Railway Station). The area you choose will depend largely on what time of day you arrive in Taegu.

Recommended at the West Chikheng Bus Terminal is *Sujong Yogwan* (tel 2386) 수정여관 Ferry, which costs W8000 a double with bathroom, TV and gallons of hot water in the evenings and mornings. It's very clean and the *ajimah* is very friendly. There are cheaper places available if this is too expensive.

PLACES TO STAY – MIDDLE
Royal Tourist Hotel (tel 253-5546/9) 24-4 Namil-dong, Chung-gu. Three-star, 50 rooms with prices from W22,000, Western restaurant, nightclub, bar, game room. English and Japanese spoken.
New Young Nam Tourist Hotel (tel 752 1001/5) 177-7 Pomo-dong. Two-star, 73 rooms with prices from

W26,500, Western, Korean and Japanese restaurants, sauna, bar, games room.
New Jongro Tourist Hotel (tel 23-7111/3) 23 Chong-no 2-ga, Chung-gu. Two-star, rooms from W25,500.
Kukje Tourist Hotel (tel 422-3131) 45-1 Kongpyong-dong, Chung-gu. Two-star, rooms from W23,000.

PLACES TO STAY – TOP END
Hanil Tourist Hotel (tel 423-5001/9) 110 Namil-dong, Chung-gu. Four-star, 100 rooms from W37,000, Western, Chinese and Korean restaurants, English and Japanese spoken.
Dong In Tourist Hotel (tel 46 7211/9) 5-2 Samdok-dong 1-ga, Chung-gu. Four-star, 92 rooms from W39,000, Japanese, Western and Korean restaurants, nightclub, bar, etc.
Daegu Soo Sung Hotel (tel 763-7311/6) 888-2 Tusan-dong, Susong-gu. Four-star, 72 rooms from W48,500, Korean and Western restaurants, bars, nightclub, disco, tennis court, swimming pool, sauna, game room, etc.

PLACES TO EAT
There are plenty of cheap restaurants around the West Chikheng Bus Terminal with a choice of Chinese, Korean and seafood restaurants.

ENTERTAINMENT
If you stay in Taegu overnight, the centre of town (around the Mida department store) is quite lively in the evenings with bars, restaurants, discos, nightclubs and the like.

GETTING THERE & AWAY
Bus
There are five bus terminals altogether in Taegu:

Express Bus Terminal 대구고속버스터미널
East (Tongbu) Chikheng Bus Terminal
동부직행버스터미널
West (Sobu) Chikheng Bus Terminal
서부버스터미널
South (Nambu) Chikheng Bus Terminal
남부버스터미널
North (Pukpo) Chikheng Bus Terminal
북부버스터미널.

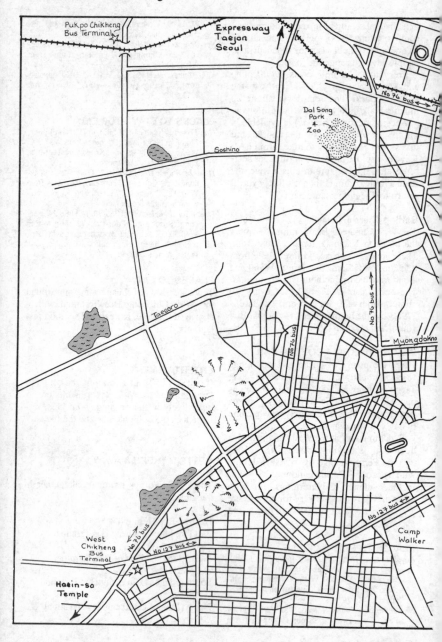

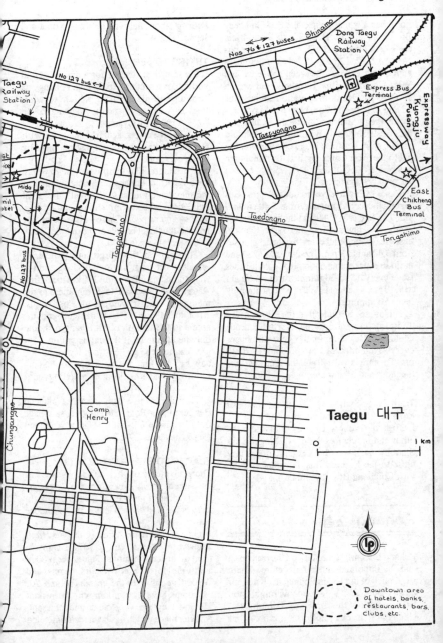

Nos 76 & 127 buses

Shinamo

Dong Taegu
Railway
Station

No 127 bus

Taegu
Railway
Station

Express Bus
Terminal

Taeryongno

Expressway Kyongju Pusan

st
ice

Mida

East
Chikheng
Bus
Terminal

nil
otel

Taedongno

Tongshimo

No 127 bus

Tongdohno

Chungangno

Camp
Henry

Taegu 대구

0   1 km

Downtown area
of hotels, banks,
restaurants, bars,
clubs, etc.

Local buses which connect the East Chikheng Bus Terminal with Dong Taegu Station and the West Chikheng Bus Terminal include bus Nos 1, 12, 22, 126 and 127. Two other buses which you can use between the East and West Chikheng Bus Terminals but which don't go past the railway station are bus Nos 33 and 120. In addition, bus No 76 connects Dong Taegu Station with Taegu Station and the West Chikheng Bus Terminal. Should you be anywhere else in the city and want to get to the West Chikheng Bus Terminal then bus Nos 1, 12, 31, 32, 35, 71, 75, 88, 89 and 101 will get you there.

Buses to Pusan leave from the Express Bus Terminal every 15 minutes from 5.40 am to 9 pm. The fare is W1980 and the journey takes nearly two hours. From the same terminal buses leave for Seoul every five to 10 minutes from 5.40 am to 8 pm. The fare is W4220 and the journey takes four hours. To Kyongju buses leave every 15 to 30 minutes from 6.50 am to 9.10 pm. The fare is W970 and the journey takes 50 minutes.

Buses to Kimchon (for Chikchi-sa Temple) leave from the North (Pukpo) Chikheng Bus Terminal. There are buses every seven minutes from 6.10 am to 10.30 pm. The fare is W1040 and the journey takes one hour and 10 minutes.

Train Taegu Station 대구역 in the centre of town is for local trains only and of little interest to travellers. Express trains from the other major centres stop at Dong Taegu Station 동대구역 on the east side of the city close to the Express Bus Terminal and the East Chikheng Bus Terminal.

Pohang 포항

Pohang is a fairly small city on the east coast and an important industrial centre. There isn't much of interest in Pohang itself and for most travellers it's just an overnight stop before taking the ferry to Ulleung-do. Ulleung-do is over 260 km north-east of Pohang, about halfway between Korea and Japan.

THINGS TO SEE

If the ferry is cancelled for a day or so and you'd like something to do then Pohang is a convenient place from which to visit Pogyung-sa 보경사 and the Pogyung Pokpo 보경폭포 below Mt Hyangro 향로 , north of the city. The area is spectacularly beautiful with numerous waterfalls, gorges spanned by bridges, hermitages, stupas and the temple itself. The temple is close to where the buses from Pohang terminate and there's the inevitable tourist village with the usual collection of souvenir shops, restaurants, *minbak* and *yogwan*. There's also a camp site beyond the ticket booth for the temple. Entry to the temple costs W400.

The trail to the gorge and waterfalls branches off from the tourist village and is well maintained. It's about 1½ km to the first waterfall and several more from there to the main falls – the first and second Pogro Falls. After that the going gets difficult and the ascent to the summit of Mt Hyangro should only be attempted if the day is young. This area can also be visited from Kyongju as a day trip by first taking a bus to Pohang followed by another from there to Pogyung-sa.

There are 11 buses daily from the Chikheng Bus Terminal in Pohang to Pogyung-sa Village from 7.10 am to 7.45 pm. The fare is W620 and the journey takes 20 minutes.

PLACES TO STAY – BOTTOM END

There are plenty of *yogwan* and *yoinsook* in the streets going back from the ferry terminal. Most of them cater for the overnight ferry trade and there's not a lot to choose between them.

One of the better ones is the *Se Hanil Yogwan* 새한일여관 (tel 2-5877), right in front of the ferry terminal. This costs W8000 a double for the downstairs rooms and W9000 a double for the upstairs rooms. All the rooms have a bathroom with hot water, TV and they are very clean and pleasant. Another place which has been recommended

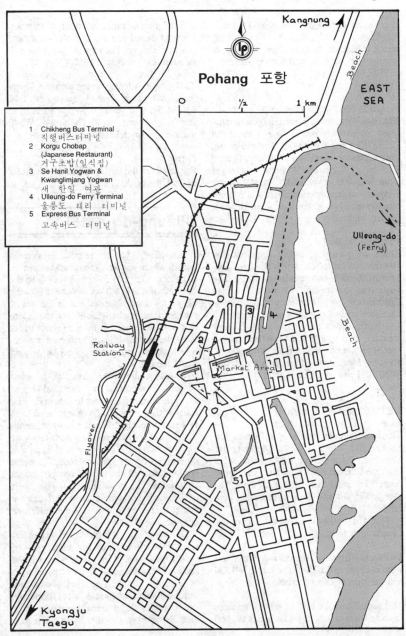

Pohang 포항

1 Chikheng Bus Terminal
   직행버스터미널
2 Korgu Chobap
   (Japanese Restaurant)
   거구초밥(일식집)
3 Se Hanil Yogwan &
   Kwanglimjang Yogwan
   새 한일 여관
4 Ulleung-do Ferry Terminal
   울릉도 훼리 터미널
5 Express Bus Terminal
   고속버스 터미널

is the *Kwanglimjang Yogwan* (tel 42-4365) 광림장 여관, 9-3 Yu Chun-dong, which is beautifully maintained, right opposite the ferry terminal and not too expensive at W12,000 a triple.

PLACES TO STAY – TOP END
The only Western-style hotel in Pohang is the three-star *Pohang Beach Tourist Hotel* (tel (0562) 3-1401/9), 311-2 Songdo-dong, Pohang, on the beach east of the city. There's a choice of Korean or Western-style rooms from W26,000 to W30,300. The staff speak English and Japanese and there are Western and Korean-style restaurants, a coffee shop, bar and nightclub.

PLACES TO EAT
There are plenty of cheap restaurants in Pohang but the place which deserves recommendation above all others is the Japanese seafood restaurant *Korgu Chobap* 고구초밥. Whatever you order is excellent and it's surprisingly cheap. It's spotlessly clean and the owner is very friendly. Two people can have fried or raw fish, soup, *kimchi*, pigeon eggs, dressed coleslaw, cockles, seaweed and rice for around W3000. If you prefer *kimbap* the price is the same.

GETTING THERE & AWAY
Bus
There are two bus terminals in Pohang, the Express Bus Terminal and the Chikheng Bus Terminal. There are express buses to Seoul from the Express Bus Terminal. These leave every 20 minutes from 6.30 am to 6 pm. The fare is W5570 and the journey takes five hours.

The following buses go from the Chikheng terminal:

To Pusan There are buses every 10 minutes from 6.45 am to 8.10 pm. The fare is W1720 and the journey takes 1½ hours.

To Taegu There are buses every 10 minutes from 5.50 am to 9.20 pm. The fare is W1460

and the journey takes one hour 40 minutes. Some of these buses are express (*kosok*) and others *chikheng*. The express buses take 20 minutes less but cost W1550.

To Kyongju All buses going to Pusan, Taegu and Seoul go via Kyongju so you can take any of these to get to Kyongju so long as they're *chikheng* buses. The fare is W540 and the journey takes 40 minutes.

Ferry
For details of the ferries to Ulleung-do, refer to the Ulleung-do chapter.

Ulleung-do 울릉도

If you have a yen for remote, mysterious islands where you won't see another traveller (let alone a tourist) from one month to the next then this is it, but get there soon because the secret is out. Isolated out in the storm-ravaged East Sea between Korea and Japan, this beautiful island requires an effort to get to at the best of times (the ferries are frequently cancelled due to gales) but is well worth the effort.

It was captured from pirates as the result of an order from King Yeji, the 22nd king of the Silla Dynasty, in order to secure the east coast of the peninsula. From then until 1884 this small volcanic island remained essentially a military outpost, but from that year on migration to the island for settlement was sanctioned by the government. From the large number of small churches you might well be forgiven for thinking that a large part of the population are not only Christian but came to the island for some religious purpose.

Due to the rugged forested mountains and spectacular cliffs which rise steeply out of the sea, the island is only sparsely populated and the farms are small. Out of a population of 20,000, 10,000 live in Dodong and another 5000 in Jeodong. Most of the people live in small villages along the coast making their living from the sea. Everywhere you

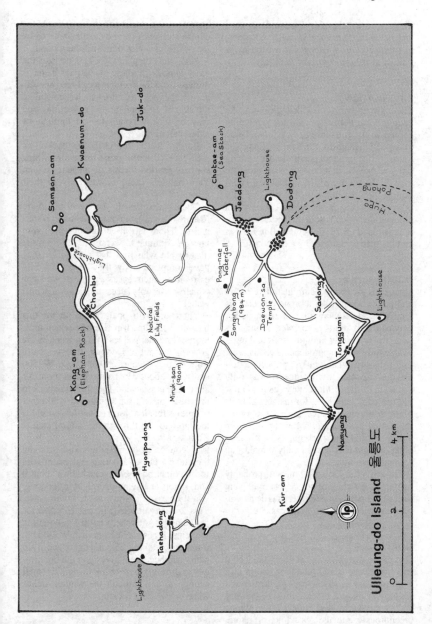

Ulleung-do Island 울릉도

look there are racks of drying squid, seaweed and octopus. There are virtually no roads, and transportation, except for two buses, is limited to fishing boats and walking.

INFORMATION

There are no banks on Ulleung-do, so take enough local currency with you (including enough to see you through a cyclone). Good maps of Ulleung-do are hard to find. The tourist office in Seoul generally has nothing but you may be able to obtain an adequate map at the tourist office in Dodong (free) though they're often out of stock. The only other possibility is the glossy booklet on Ulleung-do which is sold on the ferries from the mainland (W2000) but it's all in Korean and the map was drawn by a cartoonist.

DODONG 도동

Dodong is the island's administrative centre and largest town. Like a pirate outpost it is almost hidden away in a narrow valley between two craggy, forested mountains with a very narrow harbour front making it visible only when approached directly.

It's hardly what you might call a traditional Korean town since it was only settled in the late 19th century (there are few tile-roofed houses here, for instance) but its plain concrete facades are offset by its interesting position sprawling up the steep valley behind the harbour. Nevertheless, what it might lack aesthetically it makes up for with friendliness.

On arrival in Dodong you will probably be met by the chief of police who will want to see your passport. He's very civil and will return it to you as soon as he has checked it out.

BOAT TRIPS

One of the things you must do is take a boat trip around the island (about 56 km in all). The coast line is absolutely spectacular and it's easy to imagine that this must be the very end of the earth. Vast craggy cliffs plunge precipitously into the sea while, off-shore,

enormous sea-stacks rise up sheer out of the depths and reach for the clouds, battered by the powerful waves of the northern ocean.

Kong-am (Elephant Rock) is perhaps the most famous of these stacks. Its name is derived from the peculiar weathered appearance of the rock structure which is not unlike the skin of an elephant. On a calm day you may be lucky enough to sail through its natural arch.

Further inland the cliffs are backed by mist-covered, deep-green mountains which support gnarled forests of ancient juniper. Tiny hamlets cling precariously to their sides.

There's also the off-shore islet of Juk-do (Bamboo Island), famous for its sweet watermelon. There are three families here who bravely continue to wrest a living from the plateau but who find that every time they have to replace a cow they have to literally carry it on their backs up the stone steps which are the only access up the vertical cliff walls!

There are two boats available for this once-in-a-lifetime trip. The one which most tourists find themselves on is operated by the government out of Dodong. It leaves daily from the ferry wharf at 9 am, costs W3500 and takes about 3½ hours. It has room for about 130 passengers. The only drawback to this boat (apart from being with 130 other people) is that it doesn't call at Juk-do and is too large to sail through the natural arch at Kong-am.

If you prefer something more personal then take a bus to Jeodong and ask around for the other boat. Everyone knows about it and, if you're staying overnight in Jeodong, you'll be asked if you want to go on a trip. This boat isn't officially licensed (neither are penguins in Antarctica) but it's been going for years. It costs a little more at W5000 but it only takes about 25 passengers and it's a better trip because it gives you the opportunity to (briefly) explore Juk-do and it's small enough to sail through the natural arches when the weather is calm.

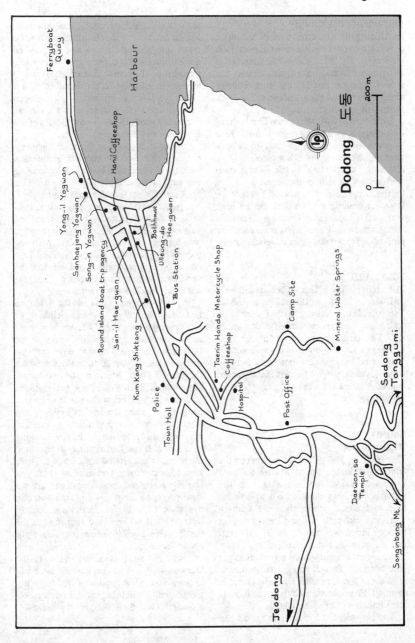

WATERFALLS & CAVES

As Ulleung-do gets more than its fair share of rain it naturally has a number of waterfalls and caves. The most accessible waterfall is Pong-nae Pokpo 봉래폭포 about five km from Dodong or just 1½ km from Jeodong along a gravel and stone walkway. The track is obvious so you cannot get lost.

Unfortunately for those who like bathing in waterfalls, swimming is not allowed here as some of the water is used to supply Jeodong. Nevertheless, it's a pleasant walk and close to the falls is the natural rock 'refrigerator' which is mentioned in all the tourist literature. Fed by a current of cold air from far underground, drinks can be kept very cool without gas or electricity. The cafe which surrounds it also offers snacks such as *pindatok* (W500) and other vegetarian food.

TONGGUMI 통구미

The small fishing village of Tonggumi, west of Dodong, is also worth making a visit to. The road from Dodong follows a tortuous path along the coastal cliffs for the whole way. This could raise the hair on your head but there's no denying that it's spectacular. You'll find the villagers extremely friendly – tourists simply don't get this far. There are beautiful views from the hill at the back of the village.

HIKING
Mt Songinbong

This is the highest peak (984 metres) on the island and is the tip of a now dormant volcano. Various pathways lead to the summit. One suggested route is to take the road to Sadong (where there's a military barracks), turn right and just keep going up through the houses and fields. You'll eventually find a trail at the end of the fields. There are occasional signs where you can get your bearings. Even if you get lost, which is unlikely, it doesn't matter since the island is so small. From the summit there are incredible views over the whole island.

Another suggested route is to follow the main street uphill in Dodong until you reach the stream. Follow the stream course for 100 metres past the last house where you will see a trail branch off to the right. Follow this straight up. The path to the summit is marked at regular intervals. After about an hour's climb you reach an area with wooden benches and tables that serve as a tea house during the peak season. It's a 1½-hour climb from here to the summit.

Instead of descending the mountain along the same path, you can take a different track which will eventually bring you to Jeodong via the Pong-nae Waterfall 봉래폭포 . This track starts from the teahouse/rest area which you passed on the way up the mountain. Half an hour down this track you will reach the first barn. Continue around it (avoiding the path forking off to the right) and down to the second barn and then follow the steep path down to the stream where you will find the small cafe with the natural cooler. From here it's a short walk down to Jeodong.

If you have the stamina and the time then instead of returning to either Jeodong or Dodong from the summit you can head north to the small fishing village of Chonbu 천부 , though you may well have to stay overnight in the village if you do this. Head towards the second crater which is tilled and complete with a small church and several farm houses. There are hot springs in the area too. From here a steep descent will take you to Chonbu. If you're lucky, a fishing-boat taxi may be available to take you back to Jeodong or Dodong. If not, find a camping spot along the beach or ask around for a *minbak*. There are a number of small restaurants where you can buy a seafood meal or you can ask the family to cook for you if you are staying in a *minbak*. To get back to Jeodong or Dodong overland follow the island ring road to the east. It's an enjoyable three to four-hour walk above the cliffs.

There is a small Buddhist temple called Daewon-sa 대원사 just off the trail that leads to Songinbong just outside of Dodong – it's signposted. It's nothing special but the bell is beautiful and the setting is very mellow.

Island Ring Trail

The ring is approximately 40 km long. Rather than take this road the whole way (which would demand two to three days) it's more enjoyable to catch a fishing boat taxi in the morning from Dodong harbour to Chonbu (negotiation necessary otherwise you'll pay at least twice what the locals do) and then walk either westward or eastward back to Dodong. Take a drink with you unless you want to pay over the odds for a soft drink or beer at the villages en route.

PLACES TO STAY

Yogwan prices in Ulleung-do rise steeply in the summer season (20 July to 20 August) when the island is thronged with Korean vacationers.

If you travelled 2nd class on the ferry, you may already have been offered accommodation with a family which lives on the island. Every ferry is met by a gaggle of *ajimahs*, all of them extolling the virtues of their *yogwan* and *minbak*. By all means, go and have a look at what's on offer but don't settle for anything you're not satisfied with – there's plenty of choice and good choices at that.

The cheapest places to stay are in rooms with families – *minbak*. The usual price is W5000 per room. For this you'll get a simple room with clean bedding and share bathroom facilities, though it's unlikely there will be hot water. Recommended is the one above the Taerim Honda motorcycle shop on the main street up the hill which has rooms upstairs. It's very clean and has separate bathroom and toilet facilities for guests.

For campers with their own tents, there's a landscaped site just below the mineral springs which costs W1500 per tent. A shower and toilet block are on site.

There's a good selection of *yogwan* available but during the summer months package tours from the mainland fill up the most popular ones and, since these people are on group tours, they tend to party into the small hours and make a lot of noise. It's great if you're in the same mood and want to join in; not much cop if you want to sleep! The

Song-in Yogwan (tel 2078) 성인여관 is one such place. It's clean but has no hot water and costs W6000 a double without bathroom plus W2000 per extra person. Much quieter is the *Yong-il Yogwan* (tel 2663) 영일여관 which is very clean and costs W6000 a double without bathroom. There's no hot water.

More expensive is the *Sanhaejang Yogwan* 산해장여관 , which costs W10,000 for a single or double with bathroom, colour TV, fan and constant hot water but the price can increase during the summer months. As the *yogwan* is opposite the ferry landing, most of the double rooms have a great view of the harbour. One traveller described this place as having 'a witch of an *ajimah*' but it seems times have changed. A recent letter complained they didn't know who was being referred to since the young woman who now runs it apparently giggles all the time and is keen on taking pictures of Western travellers posing with various members of her family.

Even if you are staying in a room with a bath/shower and you have been hiking around the island, it is worth paying a visit to the *mok yok tang* (bathhouse) in Dodong. For W1000 you'll be given soap, shampoo, body lotion, a towel and a body scrubber and your introduction to a room full of 'madly splashing bodies' all intent on the same hedonistic pursuits and a body full of tired muscles! The bathhouse is on the main street a few doors up from the harbour on the left hand side.

At Jeodong there are a number of *yogwan* around the bus station, but one place which can be recommended is the one by the big tree on the way to the Pong-nae Waterfall, though there's no sign. A double room with TV, private bath and boiling hot water costs W10,000.

PLACES TO EAT

For a very cheap place to eat, try the *Kum Kang Shiktang* 금강식당 which has Chinese food from around W800 to W1300 per dish. More expensive but certainly one of the best restaurants on the island is the *Ulleung-do Hae-gwan* 울릉도 회관 about 100 metres up the hill from the harbour front. It's fairly new and has an extensive vegetarian menu for around W1500 per dish plus seafood for W3000 per dish. The *kimchi* is excellent.

There are various other restaurants and shops on the main street but check prices before eating as they vary from day to day, especially if you order seafood.

For a cold beer try the *Son-il Hae-gwan* 성일 회관 which is a bar and 'nightclub'. There is no draught beer but a large bottle costs only W1500 (not bad considering it has to come from the mainland). They sometimes have a live band in the evenings. The *ajimah* who runs it is very friendly and according to one traveller, 'won't bat an eyelid at the spectacle of foreigners going through beer by the case'. Although you may meet local people around the island the next day who congratulate you on your bacchanalian achievement and ask how you manage to combine a night on the amber nectar with a day hiking in the mountains! This place is quite bizarre and well worth a visit. It features psychedelic wallpaper, a light-show straight out of 1968, middle-aged men wailing into microphones with sing-along tapes, 'private rooms', elaborate *anju* (snacks) and music that sounds like a sonic representation of the island's chief product – squid.

GETTING THERE & AWAY

You can get to Ulleung-do by ferry from Pohang포항, Hupo후포, and Mukho묵호. The ferries from Mukho take the least time followed by those from Hupo. Those from Pohang take the longest time.

Booking in advance may be necessary during July and August but otherwise you can buy your ticket at the boat terminal. Advance bookings can be made in Seoul or Pusan from certain travel agents. In Seoul try Lotte Tour (tel 733 0201) and in Pusan try New Pusan Tour (tel 806 8811).

Ferries are often cancelled during rough weather and this can affect the availability of tickets at either end. Be prepared to spend longer on Ulleung-do than you planned in case this happens.

GETTING AROUND

Although there are paths and dirt tracks which connect all the habitable places around the island, the only roads which exist are those which connect the island's capital, Dodong, with Jeodong, Tonggumi and Naesujeon. There are plans to construct a ring road around the perimeter of the island but work has yet to start.

Three public bus routes are currently available and if you use them you'll end up getting to know both the drivers and the people who use the buses quite well. It's a tightly knit community! Buses between Dodong and Jeodong leave every half an hour from 6.15 am to 8.40 pm, cost W170 and take about five minutes. Between Dodong and Tonggumi they leave every 40 minutes from 6 am to 7.40 pm, cost W260 and take about half an hour. Between Dodong and Nae-sujeon they leave every 45 minutes.

In addition to the public buses there are a number of minibuses available between the same towns. The fares are the same. There are also several taxis available at the standard price (minimum of W600 for the car plus the distance charge).

From Pohang

Dates	Ship	Frequency	Depart Pohang	Arrive Ulleung	Depart Ulleung	Arrive Pohang
	Tae-ah Kosok					
Nov 1-Apr 30		every 2 days	noon	7.30 pm	10 am	5.30 pm
May 1-Jul 24		every 2 days	1 pm	8.30 pm	10 am	5.30 pm
Jul 24-Aug 15		daily	1 pm	8.30 pm	11.30 pm	7 am
Aug 16-Oct 31		every 2 days	1 pm	8.30 pm	10 am	5.30 pm
	Taewon 1-ho					
Jul 20-Aug 18		daily	10 pm	4 am	9 am	3 pm
Aug 19-Jul 19		on demand				

From Hupo

Dates	Ship	Frequency	Depart Hupo	Arrive Ulleung	Depart Ulleung	Arrive Hup
	Tae-won 2 -ho					
Nov 1-Feb 28		every 3 days	2 pm	6 pm	noon	4 pm
Mar 1-Apr 30		every 2 days	2 pm	6 pm	noon	4 pm
May 1-Jul 25		daily	2 pm	6 pm	8 am	noon
Jul 26-Aug 15		twice daily	10 am	2 pm	3.30 pm	7.30 pm
			9 pm	1 am	4.30 pm	8.30 am
Aug 15-Oct 31		every 2 days	2 pm	6 pm	1 pm	5 pm

From Mukho

Dates	Ship	Frequency	Depart Mukho	Arrive Ulleung	Depart Ulleung	Arrive Mukho
	Taewon Ka-ta Malan-ho					
Apr 1-Jul 24		every 2 days	12.30 pm	3 pm	4.30 pm	7 pm
Jul 25-Aug 15		daily	12.30 pm	3 pm	4.30 pm	7 pm
Aug 16-Mar 31		every 4 days	2 pm	4 pm	2 pm	4 pm

Fares
From Pohang
1 st class	(bunk)	W27,420
2nd class	(bunk)	W18,280
1st class	(seat)	W18,280
2nd class	(seat)	W12,190

From Hupo
1st class	(seat)	W14,800
2nd class	(seat)	W10,050

From Mukho
1st class	(seat)	W18,010

Reductions are available for students and those under 24 years old.

South-East Korea

Pusan (Busan) 부산

Pusan is the second largest city and principal port of South Korea. Its population stands at around 3½ million and is rising steadily. It was the only major city to escape capture by the communists during the Korean War though at the time its population was swelled by an incredible four million refugees. Pusan has a superb location nestled in between several mountain ridges and peaks, but on the other hand this also makes for a very spread-out city and, away from the subway line, it takes a lot of time to get from one place to another.

Many travellers regard Pusan as a concrete jungle to be got through quickly, or merely as a place from which to take the ferries to Yeosu, Cheju-do or Shimonoseki (Japan) or for domestic and international flights from Kimhae International Airport. This is a great pity since it has a cosmopolitan ambience all of its own which is quite distinct from Seoul, even though it doesn't have old temples and palaces surrounded by areas of wooded tranquillity right in the heart of the city. It's a city which can grow on you if you're prepared to spend the time exploring it, and if it's wooded tranquillity that you're looking for then there are endless possibilities in the mountains which separate the various parts of the city. Indeed, some travellers have written to say that the setting rivals that of Rio de Janeiro. With certain reservations I might agree, though I think a more appropriate parallel would be Caracas.

Its distinct ambience naturally comes about as a result of constant exposure to sailors from all over the world yet, unlike many such similar places, it's a safe place to explore even at night and you're in no danger of being robbed.

ORIENTATION

The central part of the city is squeezed into a narrow strip of land between a series of mountain peaks and steep slopes and the harbour. The ferry terminals, central business district, GPO, Pusan Railway Station, and a whole collection of hotels, *yogwan* and *yoinsook* are at the southern end of this strip. Going right up the centre of this is Pusan's main road, Chungang-ro, a broad six- to eight-lane boulevard which gets incredibly busy during rush hours. The subway follows this road for much of its course.

The bus terminals, of which there are three in total, are all a long way from this area. The main two of interest to travellers – the Express Bus Terminal and the Tongbu Bus Terminal – are about 11 km to the north but within easy reach of the subway. The Tongbu Terminal is right outside Myongnyundong Station and the Express Terminal is 12 minutes' walk from Tongnae Station.

INFORMATION
Tourist Office

The tourist information office (tel 462 9734) is in the Pusan Chamber of Commerce & Industry close to City Hall. There are also tourist information kiosks at the Express Bus Terminal, outside Pusan Railway Station and at the International (Pu-kwan) Ferry Terminal.

Post

The Central Post Office is on Chungang-ro near Chungangdong Subway Station. It offers a full range of services including packing and a poste restante.

Foreign Embassies

Foreign embassies which are represented in Pusan include:

Japan
    1147-11 Choryang-dong, Tong-gu (tel (051) 43-9221)

Taiwan
 6th Floor, Tong-yang Building, 4, 2-ga Tonggwang-dong, Chung-gu (tel (051) 23-3617)
USA
 American Consulate Building, 24, 2-ga Taechong-dong, Chung-gu (tel (051) 23-7791)

Airline Offices

The main airline offices of interest – Korean Air and JAL – are along Chungang-ro between City Hall and Pusan Railway Station. Asiana Airlines main office is between the two on the road which connects Chungang-ro with the International Ferry Terminal. Thai International, SAS and N W Orient have their offices in the Bando Hotel. Delta has its office in the Ferry Hotel. There's a travel agency on the opposite side of the road from the Bando and Ferry hotels called the Jinsung Travel Corporation which handles ticketing for all airlines. The staff are friendly and efficient and speak English. Major credit cards are accepted.

Bookshops

One of the best places to find English-language books, maps, etc, is the Munwoo Dang bookshop on Chungang-ro, just before the Phoenix Hotel between City Hall and Pusan Railway Station, on the right-hand side as you walk from City Hall. There's no sign in English but you can't miss it.

Newspapers

The English-language *Korea Times* and *Korea Herald* are both available at newsstands inside both the Express Bus Terminal and the Tongbu Bus Terminal. It's unlikely you'll find them anywhere else in Pusan.

PUSAN TOWER

Finding things to do in Pusan other than going shopping or nightclubbing usually involves stretching your legs and getting a lung-full of fresh air, but in the centre itself it's certainly worth taking the lift to the top of Pusan Tower for the incredible views over the city. Photography is supposedly not allowed from the observation decks (and there are notices to this effect) but there's often a local photographer up there who does mug shots against a background of the harbour so I wonder who's fooling who? The return fare in the lift is W1000. Coffee and soft drinks are available at the top but there's no restaurant.

CHAGALCHI FISH MARKET 자갈치

Pusan's huge fish market is worth a visit for those who enjoy watching catches unloaded from the boats and the haggling which goes on between the fishermen and the buyers. It's on the harbour front south of the central business district. Get there *early* though! Things quieten down by the time office workers are on their way to work.

HAEUNDAE 해운대

Some 11 km north-east of the city centre are Pusan's beach resorts, the main one of which is Haeundae. Beaches there certainly are, and they're undoubtedly a welcome sight for those who live and work in Pusan, but they get incredibly crowded in summer. So crowded, in fact, that you'll be hard pressed to see sand for people, deck chairs and picnic paraphernalia. Travellers who have previously visited beaches in the Philippines, Thailand or Malaysia will be singularly unimpressed.

TAEJONGDAE 태종대

If the Costa del Korea doesn't appeal, try a day out at Taejongdae on Yongdo just across the bridge from City Hall. Once past the suburbs, it's a very pleasant place with beautiful views out to sea. It's not a national park so there are no entry fees. To get there, take bus No 30 from the city centre which takes about 20 minutes. Avoid taking a taxi because they go through the gate and that will cost you W2000 on top of the taxi fare.

TAESHIN PARK 대신공원

This park, high up above the city on Mt Kubong-san, north-west of Pusan Railway Station, offers a complete contrast to the frenetic commercial and industrial activity

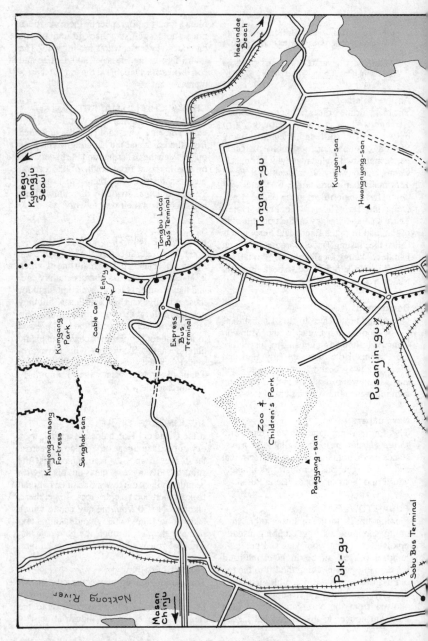

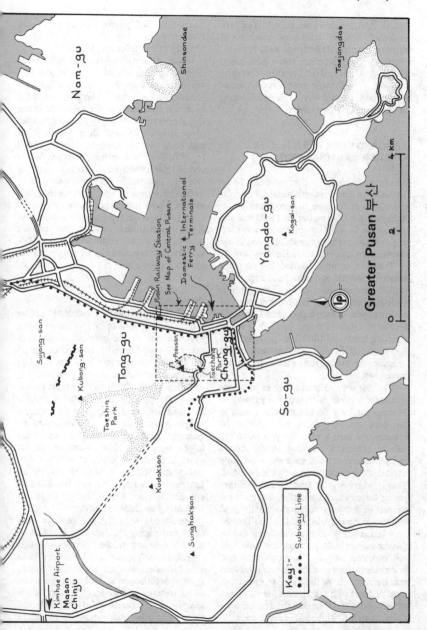

Greater Pusan 부산

Nam-gu

Shinsondae

Taejongdae

Yongdo-gu

Kogal-san

Pusan Railway Station

See Map of Central Pusan

Domestic ★ International
Ferry Terminals

Tong-gu

Sujong-san

Kubong-san

Taeshin Park

Posusan

Yongdusan
Park

Chong-gu

So-gu

Kudoksan

Sunghaksan

Kimhae Airport
Masan
Chinju

Key:-
●●●● Subway Line

0   2   4 km

below. And the views are superb! The park is densely wooded with huge conifers and there are medicinal springs as well. The simplest way to get there is to take a local bus to Dong-A University Taeshin Campus 동아대학 and walk from there. Alternatively, take the subway to Sodaeshindong Station and walk from there.

KUMGANG PARK 금강파크 & KUMJONGSANSONG FORTRESS 금정산성

Pusan's answer to the mountain-top fortresses of Seoul is north-west of the northern suburb of Tongnae, high on the ridges of Kumjong-san (790 metres) and Sanghak-san mountains. To see it properly you really need to put aside a whole day though you could combine it with a visit to the Buddhist temple of Pomo-sa, a little beyond the northern extremity of the fortress. This impressive walled fortress with four imposing gates in traditional style is the largest in Korea and covers an area of over eight sq km. Construction of the fortress began in 1703 and was not completed until 1807. It's a popular place for weekend picnics and, as you might imagine, the views from various points are incredible.

The best way to start a trek around this mountain fortress is to take the subway to Myongnyundong Station and either walk to the park entrance from there (about 20 minutes) or take a taxi. As you leave the subway station, if you look straight ahead and a little to your right, you can see the cable car installations on the mountain side ahead. This is where you're heading for. Whether you're taking a taxi or walking, first cross the pedestrian bridge to the other side of the road and stay to the right-hand side of the Tongbu Bus Terminal. Walkers should then follow this road down to the first junction, bear right and continue on past a large concrete and brick church (on the left hand side) and then take the next left. At the end of this road turn right in front of a (signposted) three-storey stone pagoda and then take the next left up a fairly steep hill. This road veers to the right

and you'll find yourself outside the park entrance gate.

Entry to the park costs W250.

Down at the park entrance there's a Buddhist temple, pavilions, an aquarium, zoo, botanical gardens, folk art exhibition hall, restaurants, a children's playground and the cable car station. Take the cable car to the top. It operates daily every 20 to 30 minutes (depending on demand) from 9 am to 7 pm and costs W1200 (one way) and W1800 (return). For children the prices are W900 and W1100 respectively. This is an exciting ride with fantastic views which takes you up 540 metres over a total distance of 1260 metres. There are no restrictions on photography. Once at the top you start walking but if you want a drink or a meal before you start then there are two restaurants up there. It's also possible to walk up here from the bottom but it's a steep climb.

POMO-SA 보모사

This Buddhist temple was founded in 678 by priest Uisang during the reign of King Munmu, one of the greatest of the Silla rulers. Uisang himself is revered as one of the greatest of the early Buddhist scholars and spent some 10 years of his life studying in China following his entry into the priesthood. Despite its proximity to Pusan, Pomo-sa is a world away from the concrete jungle down at sea level. Surrounded by peaceful deciduous forest, it is one of the largest temples in Korea – and one of the most beautiful. The Chogyemun Gate, Belfry and Main Hall, in particular, are all sublime examples of Korean Buddhist art and architecture. A visit here on Buddha's birthday is an absolute *must*!

Much of the original temple was destroyed during the Japanese invasion of 1592-3 but not before priest Sosan had defeated a Japanese army at this very same spot. Nevertheless, quite a few things remain from the Silla period including pagodas, stone lanterns and pillars. The rest of the temple was reconstructed in 1602 and there were other renovations in 1613 and

1713. Don't miss this place. It is simply incredible.

Getting there is simplicity itself. Take the subway and get off at Pomo-sa Station. From there you can either walk (about 2½ km) or take a taxi or minibus.

TOURS

The Tourist Development Corporation operates a number of bus tours to places of interest around the city and further afield. They're useful if your time is limited. Most of the tours depart from Pusan Railway Station. They include:

Historical Sites Tour

Buses leave Pusan Station daily at 10 am and 2 pm. This is a four-hour trip and costs W2000. It visits Chungyol-sa Shrine and Pomo-sa Temple.

Hot Spring Tour

Buses leave Pusan Station on weekdays at 10 am and on holidays at 9 am. This is an eight-hour trip and you visit the Pugok Hot Springs. The fare is W8400.

Holiday Tour

Buses leave Pusan Station only on holidays between 9 am and noon and visit Tongdo-sa and Naewon-sa temples north of Pusan.

PLACES TO STAY – BOTTOM END

Accommodation around the Express Bus Terminal is almost exclusively of the *yogwan jang* type and therefore expensive. Only to the north of the nearby Tongbu Bus Terminal is it possible to find ordinary *yogwan* or even *yoinsook*, but even so it's a long walk and very inconvenient. Better to take the subway into the centre of Pusan where there's much more choice of relatively inexpensive accommodation. If you do this, get off at Chungang-dong Station and head into the streets at the back of Chungang-ro away from the port side. If you arrive by ferry from Japan, Cheju-do or Yeosu, walking to this area will take you just a few minutes – no taxi is necessary.

The best area to find accommodation is

around the Bando Hotel and Ferry Hotel up against the hill. Most of the *yogwan* – and the Western-style hotels – are on the flat whereas further up the hill or alongside the steps which connect the two levels you'll find a mixture of *yogwan* and *yoinsook*.

There's plenty of choice and, if you're really short of funds, you can find very basic accommodation in a *yoinsook* for around W4000 to W5000 though all you'll get for that is a tiny room and use of a cold-water communal shower. The best of the bunch in this bracket are the *Hyundae Yoinsook* 해운대여인숙 and the *Munha Yoinsook* 문화여인숙. Both cost W5000 per room without bathroom and toilet. Neither has hot water. The Hyundae is popular with budget travellers.

Going up in price, the *Poson Jang Yogwan* 보성장여관 , on the very last street before the hillside starts, is excellent value and the owner is very friendly indeed. It costs W12,000 for a room with bathroom, constant hot water, fan and colour TV. The best rooms overlook the street below so make sure you get one of these if possible.

Of a similar standard and price and in the same area are the *Chong Hwa Jang Yogwan* (tel 463-7268) 정화장여관, and the *Cheun Cho Yogwan* (tel 44-0482/4) 천조여관. An alternative place to stay fairly close to the city centre for those who don't mind dormitory rooms is the *Aerin Youth Hostel* 애린유스호스텔 (tel (051) 27-2222/7), 41 1-ga, Posu-dong, Chung-gu. This is just below the south-western tip of Taechong Park. Local bus No 5 will take you there from the International Ferry Terminal or you can take bus No 103 from Pusan Railway Station. If you can't find either of these then walk – it's not that far. A bunk bed is a little expensive at W6000 but the facilities tend to make up for it and many travellers stay here. The staff speak English and Japanese and there are Korean, Japanese, Western and Chinese restaurants with average meal prices of US$3 to US$10.

If you're only staying overnight and catching an early morning bus and want to stay around the Express Bus Terminal then

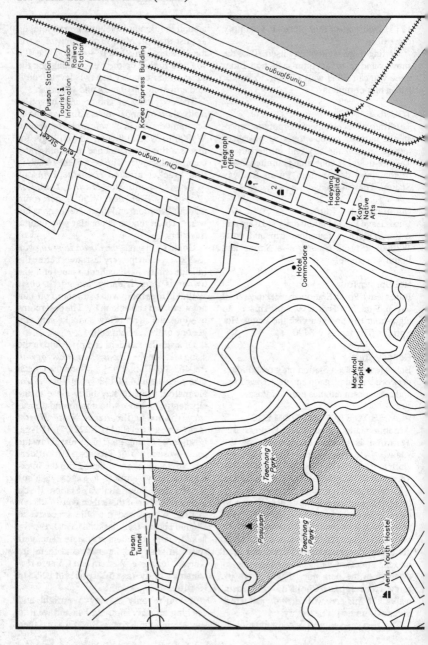

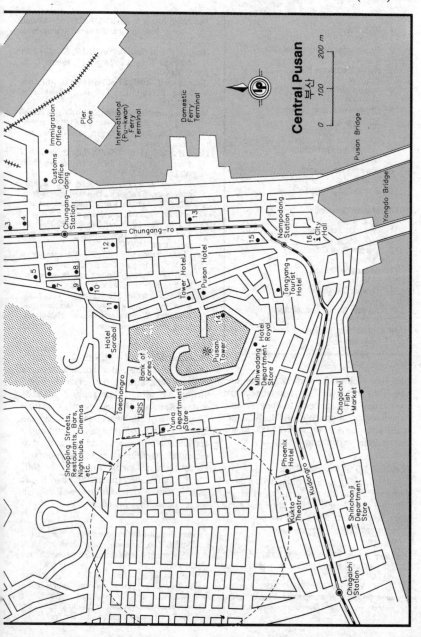

Central Pusan 부산

0   100   200 m

Pusan Bridge

Yongdo Bridge

Pier One

International (Pu-kwan) Ferry Terminal

Domestic Ferry Terminal

Immigration Office

Customs Office

Chungang-dong

Chungang-dong Station

Chungang-ro

Nampodong Station

City Hall

Tower Hotel

Pusan Hotel

Tongyang Tourist Hotel

Hotel Sorabol

Taechongro

Bank of Korea

Pusan Tower

Hotel Royal

Mihwadang Department Store

USIS

Tuna Department Store

Chagalchi Fish Market

Phoenix Hotel

Kukto Theatre

Kwangro

Shinchonji Department Store

Chagalchi Station

Shopping Streets, Restaurants, Bars, Nightclubs, Cinemas etc.

1	KAL Office 대한항공
2	Pusan International Post Office 우체국
3	Korea Exchange Bank 외환은행
4	Asiana Airlines 아시아나 항공
5	Chong Hwa Jang Yogwan 정화장여관
6	Cheun Cho Yogwan 천조장, 보서장여관
7	Ferry & Bando Hotels 훼라 반도 호텔
8	Umijong Restaurant 우미정식당
9	Poson Jang Yogwan 보성장여관
10	Munha Yoinsook 문호여인숙
11	Hyundae Yoinsook 현대여인숙
12	Central Post Office 우체국
13	Japanese Airlines (JAL)
14	Taiwan Consulate 대만 영사관
15	Korean Tourist Association 관광안내소
16	Tourist Information 관광안내소

take your pick of the *yogwan jang* around here. They stretch almost as far as the eye can see and new ones are being built every year. Expect to pay around W10,000 to W12,000 at the cheapest and up to W14,000 at the more expensive of them.

PLACES TO STAY – MIDDLE

If you're looking for something with a more Western flavour and the facilities which go with that then there's a good choice of mid-range hotels in the downtown area.

In order of price, they include:

Moonhwa Tourist Hotel (tel 806-8001/7) 517-65 Pujon-dong, Pusanjin-gu. Two-star, rooms from W17,000.

UN Tourist Hotel (tel 256-5181/4) 335-5 Amnam-dong, So-gu. Two-star, 50 rooms from W21,500, Korean, Western and Japanese restaurants, night-club, bar.

Woo Jeong Tourist Hotel (tel 807-2222) 523-1 Pujon 2-dong, Pusanjin-gu. Two-star, rooms from W20,000.

New Life Tourist Hotel (tel 67-3001/8) 830-174 Pom 2-dong, Tong-gu. Two-star, rooms from W20,000.

Oscar Tourist Hotel (tel 807-3800) 522-40 Pujon-dong, Pusanjin-gu. Two-star, rooms from W22,000.

Shin Shin Tourist Hotel (tel 88-5201/4) 263-11 Pujon-dong, Pusanjin-gu. Two-star, 65 rooms from W24,800, Korean, Western and Japanese restaurants, coffee shop.

Hotel Hillside (tel 464-0567/9) 743-33 Yongju 1-dong, Chung-gu. Two-star, rooms from W27,000.

Bando Tourist Hotel (tel 44-0561/9) 36 Chungang-dong 4-ga, Chung-gu. Two-star, rooms from W28,000, Western, Korean and Japanese restaurants, nightclub, bar, sauna, etc.

Dong Yang Tourist Hotel (tel 246-1206/7) 27 Kwangbok-dong 1-ga, Chung-gu. Three-star, rooms from W29,000.

Ferry Hotel (tel 463-0881/90) 37-16 Chungang-dong 4-ga, Chung-gu. Three-star, rooms from W30,000, Western, Korean and Japanese restaurants, nightclub, bar, sauna, etc.

Tower Tourist Hotel (tel 241-5151/9) 20 Tonggwang-dong 3-ga, Chung-gu. Two-star, 108 rooms from W32,000, Western and Korean restaurants, nightclub, bar, game room.

PLACES TO STAY – TOP END

Pusan's top hotels are to be found in three clusters, one around the city centre and strung out along Chungang-ro towards Pusan Railway Station, another around Chasongdae Park (where the old Express Bus Terminal used to be) and a third out at Haeundae beach resort. Assume that most of the hotels mentioned in this section will accept all major credit cards, that the staff speak English and Japanese and that all the usual creature comforts are available. In order of cost, they include:

Phoenix Hotel 8-1 Nampo-dong 5-ga, Chung-gu (tel 245-8061/9). Four-star, rooms from W40,000, Western and Korean restaurants, nightclub, bar, sauna, etc.

Hotel Royal (tel 241-1051/5) 2-72 Kwangbok-dong 2-ga, Chung-gu. Four-star, rooms from W41,300.

Hotel Crown (tel 69-1241/7) 830-30 Pomil-dong, Tong-gu. Four-star, 135 rooms from W47,000 to

W60,000, Western, Japanese, Chinese and Korean restaurants, nightclub, bars, sauna, etc.

Pusan Tourist Hotel (tel 241-4301/9) 12 Tonggwang-dong 2-ga, Chung- gu. Four-star, 288 rooms from W50,000, Korean, Western, Japanese and Chinese restaurants, nightclub, disco club, bars, sauna, etc.

Hotel Sorabol (tel 463 3511/9) 37-1 Taechong-dong 1-ga, Chung-gu. Five-star, 152 rooms from W59,000, Korean, Western, Japanese, French and Chinese restaurants, nightclub, bars, sauna, etc.

Hotel Commodore (tel 44 9101/9) 743- 80 Yongju-dong, Chung-gu. Five-star, 325 rooms from W61,000, Western, Japanese, Chinese and Korean restaurants, nightclub, bars, game room, sauna, etc.

PLACES TO EAT
There are several streets full of restaurants of various kinds off Chungang-ro between the central post office and the Bando and Ferry hotels. Take your pick but, if you're looking for seafood, then make sure you know the price of a meal before you order. Seafood – particularly if it's raw – can be very expensive.

One restaurant which stands out as exceptional value as far as fried fish goes is the *Songpo Haechip* 성포회집 round the back of the Poson Jang Yogwan. Here they'll serve you with a variety of fried fish complete with all the usual accompanying dishes for just W4000.

Another good place to eat if you'd like to spend a little money is the Japanese-style restaurant called *Umijong* 우미정 just down the street from the Bando Hotel. You can't miss the place with its external and internal pine-timbered decor. Here you can get excellently cooked food at reasonable prices (W3000 per dish). It's very popular at lunch times with office workers.

If you find yourself up at the Pusan Tower and feel hungry then try the small fish restaurant housed in a shack halfway up the steps leading to the south side of the Tower from the main street below (these steps take a tortuous route over the roofs of the buildings which cling to the side of the hill, and they go past a billiard hall). A whole side of fried fish here costs W1500 with *kimchi*.

Travellers in need of a break from endless plates of *kimchi* should head for 'Texas Street' where there are a number of Western-style fast-food outlets.

If you're looking for a meal at the Express Bus Terminal there are cafes inside where you can eat for W600 to W700 per dish. Opposite the bus terminal is the *Tongnae Gwan* 동래관 which offers cheap Chinese and Korean food.

ENTERTAINMENT
Most of the bars and cocktail lounges around the Hotel Royal on the bottom side of the Pusan Tower cater for Korean businessmen and are, therefore, relatively expensive. In many of them you are obliged to buy a 'snack' with your first drink and that can cost you anything from W3000 to W5000! For something more down to earth head for 'Texas Street' which runs more or less parallel to Chungang-ro from opposite Pusan Railway Station. This is Pusan's answer to Seoul's Itaewon – an area of music clubs, bars and pick-up joints that attracts American GIs and travellers. It hasn't got the same range as Itaewon but at least a few beers won't burn a large hole in your pocket.

The gaggles of heavily made-up mini-skirted girls who hang outside the doors to the clubs here might, on first impressions, suggest the raucous beer-swilling fleshpots of Bangkok and Manila. Once inside, however, such impressions rapidly evaporate. By comparison with Ermita and Patpong roads, these clubs are like a vicarage tea party. The music might be loud but the clients certainly aren't and the hostesses even less so. And there are no floor shows. You could bring an evangelist here without inviting a lecture on hellfire and damnation and the evils of the flesh!

You'll see very few Koreans in the clubs of 'Texas Street'. They go elsewhere for the pleasures of the flesh and it's a mind-boggling experience to take a look at where they go. Westerners know the area as 'Green Street' (and taxi drivers understand that) but Koreans know it as Wanwol-dong 완월동.

There's perhaps no other more bizarre experience for Westerners in Korea than to visit this area. Here are three parallel streets literally lined with brothels. But these are no ordinary brothels. Each one fronts the street with a huge plate-glass window beyond which, under intense pink lighting, sit up to two dozen women fully made up in traditional Korean costume waiting for a client to choose them. These are not strictly *kisaeng* (the Korean equivalent of the Japanese *geisha*) since real *kisaeng* would be horrified by such indiscretion. Nevertheless, this is no bawdy Texas Street. Everyone is on their best behaviour and there's not a Westerner in sight.

GETTING THERE & AWAY
Bus
The Express (Kosok) Bus Terminal 고속터미널 and the Tongbu Bus Terminal 동부터미널 are a long way from the city centre out in Tongnae suburb.

The Tongbu Terminal is right outside the Myongnyundong Subway Station so is easy to get to. Getting to or from the Express Terminal using the subway system involves a 12-minute walk (15 minutes with a heavy backpack). The nearest subway station is Tongnae. Assuming you are arriving by bus at this terminal, go out of the front entrance and turn right. About 150 metres down this road you come to a five-way road junction with a large red-brick church on the opposite side of the road. Turn right here, pass by a footbridge across the road and continue straight on down to the bottom. The yellow-painted Tongnae Subway Station faces you at the bottom of this road (Tongnae is the first subway station which is above ground going north so you can't miss it). The subway station to get out at if you want the centre of Pusan (ferry terminals and central *yogwan*) is Chungang-dong. Going in the opposite direction, take the subway to Tongnae Station, cross the main boulevard and then go straight up the road opposite the station until you reach the large red-brick church. Turn left here.

If you can find one, local bus No 57 connects the Express Terminal with Tongnae Subway Station.

An alternative way of getting to the Express Terminal is to take local bus No 35 (W120) or *chaesok* bus No 301 or 306 (W300).

A taxi into the centre will cost you around W2300. There is one other bus terminal and that is the Sobu Bus Terminal 서부터미널 in the Puk suburb in the western part of the city, about half way to Kimhae International Airport. The only time you would use it is if you needed to take a *chikheng* bus to points further west. Express buses don't leave from here. Local bus No 15 connects this terminal with the city centre.

It's easy to find the bus you want at the Express Terminal since all the signs are in both Korean and English. This is not the case at the other two terminals, where all the signs are in Korean.

The following buses are available from the Express Bus Terminal:

To Kwangju Buses every 20 minutes from 6 am to 6.20 pm. The fare is W3860 and the journey takes 4¼ hours.

To Kyongju Buses every 30 minutes from 7 am to 7.30 pm. The fare is W1150 and the journey takes one hour.

To Seoul Buses every 10 minutes from 6 am to 6.40 pm. The fare is W5970 and the journey takes 5½ hours.

To Taegu Buses every 15 minutes from 5.40 am to 9 pm. The fare is W1980 and the journey takes nearly two hours.

To Taejon Every 50 minutes from 6 am to 6.30 pm. The fare is W4030 and the journey takes 3½ hours.

To Yeosu Every 50 minutes from 6 am to 6.10 pm. The fare is W3280 and the journey takes about four hours.

Top: Autumn colours, Pulguk-sa temple, Kyongju (DS)
Left: Temple eaves, Pulguk-sa temple, Kyongju (GC)
Right: Carved temple guardian, Pulguk-sa temple, Kyongju (DS)

Top: Resting from study, Hahae near Andong (CHP)
Left: Squid drying racks at Jeodong, Ulleung-do Island (CHP)
Right: The fish market, Jeodong, Ulleung-do Island (CHP)

Ferry

Details of the international ferries from Pusan to Shimonoseki and Pusan to Osaka can be found in the Getting There chapter at the beginning of this book.

Student discounts are available on the following domestic ferries but the notice to this effect is only in Korean so you have to inquire about this.

Pusan to Cheju-do There is a choice of four ferries to Cheju-do from Pusan – two to Cheju City and two to Sogwipo via Songsanpo (on the eastern tip of the island). All these ferries depart from the Domestic Ferry Terminal in Pusan. Schedules vary from one season to another so it's a good idea to check this out as soon as possible after you arrive in Pusan. The timetables at the terminal are in both Korean and English. The cheapest fares available are those on the ferries to Sogwipo since these boats have only 2nd and 3rd classes. Even 3rd class on the ferries to Cheju City cost more than 2nd class on the ferries to Sogwipo.

Pusan to Cheju City The car ferry *Queen* sails from Pusan on Monday, Wednesday and Friday at 7 pm and from Cheju City on Tuesday, Thursday and Saturday at the same time. The journey takes 11 hours and the fares are W80,860 (special class), W32,680 (1st class bunk), W25,030 (1st class seat),

W22,270 (2nd class bunk), W14,730 (2nd class seat) and W11,180 (3rd class).

The *Tongyang Kosok Ferry* sails from Pusan daily except Sunday at 7.30 pm and from Cheju City daily except Sunday at 7.30 pm. The journey takes 11 hours and the fares are the same as those on the car ferry *Queen*.

Pusan to Sogwipo The two ferries to Sogwipo are the *Tonghae-ho* and the *Uisong-ho* which alternate with each other. One or the other of them sails from Pusan daily at 9.30 am and arrives at 5 pm. From Sogwipo there's a daily sailing at 5 pm which arrives at 8 am. These ferries call at Songsanpo. The fares on either ferry are W16,100 (2nd class bunk), W10,760 (2nd class) and W7210 (3rd class).

Pusan to Yeosu via Hallyo Waterway The journey between Pusan and Yeosu via the Hallyo Waterway National Park on the *Angel* hydrofoil is a popular trip in this part of Korea, but you should be aware that the ferries are completely enclosed by glass windows. There are no open decks and you must occupy a seat, which may face backwards. There's usually no need to book in advance but if you want to be certain then give the company a ring – English is spoken. In Pusan the number is 702-3535. In Yeosu it is 63-1824.

The schedule is as follows:

Pusan	Seongpo	Chungmu	Saryang-do	Samcheonpo	Namhae	Yeosu
7 am	8.20 am	8.40 am	9.10 am	9.35 am	10 am	10.30 am
9.10 am	10.30 am					
11.10 am	12.30 am	12.50 am	1.20 pm	1.45 pm	2.10 pm	2.40 pm
1.10 pm	2.30 pm					
3 pm	4.20 pm	4.40 pm	5.10 pm	5.35 pm	6 pm	6.30 pm
5 pm	6.20 pm					

Yeosu	Namhae	Samcheonpo	Saryang-do	Chungmu	Seongpo	Pusan
				7 am	7.20 am	8.40 am
7.10 am	7.45 am	8.10 am	8.35 am	9.05 am	9.25 am	10.45 am
				11.05 am	11.25 am	12.45 pm
11.05 am	11.40 am	12.05 pm	12.30 pm	1 pm	1.20 pm	2.40 pm
				3.05 pm	3.25 pm	4.45 pm
3.10 pm	3.45 pm	4.10 pm	4.35 pm	5.05 pm	5.25 pm	6.45 pm

The fares are as follows:

Pusan						
W5110	Seongpo					
W6490	W1460	Chungmu				
W8110	W3230	W1780	Saryang-do			
W9450	W4910	W3540	W1780	Samcheonpo		
W10,670	W6440	W5070	W3380	W1620	Namhae	
W12,960	W8790	W7420	W5620	W3830	W2120	Yeosu

GETTING AROUND

Airport Transport

There are two airport terminal shuttle buses which connect Kimhae Airport with the city. Bus No 201 runs from the airport terminal to Chung-gu (the city centre) via Kupo, Sasang, Somyon, Pusan Station and City Hall. Bus No 307 runs from the airport terminal to Haeundae Beach via Kupo, Mandok, the Express Bus Terminal, Tongnae Hot Springs, Allak Rotary and the Yachting Centre. The fare on either is W370. Both buses leave every 10 minutes from 5 am to midnight. The journey time from either the city centre or the Express Bus Terminal is about 40 minutes.

A taxi from the airport to the city centre will cost around W3200. Right outside the airport terminal is a large sign indicating (in English) what the current taxi fares are to various points in the city.

Bus

Buses which run down Chungang-ro as far as City Hall include Nos 26, 34, 42, 55, 127 and 139. The fare is W130 or W120 if you buy a token beforehand.

Subway

The subway is an excellent way of getting around Pusan though there is only one line which basically follows the main north-south road through the city. It runs from near Kudok Stadium, around the central shopping district of Chung-gu, past Chagalchi Fish Market and onto Chungang-ro. From there it continues on past Pusan Railway Station, Tongbu Bus Terminal, Pusan National University and ends up in the northern suburb of Kumjong.

It's a cheap and very convenient way of getting around. All signs are in both Korean and English. Fares depend on the distance travelled – W170 for one sector, W220 for two sectors and W250 for three sectors. There are automatic ticket vending machines at the stations as well as staffed ticket windows.

Taxi

Taxis start at W700 for ordinary cabs and W800 for air-conditioned cabs. Meters are always used. Tips are not expected.

Around Pusan

TONGDO-SA TEMPLE 통도사

This Buddhist temple was founded in 646 AD during the reign of Queen Sondok of the Silla Dynasty and is the largest and one of the most famous in Korea. Like many other Buddhist temples in Korea such as Popju-sa, Kap-sa, Pulguk-sa and Haein-sa it's situated in beautiful surroundings amid forested mountains and crystal-clear streams. There are some 65 buildings in all, including 13 hermitages scattered over the mountains behind the main temple complex.

The temple's founder, priest Chajang, studied Buddhism for many years in China before returning to Korea and making Tongdo-sa the country's foremost temple. He also brought back with him from China

**Pusan
Subway
부산
지하철**

	Nopodong 노포동
	Pomosa 보모사
	Namsandong 남산동
	Tushil 두실
	Kusodong 구서동
	Changjondong 장전동
	Pusan Univ. 부산대
	Onchonjang 온천장
Kumgang Park	Myongnyundong 명륜동
Express Bus Terminal	Tongnae 동래역
	Teachers' College 교육대임구
	Yonsandong 연산동
	Yonje 연제
	Yangjong 양정
	Pujondong 부전역
	Somyon 서면
	Pomnaegol 봄내골
	Chwachondong 좌천동
	Pusanjin Sta. 부산진역
	Choryangdong 초량동
	Pusan Station 부산역
Ferryboat Terminals & Central Yogwan	Chungangdong 중앙동
	Nampodong 남포동
Fish Market	Chagalchi 충무동
	Tosongdong 토성동
	Tongdaeshindong 부민동
	Sodaeshindong 서대신동

N.B. Chagalchi = Chungmudong
Tongdaeshindong = Pumindong

what were reputed to be part of the Buddha's ashes. They were enshrined in the elaborate tomb known as the Sokka Sari-tap which is the focal point of Tongdo-sa.

There are some exceptionally beautiful buildings here and it's well worth making the effort to stop off here between Pusan and Kyongju or vice versa. There are usually some 200 monks in residence here, so it's more than likely that a ceremony or chanting will be going on when you arrive. The temple is traditionally a Zen temple. Entry costs W300.

Getting There & Away

There are two ways to get to Tongdo-sa. The first way is to take the Pusan-Taegu *chikheng* bus from either Pusan or Kyongju. Tell the ticket office where you want to go and they'll make sure you get on the right bus, which makes a number of stops at places just off the freeway between Pusan and Kyongju including Tongdo. From where the bus drops you it's less than one km into Tongdo Village. You'll probably have to walk this stretch. At the village you have the choice of taking a taxi or walking to the temple. It's about 1½ km from the village and taxis will charge W800 to W1000 for this. If you have the time it's worth walking as the road follows a beautiful mountain stream with many rock carvings along the way.

There's also a direct bus to Tongdo Village from the Tongbu Bus Station in Pusan. The fare is W620. This way means you won't have to walk from the freeway to Tongdo Village. There are regular buses from the village to both Pusan and Ulsan. If you don't want to carry your pack to the temple you can leave it at the bus station.

NAEWON-SA TEMPLE 내원사

South-east of Tongdo-sa on the opposite side of the freeway is another temple complex, that of Naewon-sa which has a setting similar to that of Tongdo. There is a nunnery here with some 50 Buddhist nuns, and the priest, who is called Doryong, will welcome you anytime. You can get to Naewon by bus from Tongdo Village, followed by a walk along a very picturesque mountain stream. Swimming is possible in the stream in summertime.

Getting There & Away

There are direct buses from the Tongbu Bus Station in Pusan to Naewon-sa every hour from 7 am to 7 pm. The fare is W640 and the journey takes about one hour.

Chinju 진주

Chinju is a relatively small city on the Namhae Expressway about two-thirds of the way between Kwangju and Pusan. It is a convenient base from which to explore the eastern side of Chirisan National Park. Kurye, however, is a more convenient base for the western side which is where the famous temples are sited.

Chinju lies on both sides of the large Nam River, which is dammed upstream at the confluence with the Dokchon River. It's a pleasant city with a history going back to the time of the Three Kingdoms period. Like Puyo, there's quite a large, partially forested hillock overlooking the river on which most of the historical relics and sites of the city are to be found.

CHINJU CASTLE

The most interesting part of Chinju is the hillock which is actually the remains of Chinju Castle. This was once a walled fortress built during the Koryo Dynasty but it was partially destroyed during the Japanese invasion of 1592 to 1593. It was here that one of the major battles was fought in which some 70,000 Korean soldiers and civilians lost their lives. The wall was rebuilt in 1605 by the provincial commander in chief, Lee Su-ill, and it's the remains of this which you see today.

Inside the walls are several places of interest as well as a number of traditional gateways and shrines.

CHOKSONGNU PAVILION

Overlooking the river is the large Choksongnu Pavilion which was first built in 1368 during the Koryo Dynasty and used as an exhibition hall for the poems of famous scholars and civil officials. Despite having survived the turbulent years of the Japanese invasion, it was finally burnt down during the Korean War. Various efforts were made to repair it after that event but it has now been completely rebuilt in the original style.

THE CASTLE GATES

Also worth seeing are the impressive gates to the castle including Sojangdae, Pukchangdae and Yongsam Pojongsa. The latter served as the front gate for the Kyongnam provincial government during the days

1	Telephone & Telegraph Office 전신 전화국
2	Sobu Market 서부 시장
3	Commercial Bank of Korea
4	Chungang Market 중앙시장
5	Police 경찰
6	Main Post Office 우체국
7	City Hall 시청
8	Fruit & Vegetable Market 과일, 채소 시장
9	Chikheng Bus Terminal 시내 버스터미널
10	Exchange Bank of Korea 한국 외환은행
11	Narang Punshik 나랑분식
12	Ee-hwa Yoinsook 이화여인숙
13	Songjukjang Yogwan 송죽장 여관
14	Kyongnam Yoinsook 경남여인숙

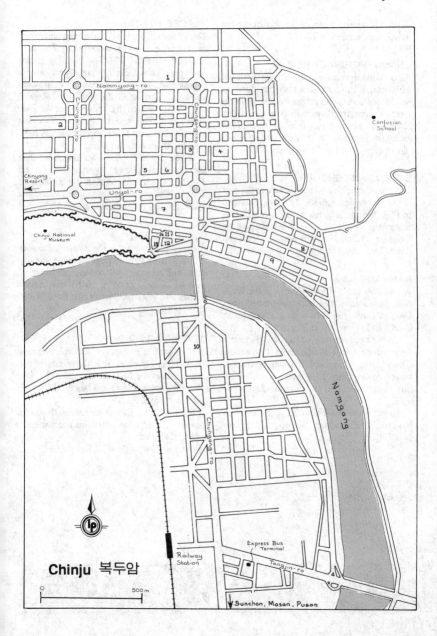

Chinju 복두암

of the Yi Dynasty when its headquarters were inside the castle.

CHINJU NATIONAL MUSEUM

Also inside the castle is the Chinju National Museum, a modern structure but done in traditional style. The museum specialises in artefacts from the Kaya period though it also has many objects dating from the time of the Japanese invasion in 1592. It's open every day except Monday. Entry costs W110.

CONFUCIAN SCHOOL

Just outside the city on the hillside to the east is the Confucian School. This was founded in 987 during the reign of the Koryo king, Songjong, as a local school. Scholars of the Chinese classics and medicine lectured there. The school is open to the public.

NAMGANG DAM

About five km west of Chinju is the huge Namgang Dam which was constructed from 1962 to 1969. The dam wall is 21 metres in height and is one km in length.

On the northern side of the dam there is a recreational and resort area known as Chinyangho. There are lookout platforms, hotels, coffee shops and restaurants. You can hire motor boats and launches are also available.

To get there from Chinju, take local bus No 16 from the centre (Unyol-ro). The fare is W120.

PLACES TO STAY

One of the cheapest places to stay, and excellent value, is the *Kyongnam Yoinsook* 경남여인숙 (tel 27184). The building is new and very clean. Both single and double rooms cost W4000 and there are cold-water showers. Similar is the *Ee-hwa Yoinsook* 이화여인숙 which has rooms for W4000 single or double, and triples for W5000. It's also a very clean place and the rooms have fans but there's no hot water.

If you'd prefer your own bathroom then try the *Songjukjang Yogwan* 송죽장 (tel 25620), which costs W9000 for a single or double. The rooms have colour TV and the bathroom has constant hot water.

PLACES TO EAT

A cheap place to eat is the *Narang Punshik* 나랑분식. It's a very large place with friendly staff and an extensive menu consisting of Korean dishes, noodles, fried rice, sandwiches and *kimbap*. Dishes cost from W800 to W1000.

GETTING AROUND

Both the railway station and the Express (*kosok*) Bus Terminal are in the section of the city south of the Nam River, about 1½ km from the centre. Take local bus No 15 if you don't want to walk.

The Chikheng Bus Terminal, on the other hand, is close to the centre on the northern side of the river.

South-West Korea

Yeosu 여수

Yeosu lies about halfway along the mountainous and deeply indented southern coastline of Korea. It's a spectacularly beautiful area peppered with islands and peninsulas. A large part of the area between Yeosu and Pusan now makes up the Hallyo Waterway National Park. One of the most popular trips in this part of the country is to take the hydrofoil from Yeosu to Pusan (or vice versa) via Namhae, Samcheonpo, Chungmun and Seongpo.

Yeosu's most famous historical associations are with Admiral Yi, who routed the Japanese navy on several occasions in the 16th century, following the introduction of his highly manoeuvrable ironclad warships or 'turtle ships'. Full-size recreations of these ships can be seen at Yeosu (the other place you can see them is in the Independence Hall of Korea outside Chonan). From being a naval base in the 16th century, Yeosu is now an expanding industrial and resort city which is worth spending a day or two exploring.

ORIENTATION

Due to the mountainous terrain of the peninsula on which Yeosu stands, the city is divided into a number of distinct parts, though the centre essentially consists of the area between the railway station and the Passenger Ship Terminal. The bus terminal is a long way from the centre (about 3½ km) along the road to Sunchon so you'll need to take a local bus or taxi between the two. The airport is even further out but a shuttle bus operates into the centre whenever there are flights. The fare is W600.

The Korean Air office is about half way between the city centre and the bus station.

CHINNAMGWAN PAVILION 진남관

Right in the centre of town stands the huge Chinnamgwan Pavilion, one of the longest pavilions in Korea. It's a beautiful old building with massive poles and beams, which was originally constructed for receiving officials and holding ceremonies and later used as military quarters. In it you can see two full-scale recreations of the turtle ships which Admiral Yi used to defeat the Japanese naval forces during the 1592 invasion.

In the summer months it's used a lot by the old men of the town as a place to gather and talk and perhaps throw down a bottle of *soju*. They're a friendly bunch and will probably draw you into conversation since very few Westerners ever visit Yeosu.

Entry to the pavilion costs W200.

CHUNGMIN-SA SHRINE 충민사

High up on the hill which overlooks the area between City Hall and the railway station is the Chungmin-sa Shrine dedicated to Admiral Yi. It was built in 1601 by another naval commander, Yi Si-eon, though it has been renovated since then. There are excellent views over Yeosu and the harbour area but it's a steep climb.

ODONG-DO 오동도

Another popular spot in Yeosu is Odong-do, an island which is linked to the mainland by a 730-metre-long causeway. It's a craggy, tree-and bamboo-covered island with a lighthouse and picnic spots and is honeycombed with walking trails. The best time to see the island is in spring when it's covered with camellia blossoms. Entry costs W400 – Odong-do is actually part of the Hallyo Waterway National Park. Local bus Nos 1 and 2 will take you here from the centre of town. The fare is W140.

A restaurant complex has been built on the island and the speciality is fresh seafood but you can forget about eating here as meals are outrageously priced at W20,000!

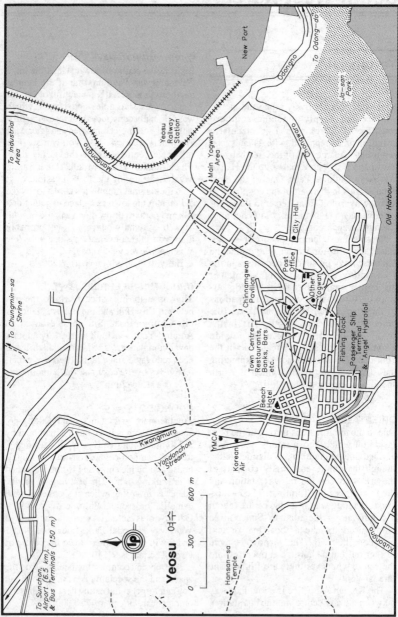

Yeosu 여수

One of the most enjoyable things to do here is to take the tourist launch around the island. The launches are berthed half way along the causeway and drop you off next to the restaurant complex. The trip costs W500 and the launches leave any time there are sufficient passengers.

HANSAN-SA TEMPLE 한산사
If you're up to a more substantial trek there is the Hansan-sa Temple, high up on the wooded mountain slopes to the west of Yeosu. The temple was built in 1194 by a high priest named Bojo during the reign of the Koryo king, Myeongjong.

The trail up to the temple is well marked and the views are superb. The best view of all is not from the temple itself, however, but from a point five minutes walk away.

To get there, take the trail through the woods to the right of the temple as you face it and descend onto a small platform where the local people do their washing. Then turn left up through an area dotted surrealistically with gym equipment and posters telling you how to do push-ups, and on to the highest point – a grassy cliff-top. The views are practically 180°. At the laundry trough you may be lucky enough to come across a shamanistic performance.

PLACES TO STAY
The majority of *yogwan* and *yoinsook* are clustered between Chinnamgwan Pavilion and the harbour front and along the road which connects this part of town to the railway station. There's hardly anywhere to stay around the bus terminal.

Places to Stay – bottom end
A good place to look for a *yoinsook* or *yogwan* is between the entrance to Chinnamgwan Pavilion and the roundabout below here on Yeosu's main drag. Just off to the left of the pavilion is the *Songkwan Yoinsook* 송관여인숙 and across the opposite side of the road down a narrow alley are a whole collection of others which include the *Shinjin Yoinsook* 신진여인숙, the *Gumnam Yoinsook* 금남여인숙, the *Tongyong Jang*

Yogwan 동양장여관, and the *Korbu Jang Yogwan* 거부장여관. Below this alley and just off the roundabout is the *Tong-il Yogwan*. They're all well-kept places and you should expect to pay W5000 to W6000 for the *yoinsook*, W10,000 for the *yogwan* and a little more for the *yogwan jang*.

There's also a good selection of *yogwan* in the streets on either side of the main drag leading down to the railway station but most are in the *yogwan jang* category.

The cheapest *yoinsook* are to be found in the streets parallel to the old fishing dock and the main drag but they're very basic and are essentially brothels intended for those with something other than the standard of accommodation on their minds. Expect to pay around W4000 to W5000 for a room.

The streets parallel to the main drag on the top side are much more salubrious and form Yeosu's central business district and shopping centre. Here you'll find the *Tonghae Jang Yogwan* 동해장여관 and the *Taewon Jang Yogwan* 대원장여관 adjacent to each other. The price for a room with shower, toilet, hot water, colour TV, fan and air-con here is W12,000 to W13,000, but the Taewon is the better of the two. These hotels are in the first street back from the main drag close to the roundabout.

There are plenty of other *yogwan jang* of a similar standard off the main road leading down to the railway station, most of them visible from the main road.

Places to Stay – middle
The best area to look for a mid-range hotel in Yeosu is along the main road halfway between the main post office and the railway station. Coming from the centre, the first you'll see on the left-hand side is the *Yosu Park Tourist Hotel* (tel 63- 2334/8), 979-1 Kwanmun-dong, a two-star hotel with rooms from W23,000. Right next door to it, and looking like a central European/French building in style, is the *Hwa-in Gak Hotel* 해인각호텔 which offers rooms for a similar price. Further down this road on the right hand side is the somewhat older *Sejong Hotel*. Down towards the bottom of this road

and close to the railway station is the *Yosu Tourist Hotel* (tel 62-3131), 766 Konghwa-dong, another two-star hotel with rooms from W25,000.

Places to Stay – top end

There's only one top-range hotel in Yeosu and this is the *Yosu Beach Hotel* (tel 63-2011/9), 346 Chungmu-dong, up on the hill at the opposite end of town from the hotels mentioned above. Rooms here with all the usual creature comforts range from W30,000 to W36,500 plus service charges and taxes.

PLACES TO EAT

There's a good range of restaurants of various categories in the central business district with the cheaper ones being closest to the old fishing dock. If you're looking for seafood, there are three restaurants on the right hand side between the traffic round-about and the dock front, but only one of them offers meals at a reasonable price – W3000 to W4000 for fried fish and the usual trimmings. The other two quote ridiculous prices, though they do specialise in raw seafood.

GETTING THERE & AWAY
Bus

The express and *chikheng* bus terminals are next to each other on the western side of the city on the road out to Sunchon and the airport.

To Pusan There are express buses every 50 minutes to Pusan from 6 am to 6.10 pm. The fare is W3280 and the journey takes 3½ hours.

To Seoul There are express buses to Seoul every hour from 6.40 am to 5.40 pm. The fare is W6120 and the journey takes 5½ hours.

To Kwangju There are nonstop *chikheng* buses to Kwangju every 50 minutes (every 20 minutes at weekends) from 6.10 am to 8.40 pm. The fare is W2050 and the journey takes nearly two hours. There are other *chikheng* buses which make a number of

stops en route but only take another 15 minutes on average.

To Kurye There are buses approximately hourly from 6.05 am to 6.40 pm which cost W1430 and take two hours. These are the buses you need if you're heading for the western side of Chiri-san National Park. There are also direct buses from Yeosu to Ssanggye-sa (in Chiri-san National Park) four times daily, the first at 8.25 am and the last at 3.35 pm. The fare is W1830 and the journey takes two hours and 20 minutes.

To Songgwan-sa There are direct buses also to this famous temple south of Kwangju seven times daily, the first at 7.55 am and the last at 2.50 pm. The fare is W1490 and the journey takes just over two hours.

Boat

All boats into and out of Yeosu dock at the large Passenger Ship Terminal at the western end of the old fishing dock. You can get boats here to many of the islands off the south coast and to the east of Yeosu. There are no ferries to Cheju-do from here.

The main ferry of interest to travellers is the *Angel* hydrofoil to Pusan via Namhae, Samcheonpo, Chungmu and Seongpo. Except during the holiday season (July and August) it isn't necessary to book in advance. The schedule for the hydrofoil is in the Pusan section.

GETTING AROUND
Airport Transport

If you arrive by air, the airport is about seven km out of town and served by local buses. There's no need to take a taxi – simply walk the few metres from the terminal buildings to the road and wait for a bus which will have 공항 in the front window. The fare is W290 and the journey takes about 40 minutes, finishing up at the Chikheng Bus Terminal.

Local Transport

Only the new Port Ferry Terminal and railway station are within walking distance of each other. The express and *chikheng* bus terminals are way across the other side of town. To get from one to the other or into the centre of town you'll need to use public transport. City bus Nos 3, 5, 6, 7, 8, 9, 10, 11, 13 and 17 go past the two bus terminals but probably the most useful is bus No 11 which connects the bus terminals with the railway station via the centre of town.

Kwangju 광주

Though Kwangju has been the capital of Chollanam-do Province for centuries and is the fifth largest city in Korea, there is precious little left of its traditional heritage. This is a sprawling all-modern concrete and glass city with few redeeming features, so it's not surprising that most travellers give it a miss or, at the most, spend a night en route to somewhere else.

In recent times it has acquired a reputation for its student and industrial worker radicalism and is also the home territory of opposition leader Kim Dae Jung. A series of events here in 1980 (described more fully in the 'History' section in the Facts about the Country chapter) culminated in a wholesale slaughter of civilians by the army in which over 2000 people lost their lives and many thousands more were seriously injured (official figures of dead and wounded were much lower but few people in Korea afford them much credibility). Chun Doo Hwan, the army commander at the time, is widely held to have been responsible for issuing the orders for the massacre and resentment lingers on at the present government's reluctance to bring him to trial. This was Korea's Tiananmen Square.

KWANGJU NATIONAL MUSEUM
박물관
Just about the only sight worth seeing, as such, is the Kwangju Museum. It was built mainly to house the contents of a Chinese Yuan Dynasty junk which sank off the coast some 600 years ago and was only rediscov-

ered in 1976. Exhibits include celadon vases, cups and apothecaries' mortars and pestles, almost all of them in perfect condition.

The rest of the museum is taken up by 11th to 14th-century Buddhist relics, scroll paintings from the Yi Dynasty and white porcelain. The museum is north of the city centre across the other side of the expressway. Entry costs W110 (W50 for students and those under 24 years old) and the museum is open daily, except Mondays, from 9 am to 4 pm (winter) and 9 am to 5 pm (summer).

MUDUNG-SAN 무등산 & CHUNG SIM-SA
Overlooking Kwangju is Mudung-san, a provincial park, at the base of which there is a resort area and, further up the slopes, the Buddhist temple of Chung Sim-sa which is surrounded by a tea plantation. This plantation is famous for its green leaf tea – established initially by a famous Yi Dynasty artist at the end of the 19th century – and there are two nearby processing factories. Thick forest covers much of this mountain and, since there are many different species of trees, it resembles Sorak-san in the autumn time.

There are plenty of streams through the forest and it's popular hiking country but once you're past the cafe, about one km into the park from the entrance, there are no more facilities. This cafe has soft drinks and snacks (such as *pindatok*). To get to the entrance of the park take local bus No 18 from the Intercity Bus Terminal (or from the bus stop in Chebong-ro, marked on the map) which costs W240 and takes about 40 minutes.

PLACES TO STAY – BOTTOM END
Probably the best of the cheapies is the *Inhwa Yoinsook* 인화여인숙 which costs W5000 for a double with bathroom (very unusual for a *yoinsook*), black and white TV and fan, but there's no hot water. The rooms are tiny but the staff are friendly. If it's full, try the *Kyubin Yoinsook* 귀빈여인숙 which

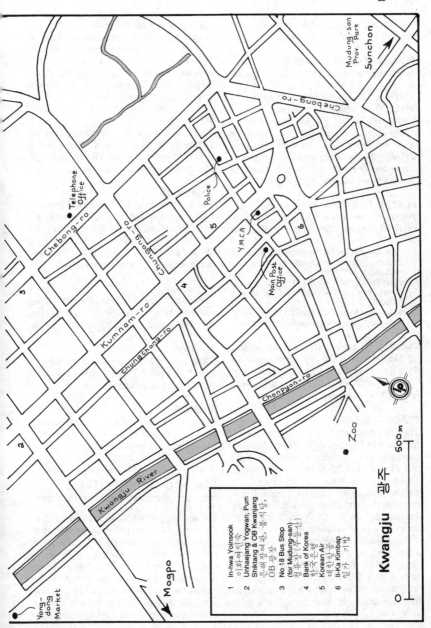

Telephone Office

Chebong-ro

Chungchang-ro

Kumnam-ro

Chungchang-ro

Chebong-ro

Police

5

Y.M.C.A

6

Main Post Office

Chonpyon-ro

Mudung-san Prov. Park

Sunchon

Kwangju River

Mogpo

Zoo

Yang-dong Market

0   500 m

Kwangju 광주

1 In-hwa Yoinsook
   이화여인숙
2 Unhaejang Yogwan, Pum
   Shiktang & OB Kwanjang
   은해장여관, 품식당,
   OB광장
3 No 18 Bus Stop
   (for Mudung-san)
   정부장 (무등산)
4 Bank of Korea
   한국은행
5 Korean Air
   대한항공
6 Il-Ka Kimbap
   일가 기밥

is the same price but without bathroom. Like the In-hwa, there's no hot water.

PLACES TO STAY – MIDDLE

A reasonably priced mid-range hotel is the *Unhaejang Yogwan* 은혜장여관 (tel 34 3502), which has Korean-style rooms for W12,000 a double with bathroom (constant hot water), colour TV and fan. There's a coffee shop on the ground floor. There are several other similar places at the same price including the *Yonsujang Yogwan* 연수장여관, *Taedojang Yogwan* 연수장여관 and the *Songkangjang Yogwan* 대도장여관.

PLACES TO STAY – TOP END

There are three top-end hotels in Kwangju itself, all of them in the city centre. They are:

Kwangju Tourist Hotel (tel 232-6231/9) 20 Kumnam-ro 2-ga, Tong-gu. Three-star with rooms from W25,000 to W33,000.
Riverside Tourist Hotel (tel 223-9111) 72-1 Honam-dong, Tong-gu. Three-star with rooms from W33,100.
Kwangju Grand Hotel (tel 224-6111) 121 Pullo-dong, Tong-gu. Four-star with rooms from W36,000.

Outside of Kwangju itself and about halfway up Mudung-san is the city's best hotel, the *Shin Yang Park Hotel*, San 40, Chisan-dong, Tong-gu (tel 27-0671/9). This is a four-star hotel with rooms from W48,750.

PLACES TO EAT

The *Il-ka Kimbap* 일가김밥 is recommended for cheap but very tasty food. As the name suggests, they only offer *kimbap* with soup and *kimchi* for W1500. Another relatively cheap restaurant is the *Pum Shiktang* 봄식당 which offers all the standard Korean dishes plus they have chicken ginseng (known as *samgaetang*) for W4000. Worth a try. There are many other restaurants in the same area.

The *OB Kwanjang Bar* is worth a visit. It's a tiny, open-plan bar with a few tables and chairs and is run by middle-aged women. Beer costs W1500 for a large bottle and they sometimes have Korean Kentucky-style fried chicken with salad, though it's quite expensive at W4000.

GETTING THERE & AWAY

Kwangju has three bus terminals. Local as well as some *chikheng* buses run from the Intercity Bus Terminal. Express and *chikheng* buses run from both the (main) Express Bus Terminal and the Honam Express Bus Terminal.

To Wando

There are buses every 30 minutes from the Chikheng Terminal (bay No 8-1 and 8-2) from 5.15 am to 7.30 pm. The fare is W2250 and.the journey takes three hours.

To Mogpo

There are buses every 15 minutes from the Chikheng Terminal from 5.30 am to 10 pm and every 10 minutes from the Express Terminal from 5.20 am to 10 pm. The fare is W1200 and the journey takes 1¾ hours and one hour and 20 minutes respectively.

To Kyongju

There are two express buses daily at 9.40 am and 3.40 pm which cost W4080 and take just over five hours.

To Taegu

There are express buses every 40 minutes from 5.30 am to 5.10 pm. The fare is W3180 and the journey takes 5½ hours.

To Seoul

There are express buses every five minutes from 5.30 am to 7.40 pm. The fare is W4530 and the journey takes four hours.

Mogpo (Mokpo) 목포

The fishing port of Mogpo is at the end of the railway line near the south-western tip of mainland Korea. Mogpo is the departure point for some of the cheapest ferries to Cheju-do (the other place being Wando further south) and for the ferries to the islands west of Mogpo, the most interesting of which is Hong-do. The town itself is of little interest and most travellers only stay

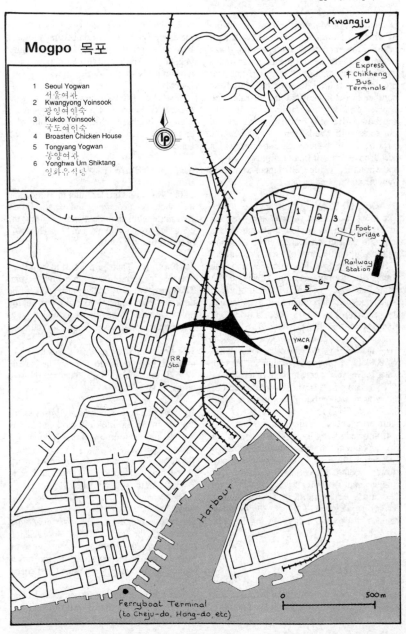

Mogpo 목포

1 Seoul Yogwan
   서울여관
2 Kwangyong Yoinsook
   광영여인숙
3 Kukdo Yoinsook
   국도여인숙
4 Broasten Chicken House
5 Tongyang Yogwan
   동양여관
6 Yonghwa Um Shiktang
   영화음식당

Kwangju

Express
& Chikheng
Bus
Terminals

Foot-
bridge

Railway
Station

1 2 3

5 6

4

YMCA

RR
Sta.

Harbour

Ferryboat Terminal
(to Cheju-do, Hong-do, etc)

0   500m

islands west of Mogpo, the most interesting of which is Hong-do. The town itself is of little interest and most travellers will stay overnight. If you have some time to spare it's worth wandering along the waterfront near the ferry terminal to see the incredible number of octopuses that are for sale – all kept alive and writhing in aerated plastic tubs and bowls! It's also worth walking around the rocky hill (Yudal-san 유달산) at the back of town for the views and sunsets. Up here are a number of small temples, pavilions and a botanical garden, all of them connected by well-maintained trails.

PLACES TO STAY

The most convenient *yogwan* and *yoinsook* in Mogpo are to be found in the streets opposite the railway station since these are within walking distance of the ferry terminal.

Some of the best of the cheapies are in the streets directly opposite the railway station immediately to the left of the footbridge which goes across the main road. They include the *Seoul Yogwan* 서울여관, *Kwangyong Yoinsook* 광영여인숙, *Kukdo Yoinsook* 국도여인숙, and *Taesong Yoinsook* 대성여인숙. The Kukdo charges W6000 (negotiable down to W5000) for a room with bathroom, and hot water is available at certain times of the day.

There are others further over to the left of the railway station but if you go there avoid the *You-Il Yoinsook* 유일여인숙 as it's the same price but very dingy.

If you're looking for something better – a Korean-style room with some furnishings, a TV and bathroom – then expect to pay around W8000 to W10,000 a double for *yogwan* and W12,000 for a *yogwan jang*. The most convenient of them are the *Tongyong Yogwan* 동명여관, *Taehwajang Yogwan* 태화장여관, and *Tongyang Yogwan* 농양여관.

PLACES TO EAT

Of all the restaurants around the railway station the one I'd recommend for value and quality of food is the *Yonghwa Um Shiktang* 영화음식점 . Two can eat *pekpan* for W2000

which includes soup and rice plus 15 other plates per person (!!) comprising mussels, fried fish, crab with sauce, *kimchi* and other vegetables. You'd find that hard to beat anywhere in Korea and the staff are very friendly.

If you're a fried chicken fiend then try the *Broasten Chicken House* (that's the way it's spelt in English) which offers somewhat expensive fried chicken with salad and *kimchi*.

GETTING THERE & AWAY
Bus

There's only one bus terminal in Mogpo and it services both *chikheng* and express buses. It's some considerable distance from the centre of town so take a local bus (No 101) or a taxi into the centre.

To Kwangju There are nonstop *chikheng* buses every 15 minutes from 5 am to 10 pm. The fare is W1370 and the journey takes one hour and 20 minutes. Make sure you get the nonstop bus as there are others which go to Kwangju but stop several times en route.

To Seoul There are express buses every 30 minutes from 6 am to 6 pm. The fare is W5520 and the journey takes nearly five hours.

To Wando There are *chikheng* buses every hour from 7.30 am to 5.40 pm. The fare is W1940 and the journey takes 2¼ hours.

To Yeosu There are *chikheng* buses every hour from 7.20 am to 6.50 pm. The fare is W3350 and the journey takes 3½ hours.

Boat

The boat terminal목포항여객터미널at Mogpo handles all the ferries to Cheju-do and the smaller islands west and south-west of Mogpo. Inside the terminal are the ticket offices, a coffee shop, pharmacy and snack bars.

The schedule for the ferries to and from Cheju-do are in the Cheju-do section. Booking in advance for these ferries isn't necessary except during the summer holidays – July to mid-August. During the rest of the year just go down to the boat terminal an hour or two before the ferry is due to sail.

Around Mogpo – the offshore islands

There are scores of local ferries from Mogpo to the small islands west and south of Mogpo. The most popular of these islands to visit are Hong-do and Huksan-do. Indeed, Hong-do is so popular with Korean holidaymakers during July and August that it's often difficult to get on a ferry and equally difficult finding accommodation if you want to stay on the island overnight. Indeed, during July you might not be able to find accommodation at all without prior booking.

These are not the only islands you can visit, of course, but if you're planning a trip around the less well-known of them then you really need a copy of the national bus, boat, rail and flight timetables and prices booklet (시각표) mentioned in the 'Getting Around' chapter. Armed with this booklet (and the coloured maps which it contains detailing boat connections) it's possible to work out a route and an approximate schedule though you'll need help with translation as the timetables are entirely in a mixture of Korean and Chinese (though mostly Korean). There are a series of coloured maps in the booklet detailing the boat connections. There's no better way of getting off the main tourist circuits than by visiting some of these islands.

HONG-DO 홍도
This is the most popular and beautiful of the islands west of Mogpo. It's comparable with Ulleung-do off the east coast in that it rises precipitously from the sea and is bounded by sheer cliffs, bizarre rock formations, and wooded hillsides cut by steep ravines. There are also many islets which surround the main

island, and sunsets are spectacular on clear days. Where it differs from Ulleung-do is that it is much smaller, being only some six km long, and the main land mass rises to only a third of the height of its eastern cousin. That doesn't make it any less interesting but the only way you can see the island is by boat as there are no foreshore roads or paths. The island is designated as a nature reserve.

Ferries to Hong-do land at Il-gu 일구 , the larger and more southerly of the island's two villages which is where the *minbak, yogwan* and telephone office are situated. It's also the only village where electricity is available (generator). Like I-gu 일구, its smaller neighbour to the north, there's a tiny cove which provides shelter for fishing boats. The two villages are connected by a footpath which follows the high ground and walking between the two places will take you about one hour.

Places to Stay
There's a good choice of *minbak, yoinsook* and *yogwan* in Il-gu at the usual prices (except during the summer holiday period when prices can double) but one which can be recommended is the *Kwangsong Yogwan* 광성여관 just below the school.

Getting There & Getting Around
Four different ferries connect Mogpo with Hong-do via Huksan-do. The *Namhae-ho* departs Mogpo at 7.30 am and arrives Hong-do at 10 am. It then returns to Mogpo and departs there at 1.40 pm, arriving in Hong-do at 4.10 pm. The *Taehung-ho* departs Mogpo at 8 am and arrives Hong-do at 10.30 am. It then returns to Mogpo and departs there at 2 pm, arriving in Hong-do at 4.30 pm. The *Namhae 2-ho* departs Mogpo at 8.30 am and arrives Hong-do at 11 am. The *Tongwon* departs Mogpo at 8.30 am and arrives Hong-do at 9 am thus making it the fastest boat. The fare on any of these boats is W2920.

HUKSAN-DO 학산도
Huksan-do lies further to the east of Hong-do, is larger and more populated than its neighbour and, in some ways, resembles

Cheju-do in that the numerous stones which litter the island have been utilised to create enclosed fields lined with dry-stone walls. Attached to rope, these stones are also used to hold down thatch roofs in windy weather. There are several villages on Huksan-do and, since the island doesn't rise anywhere near as steeply from the sea as Hong-do, farming is possible on the coastal fringes. The villages are connected by trails and you can walk around the island in a day, assuming you make an early start.

The largest village, Ye-ri 예리 , has an excellent harbour and was formerly a whaling centre. It's also where the ferries from the mainland land and where most of the island's accommodation is to be found. There's a sizeable fishing fleet which moors here. Unlike on Hong-do, you shouldn't have any problems finding accommodation on this island even during the summer holiday period.

Places to Stay & Eat

Ye-ri has a good selection of *minbak*, *yoinsook* and *yogwan* at the usual prices. Recommended are the *Taedo Yoinsook* 대도여인숙 and the *Yusong Yoinsook* 유성여인숙 which are close to each other opposite the train (there's no railway on the island but an engine, coal tender and passenger car have been set up here as a kind of children's playground).

With a substantial fishing fleet, you might expect that cheap seafood is available on Huksan-do but, as elsewhere in Korea, this isn't necessarily the case. Be sure to ask the price of a meal before you order. It can be very expensive.

Getting There & Away

All the ferries from Mogpo to Hong-do call at Huksan-do so you can use any of them to get to this island. The fare to Huksan-do is W1060.

Wando 완도

The island of Wando is off the south-western tip of the mainland and is famous throughout Korea for the quality of its seaweed (*kim*). At certain times of the year you'll see this seaweed drying in racks around the island in much the same way as squid are dried on Ulleung-do and along the north-east coast.

The town of Wando has a quiet, rural atmosphere and a look of benign neglect about it. Unfortunately most of the old tiled-roofed traditional buildings have disappeared but the narrow streets are still there. In fact they are so narrow that the somewhat decrepit local buses only go down one street. It's a very small town so you can't get lost.

There are both sandy and pebble beaches on the island. These days, the island is connected to the mainland by bridge and there is a ferry service to Cheju-do.

CHONGDO-RI 정도리

Chongdo-ri is the main pebble beach on the island and it is a very attractive sight. To get there from the town of Wando, take a local bus from the centre close to the ferry terminal and get off at Sajong-ni. From there it's a one-km walk to the beach. There's a small cafe on the beach which offers beer and soft drinks but no food.

MYONGSASIM-NI 명사십리

Myongsasim-ni (otherwise known as Myongsajang) is the main sandy beach and very beautiful. At certain times of the year it's a little harder to get to than Chongdo-ri since it involves a trip by local ferry, and they'll only sail if there's sufficient demand.

The ferries leave from the local ferry terminal which is about one km from the main terminal serving the Cheju-do ferries. The fare is W300 and the trip takes about half an hour. There are three to four ferries per day when there are sufficient passengers. Buses wait for the ferries at the far end and take you from there to the beach.

PLACES TO STAY

There's a good choice of *yoinsook* in Wando and they all charge more or less the same. The *Tongmyon Yoinsook* (tel 4539) 동명여인숙 , in front of the post office, is good value at W4000 a double. It's clean though spartan and it only has hot water in winter. Next door is the *Sujong Yoinsook* 수정여인숙 which is similar and charges the same price. At the back of the post office is the *Kwangju Yoinsook* 광주여인숙 which also has rooms for W4000 a double.

PLACES TO EAT

An excellent place to eat at is the *Haesong Shiktang* 혜성식당 on the main street. It has a good range of tasty Korean food but where it excels is in the number and variety of side dishes which literally cover the table! It's very good value at W1000 to W3000 per main dish. The *Samhojong Restaurant* 산호정 is also worth checking out. It offers Korean, Japanese and Western dishes for W2000 to W4000.

GETTING THERE & AWAY
Bus

All buses leave from the new terminal.

To Kwangju There are *chikheng* buses every 20 minutes from 6 am to 7.40 pm which cost W2570 and take about 2½ hours.

To Mogpo There are *chikheng* buses approximately every hour from 8 am to 6.40 pm which cost W1940 and take about two hours.

To Pusan There are *chikheng* buses every hour from 7.25 am to 3.10 pm. The fare is W5600 and the journey takes nearly seven hours.

Ferry

Wando is connected to Cheju-do by ferry. The schedule for these ferries is in the Cheju-do section.

If you want to explore some of the nearby islands there are ferries from Wando to Chongsan-do 청산도 , Noktong-do 낙동도 , Nohwa-do 노화도 , Cho-do 초도 and Sokhwapo 석화포 .

To Chongsan-do there is a slow boat (W830, 1½ hours) and a fast boat (W2290, half an hour). Similarly, to Noktong-do there is a slow boat (W3370, 3½ hours) and a fast boat (W6780, 2¼ hours). To Cho-do by one of these boats takes 3¾ hours (W1730) and to Sokhwapo it is one hour (W350).

If you're heading for Mogpo from Wando and would prefer to go by sea rather than by bus, there is a daily ferry which leaves Wando at 8 am, costs W3690 and takes seven hours. The ferry calls at many places en route.

GETTING AROUND

The bus terminal is a long way from the centre of town (about 1½ km). If the walk doesn't appeal to you there are local buses and taxis into the centre.

Cheju-do (Jeju-do)
제주도

Eighty-five km off the southernmost tip of the peninsula lies Korea's windswept island of myth and magic. It is to Korea what Crete is to Greece, what Mustang is to Nepal and what the Icelandic Sagas are to Denmark – something which blossomed from the same flower but which developed its own uniquely different hues. Isolated for many centuries from mainland developments, it acquired its own history, cultural traditions, dress, architecture and even language. The latter, for instance, though classified only as a dialect, was the result of the island's occupation between 1276 and 1375 by the Mongols and is as different from Korean as Provençal is from French. Mainlanders can experience difficulty understanding what is being said on Cheju-do.

There is also the enigma of the *harubang*, or grandfather stones, carved from lava rock, whose purpose is still debated by anthropologists. Certainly parallels are easily drawn between these and the mysterious statues found on such places as Easter Island and Okinawa, yet debates about whether they once represented the legendary guardians of the gates to Cheju's ancient towns seem largely irrelevant as you stand next to them in the gathering twilight at Song Eup, Cheju's ancient provincial capital. But what can be said for sure is that no other symbol personifies Cheju-do so completely as the *harubang*. They're even painted on the sides of the local buses. This is not to suggest that Cheju-do doesn't share in the Korean cultural tradition since it clearly has done for millennia, but the differences are sufficiently evocative to draw people from all over Korea – and the rest of the world – in search of legend. Cheju-do was, for instance, the last redoubt of a faction of the Koryo army which was determined to resist the Mongol armies even after the king had made peace with the invaders and returned to his capital at Kaesong. They were later slaughtered to a man west of what is today Cheju City in 1273. Later, during Yi Dynasty times, Cheju-do was the island on which the Dutch ship, *Sparrowhawk*, was wrecked on its way to Japan in 1653. Those who survived the wreckage were taken to Seoul by order of the king and forced to remain there for the next 13 years until they were finally able to escape to Japan in a small fishing vessel. An account of those years, written by Hendrick Hamel, one of the survivors, became a best seller in Europe at the time and was the first accurate description of the so-called Hermit Kingdom that Europe had received until that date.

A remote provincial outpost it may have been until recently, but over the last two decades Cheju-do has changed radically. The catalyst was tourism. It began as the favoured honeymoon destination for Korean couples drawn here by the lure of the warm south and the difficulties of obtaining a passport which would have allowed them to go further afield. The honeymooners still arrive in droves but they are now matched by Japanese tourists who arrive by the plane-load direct from Japan into Cheju-do's spanking new international airport. Indeed, Cheju is rapidly becoming Korea's second busiest

airport, and a whole new suburb consisting of four and five-star hotels, restaurants and associated services has been built on the outskirts of the main city to cater for these visitors.

Yet, while development is changing the face of some parts of Cheju-do and some of its ancient customs are on the wane (such as the island's matriarchal society exemplified by the skin-diving women who are the subject of folk songs and tourist promotion literature), the rural areas retain a timeless quality. And while it might be true that most of the tourist sights are overrun with visitors during the summer holiday period, for the rest of the year it's pleasantly uncluttered.

Geographically, Cheju-do offers some of the most outstanding features you're likely to come across in this part of the world. The island is dominated by the almost 2000-metre-high extinct volcano of Mt Halla, the highest mountain in South Korea, with its own crater lake and several well-marked hiking trails which allow you to explore its forested slopes. From the summit you will be rewarded with incomparable views on a clear day. Then there are the beaches dotted around the island; the impressive Chongbang and Chonjiyon Falls at Sogwipo on the south coast; the famous volcanic cone at Songsanpo which rises up sheer from the ocean on the eastern tip of the island, and the Man Jang lava tube cave – supposedly the world's longest – whose humid, 9°C average temperature will make you wish you were back in the balmy warmth on the surface.

Agriculturally, it's quite different from the mainland. Here there are no endless vistas of terraced rice paddies but small fields of barley, wheat, corn and vegetables, all of them enclosed by dry-stone walls to protect the crops from the high winds which lash Cheju-do at certain times of the year. Houses are similarly protected and thatched roofs held down by criss-crossed ropes attached to large rocks. Further inland there are enormous grazing pastures which support horses and cattle. Indeed, it was the Mongols who first used Cheju-do's pastures on which to rear their horses. It's also the only place in

Korea where citrus fruit, pineapples and bananas can be grown though, regrettably, that doesn't mean they're cheap!

Don't miss this island when you come to Korea, if only for the contrasts which it offers to the mainland.

CHEJU CITY 제주시

The island's capital has the most easy-going and festive atmosphere of any city you're likely to encounter in Korea. It's relatively small and compact, with everything except the bus terminal within easy walking distance of everywhere else. You'll still find many gems of traditional Cheju-style houses made of lava stone with thatched roofs and high surrounding dry-stone walls, despite the massive amount of reconstruction which has taken place recently.

In the centre of town near the Kwandokchong Pavilion you'll find an interesting and extensive daily market which sells everything from clothes to Chinese herbs, to fish to pineapples, citrus fruits and apples which are grown on Mt Halla's southern slopes.

Most of the places worth visiting are outside of Cheju City but there are a few places which you shouldn't miss.

Kwandokchong Pavilion 관덕정

The 15th-century Kwandokchong Pavilion is one of Cheju's most interesting buildings - complete with *harubang* - and the oldest of its type on the island.

Cheju Folkcraft & Natural History Museum 민속박물관

The Cheju Folkcraft & Natural History Museum, up on the hill at the back of town and close to the KAL Hotel, is excellent. In it there is a recreation of a traditional thatched house in the local style, local crafts, folklore and marine displays. There's also a film about the island (in Korean) which is shown five times daily for no extra charge. Entry costs W550 and the museum is open daily except for Monday from 9 am to 5 pm.

Samsonghyol Shrine 삼성혈

The nearby Samsonghyol Shrine, a Confucian-style mausoleum, might be worth a visit if there wasn't an entry charge but at W400 (W200 for students) entry it's touch and go whether it's worth seeing, as it's essentially just an empty house like many other such shrines on the mainland.

Yongdu-am 용두암

The Yongdu-am or 'Dragon's Head Rock' on the seashore to the west of town, which you'll find eulogised in all the tourist literature, might be worth a visit if you have nothing to do for a couple or hours but you can place it at the bottom of your priority list. On the other hand, no Korean honeymoon is complete without a photograph of the newlyweds taken at this spot.

Moksuk-won 목석원

About six km outside of Cheju City on the '5.16' cross-island highway is Moksuk-won, a natural sculpture garden of stone and wood. If you've ever found yourself taking home interesting-looking pieces of wood and stone which have been carved by the elements you'll love this place.

It was put together over many years by a local resident. It comprises objects found all over the island, many of them originating from the roots of the jorok tree which is found only on Cheju-do. The wood of this tree is very dense – it sinks in water – and it was formerly used for making combs and tobacco boxes. Along with the natural objects, there are many old grinding stones and even *harubang*. The collection is now maintained by the government.

Entry costs W300 (W100 for students). To get there, take a bus from the local bus station.

Places to Stay – bottom end

Since Cheju-do is such a popular place for honeymooners and young people on holiday, there is an excellent choice of cheap places for most of the year. You may have to do a little bit of legwork from mid-July to mid-August, however, when it gets quite crowded

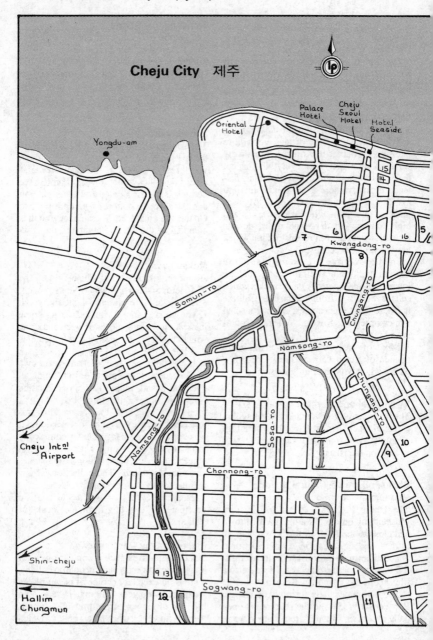

Cheju City 제주

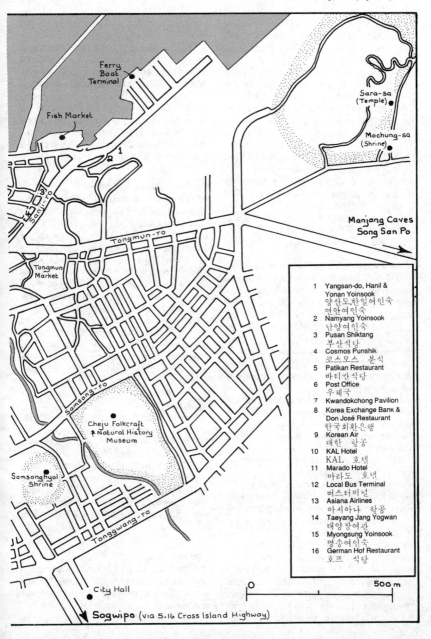

Ferry Boat Terminal

Fish Market

Sara-sa (Temple)

Mochung-sa (Shrine)

Sani-ro

Tongmun-ro

Manjang Caves
Song San Po

Tongmun Market

Samsong-ro

Cheju Folkcraft & Natural History Museum

Samsonghyol Shrine

Tonggwang-ro

City Hall

0   500 m

Sogwipo (via 5-16 Cross Island Highway)

1 Yangsan-do, Hanil & Yonan Yoinsook
양산도,한일여인숙 연안여인숙
2 Namyang Yoinsook
남양여인숙
3 Pusan Shiktang
부산식당
4 Cosmos Punshik
코스모스 분식
5 Patikan Restaurant
바티칸식당
6 Post Office
우체국
7 Kwandokchong Pavilion
8 Korea Exchange Bank & Don José Restaurant
한국회환은행
9 Korean Air
대한 항공
10 KAL Hotel
KAL 호텔
11 Marado Hotel
마라도 호텔
12 Local Bus Terminal
버스터미널
13 Asiana Airlines
아시아나 항공
14 Taeyang Jang Yogwan
태양장여관
15 Myongsung Yoinsook
명송여인숙
16 German Hof Restaurant
호프 식당

(prices also tend to be a little higher at this time). Most of the cheapies are on or off Sanji-ro, and between this road, Kwandong-ro and the sea front.

If you arrive by boat you'll probably be met by people from the various *yogwan* and *yoinsook* offering you a room. If you think what you're being offered sounds like a good deal then go and have a look.

The *Yangsan-do Yoinsook* 양산도여인숙 (tel 22-9989), only a stone's throw from the boat terminal on Sanji-ro, has been a popular place to stay for years. It's very clean and has hot water (gas heated) in the communal bathroom. It costs just W3000 a single, W4000 a double and W5000 a triple. The owners are very friendly and helpful. Ask for a room on the top floor which has an open flat roof, good views and is quiet.

Also good value is the *Hanil Yoinsook* 한일여인숙 which costs W5000 a single or double and W6500 a triple. All the rooms have fans, there is hot water in the showers and guests have the use of kitchen facilities.

Similar in price is the *Namyang Yoinsook* (tel 22-9617) which is very clean and costs W5000 a double. Hot water is available in the showers but there's only one bathroom and it's inadequate to cope with the demand when the *yoinsook* is full. You may have to wait a long time to get in here and it attracts boisterous student groups in the holiday season. The manager speaks excellent English and is helpful. Guests have the use of a washing machine.

Also in this same area, just off the main road, is the *Yonan Yoinsook* 연안여인숙 which is clean, quiet and friendly and costs W4000 a double and W5000 a triple. There's no hot water but there are clothes washing facilities.

Another very pleasant *yoinsook* is the *Myongsung Yoinsook* 명성여인숙 down an alley one block back from the sea front and opposite the Taeyang Jang Yogwan which itself is close to the Hotel Seaside. It has a leafy courtyard and costs W6000 for a room.

Going up in price, there are any number of *yogwan* and *yogwan jang* to choose from in the streets between Kwandong-ro and the

sea front, for which you should expect to pay W9000 to W11,000 and W12,000 to W14,000 respectively. All these places will have a bathroom, hot water, TV and fan, plus the more expensive ones will have air-conditioning. Recommended in this category is the *Taeyang Jang Yogwan* 태양장여관 down the first alley one block back from the sea front and diagonally opposite the Hotel Seaside. It's a very quiet place to stay, the rooms on the top floor have sea views and it costs W15,000 a room.

Places to Stay – middle

With so many tourists arriving from the mainland and from overseas, there's plenty of choice of mid-range hotels in both Cheju City and Shin-cheju. Many of these are the more expensive *yogwan jang* and named as such but others call themselves 'hotels'. There's precious little difference in terms of the quality of the rooms which they offer but the hotels often have a restaurant, coffee shop and, occasionally, a nightclub.

The most convenient of them are to be found in the streets between the seafront and Kwandong-ro (the street on which the Kwandokchong pavilion stands). They include the *Beach Hotel* 비치호텔 , *Haesang Hotel* 해상호텔 , *Namkyong Hotel* 남경호텔, *Kyong Rim Hotel* 경림호텔 , and the *Oknimjang* 옥림장 .

Further afield there are the *Daeyong Hotel* 대영호텔 , Namsong-ro, close to the Pyongmunch-on River, the *Myongsong Hotel* 명성호텔, just off Chungang-ro close to the KAL Hotel, and the *Marado Hotel* 마라도호텔 , Sogwang-ro (recommended by one traveller and costing W20,000 for a room), about halfway between the junction with Chungang-ro and the local bus station.

Places to Stay – top end

Most of Cheju City's top-range hotels are to be found in Shin-cheju (New Cheju) which is south-west of the main city but there are several others in the city itself.

In Shin-cheju there are:

Cheju Grand Hotel (tel 42-3321) 263-15 Yondong, Cheju. Five-star, 522 rooms from W70,000 to W85,000. The staff speak English and Japanese and there are Korean, Western and Japanese restaurants. The hotel has a coffee shop, bars, nightclub and sporting facilities including a swimming pool.

Hotel Cheju Royal (tel 27-4161/80) 272-34 Yondong, Cheju, Four-star, 115 rooms from W52,500. The staff speak English and Japanese and there are Korean, Western and Japanese restaurants.

Cheju Washington Hotel (tel 42-4111) 291- 30 Yondong, Cheju. Four-star, rooms from W57,750.

Mosu Tourist Hotel (tel 42-1001) 274-13 Yondong, Cheju. Four-star, rooms from W52,500.

Cheju Marina Tourist Hotel (tel 27- 6161). Three-star, rooms from W43,000.

Hawaii Tourist Hotel (tel 42-0061) 300-8 Yondong, Cheju. 278-2 Yondong, Cheju. Three-star, rooms from W43,000.

In Cheju City there are:

Cheju KAL Hotel (tel 53-6151/9) 1691-9 2-do 1-dong, Cheju. Five-star, 310 rooms from W62,000. The staff speak English and Japanese and there are Korean, Western and Japanese restaurants. The hotel has the coffee shop, cocktail lounge, nightclub, casino and sporting facilities including a swimming pool.

Cheju Oriental Hotel (tel 52-8222) 1197, 3-do 2-dong, Cheju. Five-star, rooms from W62,000.

Cheju Seoul Tourist Hotel (tel 52-2211). Four-star, rooms from W52,500.

Cheju Palace Hotel (tel 53-8811/20) 1192-20, 3-do 2-dong, Cheju 1192-8 3-do 2-dong, Cheju. Three-star, rooms from W46,000.

Hotel Paradise Cheju (tel 23-0171/5) 1315, 2-do 1-dong, Cheju. Three-star, 57 rooms from W46,000. The staff speak English and Japanese and there are Korean, Western and Japanese restaurants. The hotel has a coffee shop and bar.

Places to Eat

There are literally hundreds of restaurants to choose from. Just along Sanji-ro alone (the road leading from the ferry terminal to the first junction) there are Korean, seafood, Chinese, Japanese, Western-style and fried chicken restaurants. Many of them offer cheap food but check the prices before you eat.

The *Cosmos Punshik* 코스모스분식 on Sanji-ro has an extensive menu of Korean food which costs W1000 to W1500 per dish.

Also good is the *Pusan Shiktang* 부산식당 which serves *pulgogi* though you pay the usual price for this. There's also a lot of cheap food stalls in the Tongmun Market (above the junction of Sanji-ro and Tongmun-ro) and this is where you should head if you're looking for a lively and relatively cheap place to eat.

An excellent place to go for a meal if you're in need of a change from *kimchi* and rice is the *German Hof* on Kwangdong-ro. This is a large bar/restaurant on the 1st floor which has been decked out to resemble a German beer hall. Kitsch it might be, but the food here is excellent and remarkably cheap – expect to pay around W2500 per dish. The meals here are actually called 'snacks' but they're some of the largest snacks I've ever seen! It's also a good place to have a cold beer and meet local people and other visitors. The staff are very friendly.

For a splurge on *pulgogi* or *kalbi* you probably can't beat the *Pung Jon Shiktang* 본전식당 on the right-hand side down the main road leading to the seafront. It's a popular place to eat, the meat is superbly marinated and the food tastefully presented. Expect to pay around W5000 per person.

For a different kind of splurge, the *Don José Restaurant* (sign in English) on the top side of the junction between Kwangdong-ro and Chungang-ro next to the Korea Exchange Bank, is top value. It's essentially a Western-style restaurant with an extensive menu including such things as pizzas and superb salads. Servings are generous and you can eat your fill for between W5000 and W7000 depending on what you order.

Another place to try for a splurge is the *Patikan* 바디칸 off Kwandong-ro which is another Western-style restaurant and piano bar.

A popular coffee bar is the *Taeho Dasil* 대호다실 which is close to the post office in the basement. They have a good selection of music and they offer yoghurt in addition to coffee. There are a lot of other relatively expensive restaurants along Chungan-ro which is the road that leads from the centre of town up the hill and past the KAL Hotel.

Entertainment

Cheju abounds with nightclubs which lay on live bands, though most of them are to be found in the large hotels and cater to people with money to burn. If you plan on going to one of them then make sure you know what the cover charge will be. There are others, however, in the alleys between Kwangdong-ro and the seafront which don't have cover charges and you simply pay for what you eat and drink. Some of these clubs give the impression from their entrances that they're striptease joints, but even if that's what they aspire to be, you can be sure the entertainment will be quite tame. Like the nightclubs in the large hotels, there will be live music – usually modern Korean ballads done by a singer, electric guitarist and keyboard player with bass and drum synthesiser. Members of the audience frequently front-up to the microphone to wail and croak their way through a song.

These places can be immense fun and often contain a lively and inebriated crowd. It's more than likely you'll be invited to join a group. Single men will often be joined by one of the club's hostesses as soon as they sit down. Some charge for this; others don't.

GETTING THERE & AWAY

Air

Both Korean Air and Asiana Airlines operate flights to Cheju-do. Korean Air flies from Seoul, Pusan, Kwangju, Taegu, Chinju and Yeosu with the cheapest flights being from Kwangju (W12,800, 45 minutes), Yeosu (W15,000, 45 minutes) and Chinju (W18,800, 45 minutes). Asiana Airlines flies from Seoul, Pusan and Kwangju with the cheapest flight being from Kwangju (W12,800, 35 minutes). Korean Air also flies direct from Japan. For schedules, see the 'Getting Around' chapter.

The main Korean Air office, opposite the KAL Hotel on Chungang-ro, was being rebuilt at the time of research. However, there are two branch offices on Kwangdong-ro, another on the road leading down from here to the Hotel Seaside/Cheju Seoul Tourist Hotel and another opposite the local bus station.

Asiana Airlines main office is opposite the local bus station. There are also branch offices of both airlines in Shin-Cheju.

Ferry

There are ferries from Cheju City to Mogpo 목포 , Wando 완도 , and Pusan 부산 . On the southern coast there are ferries from Sogwipo 서귀포 to Pusan. The schedule and fares for the ferries which operate between Cheju City/Sogwipo and Pusan can be found in the Pusan chapter.

There are student discounts available on all of the ferries but you have to ask for them as the signs indicating this are entirely in Korean.

The seas in the straits between Cheju-do and the mainland are often quite rough. If you're not a good sailor it might be worth your while taking one of the faster ferries or even flying.

To/From Mogpo Three ferries are available between Mogpo and Cheju-do. The cheapest is the *Ansong-ho* which is a passenger ferry. The other two boats are car ferries though you don't need a car to use them.

The *Ansong-ho* departs Mogpo daily at 8.20 am and arrives in Cheju at 3.20 pm. From Cheju it departs daily at 10 am and arrives in Mogpo at 5 pm. The fares are W15,600 (1st class bunk), W10,440 (2nd class bunk), W6990 (2nd class) and W4700 (3rd class).

The *Tongyang Kosok Ferry 1-ho* departs Mogpo daily, except Monday, at 7 am and arrives in Cheju at 12.30 pm. From Cheju it departs, except Monday, at 4 pm and arrives in Mogpo at 9.30 pm. The fares are W21,550 (1st class bunk), W16,770 (2nd class bunk), W10,010 (2nd class) and W7610 (3rd class).

The *Tongyang Kosok Ferry 3-ho* departs Mogpo daily at 8.20 am and arrives in Cheju at 4.20 pm. From Cheju it departs daily at 10 am and arrives in Mogpo at 6 pm. The fares are the same as for the *Tongyang Kosok Ferry 1-ho*. This ferry stops at Chin-do and other places which is why it takes eight hours to reach Cheju.

To/From Wando There is a choice of two ferries from Wando.

The *Hanil Car Ferry* sails from Wando daily except on the first and third Thursday of each month at 7.20 am and arrives in Cheju at 10.30 am. In the opposite direction it departs Cheju at 4 pm and arrives in Wando at 7.10 pm. The fares are W16,240 (1st class bunk) and W7270 (2nd class).

The *Hanil 2-ho* only operates between Wando and Cheju between 20 March and 20 May, 21 July and 20 August and 1 October and 30 November. During these times it departs Wando at 10 am and arrives in Cheju at 12.20 pm. In the opposite direction it departs Cheju at 3 pm and arrives in Wando at 5.20 pm. The fares are W8710 (1st class) and W7270 (2nd class).

GETTING AROUND
Airport Transport
The airport is about two km west of the city. There's a frequent local bus service (bus No 100) which runs to/from the airport to the ferry terminal via the local bus station and Sanji-ro. A taxi will cost W1000.

Local Transport
Arriving by boat, there's no need to take a taxi or bus since most of the cheap *yogwan* and *yoinsook* are only a few minutes' walk from the ferry terminal. You probably won't have to use Cheju city buses at all except to get to the airport or to the local bus terminal (about two km).

Buses to the local bus terminal are a little more tricky since most of them are not numbered. You can find them at the bottom of the hill in the centre of town on Chungang-ro – keep asking the conductors and the other people waiting at the stop. The alternative is to take bus No 3 to the big junction past the KAL Hotel and then take another bus along Sogwang-ro where the terminal is. You'll also need to use the city buses if you need to go to Shin-Cheju.

Car Hire
There are two rental companies on Cheju-do:

Cheju Rent-A-Car (tel 42-3301/5), 271-7 Yongdong, Shin-Cheju. They also have branches at the Grand Hotel (tel 42- 3321), Cheju KAL Hotel (tel 53-6151), and at the information desk at Cheju Airport.
Halla Rent-A-Car (tel 62-3446).

Typical rates for 24 hours with unlimited mileage and including insurance would be W44,000 ('Presto'), W46,200 ('Leman') and W47,300 ('Stellar'). They also have larger deluxe cars for hire costing between W55,000 and W71,500. You can save money by only renting a car for either six or 12 hours. The rates for 12-hour hire on the above three models would be W36,200, W36,850 and W37,950 respectively.

Transport Around the Island
The local bus terminal in Cheju City is straight out of the 1970s, which is surprising considering how many foreign tourists come to the island. If it were on the mainland, then the schedule would be written in both Korean and English. Instead, it's merely chalked up in hard-to-read Korean and the organisation of the buses in the various bays is virtually unintelligible. To add to the confusion, buses are not numbered but merely have their destination in the front window. While it's high time someone injected some organisation into this mess, there's good news. And the good news is that there are plenty of buses to most places of interest around the island and, provided you have your destination written down in Korean characters along with the route you want to take, it's very unlikely you'll be sold the wrong ticket or ever board the wrong bus. The people here are very helpful.

A rough guide to the bus bays is as follows:

Bay 2 – Buses to Pyoson via Sangumburi and Song Eup. Buses terminate at Pyoson Folk Village.

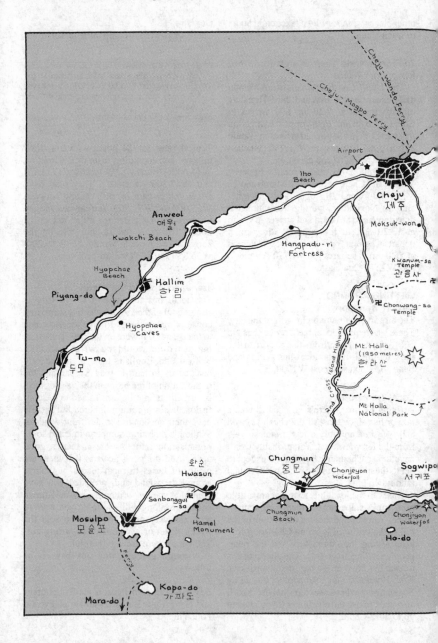

Cheju-Pusan Ferry

Hamdok Beach

Kimnyong Beach

Hamdok
함덕

Kimnyongsa
Cave

Man Jang
Caves
만장굴

Pyeongdae

U-do
우도

Songsanpo
성산포

Ferry

Songsanilchubong
성산일출봉

Shinyang
Beach

Sangumburi
Crater

Song Eup
성읍

Pyoson
표선

Namwon
남원

Su Cross Island H. Plant

Chongbang
Waterfall
정방

Chigwi-do

Sogwipo-Pusan
Ferry

Cheju-do Island 제주도

lp

0   10 km

Bay 3 & 4 – Buses to Songsanpo via the eastern coast road.

Bay 5 & 6 – Buses to Mt Halla and Sogwipo via 5.16 cross-island highway.

Bay 7 – Buses to Mt Halla and Chungmun via No 2 cross-island highway.

Bay 8 – Buses to Mosulpo and Hwasun via inland routes.

Bay 9 – Buses to Chungmun and Sogwipo via inland routes.

Bay 10 – Buses to Sogwipo via Hallim, Mosulpo, Hwasun and Chungmun via the western coast road.

Bay 11 – Buses to Hallim and Sogwipo partially via western coast road and partially via inland routes.

The other good news about bus transport on Cheju-do is that there are only four main roads which lead out of the city. The two cross-island highways skirt the slopes of Mt Halla and are the ones you will need if you're going to climb the mountain or are going to Sogwipo or Chungmun and don't want to take either of the coastal routes.

Coast Road – Soehaeson Route 서회선 The coast road going west (known as the Soehaeson route) will give you the best selection of beaches on the island. These include Iho 이호, Kwakchi 곽지, Hyopchae 협재 and, on the southern coast, Chungmun 중문. Also along this coastal road are the Hyopchae Lava Caves 협재굴 and Sanbanggul-sa Grotto 산방굴사. All buses along this road stop at both the caves and the grotto.

Coast Road – Tonghaeson Route 동해선 The coast road going east from Cheju City (known as the Tonghaeson Route) will take you to the beaches of Hamdok 함덕 and Kimnyong 김녕, the turn-off for the Kimnyong and Man Jang Caves 만장굴 and the volcanic cone of Song San Po 성산포.

Cross-Island Highway 5.16 The road which skirts the eastern side of the mountain is known as the '5.16' and buses taking this route will have '5.16' in the front window. The road passes three points at which you

can start the trek to the peak of Mt Halla and ends up at Sogwipo 서귀포.

Cross-Island Highway No 2 The other road is known as the 2nd cross-island highway and it passes two points at which you can start the trek up Mt Halla and ends at Chungmun. Buses taking this route will have '2' in the window.

Jungsanggan Route 중산간 This is a minor route which connects Cheju City with Pyoson 표선. It branches off from the '5.16' on the lower northern slopes of Mt Halla and goes past Sangumburi 산금부리 and Song Eup 성읍 to end at Pyoson Folk Village.

A few examples of schedules and fares:

Cheju City-Sogwipo (via 5.16 cross-island highway) There are buses every 12 minutes from 6.30 am to 9.30 pm which cost W930 and take about one hour. Fares and journey times are proportionally less if you're getting off at the start of the Mt Halla trekking trails.

Cheju City-Chungmun (via the 2nd cross-island highway) There are buses every 20 minutes from 6.20 am to 8 pm which take about one hour and cost W1400. Fares and journey times are proportionally less if you're getting off at the start of the Mt Halla trekking trails.

Cheju City-Song Eup-Pyoson (via the Jungsanggan highway) There are buses every 30 minutes from 6 am to 9 pm which cost W850 to Song Eup and W950 to Pyoson. The journey to Song Eup takes about one hour.

Cheju City-Song San Po (via the eastern coast road) There are buses every 20 minutes from 5.30 am to 9.40 pm which cost W860 and take about one hour. These buses will drop you at the turn-off for the Man Jang Caves. The fare to the turn-off is W530.

SOGWIPO 서귀포

On the southern coast of Cheju-do, Sogwipo is the island's second largest town after Cheju City and is connected to the mainland by ferries from Pusan. It isn't a particularly attractive town in itself but its setting at the foot of Mt Halla, whose lower slopes are covered with citrus groves, is quite spectacular. Its main attractions are the Chonjiyon and Chongbang waterfalls. It's also the nearest place to Chungmun Beach that you can find accommodation other than in *minbak* at Chungmun Village.

Waterfalls

Chongbang 정방폭포 This waterfall is 23 metres high and it's claimed in the tourist literature that it is the only waterfall in Asia which falls directly into the sea. This isn't quite correct since the Toroki Falls on the south coast of Yaku-shima in Japan also do this and are even larger than Chonjiyon. All the same, these falls are a very impressive sight and are only a 10 to 15-minute walk from the centre of town. Just off the coast you can see several small, partially forested and very rocky islands. Entry costs W500.

Chonjiyon 천지연폭포 This waterfall is on the other side of town at the end of a beautifully forested and steep gorge through which a path and bridge have been constructed. Like the Chongbang Waterfall, Chonjiyon is a 10 to 15-minute walk from the centre of town down by the fishing harbour. Entry costs W500.

Places to Stay – bottom end

There are quite a few cheap *yoinsook* and *yogwan* in the small streets around the centre of town. The *Dong-il Yoinsook* 동인여인숙 has been recommended as being a clean and friendly place.

If you're looking for a hotel with attached bathroom then try the *Jinsongjang Yogwan* (tel 62-4492), Sogwi-dong 454-38. Rooms cost W12,000 a double. They all have attached bathroom with constant hot water, colour TV and fan.

Places to Stay – top end

In the last few years, Sogwipo has become a resort town in its own right and there are a number of top-end hotels to choose from. In order of cost they are:

Sogwipo Lions Tourist Hotel (tel 62-4141/4) 803 Sogwi-dong. Two-star, rooms from W38,000.
Taeshin Tourist Hotel (tel 33-2121/9) 314-1 Sogwi-dong. Three-star, rooms from W43,000.
Sogwipo Park Tourist Hotel (tel 62-2161/7) 674-1 Sogwi-dong. Three-star, rooms from W46,000.
Cheju Prince Hotel (tel 32-9911/32) 731-3 Sohong-dong. Five-star, rooms from W62,000.

Places to Eat

The *Chunghwa Yori* 중화요리 Chinese restaurant is probably one of the cheapest places to eat at. Dishes cost from W1000 to W1500. Also reasonable is the *Kwangna-ru* 광나루식당 which is a Korean-style restaurant offering a wide variety of dishes. *Pekpan* will cost W1500 and *pulgogi* W4000. The *Seoul Shiktang* 사울식당 can also be recommended. It's a Korean restaurant with dishes ranging from W1500 to W3000.

A good place to meet local young people is the *Coffee Rain* which is a combined beer and coffee bar with a disc jockey and a good selection of records.

CHUNGMUN BEACH 중문

This is rated in the tourist literature as the best and longest beach on the island which it conceivably is, but as beaches go around the world it would hardly rate a mention. Certainly it lacks the sharp volcanic rock outcrops which can make swimming hazardous on some of the island's other beaches, such as Kwakchi, but it would still disappoint travellers who have experienced well-known beaches in the Philippines, Thailand, Indonesia, etc. Another drawback – as with all popular beaches in Korea – is the litter which is liberally strewn around the place by those with no concern for the environment or for those who will follow them.

None of this has prevented the developers from moving in, and in a big way. Chungmun is now Cheju's largest beach resort with a number of five-star hotels, condominiums, res-

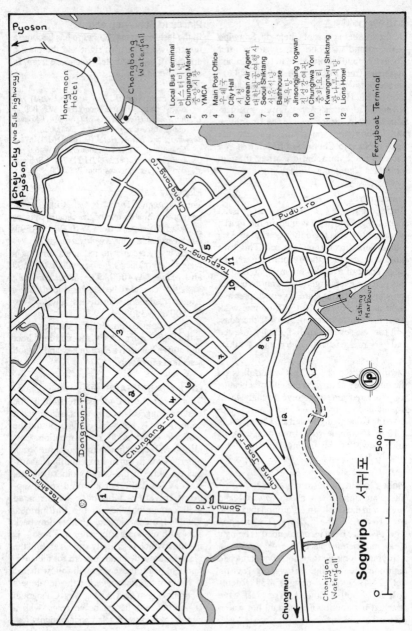

Pyoson

Cheju City (via 5.16 highway)
Pyoson

Honeymoon Hotel

Chonbong Waterfall

Ferryboat Terminal

Chungbong-ro

Pudu-ro

Daehyong-ro

5
11
10
8 6
3
7
9
4
2
1

Dongmun-ro

Chungang-ro

Tae shin-ro

Chung Jong-ro

Somun-ro

1a

Fishing Harbour

Chonjiyon Waterfall

Chungmun

Sogwipo 서귀포

500 m

0

1	Local Bus Terminal 버스터미널
2	Chungang Market 중앙시장
3	YMCA
4	Main Post Office 우체국
5	City Hall 시청
6	Korean Air Agent 대한항공포여행사
7	Seoul Shiktang 서울식당
8	Bathhouse 목욕탕
9	Jinsongjang Yogwan 신성장여관
10	Chunghwa Yori 중화요리
11	Kwangna-ru Shiktang 광나루식당
12	Lions Hotel

Top: The men's picnic, Chinju (CHP)
Left: Old monk at Tongdo-sa temple (GC)
Right: Geugrag-am Hermitage at Tongdo-sa temple (HJMG)

Top: Bridge at Chungmun Beach, Cheju-do Island (CHP)
Left: Haein-sa temple, near Taegu (GC)
Right: The beach at Wando Island (CHP)

taurants and a marine park. It also gets very crowded indeed during the summer holiday season. Other than the attractions of the beach, it's worth visiting the Chonjeyon Waterfall 천재연 폭포 (not to be confused with the Chonjiyon Waterfall in Sogwipo) which is a 20-minute walk back from the beach up to the bridge on the coastal highway. Entry costs W700.

Overlooking the beach itself is the Royal Marine Park which contains a dolphinarium, aquarium and restaurant complex. If you're interested in seeing performing dolphins after all the research that's been done into the effects of captivity on these animals then there are shows at 11 am, 1.30, 2.40 and 4.30 pm daily. If you're not interested in seeing this sort of thing then the aquarium itself isn't worth the entry fee. Entry to the park costs W3000 (W2300 for those under 24 years old).

Places to Stay

There's nowhere cheap to stay at the beach itself. This is the territory of those with money to burn. The only place you can find cheap accommodation is in Chungmun Village itself which is quite a walk from the beach and along the highway. Here there's a limited number of *minbak* and *yoinsook* to choose from at the usual rates.

At the beach itself there is the five-star *Hyatt Regency Cheju* (tel 33-1234), 3039-1 Saektal-dong, which has rooms from W70,000 to W98,000.

Places to Eat

There's a reasonably good restaurant right next to the Royal Marine Park but it's fairly expensive so if you're short on funds you'll have to eat either in Chungmun Village, where there are a few simple restaurants, or in Sogwipo.

SONG EUP 성읍

A short bus ride north of Pyoson lies Cheju-do's former provincial capital which was founded in Koryo times in the 13th century. It became the provincial headquarters in 1423 during the reign of King Sejong and remained as such until 1914 when the administrative unit was abolished. Today it's designated as a Folk Village and its traditional architecture and character have been preserved with government assistance or, at least, most of it has. Many of the traditional houses here have actually been abandoned to the tourists and, if you look closely, you'll find that concrete and asbestos are edging their way into the occupied houses. Purists baulk at this, of course, but is it feasible to expect the residents to continue living in 19th-century conditions just so that tourists can come and peek at what they'd call 'genuine' or 'rustic'?

These modern incursions aside, Song Eup is definitely worth a visit, since this is what all Cheju's villages and towns used to look like before concrete, corrugated iron and modern plumbing made their appearance and transformed the Korean landscape. There's also a good collection of original *harubang* here, though they have been removed from the village entrance and re-sited in a small park. The only other significant alteration which has been made to the village is the provision of a parking lot for coaches and cars and a number of (essentially) tourist restaurants.

There's a large sign in English and Korean in the centre of the village where the buses stop, describing the main features of the village and the history of the principal sites, so take time to have a look at it. Otherwise, take off down the narrow lanes and discover the place for yourself. Remember that most of the houses are still occupied so observe the usual courtesies regarding privacy. There are no entry fees to any of the buildings and you will not be hassled to buy tourist trash.

Places to Stay & Eat

There's a reasonable selection of restaurants ranging from simple to more elaborate along the main street of Song Eup but no *yogwan* as such. If you'd like to stay here for the night then you'll have to ask around for a *minbak*.

Getting There & Away

The schedule for the buses from Cheju City

to Pyoson via Sangumburi and Song Eup can be found in the Cheju City section. In Song Eup itself, the bus timetable board indicates there are buses from Cheju City to Song Eup and Pyoson every half hour from 6 am to 10 pm and from Pyoson to Song Eup and Cheju City every half hour from 6.30 am to 10 pm. Local people dispute the existence of the later buses and say they don't always arrive. What they do agree on is that there are buses from Song Eup to Cheju City every half hour from 7 am to 8 pm so it's best to assume that the last bus back to Cheju City is at 8 pm.

These are the same buses which run past Sangumburi.

PYOSON FOLK VILLAGE 표선.민속촌
In addition to Song Eup, there is also a specially built Folk Village (known in Korean as Pyoson Min Sokchon) just outside of Pyoson and close to the town's fine beach. It portrays 19th-century Cheju and contains three habitat zones – coastal, plain and mountain – plus there's a shamanistic area as well as official buildings to house magistrates, government officials and records. Though essentially a modern creation, all the construction here is authentically traditional and some of the cottages were brought intact from other areas and so are 200 to 300 years old. There's also a performance yard where folk songs and legends are enacted.

Like other such Folk Villages, there are a number of restaurants offering traditional food as well as *makkoli*, beer and soft drinks.

The Folk Village is open daily from 9 am to 6 pm and entry costs W2300 (W1500 for those under 24 years old and W700 for children).

SANGUMBURI 상금부리
Right by the side of the road on the way from Song Eup to Cheju City lies the huge Sangumburi volcanic crater. Larger than the one at Songsanpo, this crater is some 350 metres in diameter and around 100 metres deep. The floor of the crater is covered with grass but the steep sides are densely forested with evergreen oak and other broad-leaved

trees as well as a few pine trees. Craggy rocks line the rim. The crater is home to deer, badgers, reptiles and many species of bird. It's a spectacular sight and reminded me of similar craters in northern Kenya, of all places! There's a trail you can walk along which follows the rim but you're not allowed down in the crater itself.

You can't miss this place as it's fronted by a huge parking lot and a tourist village is nearing completion by the entrance gate.

Entry to the crater costs W500 (W270 for those under 24 years old).

Buses from Cheju City to Song Eup and Pyoson pass right by the gate and will stop if you want to get off.

MAN JANG CAVES 만장굴
East of Cheju and about 2½ km off the coast road from Kimnyong 김녕 are the Man Jang Caves. The main section of the caves is almost seven km long (!!) with a height and width varying from three to 20 metres thus making it the longest known lava tube in the world. If you've never seen one of these before then make sure you visit this place.

Take a sweater with you and a reasonable pair of shoes. It's damp down there (87% to 100% humidity) and the temperature rarely rises above a chilly 9°C. The cave is well-lit as far as a huge lava pillar (about one km from the entrance) which is as far as you're allowed to go without special permission. The caves are open every day from 9 am to 6 pm and entry costs W1000 (W500 for those under 24 years old).

Much closer to the turn-off from the main highway but alongside the same road which leads to the Man Jang Caves are another series of lava tubes known as the Kimnyong Caves 김녕굴. They're not as long as the Man Jang Caves – 600 metres divided into four parts – but they're almost as spectacular, and there are actually two tubes, one on top of the other, at this site.

These lava tubes are associated with an ancient legend regarding a huge snake which supposedly lived in them. In order to placate this snake and prevent harm befalling the nearby farms and villages, a 15 or 16-year-old virgin girl was annually sacrificed by being thrown into the cave. This horrific practice was stopped in 1514 by a magistrate newly appointed to the area. He persuaded the reluctant villagers to perform the usual ritual but to omit the sacrifice whereupon, as the story goes, the angry snake emerged, was killed by the villagers and burnt to ashes. For his pains, the magistrate inexplicably fell ill and died soon afterwards but there was no reappearance of the snake.

Unfortunately, without a powerful flash-light, you won't be able to investigate the legend of the snake since there are no electric lights in these caves and the steps leading down to them are semiderelict. Things are unlikely to remain this way for long, however, given the popularity of the Man Jang Caves and the revenue potential for opening up the Kimnyong Caves but, for the present, there's no entry charge.

Places to Stay & Eat
There's nowhere to stay at either of these caves but there is a restaurant complex at the Man Jang Caves.

Getting There & Away
To get to the Man Jang and Kimnyong caves, take a bus from Cheju City going to Songsanpo and get off at the Kimnyong turn-off (signposted for the caves). From here there are local buses to the Man Jang Caves every 30 to 60 minutes between 7.50 am and 6.30 pm which cost W170. There's a full schedule for the buses posted up in the window of the ticket office at the Man Jang Caves. Alternatively, you can hitch a ride or walk to the caves.

SONGSANPO 성산포
Songsanpo is the town at the extreme eastern tip of Cheju-do nestled at the foot of the spectacular volcanic cone of Songsanilchubong 성산일출봉 whose sides plunge vertically into the surf. If the conditions are favourable you can watch Cheju-do's famous diving women searching for seaweed, shellfish and sea urchins. It's an excellent place to watch the sun rise if you care to stay overnight in one of Songsanpo's yogwan. Indeed, the latter part of the name of this spot – ilchubong – means sunrise and there's a popular traditional song written about this place. Unlike Mt Halla, there's no longer any crater lake on the summit and the area below the jagged outer edges of the peak is continuously harvested for cattle fodder (it supports luxurious grass which is filled with herbs and wild flowers). It is definitely one of Cheju-do's most beautiful areas.

Entry to Songsanilchubong costs W500 (W270 for those under 24 years old).

Apart from walking around the crater there are boats available to sail you around but they only go when demand is sufficient and the sea is calm. The price is W4000.

Places to Stay & Eat
Facing the road which leads up to the tourist complex and entrance gate to Songsanilchubong is the Suji Yogwan 수지 where you can get a room with bath and hot water for W8000. Next door to it is the restaurant Tonggyon Haekwan 동양회판관, and on the 2nd floor there is a minbak. There's a second minbak down the alley on the left hand side as you face the restaurant. You can get a room at either for W4000 to W5000. Round the corner from the Suji Yogwan is the Songsan Yoinsook 성산여인숙 which is also a pleasant place to stay.

Going up in price, there is the Chaesong Jang Yogwan 재성장여관 opposite the post office on the bottom road which has rooms for W12,000.

It's best to avoid the restaurants in the tourist complex as they're relatively expensive. Instead, try the Tonggyon Haekwan (mentioned above) or the cheaper restaurant opposite.

Getting There & Away
There are frequent buses to Songsanpo from Cheju City which cost W860 and take about 1½ hours. Make sure that the bus you get on is going right into Songsanpo and not just to Tongnam, the town on the main coast road

where you have to turn off for Songsanpo. If you get dropped here, it's a 2½ km walk into Songsanpo.

U-DO

North-east of Songsanpo, just off the coast, is the island of U-do which is still very rural and where there are no vehicles other than a few tractors and a single minibus. It's about as far as you can get from civilisation in this part of the world, plus there are superb views over to Songsanilchubong, two sandy beaches completely free of trash, and a community of *haenyo*, Cheju's famous diving women, who work in the cove below the lighthouse. It's worth a visit if you have the time.

Places to Stay & Eat

A good place to stay on the island is the *Tungdae Yoinsook* 등대여인숙, close to the ferry pier, where you can get a room for W5000. Since there are no restaurants in this village, you should arrange to have your meals at the *yoinsook*. *Minbak* are also available but there are no signs so you'll have to ask around.

Getting There & Away

There are ferries from the port at Songsanpo to U-do. The ticket office and ferry pier are quite a walk from the centre of Songsanpo so leave yourself enough time to walk (about 15 minutes). From March to June and during October the ferries depart Songsanpo at 10 am, noon, 3 and 6 pm and from U-do at 8 and 11 am, 2 and 5 pm. From July to September they depart Songsanpo at 8.50 and 10.30 am, 2, 4 and 7 pm, and from U-do at 7.30 and 9.30 am, 1, 3 and 6 pm. From November to February the ferries leave Songsanpo at 10 am, noon, 2 and 5 pm, and from U-do at 8 and 11 am, 1 and 4 pm. The fare is W370.

HYOPCHAE LAVA CAVE 협재굴

About 2½ km south of Hallim on the north-western side of the island are a group of lava tube caves, the most famous of which is Hyopchae which was only discovered in the 1950s. Hyopchae is actually a system of several interconnected lava tubes and, although much shorter than the Man Jang Cave, is one of the few lava tubes which also has stalagmites and stalactites, due to the presence of large quantities of pulverised shells in the soil above the cave, which have been blown up from the sea shore over thousands of years. Entry to the caves costs W960 (W480 for those under 24 years old). It's advisable to hire an umbrella in wet weather otherwise you'll be soaked to the skin. They're available at the cave entrance.

There's an extensive tourist complex and a mini-Folk Village around the entrance and the paths into and out of the cave are tediously designed to force you to pass through as many souvenir shops as possible.

Also part of the complex is a Botanical Gardens, though entry to this costs a further W500 (W300 for those under 24 years old).

The other caves in this area are not commercialised and include Ssangynonggul, Hwanggumgul, Sochongul and Chogitgul. The largest and most spectacular of these is Sochongul which is some three km long. Its two entrances resemble a huge subterranean botanical gardens.

Getting There & Away

To get there take a bus going along the west coast road. You can't miss the caves as the entrance is right by the side of the road and all the buses stop here.

SANBANGGUL-SA GROTTO 산방굴사

About seven km east of Mosulpo rises the massive volcanic cone of Sanbang-sa, and halfway up its southern slope overlooking the ocean is a natural cave which was turned into a temple by a Buddhist monk during Koryo times. It's quite a steep walk up, and although the grotto itself is only of marginal interest, the views are worth the effort. Water dripping from the roof of the cave is said to be the tears of Sanbang-gok, the patron goddess of the mountain. Lower down, near the entrance, are two recently built temples where there always seems to be something going on. There's a cafe about halfway up to the grotto which is a great place to sit and have a cold drink.

Entry to the site costs W500 (W250 for those under 24 years old).

Across the other side of the road is a rocky promontory where a plaque has been erected by both the Korean and Dutch governments to commemorate the shipwreck of the Dutch merchant vessel *Sparrowhawk* in 1653. It's known as the Hamil Monument after Hendrick Hamel, one of the survivors of the disaster who later wrote a popular account of his years in Korea.

The entrance to the grotto is right beside the coast road so you can't miss it. Buses plying between Mosulpo and Sogwipo will get you there.

ISLANDS OFF THE SOUTH COAST

South of Mosulpo 모슬포 (or Taejong as it inexplicably becomes on the road signs the nearer you get to it) lie Kapa-do 가파도 and Mara-do 마라도 , the most southerly points of Korea. Both are inhabited. Kapa-do, the nearest and largest of the islands, is flat and almost without trees, and crops have to be cultivated behind stone walls to protect them from the high winds which sweep the island. Many of the inhabitants are fishers.

Unlike Kapa-do, Mara-do rises steeply from the sea and its grassed top supports cattle grazing, though it is only half the size of Kapa-do and there are only some 20 families living there.

Places to Stay

Minbak are available on Kapa-do in the village where the ferry docks, but there are no restaurants so you'll have to arrange meals with the owner of the *minbak*.

There's nowhere to stay on Mara-do but if you find yourself stranded there ask if you can sleep on the floor of the island's only school if you don't have a tent. Likewise, there are no restaurants so you need to bring all your own food and drink as well as cooking utensils.

Getting There & Away

There are two daily ferries from Mosulpo to Kapa-do at 8.30 am and 2.30 pm which take about half an hour and cost W360 (half-price for children). To Mara-do there is one ferry daily from Mosulpo at 10 am which takes about 50 minutes and costs W510 (half-price for children). Neither of these ferries sail in rough weather.

The ferry terminal in Mosulpo is down by the fishing harbour and is about one km from the centre of town which is where the buses drop you. There are *yoinsook, yogwan* and restaurants in Mosulpo if you prefer to stay overnight in order to catch the morning ferry. It's possible to miss this ferry if you attempt to get to Mosulpo from Cheju City by early morning bus.

TREKKING ON MT HALLA

Walking to the top of Mt Halla is one of the highlights of a visit to Cheju-do, but make sure you get off to an early start. No matter how clear the skies may look in the morning, the summit is often obscured by cloud in the early afternoon which is when you should be on the way down. Anyone can do this trek. No experience is necessary and no special equipment required. Just make sure you have a decent pair of jogging/hiking boots and something warm (it gets chilly up there at nearly 2000 metres).

There are five well-marked trails – three coming in from the east and two from the west – and they all connect with one or other of the two cross-island highways. The whole area is now a national park and entry to it costs W200. Detailed trail maps are available free of charge at all the ticket offices which are at the beginning of the trails.

The two shortest trails are the ones coming in from the west side – the Oh Sung Sang 어승생 and the Yong Sil. It takes the average person about 2½ hours to climb to the summit along either of these and about two hours to get back down again. Coming from the east side you should plan about four or five hours to the summit. If you have camping equipment there are several sites where you can pitch a tent. Close to all the ticket offices are places where you can buy soft drinks, snacks and even *soju*.

Contrary to what the trekking map suggests, the Oh Sung Sang and the Yong Sil trails no longer connect with one another due to a rock slide, and the path now detours south to join the Tun Nekah trail which you then take to get to the summit. Likewise, the last 50 metres or so of the Oh Sung Sang trail are virtually impassable so if you want to reach the top then take a different trail. This was the situation in 1989 but it's likely work will be done soon to remedy the situation.

There's quite a large and active Buddhist monastery – Kwanum-sa 관음사 – close to the trail of the same name.

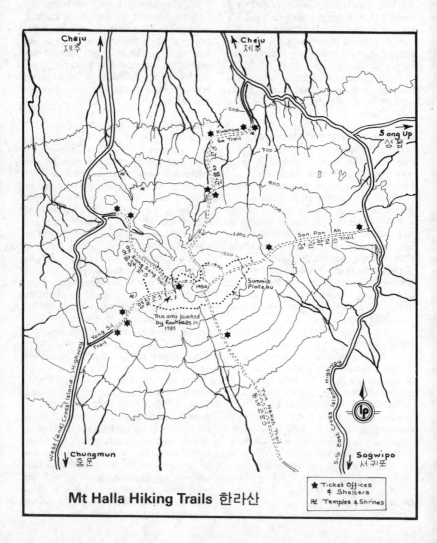

Mt Halla Hiking Trails 한라산

Places to Eat

There are a number of restaurants at the start of some of the trails. The one at the start of the Son Pan Ah trail is open year round as is the one at the '1100 Meter Rest Area' about halfway between the trail entry points on the western side of the mountain (on the 2nd cross-island highway).

Getting There & Away

To get there from Cheju City simply decide which trail you want to start off on and then take the appropriate bus along either the '5.16' or the 2nd cross-island highway. Tell the driver or his assistant which trail you want to go on and they'll make sure you're put down at the right spot.

Chiri-san National Park
지리산   국립공원

This huge national park east of Kwangju and north of Yeosu/Suncheon offers some of Korea's best hiking possibilities and is peppered with famous temples among which are Hwaom-sa and Ssanggye-sa.

The most popular base from which to explore this park is the town of Kurye 구례 though, if you prefer it, it's just as easy to find accommodation or to camp in or around the tourist villages below either of the two temples mentioned above. There are direct buses both to Kurye and to Ssangye-sa from both Kwangju and Yeosu as well as a number of other towns in the vicinity. Likewise, there are frequent local buses from Kurye to both Hwaom-sa and Ssanggye-sa.

HWAOM-SA 화암사

Probably the most famous temple in Chiri-san National Park and certainly one of the oldest, Hwaom-sa was founded by priest Yongi in 544 AD after his return from China and is dedicated to the Virochana Buddha. The temple has suffered five major devastations including the Japanese invasion of 1592 but, luckily, not everything was destroyed in those various cataclysms. It was last rebuilt in 1636.

The most famous structure surviving from the old days is a unique three-storied pagoda supported by four stone lions as well as Korea's oldest and largest stone lantern. The huge two-storied Kakwang-jon Hall, whose wooden pillars tower nearly 49 metres, was once surrounded by stone tablets of the Tripitaka Sutra (made during the Silla era) but these were destroyed during the Japanese invasion. Many of the pieces have since been collected and are preserved at the museum.

Entry to Hwaom-sa costs W950 (less for students and those under 24 years old).

The tourist village below the temple has the usual collection of souvenir shops, restaurants, *minbak* and *yogwan* plus you can camp if you have your own tent.

Getting There & Away

There are *chikheng* buses from Kwangju to Kurye from the Intercity Bus Terminal every 20 minutes from 6.30 am to 8.10 pm. The fare is W1300 and the journey takes 1½ hours. From Kurye there are local buses every 40 minutes from 7.50 am to 8 pm which cost W170 and take about 15 minutes.

There are also direct buses from Suncheon to Hwaom-sa twice a day at 10.35 am and 4.25 pm. The fare is W840 and the journey takes 1½ hours.

SSANGGYE-SA 쌍계사

East of Hwaom-sa is another famous temple, Ssanggye-sa, one of the principal temples of the Chogye Order of Korean Buddhism. The temple was originally built in 722 to enshrine a portrait of monk Yukcho which two Silla monks brought back with them from China. The temple was originally named Okchon-sa but received its present name from Chonggang-wang around 886 in tribute to the Zen monk, Chingam-sonsa, who enlarged the temple in 840 after he returned from studying in China. Chingam-sonsa was also responsible for establishing the tea plantations on the slopes of Chiri-san using seeds which he brought back from China. The temple has been renovated several times by a number of prominent monks and there are several national treasures listed here.

This temple has a sublime setting amid steep forested hillsides and is entered by a series of massive gateways housing the various guardians of the temple. A crystal-clear rocky stream spanned by a bridge divides the compound into two halves, and if you follow the path which crosses this stream further up into the mountain it will take you to the waterfall of Pulil-pokpo 불일폭포. It's about two km from Ssanggye-sa to the falls.

Entry to the temple costs W950 (less for those under 24 years old).

Places to Stay & Eat

Buses to Ssanggye-sa terminate in a small village on the opposite side of the main river from the temple, so to get to the temple you first have to cross the river bridge. There are restaurants, souvenir shops and *minbak* both in the village where the buses stop and along-side the tarmac road which leads to the temple beyond the ticket office, plus there's even a *yogwan* which styles itself *jang* just before the first gateway of the temple (surely wishful thinking judging from the stan-dard!). Expect to pay around W5000 for a room at a *minbak*. You can camp either in the village where the buses stop (thus avoiding repeated entry fees) or alongside the stream below the temple compound.

Getting There & Away

There are local buses direct from Kurye to Ssanggye-sa approximately every hour from 8.15 am to 6.20 pm. The fare is W400. It's a beautiful journey. There are similar local buses direct to Ssanggye-sa from Hadong to the south-east.

If you're heading up this way from Yeosu, there are direct buses to Ssanggye-sa daily at 6.35, 7.33, 8.17, 11.27 am, 1.40 and 2.25 pm. The fare is W1830.

TREKKING

Chiri-san National Park is honeycombed with well-maintained trails which will take you up to the ridge which forms the back-bone of the park. Up here are many peaks over 1500 metres high including South Korea's second highest mountain – Chiri-san at 1915 metres. The area is noted for the variety of its fauna and flora.

There are camp sites with basic facilities at many places within the park as well as a total of seven shelters where those without tents can find dormitory accommodation. All these shelters are situated along the saddle of the mountain ridge which forms the back-bone of the park. You need to bring your own bedding, food and tea/coffee though there is a limited range of canned and packaged foods for sale at inflated prices at the shelters. All the shelters have access to spring water.

If you're going to do some trekking in this park get hold of a copy of the National Parks Authority's leaflet, 'Chirisan National Park', which has a map of the area indicating the road-heads, trails, camp sites, shelters, temples and other points of interest. It's suf-ficiently accurate for most people's purposes though if you intend to get off the marked trails then you'll need one or more of the topographical maps produced by the national cartography service – available from the Kyobo Book Center, the Chong-no Book Center or the Jung-an Map Shop in Seoul. You won't find these maps at the national park ticket offices so you need to plan ahead.

Kurye 구례

Kurye is probably the best gateway to Chiri-san National Park – at least for the southern part of the park. It's a small town just south of the western end of the park and connected to Kwangju, Yeosu and Chinju by frequent buses. There's also a railway station with connections from Chonju and Suncheon but the railway station is some seven km south of the town. In Kurye, there's a good selec-tion of *yoinsook*, *yogwan*, restaurants and shops where supplies can be obtained.

PLACES TO STAY & EAT

Most of the *yoinsook* and *yogwan* in Kurye

are clustered around the bus station so you don't have to walk very far to find a room which suits your pocket. The *Okchong Jang Yogwan* 옥천장여관 has been recommended as a good place to stay. It's very clean and costs W10,000 a double with bath, colour TV and hot water. Also very popular is the *Shinhung Jang Yogwan* 신흥장여관 , a new red-brick building very close to the bus station and the tallest in Kurye. The entrance is around the corner from the bus station and left along one of the main streets. It's spotlessly clean and friendly though somewhat expensive at W15,000 for a room with bath and toilet, constant hot water, fan and colour TV.

One of the best places to eat here is the *Jin-mi Shiktang* 진미식당 which is around the corner to the right as you leave the bus station. The owners of this restaurant are very friendly, familiar with foreign visitors, and the food is excellent (the restaurant is also recommended in the Japanese budget travel guide to Korea). They have the usual range of Korean dishes and you can eat for between W2000 to W5000 depending on what you order.

GETTING THERE & AWAY

The bus station in Kurye handles both *chikheng* and local buses. The timetable is entirely in Korean but it's fairly easy to work things out as it's so small.

To Kwangju

There are nonstop *chikheng* buses every 10 minutes from 6.15 am to 9 pm. The fare is W1300 and the journey takes about 1½ hours.

To Yeosu

There are *chikheng* buses every 45 minutes from 5.40 am to 8 pm. The fare is W1430 and the journey takes 50 minutes.

To Pusan

There are buses every 40 minutes from 7 am to 6.40 pm. The fare is W3090 and the journey takes nearly four hours.

North Korea

INTRODUCTION

Since North Korea was opened up to individual Western travellers in 1989, it's now just a formality getting a visa, though there are still a number of major restrictions which you should take into consideration before visiting.

The most important one is that you must submit a proposed itinerary of where you want to go and have it approved by the tourist bureau in Pyongyang before your visa is issued. At the North Korean Embassy in Beijing (China), this takes only a day. Elsewhere it will take longer. Also – and perhaps more important – once your itinerary has been approved, you must pay for the entire trip in advance in hard currency before your visa is issued. There's no way you can simply just go there.

Once you get there, you must be accompanied at all times by a (male) guide (whose fees you will already have paid) except in a few places where you are allowed to walk around alone – basically Pyongyang and a few of the beauty spots – though this is only reluctantly conceded. Guides are available who can speak English, French, German, Chinese, Japanese and Russian as well as a number of other languages.

In addition you will have to stay at certain designated hotels everywhere you go. These are modern, multistar hotels which have been built specifically for foreign tourists/business people and, as you might expect, they're expensive, though there are several grades of them. Local *yogwan* undoubtedly exist, though not anywhere near in the same numbers as in South Korea, but you're not allowed to stay at them. And since you must stay in the large tourist hotels, this also limits where you can go.

Eating out at local restaurants is easier to arrange, and if you want to do this, you should make this clear to your guide. Doing this will also ensure that you have a chance to savour the local cuisine (essentially the same as in South Korea) instead of the standard 'international' dishes offered by the large hotels.

All in all, it's going to be an expensive trip and you're looking at between US$80 and US$120 per day all-inclusive, depending on where you elect to stay and where you want to go.

So why go?

There are a number of reasons, and probably the one which draws most Western people to this country is pure curiosity. North Korea, like Albania, is one of the world's most closed countries – so closed that few people outside of the Communist bloc have visited it since the Korean War. It's also one of the few remaining Communist countries in the Stalinist tradition, though in North Korea's case this has been augmented with its idiosyncratic leader's ideology of *juche* (self-reliance) which has resulted in the country spurning overseas aid and accelerating industrial development at the expense of agriculture. It also has the world's fifth largest standing army, estimated at 850,000 men, and is believed to be developing a nuclear capacity at its reprocessing centre near Yongbyon, north of Pyongyang.

The answer to why it's been so closed for so long and why it sees fit to spend such an enormous amount on its armed forces lies principally with Kim Il Sung (the 'Great Leader'). He has totally dominated the politics of North Korea ever since WW II and has been grooming his son, Kim Jong Il (the 'Dear Leader'), to take over after his death. If there's anyone who has outdone Stalin or Mao Zedong in the cult of personality then it has to be Kim Il Sung. Not only is his word God's will, but huge statues and portraits of him litter the North Korean countryside and the cities. You need never be in doubt as to whether someone is a North Korean or not. Everybody, young or old, at home or abroad, wears a small metal badge with the face of the 'Great Leader' on it, and though it's not a crime to fail to wear such a badge, it definitely singles a person out as requiring special treatment of one sort or another. You may take with a pinch of salt claims by North Koreans that prisons don't exist, though they do admit to maintaining 're-education centres'.

This sort of cult following and passionate belief in every gem of wisdom which falls from the 'Great Leader's' lips is a cornerstone of the education system and no-one escapes it. It even has its attraction for some university students in South Korea, who display the utmost naivety by uncritically espousing his totalitarian strictures on the evils of South Korea's political, economic and social policies and his passionate anti-Western rhetoric. Of course, many things are far from perfect in the South, but it's true to say that few would prefer Kim's brand of utopia, given the choice.

It may seem incredible to a Western liberal accustomed to multiparty democracy that such Orwellian rigidity and conformity could be maintained in the late 20th century, but it does and is likely to remain in place until Kim Il Sung dies. After that, anything could happen, particularly because Kim Jong Il lacks the charisma of his father. Change, however, is unlikely to be precipitous. People indoctrinated for decades to worship Big Brother and lacking any history of democracy and personal choice are not suddenly going to embrace an ideology which they have been taught to condemn passionately as evil. A parallel with the collapse of Communism in Eastern Europe isn't really appropriate.

Information about the rest of the world is hard to come by in North Korea. The press is rigidly controlled and prints only what the government tells it to print. Likewise, TV programmes are all designed to reinforce the reigning ideology. Travel restrictions, too, are very tight for North Koreans. Even within the country, special permission is required for a change of location. Those who are allowed to go overseas for study invariably have to choose a Communist country as their destination. Most go to Chinese univer-

sities, though for a few Tanzania is a possible alternative. At all these universities where there's a Korean contingent they form an exclusive bloc and never, at any time, socialise with non-Koreans, even at a departmental level. In addition, there's always a political cadre to keep watch over them and report any infractions. Likewise, all North Korean business people are required to attend special political education classes once a week to keep them doctrinally pure.

Another of the major contrasts to be seen here in comparison to the South is the almost total lack of pollution, whether it be industrial waste or just pure trash. The one thing which strikes most visitors to North Korea is its squeaky-clean appearance. This is a function not just of the lack of consumer goods and their packaging but of determined policies which keep it that way. The streets of Pyongyang are washed down twice a week, and before dawn each day street cleaners are out sweeping up any litter or leaves which they can find. You'd be hard-pressed to find a single piece of paper on the streets despite the total absence of litter bins. Even in the countryside, women are assigned a particular stretch of the main road to sweep and keep clean – each and every day. It's a far cry from the situation in South Korea where litter has become a major eyesore – especially plastic rubbish which clogs many a major river and fouls up popular beauty and picnic spots.

The capital, Pyongyang, is a superb example of the regime's determination to project its own image of progress, discipline and the wellbeing of its citizens. You won't find here the hustle and bustle, the noise and smells of other cities in Asia. Kim Il Sung's version of the model Communist capital city excludes people with disabilities, the very old, bicycles, animals, street vendors and even pregnant women. In fact, there appear to be very few people about at all despite its population of over 1½ million. It's said that only those with proven records of unswerving loyalty to the country's leaders are allowed to live in Pyongyang.

The apparent lack of people is also one of the most striking features of the countryside (or, at least, of that part which you're allowed to see) and you may get round to wondering where all those 20 million people actually live and work.

The other major contrast is the lack of traffic on the highways. Most of what you'll see will be army vehicles. There are very few passenger cars, since North Korea has no manufacturing plants and must import them from abroad. As a result, there's nothing remotely like the traffic congestion and vehicle exhaust pollution which characterises many South Korean cities.

As far as Buddhist temples go, they do exist, and in some cases have been renovated, but they no longer function, as the religion is regarded as an expression of so-called bourgeois mentality and is proscribed. Confucianism has been similarly suppressed. The traditional arts associated with such temples and shrines, on the other hand, have been harnessed to serve the greater glory of Kim Il Sung's 'vision'. Christians and Christian churches do exist here though they're few in number and any belief in the holy trinity is likely to be expressed in the form of the 'Great Leader' (Kim Il Sung), the 'Dear Leader' (Kim Jong Il), and the holy spirit of *juche* – the national ideology of self-reliance.

So why has the country opened its doors to the bourgeoisie of the world? The main reason is economic. Despite appearances to the contrary, North Korea's economy is on the skids and the country desperately needs hard currency. It's also worried that in the current climate of detente and cooperation between the Communist and capitalist blocs it will find itself totally isolated, particularly from its neighbours and former sources of aid – China and the USSR – which show an increasing interest in doing business with Seoul.

VISAS

North Korea was opened up to Western group tourism in 1986 and to individual Western travellers in 1989, so getting a visa is now just a formality, though subject to the restrictions mentioned in the introduction

and below which make it an expensive prop-osition. Even citizens of the USA are allowed to visit, despite North Korea's vehemently anti-US stand. The same goes for Japanese nationals. Only Israelis are prohibited entry.

Since there are so few North Korean embassies outside of the Communist bloc (there are none in Japan, the UK or USA, for instance, though there may well be soon in Japan, following recent high-level discussions about establishing diplomatic ties), most people apply for their visas at the embassy in Beijing (China). The embassy is in the Jianguomenwai compound, Ritan Beilu, Chaoyang District. There's also an embassy in Paris for those who wish to arrange their visa beforehand.

At the Beijing embassy, you first have to register in a log book and then give them a proposed itinerary of places which you wish to visit. This has to be confirmed with the tourist bureau in Pyongyang, which usually takes a day, after which you must pay for the entire trip in advance in hard currency. Two photographs are required and there's a 15 FEC visa fee.

If you're with a group of over 16 people, the tourist bureau allows the 16th person to visit free of charge.

The visa is not stamped into your passport (which might prejudice future visits to the USA or South Korea) but onto a separate sheet of paper which is stapled to your pass-port and will be retained by the immigration authorities on leaving North Korea.

Whatever else you do, if you want to be an independent traveller and before you apply for your visa, work out in advance your itinerary and timing and have this written out clearly and simply. This is easier said than done since there's very little literature avail-able. The first thing to do is to write to the Korea International Tourist Bureau, Central District, Pyongyang, Democratic People's Republic of Korea (Telex 5998 RHS KP), and request a copy of their brochure entitled *Ryohaengsa*. It's printed in several lan-guages – English, German, French, Japanese, Chinese, etc. This is a full-colour brochure describing all the major sites open to foreign tourists, the hotels, an airline schedule, and a breakdown of seven suggested itineraries ranging from three days to 16 days, but no prices.

You cannot get this brochure at the Beijing embassy.

Most of the suggested trips originate from Pyongyang, so in preparing your itinerary try to minimise your time in Pyongyang, as touring the capital can be slotted into your stopovers here. It seems you don't have to take any of the suggested trips if you can put together your own and have it accepted. This isn't as difficult as some people would have you believe.

Travel pamphlets can be purchased at the Koryo Hotel in Pyongyang, but by then it will essentially be too late, and in any case they're brief. The only other source of information is the book *Korean Review* by Pang Hwan Ju (Foreign Languages Publishing House, Pyongyang, 1987), which gives information on North Korea's flora, fauna, minerals, history, economy, politics and sightseeing.

For those whose time is limited, the only UK travel agent which deals with trips to North Korea is Regent Holidays Ltd (tel (0272) 211711), 13 Small St, Bristol BS1 1DE, but be warned that they occasionally cancel trips.

MONEY

The unit of currency is the won, which is worth 100 jon.

In addition, there are three types of North Korean currency. The first is coloured green (for won) or blue (for jon) if you're converting hard currency. The second is coloured red (for won) or pink (for jon) if you're exchanging 'nonconvertible' currency (basically Communist bloc and Third World currency). The last is local currency for use by Koreans only. Local currency comes in both banknotes and coins whereas green/blue and red/pink currency comes only in banknotes. As a foreigner, you must pay for hotels, restaurants and goods bought in stores in either green/blue or red/pink

banknotes and change will only be given in matching notes.

Red/pink currency is North Korea's way of saying it doesn't particularly want roubles or the like. There are, for instance, certain limits on consumer goods that can be bought with red currency. The object of this is to prevent East Europeans and particularly people from the Soviet Union from stripping stores bare – something which wouldn't be too hard to do! There are also two sets of prices for certain goods – a green price and a red price. The red price is often up to six times greater than the green price.

The only time you're likely to need local currency is if you use the metro in Pyongyang since the escalator takes only coins.

There's no black market but you can, if you meet the right people, swap green for red or local currency. Foreigners must exchange money at hotels.

Currency declaration forms are usually issued when you get your visa or at the border/airport on entry and you must fill in an exit currency form when you leave. It's probably best to make sure you get a currency form to avoid hassles on leaving, but if you don't it seems that the guides assigned to you can generally sort things out without too much trouble.

GETTING THERE & AWAY
Air

There are flights between Beijing and Pyongyang by either the Chinese national airline CAAC or the North Korean airline on Wednesday and Friday, which take two hours. In the opposite direction they depart on Wednesday and Sunday.

There are flights between Khabarovsk and Pyongyang in either direction on Thursday and Saturday by either Aeroflot or the North Korean airline and between Moscow and Pyongyang by the same airlines on Tuesday and Sunday. From Pyongyang to Moscow, the flights depart on Monday and Tuesday.

There are also flights between Berlin and Pyongyang via Moscow in either direction on Thursday.

You're advised to book as far in advance as possible for any of these flights, as demand for seats is heavy. Sunan International Airport is 24 km from Pyongyang and takes about 20 minutes by car.

Train

There are four trains per week in either direction between Beijing and Pyongyang via Tianjin, Tangshan, Jinxi, Dandong and Sinuiju. The Chinese trains leave on Wednesday and Thursday and the North Korean trains leave on Monday and Saturday. All these trains leave Beijing at 4.48 pm and arrive at Pyongyang the next day at 4.20 am (about 15½ hours). The trains arrive at Dandong (the Chinese border) at 8.25 pm and stay there for 1¾ hours for immigration and customs formalities. They arrive Sinuiju (the North Korean border) at 10.05 pm and stay there for 2¼ hours for the same reason.

There's little difference between the Chinese and North Korean trains except that the North Korean ones don't sport the infernal music and comedy shows which blare out at you from both the compartments and the corridors of the Chinese trains. Also, the Chinese trains have female attendants exclusively whereas the North Korean trains have male attendants exclusively.

Customs and immigration at either border are brief and relatively casual and your passport will be taken away for stamping.

The North Korean train is actually just two compartments attached to the main Beijing-Dandong train, which are detached at Dandong and then taken across the Yalu River bridge to Sinuiju, where more carriages are added for local people. Non-Koreans remain in their original carriages and are soon presented with a menu (complete with colour photographs) of what's for dinner. It's all very civilised. Make sure you have some small denomination US dollar bills to pay for the meal, as this is not included as part of the package deal you paid for in Beijing. There are no facilities for changing money at Sinuiju or on the train. The dining car is for the use of non-Koreans only.

This train will be your first introduction to North Korea and the contrasts with China will be quite marked. Everything is squeaky-clean and the stations en route will be almost deserted except for a few young children and old people.

Your guide will meet you on arrival at Pyongyang Railway Station and accompany you to your hotel. Likewise, when you leave North Korea, your guide will bid you farewell at Pyongyang Railway Station and you travel to China unaccompanied.

The Trans-Siberian

When leaving North Korea, you can link up with the Trans-Siberian train at Sinuiju/Dandong in China. To make this connection you need to take the noon train from Pyongyang on Saturday which arrives in Moscow the following Friday. There's also the possibility of crossing directly from North Korea into the USSR in the north-east via Hasan and Tumangang and then taking the Trans-Siberian to Moscow. This connection leaves Pyongyang on Monday and Wednesday at 5.30 pm. These trains arrive in Moscow on Monday and Wednesday respectively.

Boat

A passenger ship, the *Sam Jiyon*, plies between Wonsan on the east coast of North Korea and Nagasaki (Japan) once a month. It's a North Korean ship and is primarily intended to enable Koreans living in Japan to visit their homeland – most of the Koreans living in Japan originally came from North Korea. It's popular with youth groups from Japan, who get VIP treatment on arrival in the North, and is a possible port of entry if you already have a visa for North Korea.

If you have limited time at your disposal, you'll need to know the departure dates of this ship. North Korean embassies *may* know the details but don't be surprised if they don't. In Japan, contact Korean organisations at a university.

GETTING AROUND

Public transport isn't anywhere near as well

developed in North Korea as in the South. There are certainly railways which connect the major centres of population and you're allowed to use them (accompanied by your guide) but they generally don't go to places of tourist interest. There are hardly any public buses in the countryside or between major cities, a reflection of the fact that North Koreans are not allowed to move freely around their own country without permission. This means that most of the time outside Pyongyang you'll have to travel by car along with your driver/guide, which will naturally limit your chances of meeting local people. On the other hand, if you can't speak Korean then this is probably an advantage of sorts, though it does mean you'll stand out a mile as a foreigner.

Being conspicuous is no great disadvantage in itself since Confucianism still rules, though under a different guise. Children will wave at you as you pass by or bow deeply to you if you happen to stop and get out on the streets. They've been encouraged to give visiting foreigners a warm welcome.

Yet there is a distinct lack of traffic in the countryside. Most of the vehicles you'll see will be military transports – many of them with their bonnets up being fixed. What you will notice – and this is the major contrast with China – is a distinct lack of bicycles. There are none in Pyongyang and very, very few elsewhere. Presumably this indicates an official ban on their use. One traveller did come across a few bicycles in a department store in Pyongyang but they were tucked away in a corner and had no price tags on them. Certainly you cannot rent them anywhere.

Finally, even if you did have your own transport, you'd be hard-pressed to find your way around either in the cities or in the countryside because there are no street signs in the cities or direction signs in the countryside and road maps are almost impossible to find. The only street map you'll find available is for Pyongyang.

PYONGYANG

Being the capital, Pyongyang is the showpiece of North Korea and is peppered with distinctive landmarks and monuments, many of them in honour of the 'Great Leader'. Two of the principal ones are the huge Koryo Hotel, which you can see even from the airport, and the 170 metre-high Juche Tower, crowned with a beacon which flickers at night. There's also the extraordinary 13-lane boulevard which connects the city centre with the outer suburb of Kwangbok over three km away – a ridiculous extravagance given the scarcity of traffic, though no more of a profligate waste than many of the other grandiose monuments.

Like Seoul, the city is built on the banks of a major river, in this case the Taedong, but unlike the Han River the Taedong appears to be refreshingly clean. Like the Han, it often freezes over in winter. One of the major sights here are the two mid-river fountains which rise to a height of 150 metres. Your guide will proudly tell you they're the highest in the world, and this is probably true (Canberra's single jet reaches only 140 metres and the one in Geneva only 122 metres).

Things to See

Your first day out in Pyongyang will undoubtedly be a guided tour of the monuments by car. How many of them you will see depends on the time available and what preferences you express. It's a good idea to make your preferences known as early as possible after arrival in North Korea or even beforehand if you want to be sure of being taken to the ones of your choice.

One of the principal monuments is the **Tower of the Juche Idea** which, though uninspiring architecturally, rises 170 metres and which you can get to the top of by express lift for an unencumbered view of the city. The ride costs W5. In an alcove at the bottom are commemorative messages from various parts of the world hewn in stone and brick extolling the concept of *juche*. The tower stands opposite the fountains in the Taedong River.

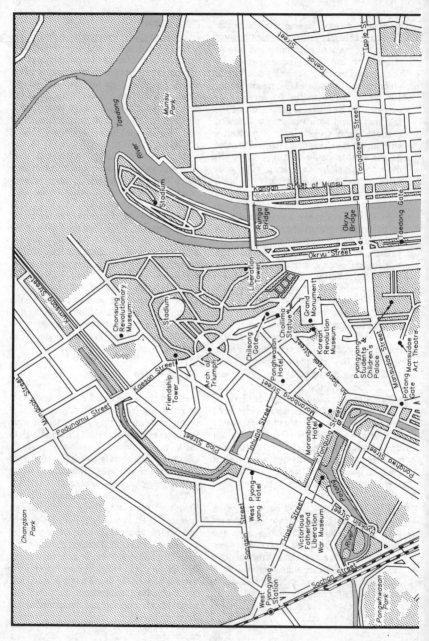

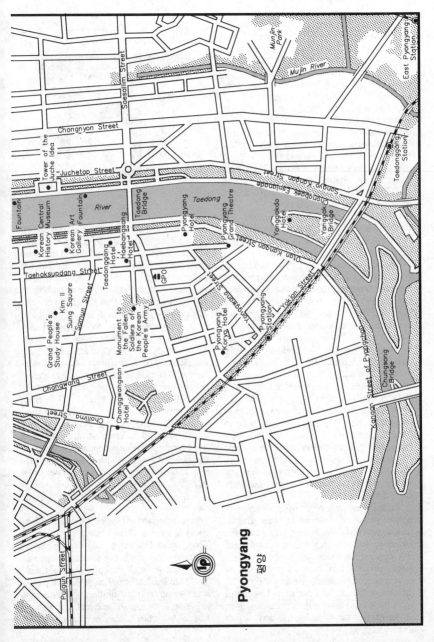

Pyongyang

Others are the **Arch of Triumph**, which marks the spot where Kim Il Sung made his rallying speech following the departure of the Japanese, and which is a full three metres higher than its counterpart in Paris, and the **Chollima Statue**, a bronze Pegasus representing the high-speed progress of the socialist reconstruction of North Korea. On Mansu Hill, overlooking the Taedong River, is the **Grand Monument** itself – North Korea's answer to Taiwan's Chiang Kai-Shek Memorial Hall. As you might expect, this is where an enormous and highly polished bronze statue of the Great Leader stands, flanked by carvings of oppressed but ultimately victorious workers.

Of a more traditional nature are the **Chilsong and Taedong Gates**, two of the old city's gates, the latter with a two-tiered roof similar to its counterpart in Seoul.

For an exposition of North Korea's version of the country's history there is the **Korean Central History Museum**. The counterpart to the South's Independence Hall outside Chonan, the museum houses exhibits, artefacts and drawings tracing Korean history from prehistoric times right up to the revolution. Your guide will provide a running commentary.

Other institutes which may well be worth a visit include the **Students' & Children's Palace**, established in 1963 as a centre for after-school activities and where you can see students doing everything from pingpong to dance, gymnastics and music, and the **Pyongyang Embroidery Institute**, where you can see an exhibition of very impressive embroidery as well as prototype designs which are then copied by manufacturers around the country.

Since Pyongyang is one of the few places where you'll be allowed to walk around unaccompanied (with a little gentle but persistent persuasion), it's a good idea to take this opportunity once you've been chauffeured around the main sights. If you request it, you can, for instance, be dropped on the far side of the city at Liberation Tower and walk back from here to the centre calling in at department stores along the way if you

Arch of Triumph

want. You'll also see many local restaurants, though it's unlikely you'll be able to sample them as they're invariably full and there are often queues outside which stretch down the pavement.

You should also utilise your walkabout to call in at a metro station if only to see the extravagance with which the stations have been constructed. Each is differently designed, with varying bronze sculptures, murals, mosaics and chandeliers, and all the pillars, steps, corridors and platforms are fashioned in marble. The trains themselves are nowhere near as impressive, being dim and dingy. There are 17 stations in all served by two lines covering a total length of 24 km and the present system was completed in 1978. There are plans to extend it to Nampo and Mangyongdae. Each station has a map of the system indicating where you are. The cost of a ride on this system is a standard 10 jon and it's a very convenient way of quickly visiting different parts of the city.

If walking around the city, beware of jay-walking even if there's not a car in sight! There are underground walkways or pedestrian crossings at all major intersections and *everyone*, without exception, uses them. There are also traffic police at all such points standing on wooden plinths. If you attempt to jay-walk the nearest one will give a sharp blast of her whistle (they're mostly women) and a smart remonstration will quickly bring you back in line.

It's unlikely you'll ever use the urban bus network as the queues are phenomenally long and the buses crammed to bursting point but, if you do, they run until 10 pm each day. Women with children form separate queues and have priority in boarding buses.

Places to Stay

Wherever you choose to stay in Pyongyang it's going to cost you heavily (unless you have contacts and/or are a member of your local Communist organisation). On the other hand, there is a choice between deluxe, class A, class B and class C accommodation. You'll probably be pressured to stay at the deluxe *Pyongyang Koryo Hotel* (tel 38106) which is 45-storey high, in the centre of the city and where most foreigners stay, but it's not the only choice in this category. There's also the *Tourist Hotel*, about seven km from the city centre, the *Angol Hotel*, at a similar distance from the centre, and the *Yanggakdo Hotel*, about four km from the centre. A huge new development is projected about four km from the centre to be known as the *105-Storey Hotel* in the shape of a pyramid with 3000 rooms, but whether it will ever be built is another matter.

Further down the scale in the class A are the *Potonggang Hotel* (tel 48301), a fairly modest hotel about four km from the centre with 161 rooms, and the *Youth Hostel*, about 10 km from the centre with 465 rooms. The latter, of course, doesn't even faintly resemble youth hostels of the type found in Europe, America or Australasia.

Class B hotels include the *Changgwangsan Hotel* (tel 48366), about three km from the centre, the Pyongyang Hotel (tel 38161), in the heart of the city, and the *Taedonggang Hotel* (tel 38346), also in the centre of the city.

The only class C hotel where you can stay is the *Haebangsan Hotel* (tel 37037) which has 83 rooms and is also in the centre of the city.

Around Pyongyang

The major site of interest is the outer district of **Mangyongdae** – the so-called 'Cradle of the Revolution'. This where Kim Il Sung was born and spent his childhood. His old thatched house here, set in carefully tended gardens, has been turned into a shrine, and houses photographs of his family as well as a few everyday household utensils to indicate the humble background from which he came. The surrounding pine woods hold the burial mounds of his relatives. There's also a marble observation platform overlooking the Taedong River at the top of Mangyong Hill.

Near to Mangyongdae are two funfairs and pleasure grounds which you'll be told receive over 100,000 visitors a day, but you can take that with a pinch of salt.

On the way back from Mangyongdae, it's worth making a detour to see **Kwangbok Street**, a Kowloonesque suburb visible from high points in central Pyongyang. It's essentially a linearly laid-out suburb of high-rise apartment blocks, which stretch for over three km on either side of the virtually empty 13-lane highway.

AROUND THE COUNTRY

What you get to see outside of Pyongyang depends entirely on what sort of itinerary you presented at the time you applied for your visa. It will also be limited to the places where tourist hotels are located. The following is a selection of places but isn't meant to be exhaustive. If you wish to go elsewhere then it's worth attempting to get permission. Few such requests, it seems, are refused, though they may initially cause raised eyebrows. On the other hand, if you do succeed in getting permission to visit places which aren't on the suggested tourist circuits, you must be prepared to accept last-minute cancellations. This even happens to group tours occasionally.

Mt Myohyang

A visit here from Pyongyang can be adequately covered in a day trip using the train as your means of transport. It's 160 km from the capital.

The train leaves Pyongyang daily at 6 am and arrives at Hyang-san at 9 am. On the return journey, the train leaves Hyang-san at 7 pm and arrives Pyongyang at 10.20 pm. Breakfast is taken on the train in the foreigners-only dining car.

The main centre of interest in Hyang-san is the International Friendship Exhibition (IFE) centre, about three to four km from the railway station. It's another of those monuments to the greater glory of the 'Great Leader' and, to a lesser extent, of the 'Dear Leader'. It's a six-storey building in traditional Korean style which houses gifts given to Kim Il Sung and Kim Jong Il from all over the world and is magnificently set amongst densely wooded hills. You need to be on your best behaviour here as the building is maintained as a hallowed shrine. Shoe covers must be worn when walking around and you'll be escorted by a woman in traditional Korean costume. The building has been lavishly endowed with marble stairways, huge bronze doors and thick carpets. There are no windows and each room is thermostatically temperature-controlled.

The gifts are quite interesting, and range from a bulletproof car from Stalin to carvings, pottery and paintings, many of which are exquisitely executed. They're arranged by country with a note, in English, of who sent them and when.

When you've seen the exhibition, it's possible to go for a three-km hike up the Sangwon Valley, via a clearly defined pathway, stone steps and a suspension footbridge to three sets of waterfalls (Kumgang, Taeha and Sanju). Nearby, there's an observation platform from which you can view the surrounding countryside. A short hike above the falls is a Buddhist temple – Sangwon-sa – which is in good order though no longer used.

There's also the Buddhist temple Pohyon-sa, just a short walk from the IFE at the start of the hike up Sangwon Valley, which consists of several small pagodas and a large hall housing images of the Buddha, as well as a museum which sports a collection of wood-block Buddhist scriptures.

The village of Hyang-san itself consists of just one main street lined by traditional Korean houses. Close by (about one km from the railway station) is the *Chongchon Hotel* which is where you will probably be based for the day. Other hotels in this vicinity include the modernistic *Hyangsan Hotel*, about halfway between the station and the IFE, and the *Chongbyong Hotel*. All these hotels are class A.

Kaesong

Kaesong is one of the few North Korean towns where burial sites of the former kings and queens of Korea can be seen. You can see here the burial mounds along with associated statuary of King Kongmin (the 31st Koryo king, who reigned between 1330 and 1374) and his queen about 13 km from the centre of the city. It's a very secluded site and there are splendid views over the surrounding tree-covered hills from a number of vantage points. You'll need a car to get there.

In the city itself are a number of 'obligatory' tourist sights. Included among them are the **Sonjuk Bridge**, a tiny clapper bridge built in 1216 and, opposite, the **Pyochung Stele**, similar to those at the shrines outside of Kyongju and elsewhere in South Korea. A short drive from town is the **Songgyungwan Confucian College** which was originally built in 992 and rebuilt after fire in the 17th century. Today it's a museum of vases and other relics. The buildings surround a wide courtyard dotted with ancient trees.

Kaesong itself is a modern city with wide streets and of scant interest, though it does have an interesting old part consisting of traditional tile-roofed houses sandwiched between the river and the main street. There's also the Nam (South) Gate at the beginning of the main street which dates from the 14th century. From the main street, a wide driveway sweeps up Mt Chanam on top of which there's a massive bronze statue of – guess who?

If you stay in Kaesong, you'll be based at the *Channamsan Hotel*.

To get to Kaesong you can either take the train or a car, though a car is preferable if you want to see the towns en route. The driving time between Pyongyang and Kaesong is about 3¼ hours with a tea stop at a tourist halt built on a rocky outcrop overlooking the Sohung River along the way. The road is badly rutted but no worse than many other roads in Asia.

Panmunjom

The eternal fascination which this 'Truce Village' exerts on travellers both in the South and the North is hard to comprehend. Perhaps it's more understandable in the South as it promises a glimpse of 'the forbidden land'. When you're actually in 'the forbidden land', however, there seems little point in coming here just to gawk at tourists and soldiers on the other side.

If you're dead set on going, on the other hand, you need special permission, and this has to be reconfirmed on the actual day of your visit. Your guide will do this for you.

To get there, you drive out of Kaesong to a sentry box and tourist shop at the entrance to the DMZ where a military officer gives you a brief rundown of the history of Panmunjom aided by a large model of the truce village. After that you'll be escorted to the Joint Security Zone by military officers in a car. From the car park, you enter a large building that faces the row of huts which straddle the demarcation line and then exchange glances with burly US marines and the tourists on the other side in their pagoda viewing tower. After that, it's back to the main building for an exposition of the North Korean view of things, and then back to Kaesong. All very gripping stuff.

The Diamond Mountains (Kumgang-San)

North of Wonsan on the east coast, the Diamond Mountains are the North Korean equivalent of the South's Sorak-san and Odae-san mountains – an area of outstanding natural beauty. The usual route there is by car from Pyongyang to Onjong-ri via Wonsan along the new highway (around 315 km or four hours in all). The first part of the journey to Wonsan can also be done by train, though it's not so interesting doing it this way.

Going by car, you call off at a tea house at Sinpyong Lake – a very attractive area and a centre of honey production. The new road is quite spectacular and involves passing through 18 tunnels between Sinpyong and Wonsan, the longest of which is some 4½ km long. The port city of Wonsan itself was shelled to rubble in the Korean War, so it's an entirely modern town with a seven-lane boulevard leading down to the waterfront. Tourists are taken to the *Songedowen Hotel* and the adjoining *Kumgang Restaurant*.

From Wonsan, the road more or less follows the coastline, and you'll get glimpses of the double electric fence which runs the entire length of the east coast – like its counterpart in South Korea. They'll be an obligatory stop for tea at Sijung Lake. Your final destination is the village of Onjong-ri and the *Kumgangsan Hotel*. The hotel is quite a rambling affair consisting of a main building and several outer buildings which include chalets, a shop, dance hall and bathhouse (fed by a hot spring). The village itself, 15 minutes walk from the hotel, is worthy of a guideless visit and consists of a cluster of traditional Korean houses and small front plots crammed with vegetables.

Much like Sorak-san in the South, Kumgang-san is divided into Inner, Outer and Sea Kumgang, and the main activities here are hiking, mountaineering, boating and sightseeing. The area is peppered with former Buddhist temples and hermitages, waterfalls, mineral springs, a lake (Samil Lake) and museum. It's up to you how long you spend here and what you do, but maps of the area are provided to help you decide where you want to go.

Two of the most popular excursions are to **Kuryong Falls** and **Samil Lake**. The falls are a 15-minute drive from the hotel via Onjong-ri along an unsurfaced road through conifer forest to the *Mongran Restaurant*. The restaurant is hemmed in by steep rock faces and its balcony overlooks the waters of the river which flows down from the falls. It's a pleasant place to eat lunch. From the restaurant it's a 4½ km walk along footpaths, over rocks and across suspension bridges to the falls. Your guide will regale you with legends about the area and stories about the rocks, which supposedly resemble animals such as elephants, frogs, turtles, etc. At the falls, which are some 70 metres high, there's a viewing platform. It's a very attractive area and popular with artists (many of the paintings you see in Korea were inspired by the views in the area).

Samil Lake is located in an area of conifer forests and was once connected to the sea, and although you can see the ocean from here it's not permitted to go to the seashore at this point. Boats are available for hire at the lake, and for meals there's the *Danpung Restaurant* on the lakeside.

This is just a brief sketch of what is possible in the area.

Mt Paekdu

The highest mountain in the whole of Korea at 2750 metres, Mt Paekdu sits astride the Korean-Chinese border in the far north and is heavily symbolic of the struggle against the Japanese. It's here that Kim Il Sung established his headquarters and where it is claimed that his son was born (though that is disputed – some sources maintain that Kim Jong Il was born and brought up in the USSR). Atop the now-extinct volcano is a crater lake (Lake Chon) which is some 14 km in circumference and reaches a maximum depth of 380 metres.

Hotels to stay at in this area include the *Hyesan Hotel*, in the town of the same name, the *Samjiyon Sin Hotel*, some 67 km from Hyesan, and the *Onsupyong Hotel*. The first two are class B hotels whilst the latter is a class C hotel.

Access to this area is by air or train followed by car.

ACKNOWLEDGEMENT

This chapter was constructed from a long letter and subsequent correspondence sent to us by Stephen Bailey (UK) who visited North Korea in 1989. Many thanks, Stephen!

Index

Dear traveller

Prices go up, good places go bad, bad places go bankrupt ... and every guidebook is inevitably outdated in places. Fortunately, many travellers write to us about their experiences, telling us when things have changed. If we reprint a book between editions, we try to include as much of this information as possible in a Stop Press section. Most of this information has not been verified by our own writers.

We really enjoy hearing from people out on the road, and apart from guaranteeing that others will benefit from your good and bad experiences, we're prepared to bribe you with the offer of a free book for sending us substantial useful information.

Thank you to everyone who has written and, to those who haven't, I hope you do find this book useful – and that you let us know when it isn't.

Tony Wheeler

The latest news from Korea is that ferries are now plying the route between South Korean ports and mainland China.

Traffic congestion is becoming a problem in Korea, and is getting quite bad around the major centres of Seoul, Inchon and Pusan, where drivers should expect long delays at the cities major entry and exit points. The worst place is the Seoul to Pusan corridor where the average travel time for the 420 km trip has doubled to 14 hours over the last five years. The present government is planning to build a high speed rail link between the two cities to alleviate the problem.

There don't seem to be any new developments on the reunification of North and South Koreas.

The information in this Stop Press section was compiled with the help of letters sent to us by the following travellers: Rex Alexander, Robert L Aronoff (USA), Scott Frost, Jody Grant, Grahame & Rose-Anne Manns (AUS), Molly Martell, David C Matton (C), and Jeffery Wright (USA).

SOUTH KOREA

The new telephone number for the United Service Organisation (USO) in Seoul is ☎ 795 3028.

Money & Costs

A traveller found the best exchange rates at the Bank of Seoul followed by the Bank of Pusan. By far the worst was Korea Exchange Bank, who charge an exchange fee for each separate travellers' cheque. It pays to shop around as the situation changes constantly.

The official current exchange rate is US$1 to W787.60.

Places to Stay

You need to book ahead for youth hostels during October and November, which is the graduation period when many students travel – all hostels outside Pusan and Seoul are almost completely booked up. Even if you can get in without a booking, you might not get much sleep as the teenagers make plenty of noise all night.

Getting There & Away

Air The airport tax in Seoul is now W9000.

Boat There are now two new boat routes between China and Korea. One is between Tianjin, the nearest port to Beijing, and Inchon. The trip to Tianjin takes 27 to 30 hours, but if you are coming from China on this route, the trip takes about 40 hours, as you are required to spend a night on the boat due to restricted port hours in Inchon. Tickets are available at the Seil Travel Agency in both Seoul and Pusan. A one-way ticket is from US$160. A student discount of 10% is available if you have an international student card. While the tickets for Tianjin state that the arrival place is Tianjin, you actually arrive at the Tianjin Passenger Terminal in Tangu, which is 70 km from Tianjin. To get from the Tianjin Passenger Terminal in Tangu to Tianjin, take a taxi (about Y25) or a bus No 108 to the Tangu Main Station, from where there is a train to Tianjin.

The other route has a twice-weekly boat service between Weihai, in Shandong Province, China, and Inchon every Wednesday and Saturday at 4 pm. A one-way ticket to Weihai is US$90 (economy class), US$110 (2nd class), and US$130 (1st class). Tickets are available in China from CITS in Weihai at the boat harbour. In Seoul, tickets can be bought from the Universal Travel Service (UTS) behind the City Hall, just near the Seoul city tourist information centre, or from the Unification Church's Seil Tour System, 3th(!), Dowon Building, 292-20 Tohwa-Dong, Mapo-Gu, Seoul (☎ 701 6611). CTS in Seoul will get you a Chinese visa but will charge you US$100. It's cheaper to get a Chinese visa before coming to Korea, but don't forget that Chinese visas are only valid for three months from the date of issue. At the time of writing, there is no Chinese embassy in South Korea.

You might also be delayed by customs due to the lack of diplomatic relations between China and Korea. One traveller reportedly arrived in Tangu at 8 pm but did not get off the boat until 1 am.

Travellers have reported that there are two new services plying the route between Pusan and Hakata, Japan – a jet boat and a ferry. The jet boat is called the *Beetle*, takes around 3½ hours to make the crossing and costs roughly the same as the 2nd-class ticket on the Pusan to Shimonoseki ferry. The jet boat departs daily from each post. The Japanese Tourist Office on Kyushu can book your ticket and they have also been offering a concession-priced rail ticket to Hakata.

When arriving at the Osaka ferry terminal from Pusan, beware as there is no currency exchange on the ferry nor in the terminal itself. There is a free bus that will take you to a subway station just outside immigration.

The ferry departs Hakata Port on Tuesdays, Thursdays and Saturdays at 5 pm and arrives at Pusan Port at 8.30 am on the following morning. On the return journey, the ferry departs Pusan Port on Mondays, Wednesdays and Fridays at 5 pm and arrives at Hakata Port the next morning at 8.30 am. Enquiries can be made through the Hakata Port International Boat Passengers Terminal (☎ 271 7677).

Naksan

The Naksan Beach Youth Hostel is apparently closed during the off-season. During this time it is also difficult to find food, other than all sorts of dried sea urchins and digestive biscuits.

Pukansansong

One traveller had a problem with the military at the North Fortress of Pukansansong, near Seoul. It is advisable not to walk too close to the fortress, and definitely do not try to photograph it. Apparently, you can walk along the military road to view Seoul from the north only during the day. It is not possible to stray off the road or take photos like he did.

Taroko Gorge

The Pao-Ma-Charng trail has been washed out by a landslide in early 1992. It might be closed for a long time, so it is advisable to cheque the condition of the trail before you set out.

Travellers' Tips & Comments

I found hitchhiking quite easy in Korea. Koreans don't seem to do it, but they accept it as a foreign eccentricity and recognise the 'thumbs up' sign. You will usually be expected to tutor the driver in English for the trip's duration, but it's not a bad deal. Of course, the buses are so cheap and comfortable, hitching is only useful for short distances or places inaccessible by bus.

The Korean Herald and Korean Times periodically have advertisements for English teachers. These are English papers and are easily obtainable at newsstands in Seoul.

Eric Thurston – Canada

Our two male guides were very reluctant to let us out on our own in Pyongyang. Visits to department stores appear now to be carefully arranged for the benefit of visiting Westerners. At the appointed hour, we were taken in to the store, and even managed to buy something. However, none of the Koreans in the store appeared to be buying anything, but were standing around awkwardly trying to look normal, and failing. This was all undoubtedly staged.

In Pyongyang, the 105-storey, 3000-room hotel, in the shape of a pyramid has now been built – at least its outer structure exists. It's called the Ryugyong Hotel. Whether there is anything inside is a matter of conjecture – it is still under construction. It has no glass in its windows and now a fair number of them appear to be bricked up!

Paul Radmore & Margaret Leszcynska – UK